COLLECT THEM ALL

"What I do not know—indeed, what none of us know—is how many cardinals have escaped Borja's agents and survived to attend?"

"And why is that important?" Vitelleschi asked archly.

Bedmar smiled patiently. "Father, the Jesuits have been an eminently practical order since their founding. Indeed, had they not been, they would not have had one tenth the success they have enjoyed around the globe. And so, I press the practicality of my question to His Holiness: how many of us are there? Enough to make a stand—or just enough to make for a memorable collection of martyrs?"

1636
THE VATICAN SANCTION

ERIC FLINT
CHARLES E. GANNON

1636: THE VATICAN SANCTION

This is a work of fiction. All the characters and events portrayed in this book are fictional, and any resemblance to real people or incidents is purely coincidental.

A Baen Books Original

Baen Publishing Enterprises
P.O. Box 1403
Riverdale, NY 10471
www.baen.com

ISBN: 978-1-4814-8386-5

Cover art by Tom Kidd
Maps by Michael Knopp

First printing, December 2017
First mass market printing, March 2019

Library of Congress Control Number: 2017042953

Distributed by Simon & Schuster
1230 Avenue of the Americas
New York, NY 10020

Pages by Joy Freeman (www.pagesbyjoy.com)
Printed in the United States of America

This book is dedicated to
our copyeditor Modean Moon,
who has been standing invisibly beside
every author in the Ring of Fire series.
Her exceptional work has been and remains
extremely important to the success of the series.

Contents

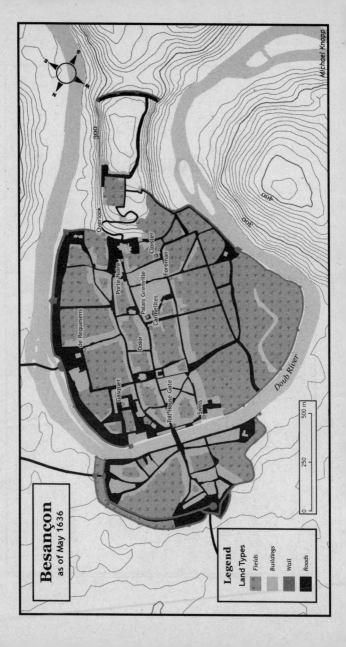

Besançon
as of May 1636

Michael Knopp

Overlook
Cloister
Foreman
Porte Noire
Palais Grenville
de Requesens
Carmelites
Dolor
Gasquet
Toll House Gate
Swiss

Doub River

300
400
300

Legend

Land Types

Fields
Buildings
Wall
Roads

0   250   500 m

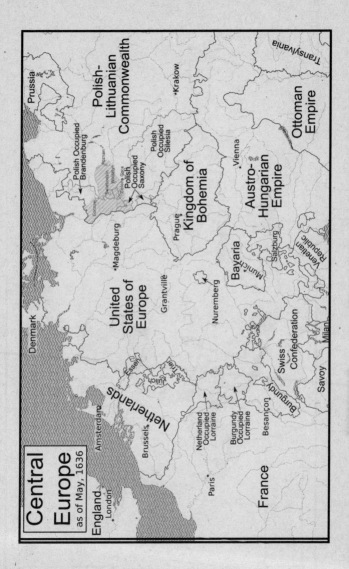

Central
Europe
as of May, 1636

England
• London

Denmark

Amsterdam

Netherlands

Brussels

Prussia

Polish Occupied Brandenburg

Poznan

Swiebodzin
Zielona Gora
Wschowa

Polish Occupied Saxony

Polish-
Lithuanian
Commonwealth

• Krakow

Polish
Occupied Silesia

• Magdeburg

United
States of
Europe

Grantville

Essen
Trier
Julich

Nuremberg

Prague •

Kingdom of
Bohemia

Vienna
•

Wien

Austro-
Hungarian
Empire

Transylvania

Ottoman
Empire

Munich

Bavaria

Salzburg

Venetian
Republic

Netherland
Occupied Lorraine

Burgundy
Occupied Lorraine

Besançon

Burgundy

Swiss
Confederation

Savoy

Milan

Paris •

France

Prologue

We are the fruit thereof

Silhouetted by the light he carried to lead the way, the bent man glanced back at Wilbur Craigson and pointed at the crudely mortared wall. Hunching further to keep from grazing his shaggy head against the ceiling, the aged fellow gestured toward the mismatched bricks repeatedly, as if seeking to underscore that it was, in fact, a wall of particular excellence or significance. Which it certainly did not appear to be.

After checking to see that Craigson was paying attention, his silent guide moved closer to the old brickwork, gnarled hands moving toward it as if trying to conjure forth a spirit of the earth.

Craigson produced the sap he had been carrying in his left pocket and, in one smooth motion, smashed it across the lower rear of the man's head. Who—long gray locks bloody in the light of the falling lantern—fell, nerveless as the rocks in the wall.

Craigson quickly scooped up the guttering lantern, then produced a much smaller lamp which he had been hiding in his long cloak. He advanced the wick, lifted the lamp as the flame grew, examined the man's wound, checked for a pulse: yes, faint but steady. Craigson set his lamp down carefully, unsheathed a long, well-made dagger, and quickly and expertly cut the man's jugular and carotid. With both severed, he estimated that his guide would exsanguinate within two minutes. At the very most.

He retrieved the purse of silver that the fellow had received from Craigson two hours ago, reached for the bag of lime he had secreted in the windowless room some days before, and began spreading it upon the body.

By the time the wick was burning down, Wilbur Craigson was done and had propped the corpse up against the wall which abutted the one that had been the object of their visit. Dusting his hands off, and then grabbing a handful of bagged sand to scour away what little blood had spattered on them, he walked to the wall, inspected it briefly, found the section the man had been indicating when felled. Satisfied that it was adequate for his purposes, he turned, preparing to dim the light and return to the streets of Besançon. His rent for this mostly useless storage room, paid four weeks in advance, ensured that the owner would not trouble him to relocate, nor come knocking: with the city virtually overrun by villeins, aristocrats, and all social stations in between, it had been feasible, if unusual, that the room had commanded any rental interest at all.

Exiting and cinching the door closed behind him, Wilbur Craigson produced the crude iron key and fastened the equally crude iron lock. As it snapped shut, he reflected that he was becoming either dangerously sentimental or cavalier: he had used his given name when introducing himself to this man.

He had, after all, been grimly certain that the knowledge of it would die with the old fellow. But still, Craigson had long experience with just how profound the vicissitudes of fate could be: using his real name was a wholly unnecessary risk. So why had he done it?

Was it because he was finally drawing close to the vengeance he had been nursing for almost two decades? Or because his poor guide had not deserved the end to which he came? The end which Wilbur foresaw from the moment he located him in the worm-eaten flop house, paid for with meager savings from a life of hard work he was no longer fit and able to perform?

Wilbur Craigson pocketed the key, turned, resolved not to use his given name—and risk discovery—again, not until his retribution was concluded. Which meant that now, as he prepared to return to the streets of Besançon, he would have to readopt the identity and name that he had assumed for so long it felt more natural than the one he had been born with.

It was time, once again, to become Pedro Dolor.

Part One

Monday
May 5, 1636

In verses wild with motion, full of din

Chapter 1

Sharon Nichols peripherally detected a hint of motion in the sky and scanned above the low, tiled roofs that screened the Doub River from view. Just to the right of St. Madeleine's gothic steeple, a small oblong was descending from the low clouds, like a bit of gray fluff shearing off from the cottony white cumulus. That was probably the dirigible they had been waiting for. Probably.

She turned toward her husband, Ruy Sanchez de Casador y Ortiz, who was deeply involved in a discussion with two recently arrived Burgundian guards who were not from Besançon themselves. They were still getting used to distinguishing local peddlers from the regional traders who, for three weeks now, had been rigorously screened before being allowed into the main city. More and more of them were being turned back across the old Roman bridge into the less densely built, and less affluent, district on the other side of the Doub: the Battant. As security tightened, more were forced to remain there, resolving themselves to trade as best they could in the markets that had sprung up between the margins of that district's curtain walls and the vineyards which surrounded them. Which in turn meant that lodging—even in barns and hastily improvised shelters—had become exorbitantly expensive, if available at all.

Of particular annoyance to Ruy and the various officers of the city's temporary and multitiered security forces were the new arrivals who (daily, it seemed) attempted to pitch tents, erect market stalls, or both, along the margins of a field in the north reaches of the Battant. But as surely as those hopefuls arrived, they were just as surely shooed away; that enticing stretch of close-mown grass was the marshaling field of the city's makeshift aerodrome. The dirigibles—inbound mostly from the United States of Europe, but also from the Lowlands, Bergamo, Venice, and even Austria—had been arriving with increasing rapidity through the month of April. However, even as May brought improved weather, the rate at which the comparatively well-heeled air travelers arrived had begun to diminish.

Sharon turned back toward the north, marked the progress made by the gray oblong, which was now close enough to see in greater detail. Its lines were more trim than most of the airships which had been arriving, and there were more catenary wires draped across its back to hold up a larger and more enclosed gondola beneath it. It trailed less smoke, which meant that it was not running a burner to keep the envelope inflated with hot air; the only fuel it was burning was to power the lawnmower engines that spun its propellers. As it angled lower, toward the pennons flying over Besançon's walls, she had no doubt left:

this was definitely a hydrogen airship—and therefore, the one they had been waiting for.

Sharon turned toward her husband. "Bedmar's here."

Ruy glanced at her, a smile creasing lean cheeks already well-equipped with wrinkles. Thirty-three years Sharon's senior, Ruy's face was the only physical signifier of his age. Almost wasp-waisted and with an erect bearing that connoted both vigor and long decades of service to the Spanish crown on five continents, the crow's feet at the corners of his eyes and deepening smile lines merely made him look mature. And if there was any gray in his mustache or painstakingly styled beard, she could not see it—although Sharon did wonder if the occasional glints she noticed there were the reflections of pomade or the start of a few telltale strands of silver.

His eyes briefly left hers, scanning the sky. "Yes, my love. At last, Bedmar arrives. The old scoundrel."

Which, had Ruy been anyone else, would have been an outrageously disrespectful comment. Alfonso de la Cueva-Benavides y Mendoza-Carrillo, still referred to by his former title, the Marqués de Bedmar, was now the cardinal-protector of the Spanish Lowlands and also Philip IV's ambassador extraordinary to that same turbulent state. And, just a year ago, Ruy had been his adjutant, right-hand man, intelligencer, and senior bodyguard, as he had been for more than a decade before marrying Sharon. Consequently, he had an easy familiarity with Bedmar that few others enjoyed. But neither he nor Sharon were certain of the cardinal's attitude toward Pope Urban or his summons to an ecumenical colloquy in Besançon.

Ruy placed a strong, sinewy hand on his wife's full

arm, left it there, a faint additional pressure conveyed through the palm. "I reiterate, my heart, that you need not be here to meet the cardinal."

"And I reiterate that as the USE's papal ambassador, and sponsor for this event, it is my duty to receive him."

Ruy's smile became slightly strained. "He is no more or less a cardinal than the others whose arrivals you have missed." A genuine twinkle rekindled in his eye. "Unless, of course, your ulterior motive is to press him to divulge the details of my behavior before I met your magically-redeeming self. Before I can swear him to secrecy, that is."

Sharon smiled. "Ruy, I can find out about that at any time, if I want, and without the cardinal's help. Of which you are aware. So here's what I *do* want to know: why are you trying to get me to leave before he arrives?"

Ruy, who was usually compliant in the extreme, frowned slightly. "My beauteous wife, despite your many charms—those both subtle and bountifully obvious—I am compelled to confess that I am no more likely to be distracted from my curiosities than you are. You have not yet explained why you feel the need to be here to receive Bedmar. But let us make a happy truce: to promptly and frankly reveal our concerns to each other."

"Fine. You first."

Ruy may have suppressed a sigh. "You are a hard taskmaster, beloved wife. Usually, I take singular joy in that quality of yours—"

"Ruy, are you capable of conversing without flirting?"

"With you? I fear not, my love, but I shall endeavor

to do so now. To answer your query, I fear for your safety."

"My safety? From whom—or what?"

Ruy shook his head. "That is another question. First, I shall have the answer to my own query."

Sharon smiled, worked in a coy upturn of the left side of her mouth, saw Ruy respond, but without any perceptual loss of resolve. "Okay, okay." She let the smile drop, kept herself from biting her lip instead, glanced at the rapidly descending airship. "It's important that we—the USE—engage Bedmar officially. As quickly as possible."

Ruy shook a remonstrating index finger when he saw that Sharon meant to let that suffice as an answer. "My delightfully shrewd wife, that answer is no answer. The same could be said of any of the cardinals and other religious luminaries who have already passed through this gate." He gestured briefly at the archaic archway near which they stood: the Toll Gate. It was also referred to as Porte Boucle, since it was the one means of entering the core of Besançon, or colloquially, the Buckle. The Old Town of the city sat between the curving banks of the Doub which, here, were bent in the shape of an oxbow, or, as some preferred, a buckle.

Sharon sighed. "Bedmar's a diplomatic lynchpin. He answers to both Madrid and the Church. And those two authorities are diametrically opposed over the topic Urban is going to bring up here in a few days."

Ruy nodded slowly. "Which is hardly news to me, my heart. So you must be aware of a new complication, since Bedmar's attendance effectively affirms that he has moved from Philip's orbit into that of his brother, Cardinal-Infante Fernando—or, I should say,

Fernando, King in the Lowlands, since that is the title he now goes by."

A title likely to plunge the House of Hapsburg into a civil war. Damn regal pride! "It's not that there's new uncertainty, Ruy. It's that we have news that Bedmar probably hasn't heard yet."

Ruy's unblinking eyes were patient but insistent.

Sharon made sure her voice was so low that almost she could not hear her own words: "Madrid is not likely to see any silver from the New World, this year."

"So bad a year in the mines?"

"Ruy, I'm not talking about a reduced shipment. I'm talking about *no* shipment."

Ruy's eyes widened slightly. He leaned back slightly, coming fully erect. "Ah. I see. Yes, that could change things."

"Yes, it really could. So, now: your turn. Exactly why am I in danger meeting the cardinal?"

"The danger is not to you, specifically, my heart. It is because you will be close to Bedmar."

"And that will do what? Make some old geezers in Madrid angry at me? Well, *more* angry at me?"

"No: it will place you where an attack on Bedmar may also become an attack upon you."

"An attack? On Bedmar? Here?"

"Beloved, whose very breath is as air to me, we are not here only to guard Pope Urban." He waved his hand to take in the many layers of security. "Cardinal Borja may remain upon the papal throne he usurped in the Holy City, but his reach is long and he may not be done with killing cardinals. And Bedmar may be a target of special interest. Even though Madrid has washed its hands of Borja, Philip might still provide Borja with the encouragement—and perhaps the means—to dispose of a mutually disloyal Spanish cardinal."

Sharon nodded, scanning the long line of waiting commoners, and the much shorter and better dressed "fast lane" that had been set up for dignitaries, aristocrats, officials, and known couriers. People she had presumed to be bored a minute ago now looked carefully expressionless, as if attempting to conceal their true purpose. The irate looked personally and immediately dangerous. And visitors from afar radiated danger, their calm faces hiding agendas as undiscoverable as the imaginary weapons buried in their towering piles of chests and traveling cases.

Which is all total bullshit, of course. Sharon took a deep breath.

"I am sorry if I have distressed you, my lovely wife," Ruy murmured.

Sharon smiled, put a hand on Ruy's, which had never left her arm. "I overreacted. Like a dope. But I also needed that reminder of the danger that may lurk around us. You've been screening visitors for so many weeks now, and with so little cause for alarm, that I guess I just got used to it."

In point of fact, she realized with a second look and a start, Ruy's security precautions actually *had* changed from what she had first seen five weeks ago, when the first of the representatives to Urban's colloquy had begun to arrive. The primary screening was still being conducted by the local militia. They spoke the local patois, often knew the families of vendors and tradesmen, and were able to joke about recent events. It was both a casual and efficient means of sorting out the known persons from the unknown.

Never far off from the militia, but always standing two or three paces away from the line itself, were Burgundian regulars. Or so they called themselves: to Sharon, the lack of national uniforms among the armies of Europe made it impossible to keep them apart or to really think of them as true soldiers at all. They almost all had off-white (or maybe just dingy) shirts and dark trousers. Their only definitive identifiers were their arm bands or tassels of orange and dark teal: the colors of their ruler, Grand Duke Bernhard. Originally a German noble of the powerful Wettin family, he had essentially stolen a number of provinces at the end of the abbreviated Thirty Years' War, collectively labeled them Burgundy, and ruled there only because, as the old axiom had it, might makes right. And he still possessed the greatest might in the region.

The Burgundians' equipment was dated: brigandines that had seen better days and shabby old swords. But soon Sharon overcame the initial impression of anachronisms on parade and perceived the methods in the madness that had inspired Ruy to assign the regulars to this duty. Although few were *besontsins*, they still knew the local patois and could easily follow what was transpiring between the militia and the throngs attempting to enter the city. On the other hand, few had relatives here and so were not merely at a physical remove, but a socially impartial distance, from the often impatient crowd. Lastly, since any problems were likely to start with a physical altercation of some kind, their armor and swords were significant disincentives but divorced from any possible escalation to firearms. On the other hand, if a troublemaker in the line did

produce a hidden gun...well, there were other forces
to deal with that.

Lurking less obviously near street corners, the walk-
ways down to the quay, and around the gate itself was
a far more professional and uniform set of soldiers: the
Irish Wild Geese. Commanded by Owen Roe O'Neill
himself, several had been on hand to fight off Urban's
would-be assassins last year. Well trained with both
swords and pistols, their heavy, custom-built pepperbox revolvers rode at their hips, occasionally clacking
against their cuirasses. The almost uniform light eyes
and fair hair that peeked out from beneath the brim
shadows of their capeline helmets marked them as
strangers to the region, as did their language: a mix
of English and Amideutsch that labored up through
heavy brogues. They were watchful and serious, befit-
ting their new status as the Pope's Own: the Holy
City's Swiss Guard had almost all been slain during
the siege of the Castel St. Angelo.

Last and least obvious of all were the figures only
visible as half seen shadows in a few ground-floor
doorways, on a few balconies, and a single silhouette
holding a long, thin-barreled rifle up in the bell-tower
of St. Madeleine: two squads of the crack Hibernian
Mercenary Battalion. Officially soldiers of fortune, they
were under exclusive contract to the up-timer-dominated
government of the State of Thuringia-Franconia and had
proven their worth several times in Italy and Mallorca
during the previous year. Wearing buff coats tailored
after up-time military style, they remained all but hidden, their individually-crafted Winchester .40-72 lever
action rifles and percussion cap revolvers usually well
out of sight, both to retain surprise and avoid attracting

undue notice. Two on the closest balcony were hunched intently over a small box: a primitive portable radio, several of which were being used by Ruy's security assets to keep each other apprised on traffic and individuals of interest throughout Besançon. And almost invisible at this distance, the silhouette in the bell-tower continued to turn slowly, one hand holding unseen binoculars to his eyes while the other cradled the rifle with a long tube atop it: a scope.

Ruy had been quick to see the advantages of the Hibernians' up-time methods, particularly those made possible by multiple portable radios. But this layered security approach also brought a problem that was equally anachronistic, but quite familiar to Sharon: turf wars.

The local cops—the militia—were ticked off that the State Troopers—the Burgundians—were really calling the shots. They were annoyed, in turn, by the President's Secret Service—here, the pope's Wild Geese—who could interfere whenever they wanted to. But even those professional bodyguards had to coordinate with the Hibernians, who were the equivalent of a SOCOM unit possessing the demeanor of the SAS. Who all ultimately answered to the national intelligence apparatus: Ruy and his immediate lieutenants. *Just like home.*

Or maybe not. Sharon could feel her smile droop as she noticed anew the shabby pomp of the sun-bleached national and city pennants that fluttered all around them, the omnipresent stink of both equine and human wastes, the borderline malnutrition in many of the less-well-attired persons in the crowd, their yellowed and crooked teeth, and the paucity of signage that sported words in addition to simple icons.

No, Sharon reflected, suppressing a shake of her head, *this isn't home. And not because the conditions here are worse. In a lot of ways, it's better. Hell, I'd rather be burned for being a witch than for being black. But this will never look* normal *to me, to eyes that grew up filled with images of a world almost four hundred years further along than this one, no matter its own ugliness and horrors.*

She turned, back toward Ruy, watching him receiving reports, giving orders, shuffling his men around with the surety of a master chess-player navigating a practice match. To him, this was all a brave new world of wonders: he marshaled forces by radio, had a .357 magnum in a shoulder holster, had seen the surface of a moon through a telescope, had watched a video of *El Cid*, and had dipped into dozens of up-time books with the same luxuriant delight evinced by a man of humble means who suddenly finds himself furnished with unlimited aristocratic delights and diversions. And yet, as he often and emphatically pointed out, the greatest gift that the future had conferred upon him was his beloved wife.

Who, for one small moment, envied that her husband was enchanted and excited by changes that seemed only wondrous and future-looking. Because for a foresightful up-timer, not only was this world a vast slip backward in health, in justice, in safety: it was also ingenuously caught up in the first, misleading blush of enthusiasm for all the improvements that had come from the future. Soon enough, Sharon feared, the long-term consequences of those changes would be felt, and a backlash against the new would arise. As it always did.

A door, groaning heavily on its hinges, opened slowly behind her. She glanced back, wearing a small, reassuring smile by the time she turned to face—

Larry Mazzare, Cardinal-Protector of the United States of Europe, emerged from the combination toll- and customs-house that extended away from the southwest side of the gate. Two Wild Geese flanked him as he squinted into a beam of sudden sunlight; the clouds were finally parting.

Larry had aged since they had arrived down-time, five and a half years ago. There was more gray in his hair, more lines on his face, and his simple Sunday-black had been traded for the heavy and many layered raiment of a post-Renaissance cardinal. A trade he had not welcomed, and which he did not maintain at home, but here, in Besançon and on the pope's business, he had little choice. He noticed Sharon, nodded at her, at Ruy, and asked, "So . . . he's here?"

Ruy nodded. "Yes. Bedmar has landed. He is on his way."

Chapter 2

Larry Mazzare moved to stand beside Sharon and Ruy, but the Wild Geese with him—Cormack McCarew and Daniel O'Dempsey—crowded protectively in front of him. Larry sighed: leave it to young Irishmen to be not only ready, but eager, to take a bullet for a trusted counselor of the pope.

Daniel—who everyone wound up calling "Danny-o-Dee"—raised an eyebrow in mock recrimination as Larry tried to press forward. "Yer makin' our job a trial, y'ar, Your Eminence."

Mazzare frowned back, not entirely joking. "You call me 'your eminence' one more time, Danny, and I'll have your hide."

"Yer welcome to it—Your Eminence."

"Danny—"

"All right, then Fahther, but it *will* be my hide f'sure if anyone hears me bein' so familiar with yeh."

Cormack McCarew nodded. "He's right, Your Eminence. And don't waste your evil eye on me: I've sworn me duty t' God, and if't please you, I'm more feared of His wrath than yours."

Larry didn't find it too hard to suppress a smile. McCarew and Danny-o-Dee were among the youngest of the Wild Geese, as cute as a pair of spring-born pups, and so utterly earnest that it was impossible not to be charmed by them. But for all of that, they were also tiresome sticklers for the details of their duty: to stick with Mazzare no matter where he went, no matter what he was doing. No exceptions. Which led to some truly frustrating moments at the privy and in the bath. Urban had a similar security detail and similar exasperations.

Larry eventually came to stand by Sharon, with Ruy to her left. "The radio report has Bedmar passing the waypoint at St. Madeleine now. The entourage is moving quickly."

Ruy nodded. "Was there any indication that his arrival attracted any special attention?"

"No. Your decision to use sedan chairs instead of carriages seems to be working. The locals have now seen so many people carried that way from the aero-drome that they don't take any special note."

Sharon leaned toward Larry. "You must be relieved."

"Why?"

"Because Bedmar is the last cardinal you have to wrangle. To say nothing of the Protestants and the rest."

Larry shrugged. "Heck, Sharon, I guess you could say I brought it on myself. I *could* have kept my big yap shut about the up-time documents of the papacy, the Church, and especially Vatican Two...but I didn't."

Sharon looked at him. "I don't claim to understand much about the chats a priest must have with God, but you've made it pretty clear you felt you had to." She smiled. "To quote a movie that's set in my old home town, 'You're on a mission from God.'"

Larry stared at her. "I may wear white shirts and black suits, but I do not wear black horn-rim sunglasses or claim to be a Blues Brother."

Sharon laughed, her chin lifting into the sound. Her face was not quite as full as it had been when they had arrived in 1631, and although she was still a heavily built woman, she was more athletic and toned, now. The last two years had involved a lot of rigorous travel, often under the threat of pursuing assassins, all on a diet in which refined starches were sparse and refined sugar downright rare.

"Frankly, Sharon, I should be thanking you."

"For what?"

Larry waved a hand at the long line that snaked away from the gate, the soldiers, the busy bridge. "For arranging to reserve lodging for over a hundred dignitaries, and then three hundred more scribes, guards, clerks, personal assistants, and other members of various entourages. Convincing Bernhard to go along with it, and to conveniently be out of town. And above all, getting Gustav Adolf to pay for the majority of it. I suspect that was the hardest trick of all."

Sharon's smile became sly. "Yeah, well, I had a secret weapon."

Larry smiled back. "You mean Mike Stearns?"

"The one and only."

Larry nodded. The de facto leader of the displaced American up-timers, former union official Mike Stearns, was notorious for combining forces with Ed Piazza, the former high school principal who was now the president of the State of Thuringia-Franconia and expected by most people to become the next prime minister of the United States of Europe in the coming elections. Stearns and Piazza employed a kind of tag-team advocacy to wrestle Gustav—or more properly, Gustav II Adolph, King of Sweden, High King of the Union of Kalmar, and Emperor of the United States of Europe—into supporting the projects they really wanted. Gustav, a staunch Lutheran, would have pushed back hard on funding a papal colloquium, ecumenical or not. Clearly, Mike and Ed had successfully justified it as being essential to the future health of the USE.

"Besides," Sharon continued after a moment; nodding toward Burgundian regulars, "Bernhard was going to be out of town anyhow. It's the start of campaign season."

Which was true enough: Bernhard's version of Burgundy was not a pleasing geopolitical construct to most of the region's powers. It ran roughshod over the historical claims of France's Capetian dynasty, made a mockery of Madrid's Hapsburg-legitimated dominion of the region since 1519, violated Besançon's own status as a semi-independent city of the now defunct Holy Roman Empire, and had quickened a surge of preemptive defensiveness along the south-flanking border with the Duchy of Savoy. To put it lightly, Bernhard's arrival had earned him more than a few restive neighbors.

Bernhard's response to these pressures was exactly what Larry had come to expect from the monarchs of the seventeenth century: he went to war. In Bernhard's defense, his campaign was neither impetuous nor ill-considered. His relatively recent marriage to Claudia de Medici, the regent and current ruler of Tyrol, had enabled him to transform his two-year standoff with the Swabian-based Swedish forces into an undeclared armistice. Tyrol was the newest state in the constellation of the USE, and so Gustav's troops could hardly launch attacks against Bernhard without causing both a multifaceted intranational *and* international incident with his wife's polity.

Having thus wrought a political solution to the very real danger beyond the Rhine on his eastern flank, Bernhard immediately reinforced his western border, and was now busily snapping up some undefended autonomous real estate to his north. Out of the goodness of his autocratic and acquisitive heart, he was determined to offer those lands the security of sheltering beneath the new Burgundian—which was to say, Bernhardian—flag. It was, so to speak, an offer they could not refuse. Consequently, with his visiting wife and newborn son safely ensconced closer to his intended area of operations, devoutly Lutheran Bernhard had also managed to be out of town at exactly the moment when it would have been most awkward to be present: the commencement of a colloquium during which his rising star would have been outshone by sharing the local political stage with no less a luminary than the pope.

Larry's thoughts were interrupted by the arrival of a breathless runner, who leaned quickly toward Ruy. The hidalgo acknowledged the message with a quick nod, then turned to Sharon and Larry. "Bedmar's entourage is starting across the bridge. We will be at pains to greet him in such a way as to avoid rousing suspicions as to his importance, so we must not appear too protective or hasty. But nor may we indulge in lengthy greetings and conversations."

Sharon nodded. Larry merely folded his hands. His part in the scripted reception—peeling off with a picked and hidden formation of Owen Roe O'Neill's

Wild Geese and escorting Bedmar to his protected lodgings—would commence soon enough. Until then, he was merely a spectator. And maybe, a calming distraction for Sharon, who was starting to appear a little anxious. "I imagine you're looking forward to seeing the back of Bedmar's arrival, too."

Sharon replied with a sound that was part sigh and part grunt. "We're still waiting for the Russian orthodox contingent, who should have come in on yesterday's dirigible. And two of the Lutheran theologians haven't shown, yet—even though, by all rights, they should have been the first to arrive." She sighed. "At least I didn't have to juggle all the balls myself at the outset."

Larry nodded his understanding. In the earliest phases of organizing the colloquium, Sharon had delegated various organizational tasks to up-timers who were already located in Besançon and whose skills were suited to her needs. Unfortunately, that came to a grand total of three persons—well, more like two and a half: Lisa Lund, who had formerly been an interpreter and clerk; the similarly skilled Carey Calagna; and her fifteen-year-old daughter Dominique Bell, who was a pretty sharp cookie and was a match for most down-time scribes when it came to reading and writing.

The rest of the displaced Americans in the region were located across the north loop of the Doub in the small hamlet of Bregille, where, future maps indicated, two smaller bridges would be built over the shallows that were currently used as occasional livestock fords and for the setting of weirs. Hired by Bernhard to oversee the creation of a variety of (comparatively) modern construction and fabrication shops, the Americans had chosen Bregille for its direct and largely untrafficked river access: a major advantage for reducing the expense of receiving raw materials and, eventually, shipment of finished goods. Located well beyond the roadway bottlenecks of both the Battant and the Buckle, land was cheap there and unburdened by special tolls and tariffs.

However, as Sharon had emphasized when discussing security provisions with Ruy and Larry half a year ago, she would still have been happier if the up-timers in Bregille had been a hundred miles away. A ruthless and well-informed adversary—such as the one they'd faced in Italy—could use them as hostages, since it was known that most of the time-marooned Americans tended to watch out for each other to a certain degree, enough for that instinct to provide leverage over them. And any well-informed adversary would know that Sharon Nichols remained the USE's representative to Urban, and so, knew that to be an emotional screw they might hope to turn.

Consequently, Sharon had cut what little contact she had with the small up-time enclave in Bregille and had dismissed Lisa, Carey, and Dominique by late March, pressing bonuses upon them along with entreaties to continue with their daily lives as unobtrusively as possible, and to use their up-time skills—and modest celebrity—as sparsely as they might.

Sharon glanced away from where the three sedan chairs, porters, mules, and several unusually strapping attendants were making their way across the Pont Battant with the rest of the traffic. She looked over her shoulder at Mazzare. "To be honest, sometimes I tell myself I'm a self-indulgent wimp to complain at all, since I'm mostly just the figurehead of the USE's involvement here. It's other people who've done the really heavy lifting."

Larry shrugged, understanding what she meant even if he didn't agree with her self-dismissive summation. Financial arrangements for the colloquium had been handled through banks and money trading channels in Magdeburg, with some transfers taking place through the Jewish shadow-network overseen by relatives of Mike Stearns' wife, the Abrabanels. Arranging for airship transport for various dignitaries who had to travel long distances—often over forbidding or unsecure territory—was handled by the burgeoning air service company known as Upward Mobility LLC, which was owned by recent émigré Estuban Miro. Ruy had arranged for all the security, its provisioning, its billets, its standing orders and duty rosters. Communications—both radio operation and messenger contracts—had been overseen by Odo, the radioman who'd been with her from her first days in Rome and Captain Taggart of the embassy's Marine Guard who'd been with her since she left Grantville.

But there had been a less obvious—albeit desperately important—element to the USE's support of this meeting of Europe's various religious leaders: coordinating the preparatory intelligence. The Roman Catholic cardinals who were attending did so at the risk of their lives. Any of Borja's agents who detected their travel were certain to have orders to eliminate them, garnished with the promise of a substantial reward. Word had it that this bounty now included any cardinals who could not be found in their villas and palaces in the Lazio, the broad environs around Rome. It was further rumored that even distant cardinals whom

Borja's messengers failed to find ensconced in their dioceses were, by process of bloodthirsty deduction, also presumed to be Urban's creatures. Many considered this report to be a sensationalistic invention, but from what Mazzare knew of the papal usurper, it was entirely within his character and the scope of his well-manicured barbarity to make just such rash presumptions and issue correspondingly ruthless orders.

The identity of the intelligence chief responsible for contacting those many prelates and arranging for their travel and security was only known to Larry himself, Sharon, Ruy, and a handful of others: Estuban (but really, Ezekiel) Miro, the same fellow who had arrived in Grantville less than two years ago, and had made his fortune through the development of air travel. He had succeeded handsomely, and the magnitude of that success was increasing weekly, it seemed. Also, that role gave him the perfect cover to handle matters of confidential travel. Although he was Europe's primary provider of dirigible services, it was also within the scope of his activities to arrange for air travelers' connections to carriages, mounts, and other means whereby they would journey onward from the aerodrome where they disembarked. Consequently, Miro was able to track and subtly shift schedules as needed, all within the scope of his routine operations. It also afforded him the opportunity to ensure that certain unremarkable (yet discreetly well-armed) "fellow travelers" were present at every departure, at every arrival, on every flight that carried carefully nondescript travelers who just happened to be hiding red birettas in their luggage, which was carried by unusually muscular valets.

It was little different when it came to arranging for the travel of the non-Catholic religious figures, although they had been easier to contact. Unlike the understandably reclusive cardinals, very few of the Protestants were trying to remain hidden. However, Miro had been at considerable pains to select and prepare messengers who would not only exercise great discretion when bringing the various theologians a carefully worded invitation to Urban's ecumenical colloquium in Besançon, but who could tactfully allay their suspicions even while pressing them to appreciate the dire importance of their attendance. That several of the Protestant luminaries had stonily refused to conduct any of their travel by dirigible had not made the security arrangements any easier.

But within the minute, the most worrisome of all those arrangements would be behind them: the sedan chairs bearing Bedmar's entourage had swung around the far end of the uneven line that stretched halfway back to the bridge.

But they were not alone. A distinctly alien group came along directly behind them on horseback. Large burly men with sabers, long curved axes, and strangely peaked helmets surrounded a thin, gold-clad figure kept carefully, protectively, in their midst.

Owen Roe O'Neill, emerging from the toll-house, stopped, stared. "What in the name of all that's holy—?"

Larry answered. "Russian Orthodox." He turned to Sharon. "I thought they were coming by dirigible."

"They did, at least as far as Basel," she answered, then caught her lower lip between her teeth. "Damn, we're going to need a bigger escort. That's two big holy rollers at the same time." Her eyes opened wider as she evidently reconsidered her use of the colloquialism, "holy roller." She turned toward Larry. "Larry, uh, Father Mazzare, I—I'm—"

"I find a little irreverence refreshing. Although, you probably don't want to repeat that phrase in *their* presence."

Ruy's eyes, which were watching the Burgundian soldiery and the Wild Geese reposition themselves with the smooth ease of a much-rehearsed change of formation, may have twinkled. "I agree with Cardinal Mazzare—but I would enjoy seeing you call Bedmar a 'holy roller' to his face, even so."

Sharon smirked. "I bet you would. You'd probably—"

From just behind the Russians, a sudden commotion fumed and frothed along a short section of the line of regular entrants. Launching outward were almost a dozen thin figures, most clad in fragments of armor. Several carried short swords; one had a halberd. Their clothing was even more irregular, but almost all had wide knee-length breeches or a hip-length doublet. One or two had shirts with striped sleeves, or short-capes of either black or gray. Or maybe the gray ones were simply very worn versions of the black.

The *besontsin* militia, which had not yet reached this part of the line, recoiled, crying out for aid and weapons. The Burgundians collapsed inward toward the disturbance, swords clearing sheaths with ringing hisses.

And, despite a lifetime in priestly vestments and striving to be Christlike in thought and deed, the first words that flitted through Larry Mazzare's mind were:

Oh, shit.

Chapter 3

Ruy's alacrity never failed to startle Mazzare, though he had seen it in action several times. Before the American priest could have formed the thoughts necessary to give orders, the hidalgo was shouting abbreviated commands, racing forward. The Wild Geese suddenly became an outer security cordon, with several of its senior members trying to rein in the Burgundians.

But if the militia or regular soldiers had heard Ruy—or Owen Roe O'Neill, whose long-legged sprint carried him toward the unresponsive sergeant of the Burgundians—they gave no sign of it. They closed in on the strange group that had emerged from the line and seemed to be striving to reach Bedmar.

"Damn it," Sharon hissed. She turned toward the young Hibernian who both carried a portable radio and was detailed as her assistant. "Are your snipers ready?"

"Ready, ma'am," he said, glancing up at the various vantage points where the elite troops were already sighting along the barrels of their large-bore Winchesters down toward the ragged pack that was approaching the three sedan chairs.

However, to get to Bedmar, the unruly ragtag group had to brush alongside the Russian horsemen. Who, seeing the trajectory of these unlikely threats, drew weapons and, with admirable swiftness, reformed so that three of their number were countercharging while the remainder closed ranks around their glittering patriarch, faces and blades affirming a fell readiness to take on the entirety of Besançon.

Bedmar's own group had halted. In the next instant, the veiled sedan chairs each emitted a ready warrior in a most nonclerical rush of plate-armored limbs and readied swords. Which meant one of three things: that Bedmar was not traveling with his entourage, that he was disguised as one of its lesser members, or that he was one of the redoubtable combatants now positioning themselves behind the charging Russian horsemen.

Larry Mazzare had proven his mettle and resourcefulness defending Pope Urban in Italy, but the suddenness with which the open space before the toll-house was turning into a battlefield caught him so off-guard that all he could do was accept the certainty that a bloodbath was imminent. Ruy, despite his speed and agility, was not going to be able to reach the point of contact in time, not before the Russians had charged headlong into the slowing, and possibly startled, group that had emerged from the line. He glanced over the stunned faces of tradesmen and fishmongers toward Owen Roe O'Neill.

Who turned, nodded at an adjutant, then pulled a weapon from where it was slung across his back: a Russian SKS. The adjutant raised what looked like a cumbersome trumpet and blew a shrill, sustained peal on the instrument.

The tatterdemalion detachment from the line halted; the Russians drew up their protesting horses; Bedmar's troops looked over, uncertain what this clarion call might signify. And in the moment of silence that followed:

"*Halt! Arrêt! Detener!*" Ruy's sword came out along with this high, clear shout, and if his French accent wasn't much better than his German, it did not seem to impede anyone's understanding of his command or the presumption of authority in his voice.

The drawn weapons lowered slightly, and if the faces of the various groups were still fierce and furrowed in wariness, the expressions were now more defensive than aggressive. The voice of the trumpet—a call to attention recognized by fighting men of every nation— had paused them, reflex keeping them momentarily poised and expectant for a signal to further action.

By the time the first of them were recalling that, because they recognized none of the local authorities, they had no reason to heed this foreign trumpet, Ruy had managed to work his way between the brooding Russian cavalry and the bewildered ragtag collection of what appeared to be commoners playing at soldier. Raising a hand to hold back the Russians, the hidalgo half raised his sword in the direction of the ragged group who were clutching their weapons. "What is the meaning of this display?" He scrutinized them; even at his greater distance, Larry could now discern that many of them were quite young.

Their apparent leader—a good-looking young man with golden hair and a nose like a perfect right triangle—bowed. "If it please the captain, I am Ignaz von Meggen, the great-great-grandson of Jost von Meggen." He said it with studied humility.

Ruy, who had been admirably prepared for every eventuality that had presented itself so far, suddenly seemed at a loss. "I see," he said, frowning.

Larry started moving forward, Sharon trailing a step behind him. Ruy was still struggling to find an adequate response. Clearly, the young man presumed that his family name would make his presence and intent clear. It was equally clear that he was coming to realize that this could not be further from the case.

More earnest than before, he attempted to provide greater clarity. "I refer to Jost von Meggen of Luzern."

Larry spread his arms as he approached: a gesture someplace between a greeting and a blessing. "Young Herr von Meggen, I am not familiar with the families of the Swiss cantons. Perhaps you would be so kind as to acquaint me with the details of your own."

Ignaz made another slight bow—both a polite response to the introduction and a signal of his intent to comply with the request—and then stopped, glancing more closely at Mazzare. "Your accent is peculiar, Father—er, pardon, Your Eminence. Might I ask where you call your home?"

Well, now was as good a time as ever. "Perhaps you have heard of the town of Grantville?"

Young von Meggen was suddenly very straight. "You are an up-timer." Larry could see the deductive dominoes falling behind the young fellow's eyes: he might be ingenuous, but he was not slow-witted. "You are the cardinal-protector of the United States of Europe!" And he was on one knee with remarkable speed. His younger companions followed his lead promptly; the older ones in the rear seemed less enthusiastic doing so. "Your Eminence, I apologize for having had no means of identifying you from the outset."

Larry stepped forward, took the young man by the shoulders, and raised him up. "Well, that makes us equal, then. So tell me of the family von Meggen of Luzern."

Ignaz complied quickly. And loquaciously. However, although it was long in the telling, it also had the effect of boring, and thereby calming, the various armed men who had been ready to commit mayhem only scant minutes earlier.

"So," Larry said, in an attempt to summarize, "your great-great-grandfather was the first Swiss commander of the Papal Guard after the Sack of Rome in 1527."

Ignaz nodded; his hair bobbed and shone. Well back in the crowd, some young female voices murmured appreciatively. Whatever else you might say about Ignaz von Meggen, he was a handsome fellow. Ignaz, oblivious to the signs of attention from the opposite sex, stared expectantly at Larry. "So, clearly, you know why we are here."

Suddenly, Larry found himself in the same situation as had Ruy. He put on his best smile and shook his head.

Ignaz von Meggen's face grew very pale, then very red. "Is it possible?" he said loudly, staring back at the crowd as if seeking their sympathy. "Can it be that the sacrifice of so many fine men is so quickly forgotten?" As his volume built, so did his passion; as surprise became bitter disappointment, a measure of anger crept in as well. The militia's and Burgundians' stances began a subtle shift back into combative readiness; just behind, Larry could hear the Russians shifting in their saddles, the horses moving restlessly in anticipation of renewed action. Mazzare swallowed, decided to risk stepping closer in an attempt to calm the charming young hothead...

A stooped, almost hunchbacked, figure stepped sideways out of the line. "If it please Your Eminence, Your Lordships, I think I can explain."

Ruy's sword came up slightly. "And who are you?"

"A fellow traveler with the lad and his companions."

Larry stared at the man's rough clothes; the mule-drawn cart and large, sleepy-eyed assistant he had been standing with; and his own unfortunate facial features. They might have been at least plain, once, but now they were dominated by a nose that resembled a squashed turnip and an uneven jaw that worked with a sideways motion and occasionally revealed an uneven row of mostly shattered teeth.

Ruy's tone was dubious. "You are part of his company, then?"

"Sorry, no, my lord, I am not. I started out closer to Zug, heading to Zurich, then the Bozen pass to Basel and so to here. Same route the young freiherr was on, if't please you."

"I see," Ruy muttered. "You mentioned an explanation?"

Young von Meggen's chin came up with his obvious intent to try again, but he accepted a deferential stilling gesture from the turnip-nosed man. "Yes, lord. It's a matter of the date, you see. May 6. Tomorrow." Even he seemed a bit surprised when this did not kindle any discernible flickers of understanding in the eyes around him. "No doubt it's more significant to us in the cantons—the Catholic ones, that is—than elsewhere. That's the day that almost all of the first Pontifical Swiss Guards were slain defending Pope Clement VII during the Sack of Rome. Since then, it's been the day that new members of the Guard are sworn in."

Ruy did not manage to keep all the incredulity out of his voice. "And these...young men...intend to present themselves here, to Pope Urban, for that purpose? To take service with him?"

This time, Ignaz would not be stilled. "As did our fathers before us, sir! And having word that the Holy Father is here, and of the new massacre that befell our countrymen in his service last year, we felt it our duty—both to our families and our faith—to offer our swords and our blood to him and to Mother Church."

Ruy swallowed, looked helplessly back at Larry, who managed not to shrug.

Turnip-Nose took a shuffling step closer. "My lord, Your Eminence, a word, if I might."

Ruy nodded, waved him forward with the hand that he had been using to hold the Russian cavalry motionless. A stern look kept the militia and Burgundians back...but Ruy pointedly did not glance at Larry's two Wild Geese guards, who drifted slowly, unobtrusively, closer. "Be quick," the Catalan murmured when the fellow had approached.

"Yes, lord. There's more at work here than youthful impetuosity. Service to the pope runs long in some of our families, particularly the ones who've shed blood as pikemen. But the wealthiest families...well, they often secure a place in Rome at the expense of the lesser ones."

Larry frowned. "How does that impact Ignaz? He

claims his family was one of the first to serve in the Papal Guard."

The tradesman bobbed once. "Yes, Your Eminence. That is true. But it is also the *last* time they served. Other, more influential families shoved this lad's aside. At least that's how we heard it in the towns outside Luzern itself."

Mazzare crossed his hands. "And now, in the wake of the destruction of the Swiss Guard at the Castel St. Angelo last year, he hopes that the von Meggen family might once again have the opportunity to serve?"

"That's the gist of it, sir. Don't know much beyond what he shared over campfires on the trail, Your Eminence. Can't say I know much about his family, either, except to say that none of it is bad. Can't say the same for some of the others who've always had sons carrying halberds and wearing papal colors south of the Alps."

Ruy looked narrowly at the crooked man. "And what is your interest in this, that you stand forward to take his part?" Mazzare almost started at the sudden accusation in Ruy's tone.

So did the man. "My lord, I'm . . . I'm a father. I have idealistic sons. Fewer now than before, to speak plainly. And I've seen where their grand ideas and big mouths can land them, early graves being not uncommon ends. So why should I let some other man's son share that fate, especially when the son's father is no longer on this side of the grave to help?"

Ruy was clearly trying to maintain his hard exterior, but his voice belied a softening behind it. "He is the eldest male von Meggen remaining?"

The other looked down, scuffed in the dust. "I was not so bold as to ask it that directly, sir. But it seems so. Family's fallen on hard times." He looked up. "Most of the battles of the past ten years were south, in the Valtelline, but they sent us their share of hardship, too. If you take my meaning, my lord."

Larry took a half step forward. "We take your meaning and appreciate your willingness to help a fellow traveler. Don't we, Colonel Sanchez?"

Ruy nodded but peered more intently at the trades-man. "What is *your* business here in Besançon?"

The man hitched around, favoring what seemed to be a bad hip, gestured at his donkey cart and enormous assistant. "Nails and ironmongery, my lord."

"You will no doubt welcome our inspection of your goods?"

The man looked stunned. "You are more than welcome, my lord." He bowed out of the way, hastily gestured to his assistant, who fumbled uncertainly in response. "Apologies, sirs; Otto does not always understand what I ask him to do. With your leave, I shall have him open the casks so you may—"

Ruy shook his head sharply; Larry couldn't be sure if he was annoyed at the turnip-nosed man or at him-self. "No need. We thank you for your assistance." He motioned Ignaz closer. "Young Freiherr von Meggen, you are fortunate in the acquaintances you have made along the road, for without this one's intercession, your actions might have led you to a bad end."

Ignaz nodded. "My regrets, sir. I was overcome by my ardor and eagerness to serve my pope."

Ruy's left eyebrow raised slightly. "I do not see why that would inspire you to suddenly fly in pursuit of the sedan chairs." He gestured behind at Bedmar's entourage.

Von Meggen nodded in the same direction. "I saw that, sir."

Ruy and Mazzare turned.

The rearmost of the papal sedan chairs, which had been left at the aerodrome for the express purpose of carrying Bedmar through the gates incognito, no longer had its concealing shroud firmly attached to the back. Instead, having slipped, it revealed the crossed keys symbol of the Holy See.

Ruy shared a rueful look with Mazzare, then turned back to Ignaz. "While your enthusiasm to serve your pope is laudable, Herr von Meggen, your impetuosity was nearly your undoing—yours and all your men. You must learn to temper your passions, if you are to become an officer worthy of the position to which you aspire."

Ignaz almost came to attention. "Yes, sir."

Ruy nodded, seemed to be trying to suppress a grin as he lifted his chin, spoke so all around him could hear. "And since you have now all been questioned, you may enter Besançon at your leave. Be warned: lodgings are sparse, now. Secure rooms swiftly."

Ignaz pressed a half step closer. "But Colonel, Your Eminence, there is the matter of presenting ourselves to the Holy Father on the morrow, to swear obedience to his..."

Ruy held up his hand. "I have no authority in these matters, Herr von Meggen." Then his eyes were suddenly lost in a crush of mischievous crow's feet: "However, Cardinal Mazzare is one of His Holiness' closest and most trusted counselors. Surely he will be able to offer you guidance in this matter." The spry hidalgo moved off to shoo the shabby imitation Swiss Guards out of the line, while gesturing for two militiamen to help Turnip-Nose and his sizable assistant Otto move their recalcitrant mule.

Larry stared after him, tamping down uncharitable thoughts that he was ultimately able to constrain to, *Thanks a bunch, Ruy.*

Ignaz actually had his hands clasped in some mixture of anxiousness and supplication. "We are entirely at your disposal, Your Eminence. We will happily wait upon the Pontiff's pleasure—in the street, if necessary—so that we might—"

"No, no; that won't be necessary." Mazzare thought quickly. "Tomorrow morning, before first mass, come to the square just north of St. John's cathedral. Your first test will be patience, as I have no idea what the first half of the day will hold, or even if the pope may see you and receive your oaths of service. In the months since the Second Sack of Rome, he has had to take on a new guard, and it may not be immediately convenient to take on more. However, the Holy Father holds his children of the Swiss Cantons particularly dear and would not wish to send you away without a better idea of how your love may best serve Mother Church. So present yourself on the morrow, as I have directed, and we shall proceed from there."

Ignaz's face had cycled through crestfallen frowns and almost trembling smiles of hope while Larry had spoken. He ended on the latter. "Yes, Your Eminence. Your words shall be our law." With a swift nod, he bowed himself back and in the direction of his men.

Who were being impeded by a thin fringe of militia and Burgundians, backed by the sergeant of the regulars. Larry looked for Ruy: he had joined Sharon over by the Russians in an attempt to forge enough of a conversational link to explain the misunderstanding and calm them. A few gusty laughs from the horsemen told Mazzare that Ruy was succeeding in his soldier-to-soldier communicative efforts. Larry turned toward the militiamen. "Stand aside, my sons: these Swiss are our friends and devoted to the pope."

The *besontsin* guards eyed them darkly. The Burgundian sergeant looked like he was ready to spit. If a cardinal hadn't been standing in front of them, Larry had no doubt he would have. "You mean these Protestants?"

Larry felt a flash of anger ring his neck where his collar touched it. "These men have professed themselves as Catholics. But all you need to know is that these Swiss pikemen have been cleared to pass."

One of the *besontsins* sneered. "More like Swiss pike*boys*."

Larry saw Ignaz von Meggen turn, red-faced, with his hand moving toward his sword.

A very loud, authoritative voice froze him in mid motion, startled the militia and Burgundians into something approaching attention: "Where did you get the gear?" It was Owen Roe O'Neill, who had just wound his way across the line of commoners, one of his men, Oliver Fitzgerald, in tow. He nodded at the sword that Ignaz had been about to draw.

The young Swiss sounded defiant and pained, all at once. "Our dead fathers and brothers."

"And how did they die, again?"

"Most of them . . . defending the pope during the sack of Rome, last year."

Owen Roe didn't change the position of his head, but his eyes flicked over to stare at the Burgundians.

"So you'd be eager to skewer the sons of men who fought and died for the pope?"

"They did it for coin, Colonel. Might have claimed a different faith to get it, too. Lots of those Alpine valleys are pretty poor."

Before von Meggen could offer a retort, Owen shook his head. "Not what I heard about the mess in Rome, last year. And I heard it from one who was there, who saw the Pontifical Guard die, almost to a man."

"Oh," drawled the Burgundian sergeant, almost dismissively, "and who would that be?"

O'Neill's eyes were untroubled, but he started forward quickly. "You'll be watching your tongue, lad. Or I'll be having it out of your head."

The sergeant looked away. When he spoke, his voice was no longer that of a man barely concealing contempt, but beating a hasty retreat to save what face he could. "I'd still know who saw this sacrifice of the Pontifical Guard."

A familiar voice came from behind Larry. "Why, that would be my own undeserving self, Sergeant." Ruy concluded on a smile, then glanced at O'Neill. They exchanged knowing looks.

And suddenly Mazzare understood: this too had been a contingency, had been a planned response to a possible discipline problem among the local troops. Which meant that O'Neill's very loud voice had been a signal, that this countermove against insolence from the Burgundians and *besontsins*—neither of whom liked being outplaced (and obviously outclassed) by Sanchez's and O'Neill's men—was yet another contingency that they had put in place.

Ruy had fixed the Burgundian sergeant with an

intent stare. "In my experience, coin alone does not buy loyalty unto oblivion. Honor, love, integrity: those are the virtues that compel men to serve unto their own death. They are also virtues that Our Savior extolled."

Sharon had arrived to stand alongside her husband. She looked down the line, chin in the air. "I see we have some *genuine* Protestants back there. Famous ones, too." She smiled and waved several modestly-dressed gentlemen forward. "Reverends, I'm sorry I didn't see you waiting in the main line. I wonder: could we trouble you to shift over into the line for arriving dignitaries?"

Two middle-aged men did as Sharon asked, each followed by an assistant.

Mazzare saw their faces, started, leaned toward Sharon. "Are those—?"

"Not a word yet, Father," Sharon whispered out of the side of her mouth. As the newly detached group came forward, she raised her voice so all could hear. "Reverends, I wonder if I could trouble you to share your names and credentials?"

"Certainly," replied the older one. "I am Johann Gerhard, Senior Professor of Theology at Jena and not entirely unknown to Cardinal Mazzare, I think!"

He and Larry exchanged smiles.

"And my shy English friend here has less confidence in his French, but he is—"

"—but he is quite capable of speaking for himself, Johann!" The younger man turned to Sharon, made a deep bow, and, in Oxbridge English, announced, "The Reverend John Dury, Ambassador Nichols. A disciple of Calvin. My credentials are—dubious, madame."

Larry smiled. "A unifier of faiths is frequently an

itinerant: hard to come by a title that way. But we know your work, Reverend, and are glad you consented to come."

"So," Sharon concluded, turning to the Burgundian sergeant with a smile that was anything but cheerful. "Since you seem determined to ascertain the religion of the people who want to enter Besançon, here are a half dozen Lutherans and Calvinists who also happen to be our guests. Are you going to detain and question them?"

The Burgundian sergeant stammered but ultimately fell quiet.

Owen Roe O'Neill came level with the soldier and patted that worthy on the shoulder. "A wise reply. Now, find such militiamen as can be trusted to help all these men to find lodgings."

Chapter 4

Ruy Sanchez de Casador y Ortiz turned away from the mollified Burgundian sergeant, nodded appreciatively at O'Neill, sent his wife a grateful kiss through his eyes, and focused on the now thoroughly bored Russians. Some of them had known just enough Turkish that he had been able to reassure them with a joke about militiamen who thought they were soldiers, and soldiers who thought they could think. But now, he found a more difficult task before him: communicating with the Patriarch of Moscow and All Rus.

Ruy had a little Greek, and he took a stab at introducing himself. At which point a slim young fellow in hardly any armor at all interceded. "We may converse in English—or Amideutsch, if that would be convenient, Colonel Sanchez." The young man bowed slightly in his saddle. "I am the interpreter and, I think you would say, purser, for Patriarch Joasaphus and his party. The patriarch would welcome an explanation for the agitation just resolved."

Ruy explained as succinctly as he could, Sharon coming alongside him as he did.

She nodded agreement as he concluded, adding, "We welcome His Holiness and ask that you follow the guards which Colonel Sanchez will now provide for escort to the lodgings we have set aside for you. Please convey to them any additional needs and we will meet them as best as we might." Sharon's smile became a little crooked. "As you might suppose, since we are not meeting in Rome, we also lack the amenities that would have been available there."

Joasaphus—a tall, thin man with a dour hermit's face—muttered something to the interpreter, who nodded his understanding, and seemed to suppress a smile. "His Holiness understands and even welcomes these less opulent conditions. To paraphrase, 'gold blinds men to truth, and so, blinds them to the will of God'—and so, feels that this venue is more promising than those which might have been better appointed."

Sharon smiled; Ruy did his best to keep his focus on the patriarch rather than his wife's dark, beautiful face, full lips, and flawless skin. "We are very grateful to have His Holiness' wisdom for this colloquium. It also seems he does not particularly need an interpreter."

The interpreter smiled. "The patriarch finds it far easier to understand English than to speak it. And only when it is spoken at a measured pace, as you just did. He looks forward to meeting with the leaders of the other churches and wonders if that will take place tomorrow."

"No, the day after. Please impress upon His Holiness that we wish to give our visitors time to settle in and, to the extent possible, acclimate to the language and customs of Besançon. We shall send a messenger later today with an outline of the itinerary."

The interpreter began turning his horse. "Patriarch Joasaphus is most grateful, Ambassador Nichols." The lean, gilt-garbed patriarch raised a thin-fingered hand in farewell, maybe blessing and, his bodyguards clustering close around him, rode slowly after the guides and guards that Ruy had provided.

Ruy glanced at Bedmar's group, who were still standing, arms at the ready. Obviously, none of the heavily armored men who had debouched from the sedan chairs were Bedmar himself. Only one was anywhere near short enough, and he was far too young: Alfonso was now more than sixty, and, word had it, was even less dedicated to daily exercise than he had been just a year ago.

A shapely hand was tugging at his elbow: his wife's, who was facing the other direction and saying, "Thank you for your patience in becoming part of our object lesson in religious tolerance, Reverends."

Ruy turned, found himself facing the two Protestants. The older, German one was nodding. "Dury and I have devoted much of our life to similar exercises—although sometimes, I confess, the task can seem Sisyphian."

The Englishman shrugged. "That is because you refuse to threaten with the stick when the carrot doesn't work, Johann." If they had not known each other when their journey to Besançon had started, they had apparently become not merely friendly, but informal, as companions on the road.

Which reminded Ruy to make his now-standard inquiry of those guests who had any prior familiarity with the region. "Reverends, before domiciling you, I would appreciate anything you might tell us about conditions along the route you took to reach us."

Dury shrugged. "There is little to tell. I had already traveled to Jena, where I met this fellow waiting for the same balloon."

Ruy nodded. That had been part of Miro's plan: to put the attendees on the same flights, and thereby minimize both the number of security overseers, and also the number of seats that might be filled by unknown persons.

"From there," Johann Gerhard was saying as he waved at the sky, "it was just a matter of counting clouds."

"And landing," Dury added with a shudder.

"Yes," Gerhard agreed with a small sigh. "One of the landings was a bit...sudden."

"It was at Biberach," Dury declared, his face paler than it had been a moment before. "Wind forced us down too quickly."

"It was Basel," Gerhard corrected mildly, "where we caught a bit of an alpine draft upon our descent. But the...eh, 'pilot,' was quite skilled. He aimed up into the wind until it calmed, then alit in the marked field. Most exciting. And wondrous."

Dury's pallor suggested he had other associations with the episode.

Sharon nodded at Gerhard, and Ruy could tell, by the way she had leaned forward very slightly and the way her eyes moved from the face of one reverend to the other, that she was going to try to change the topic away from flying. "Well, we are delighted and relieved you are here. We were informed, however, that both of you had planned to travel on the roads."

Gerhard brushed a finger across his mustache; a gesture not dissimilar from the one that Ruy affected every once in a great while, although Sharon insisted he did it several times an hour. "That had been my intent. But weather delayed me. March was rainy and trade goods had been moving very slowly from town to town—so slow that, by April, teams could not be contracted. Merchants had them reserved at premium rates. So, while I waited, I received this fellow's letter, introducing himself and wondering if we might travel together. Well, I'd never met the troublemaker before, and I had to wait anyway.

"But by the time the weather cleared, it was equally clear we would never make it here in time by wagon or even coach. So I recontacted Herr Miro in Grantville and we were fortunate: he still had seats on his wonderful dirigibles."

"They would be more wonderful if they stayed closer to the ground," Dury groused.

What would have been even more wonderful, Ruy reflected, would have been if they'd traveled by road from Basel. That way, they would have heard travelers' tales of the conditions in the various Alpine passes and roads that attendees might be trying to use to reach them from Italy. More specifically, poor road conditions meant that some of the Italian cardinals might still be coming, just couldn't get through yet. At last report, the closer passes—the Bozeberg, Belchen, and less-frequented Chilchzimmersattel—were clear, and there had been no word of late season snows in the farther Brenner and Bozen passes.

Ruy had enough presence of mind to add his welcome and good wishes to those of Sharon, who, once the theologians had been sent on their way with guides, half turned to him. "Ruy, what's the matter?"

"I am afraid we may have admitted the last cardinal we may hope to see."

"Well," put in another voice, "not the *very* last, I hope."

Ruy shook his head, turned. Bedmar was standing behind him, hands on hips, wearing the almost ankle-length frock of a Church scribe. Ruy could not keep a mischievous curl from bending the left side of his mouth. "Your Eminence," he said with a bow.

Bedmar laughed, but returned the bow for the benefit of the scores of befuddled—and a few bemused—on-lookers. "A rascal as ever," he snickered. "I would ask you how you have been, Ruy, but you would report the same rude—nay, satanically gifted—health that you have always enjoyed. Besides, such a query would delay the most pleasant part of this reunion: reacquainting myself with your wife, Ambassadora Nichols."

Sharon came forward with a wide smile, but Ruy knew the look: it was disarming, and yet, a bit guarded. Her contact with Bedmar had been scant, but she had heard many stories of the years that Ruy and Bedmar had spent together. "Your Eminence," she said with a slightly formal bow.

Bedmar was nothing if not perceptive. His smile was almost apologetic. "And I can tell from the look in your eye, Ambassadora Nichols, that my old friend has now given you a full account of our times together. As a good husband should." He blew out his cheeks, exasperated. "I can only hope there shall be an opportunity for us three to dine together, that I might improve your opinion of me. And I shall further hope, when formal courtesies are no longer necessitated by this public setting, that our conversation shall be more relaxed. But, for the nonce, I must convey my congratulations on your security. Ruy, you have, if anything, become a more accomplished war-dog with each passing year."

"I avail myself of new insights wherever I might find them," Ruy replied, with a brush at his moustache. See, he didn't do it *that* often—did he? "And ready access to the full collection of books in Grantville has been uncommonly enlightening. You are to be congratulated on your own precautions, Your Eminence."

Bedmar sighed. "I wish I could take credit for that ploy, my dear Sanchez, but since lying was still a sin when I consulted my breviary this morning, I must give credit where it is due." He turned to the oldest of the three men who had emerged from the sedan chairs. "May I present, Captain Achille d'Estampes de Valençay, knight of the Sovereign Order of Malta. And in your timeline, Ambassadora, eventually the general of the papal army under Pope Urban."

Ruy extended a hand and put a winning smile on his face as he mentally consulted the dossiers that Sharon had reviewed with him. Urban had sent a secure document to Malta half a year ago, inform-ing de Valençay that he had been made a cardinal *in pectore:* "close to the chest," and so, undisclosed. Urban had sent out many such notifications, most of them following patterns of loyalty he had observed in both this world and, evidently, the other. There, Achille d'Estampes de Valençay had been given a biretta in 1643. And this was not the only way in which the arrival of the up-timers had been favorable to his fortunes: since the disruption in the original progression of the Thirty Years' War had prevented the Battle of Castelnaudary from ever being fought, he had not taken the side of Gaston's ally, Henri II de Montmorency, in an attempt to strip Richelieu of his royal influence. Nonetheless, the Grey Eminence, familiar with the up-timer histories, had taken the precaution of ensuring that the much-honored Achille be deprived of an appropriate command, resulting in his return to Malta.

Achille stood at least three inches taller than Ruy's own medium height, and if the hidalgo had a panther-like build (well, perhaps only a cheetah now—but still as swift!), de Valençay was decidedly a tiger. His rapier was of the heaviest kind—almost a longsword—and his service as a colonel and even a fleet commander had not leeched any of the taut, lean readiness out of his body. At forty-three, he wore his heavy cuirass and helmet with the indifferent ease of men half his age. Ruy found himself assessing the way this chevalier wore his sword and moved: an old reflex for assessing possible opponents, working out optimal tactics in advance. But this time, there was a faint twinge of jealousy, of being the older rooster meeting a younger one who might be every bit as capable in a fight. Not as polished, probably, but strength and size might offset that difference.

Ruy almost had to physically shake himself out of the competitive mindset. "Captain, your reputation precedes you, and your most recent ruse adorns it even further."

Valençay bowed as they finished shaking hands. "And you, sir, are becoming something of a legend. I welcome the chance to make your acquaintance. Allow me to present my traveling companions, and fellow-protectors of His Eminence Cardinal Bedmar: my brother Léonore and Giovanni Carlo de Medici."

Ruy peripherally noticed Sharon stand a bit straighter beside him. And for good reason: Giovanni Carlo de Medici, or Giancarlo, was not merely one of the most able young nobles—and eligible bachelors—in all of Italy, but was the nephew of Bernhard's wife, Claudia de Medici, although only six years younger than she. And he was fairly sure he knew what his wife was thinking: here is a prime scion of the royal house of Tuscany acting the part of a cardinal's bodyguard, when he himself might need protecting against assassins' knives. Borja's agents had learned that he, too, had been fated to become a cardinal in later years, and for him to be at Urban's colloquium was akin to volunteering for a death sentence. Léonore was, by comparison, decidedly less tigerish than his older brother, just as his eyes were less piercing and his handshake less viselike.

Ruy turned back to Bedmar. "You are singularly fortunate in your retinue, Your Eminence."

Bedmar nodded, but his face had become grave. He turned to the others, who were almost his peers, and asked them, graciously, if they would be so good as to spread word that the entourage would be moving soon again. The three exchanged knowing looks, proffered bows to Ruy, Sharon, and then Larry, who had not yet come forward, and set about ordering their small group; it responded and moved with the precision of a military unit.

"I see you are taking no chances in your travels," Ruy observed with a pointedly flat tone once they had left earshot.

"Quite true," Bedmar countered. "Although, in point of fact, we are all helping each other. Achille received a summons from Urban, I am told, and I can well guess its nature. Giancarlo, having had the promise of a biretta in your world, has now attracted the baleful attention of Borja in this one. So just as I am made safer by having three such soldiers with me, I offer a measure of protection to them."

Sharon nodded. "Because unless someone after them also has orders to kill you, they can't take a chance of exceeding their . . . authority."

Bedmar smiled at the euphemism. "And so, here we are, arrived in safety, due in no small measure to your excellent network of aerodromes. In fact, so far, there is only one disconcerting aspect of my reception here."

Sharon leaned forward. "Please, tell me."

Bedmar smiled. "That my brother in faith has not stepped forward to greet me." He shot a quick glance over Sharon's shoulder at Larry Mazzare, who stood, hands folded, ten feet behind her.

"I did not want to interrupt what was sure to be a reunion of friends," Mazzare said quietly. And Ruy also detected a hint of caution and reserve.

So, apparently, did Bedmar. "Your Eminence, when last we met in Venice, circumstances ineluctably made us enemies. Respectful and honorable, yes, but enemies nonetheless."

Larry did not change position or posture. "Indeed, Your Eminence. And now?"

Ruy saw Sharon suppress a start: clearly, Larry had not informed her that this was the tack he intended to take upon Bedmar's arrival.

Bedmar folded his hands, studied Larry carefully. "And now," he repeated, "I find you a changed man, and us in very changed circumstances. We have always been brothers in the Church, Your Eminence; we are now fully peers, as well." Bedmar smiled. "Indeed, you may have the advantage of me."

Larry raised an eyebrow, his tone no less wary. "In what way?"

Bedmar put out appealing hands; they were large hands, almost comically so, given that he barely stood five foot six in thick-heeled boots. "Surely you see that, by coming here, I am not endearing myself to Philip of Spain, and even less to his minister Olivares. I am the only Spanish cardinal who has not proclaimed for Borja. Now, I am an honored guest in the camp of his mortal enemy. What level of favor do you expect I enjoy in Madrid?"

Larry nodded. "Reduced, certainly—but not irre-deemable. In fact, it may yet prove advisable for at least one of the 'Spanish cardinals' to remain unsoiled by support of Borja. That lack of unanimity could become a fig-leaf of legitimacy if Philip eventually wishes to claim that he did not expressly order his cardinals to declare for the homicidal madman cur-rently maintaining a rule of terror in Rome."

Bedmar looked down, frowned. "And you presume I am so farsighted?"

Larry folded his arms. "I don't know; are you?"

Sharon almost gasped. "Lar—Cardinal Mazzare!"

"No," Bedmar interrupted. "He is right. And it confirms what I have heard of Cardinal-Protector Mazzare. He has risen to his august position not merely by dint of being the senior Catholic among you up-timers, but by his shrewdness." Bedmar stood straight. "Very well. I may not divulge the full details of the political circumstances under which I have traveled here, but let me make this very clear: I come to you—first, foremost, and only—as the cardinal-protector of the Spanish Lowlands, and of Fernando, the king in the Lowlands. And his desires match the mandate of both my conscience and my vows: to safeguard Mother Church, and, if it is possible to do so without compromising her, to put the sectarian strife with the Protestants to an end." He paused to let his words sink in. "Is that clear enough?"

Mazzare nodded slowly and stepped forward. "It is, Cardinal Bedmar." He looked sideways at Sharon. "My regrets, Ambassador, but I am a son of the Church first—even before I am a citizen of the USE and Grantville."

Sharon nodded slowly, her eyes calm—but if Ruy was any judge of his wife, she would be taking Larry Mazzare aside at some time in the very near future for a forthright and lively exchange of opinions.

Bedmar closed the remaining distance to Larry and offered his hand. "I apologize for the liberties I took when we first met in Venice. It is an old military instinct to put a potential adversary on the back foot, to push him in conversations, to test limits and boundaries, all under the guise of diplomatic banter. I did so there. I will not do so here—with you, or anyone. Times have changed. I will not claim that I have as well, but I am reformed in some of my least dignified habits. These days leave no room for pettiness if we are to caretake the future well-being of Holy Mother Church and the innocents who might yet die in sectarian strife."

Larry offered his hand in return. "We are certainly agreed on that."

Bedmar nodded soberly. "I think you shall find that, since you and I last met, we are in agreement on much, much more." He put his other hand atop theirs and then withdrew towards his entourage. "I suspect it is not part of your protocol to keep vulnerable persons loitering about as easy targets."

Of the many things Ruy had ever imagined, or knew, Bedmar to be, "vulnerable" or "an easy target" were not among them. "Yes, let us go."

Chapter 5

As the sand in his hourglass passed the two-o'clock mark, Javier de Requesens y Ercilla put down his midday meal—a small, fantastically expensive roll—and glanced up at the thick, almost basilicate, bell-tower of St. Paul's. When he had started reviewing the reports to synopsize for his next transmission to Madrid, it had been eleven AM. The tip of the church's shadow had been upon the sill of his window as he opened the cedar shutters upon a day in which the sun proved elusive, capriciously flitting in and out of the clouds like a coquette changing dance partners at a court ball.

However, despite his lesser grandee origins, Javier had not spent much time at any court or attending balls. Which was a pity, because he was quite sure that his graceful footwork, deft conversational skills, and ability to convince dull social superiors that they were in fact every bit as fascinating and compelling as they believed (or hoped) themselves to be would have won him much favor in any of the ducal courts or even those at Madrid itself.

He looked out his window, ostensibly the best view

(and room) in *L'Auberge de Boucle d'Argent*. Beyond St. Paul's bluff sides and steeple, beyond the curtain wall that encircled Besançon, he stared at the northern horn of the River Doub's oxbow curve. The water was streaked and speckled by white, there: the current picked up speed as it flowed around the corner and made for the Pont Battant. It was truly a shame, he thought with a sigh, that instead of a life as a courtier, he had been compelled to make his way in the world by serving as an incognito factotum for any one of a dozen intelligencers to whom Olivares commended his services. His education at Salamanca and facility with languages made him an excellent foreign agent, and his aristocratic background and ambitions made him somewhat less susceptible to outright treachery, although it was presumed that a man in his position would of course accept the gratuities and gifts that, in any other line of work, would have been known by a more distasteful (if accurate) term: bribe.

It wasn't very hard work, gathering intelligence and relaying orders with reasonable subtlety. And what was often the greatest inconvenience of all—relocating and establishing a legitimate reason for being in the environs to which he'd been assigned—had been unnecessary this time. One of Olivares' innumerable section chiefs had been tasked with developing a portfolio on the new power in what had formerly been the Imperial city of Besançon, but which Bernhard had then grabbed during the extraordinary cascade of unforeseeable developments that had followed the up-timers' arrival at more or less the epicenter of the Thirty Years' War. It had been, in their world as well as here, not so much one war as a flurry of separate disputes that roared, sputtered, and roared again in rhythm with the changing fortunes and desires of various states and faiths, all of which draped themselves in high-sounding language and testimonies of holy purpose.

But by late 1634, those guttering fires had all but burned out and Bernhard seized Besançon as his capital. That it had been, for centuries, a free city of the Holy Roman Empire under the protection of the Hapsburgs had not served as a brake upon his ambitions.

Subsequent political events proved Bernhard's usurpation to have been as canny as it was bold. The city had passed from Spanish to Austrian oversight at the end of the last century, and the Austrians were now preoccupied with the looming likelihood of an Ottoman incursion. Between that concern, their decision not to garrison the city with foreign troops, and the expanses of very rough—and unallied—terrain between their country and Burgundy, the Austrians had accepted its loss with something approaching aplomb.

This put the onus of a decisive reaction back upon Spain's shoulders. But the same turmoil that had allowed Bernhard to grab Franche-Comté had cut the famous Spanish Road which had led from Spanish holdings in Italy all the way through to the Lowlands. Now interdicted at multiple points by multiple potential antagonists, Madrid had conceded that for any foreseeable future, and perhaps for all time, the overland artery that had fueled her European possessions with the blood of once-feared Spanish tercios had been irreparably severed.

However, that did not mean Spain ceased to have any interests in Besançon. There was no shortage of Spanish money and trade still invested in the city, as well as loyal allies who lamented the recent passing of the Hapsburg dominion over the place. And besides, Bernhard was unlikely to remain sated with the scope of his conquest for long. Like a shark, he was likely to die if he did not keep moving and devouring more of the land that provided the sustenance sought by all rulers: resources, taxes, young men who would take an army's coin.

And so, Javier de Requesens y Ercilla had arrived in Besançon in late September, 1634, shortly after the open hostilities between Bernhard's forces and those of the Swedish general Horn had diminished to sullen border-watching and occasional skirmishes when patrols led by overly ambitious young officers blundered into each other. War was, Javier affirmed as he organized the reports he had been busy emending for maximum brevity, a very foolish business.

However, if it were not for the acquisitive nature of kings, who knows what employ he himself might have? He was but the fourth son of a branch of the Requesens that had watched their fortunes fall along with their increasing distance from the House of Zuñiga, one of the twenty-five families made Immemorial Grandees of Spain and a frequent source of Madrid's leading ambassadors and intelligencers. Indeed, if Philip IV had not called Don Pedro de Zuñiga out of retirement in 1632 to provide a practiced Anglophone perspective upon the newly arrived up-timers, Javier feared he might have wound up overseeing some miserable collection of *fincas* where tenant farmers tilled the soil on one of his family's dwindling tracts.

But the senior Zuñiga had remembered his family's connection to both the Requesens and Ercillas, and accordingly asked for Javier: a suitably tactful individual, fluent in four languages, and eager to advance but without the delusions of grandeur that would make him more a liability than an asset. And so he had been plucked from his nuclear family's fate of increasing obscurity and become an object of pride. Javier's branch of the Requesens might still be counting fewer silver coins every year, but now, one of their number was once again carrying out important business for the Empire, had put the family name back on the lips of counselors and courtiers in Madrid. In the status-obsessed society of seventeenth-century Spain, that was almost as good as currency itself.

Javier glanced at the sundial; it would be time to turn on the radio soon. But not to relay information to the obscure factotum that Zuñiga trusted with matters in Besançon. Rather, Javier was scheduled to communicate with his second, surreptitious employer: Cardinal Gaspard de Borja y Velasco. How the would-be pope learned of Requesens' fortuitous presence in Besançon was as great a mystery as how he had learned, earlier than most, of Urban's establishment there. But that was immaterial to Javier. Borja paid good coin for the simplest of services: to relay reports from, and convey coded orders to, some creature of his who was currently in the city.

The sand in the glass ran out with the invariable appearance of suddenly increased speed. Javier reflected that life probably felt like that, too, when one came closer to its end. He reached over, turned on the radio, waited for the first signal, and hoped the earlier clouds did not portend difficult weather to the south and equally difficult transmissions. If so, he might be here for as long as four hours, working the same signals over and over again until the messages were complete. The mere prospect of such a dull routine drew forth a great sigh from him, and Javier de Requesens y Ercilla freely admitted to himself that he sighed a lot. It was, after all, the inevitable burden of a refined and sensitive soul such as his.

The radio crackled and began emitting a stream of coded signals, the first of which was a cipher that indicated that he was to receive a message before sending his report.

Javier rolled his eyes. More work. Well, at least the signal was clear, so he might not have to endure the additional burden of suffering through the monotony of oft-repeated messages.

Estève Gasquet glanced at sudden movement in the narrow street that separated his attic rooms and the small chapel that stood beside the entry to the Hospital of the Holy Spirit. It was one of his men—Peyre, from the size of him—who disappeared beneath his field of view, no doubt soon to pound up the narrow and rickety stair. Sure enough, the accomplished Pyreneeian strangler's heavy tread began thumping closer. Which meant that an incoming message from Rome was likely.

Gasquet turned his back to the narrow dormer window. He wished he could shut out the smell of fish and infrequently removed garbage that were the hallmark aromas of the hospital district: an overcrowded cluster of shabby buildings shoved up against the walls separating them from the quays where the northern curve of the Doub's oxbow bent the river and accelerated its flow toward the bridge. Still, as flophouses went, this was better than most. It was clean, if dingy, and while the neighborhood was anything but appealing, it was mostly safe. The much maligned Protestants of the city had increasingly drifted into this quarter since the failed Huguenot attack half a century ago, paying a price in prejudice for an incident that few of them had supported. Those Jews who did not make their living out in the Battant congregated here also, probably because the presence of the hospital seemed to prick the consciences of most of those whose prejudices might boil over into violence. Somehow, the typical bigot's dusk-stimulated appetite for thrashing or raping a few nonbelievers was undermined when they could hear the Hospitallers just a few doors away, murmuring vespers and beseeching the Holy Spirit to fill them with greater depths of charity and humility. Gasquet did not quite sneer at that thought: what idiots they all were, one half sacrificing themselves to help those halfway to the grave, and the other half risking violence without any hope of gain. All fools driven by ideas, beliefs, urges as insubstantial as the dead ancestors who had imposed these rituals upon them, rather than inculcating them with an appreciation for the only thing that mattered, the only thing that was tangible in this material world: material gain.

Beyond the old sheet that he had hung as a privacy blind—no sane leader ever lived without some physical boundary that reminded his men of the separation in their status and station—Gasquet heard Peyre emerge into the attic, breathing heavily. "News," he gasped.

Estève pushed around the side of the sheet, strode toward Peyre. "Let's have it, then."

"Two things," Peyre panted. "First, there's a message at the drop."

Gasquet nodded, glanced at the smallest of his six men, Chimo. "Get it."

The little Catalan was on the narrow stairs and heading down before Peyre could wheeze out. "Not yet."

Gasquet frowned. "Why?"

"You'll want to send a message of your own. Now. Before decoding the new instructions from Rome."

"I'm guessing that's due to the second bit of news you have for me."

Peyre nodded, finally straightening back up. "The Swiss. They're on the way."

"All of them?"

"No, no. Just the ones who know to look for us. I saw them all come into town a while ago. They split into two groups to look for lodging. One group is headed this way."

"So they found the message drop outside the Battant. Good."

"Very good," Peyre suggested. "Word is there are no rooms left in the Buckle. Everything is taken. Stables, attics, cellars."

Gasquet's lieutenant, Donat Faur, drew alongside, nodding. "Makes sense," murmured Estève's fellow *Prouvènço*. "The militia has been warning people that, after today, there will be no new entries allowed."

"You mean they're closing the city?" Chimo squawked.

"No," Peyre corrected irritably. "Anyone who has been allowed to enter up until now is either known personally or has been given a written pass with a seal. Same thing for boats on the Doub: they either have papers or they have to find mooring over in the

Battant. The last of those permissions were issued today. And anyone with a pass has been told to expect to be detained at the Porte Boucle until someone can be found who remembers providing them with the pass. Personally."

"So we won't be sneaking anyone else into the city by using a 'borrowed' pass, then," Faur muttered with a bitter smile.

"Not unless we want to attract attention. No: we have all the forces we're going to have."

"Which is why I figured you'd want to speak with the Swiss, find out how many more bodies we can count on."

Gasquet nodded, heard faint voices in the street, threw back his privacy sheet, glanced down.

"Looks like they're here. Brenguier," he said, gesturing to the swart, rangy Occitan lounging in the far shadows. "You speak the best German and spent time in Geneva, so you'll meet them downstairs. Make your greeting of them public, like they're friends, people you've known for years."

Brenguier nodded, shifted the scabbard of his large dagger to his back, pulled his loose shirttails over it, and pattered down the stairs quietly.

Chimo chewed determinedly on one unwashed cuticle. "I hope there are lots of them. The Swiss, I mean." He looked around the attic. "But then they won't fit."

Gasquet managed not to roll his eyes. "They are not staying with us. We need to stay separated until we act. We will coordinate through drops, but we have to set them up first, get an idea of their numbers, agree upon a new code."

"Why? No one's found our messages, so how would the pope's soldiers know our code?"

Donat breathed deeply, as if sucking in an extra reserve of patience for Chimo. "No one's found our messages *so far as we know*. But if they have, then now is when we must change the code: the one time we will see our allies and make our plans face to face. Otherwise, if the opposition has deciphered the code we've been using so far, they would begin learning our true intents."

"Yeah, okay—but wouldn't it be safer not to meet at all then? Just to tell the Swiss to use a new code when we put out the next drop?"

Gasquet heard the sound of more feet mounting the stairs; three pairs, if he was correct. And he did not want Chimo to still be displaying his ignorance—and stupidity—when the Swiss came through the door, so he explained the matter sharply: "We don't have any jointly agreed upon drop point in this city, dolt, so how would that work? And even if we did, how would they know the first message from us wasn't actually from the opposition, using our code, to trick the assassins among the Swiss to reveal themselves?"

Chimo's mouth was hanging open slightly. "But—"

"No more questions, Chimo. We don't have the time to get it all through your thick skull. Now, we meet our allies." *Which means I have another job to do: to let them know that I'm in charge and that they're here to follow orders, not give them.*

Chapter 6

The heavy, muffled tread on the stairs suddenly became sharper, louder as a blond head with a pageboy haircut crested the floorboards where the attic communicated with the lower level. Another head, black-haired and tousled, followed. Brenguier waved a hand over the lip of the stairwell, signaling that he would remain below, on the lookout.

The two Swiss were in ratty garments that might once have been military uniforms. The blond one waved off the stares from Gasquet and his group. "Pontifical Guard rags. Don't laugh; they got us in."

"That and the choir boy who thinks he's our leader," the other added. "Hard to believe he can be stupid enough to think men of our experience would follow him here to try to commit holy suicide by pledging ourselves to a doomed pope."

The first shrugged. "Von Meggen's from a known family. That means something to lots of people. Sure meant something to the armored fools who saw us through the toll-gate today."

Gasquet leaned his left shoulder against a rafter.

"Not all of the pope's men are fools. Don't underestimate them."

The blond one looked at him. "So who are you?"

"I'm Gasquet. The man who'll be giving you your orders."

The one with the tousled hair started to push forward. "Hey, who do you think—?"

His friend held him back. "So you're the one getting instructions from Rome."

Gasquet did not need to answer, so didn't. "And who are you?"

The blond one, realizing that there was not going to be any congenial give-and-take, evidently decided to stake out his own territory by making the limits of his deference clear: he grabbed a chair, swung it under him, sat. "I'm Norwin Eischoll. My companion is Klaus Müller. There are four more of us who were sent to join the choir boy as cover for our mission. Two others attached themselves along the way. Their papas were not former Papal Guards; they were just hoping to hire for coin and see Italy. But I think we may be able to convince them to consider joining our mission for a better sum."

Gasquet shook his head. "I don't have any money for more sell-swords. If you bring them around, you'll have to pay for them out of your own pocket."

Norwin smiled. "Will I? If the enemy doesn't take care of them, I can shortly afterwards."

Gasquet nodded slowly, returned the smile, thought, *He's practical, focused, ruthless. He's a good addition and will control the Swiss well. And he's too dangerous to be left alive once we're done. Probably thinking the same about me. Well, that's the nature of our business.* "And how did you get the weapons through the gate?"

Norwin shook his head. "We didn't. Instead of meeting the contact to get them, we got a message indicating that security was too tight at the Pont Battant, and they were being brought in another way."

Gasquet waited. "And?"

"And what?"

"What's the other way?"

Norwin smiled. "You're not the only one getting confidential messages, Gasquet. We were assured they'd be ready soon enough. The day after we secure permanent lodgings, Klaus here is going to go to the fountain of Neptune in front of the Carmelite abbey at noon. He'll stand there for ten minutes with a big, uneaten roll. And then he'll return to us. A runner will come to our rooms by the end of the day. He'll have the location of a dead drop for all subsequent messages." Eischoll's smiled broadened. "From the look on your face, it must sound familiar."

Gasquet was suddenly glad that the orders from Rome had been very explicit about him being in charge—because he would not have liked having to vie for control of the operation with Norwin Eischoll. "Somewhat."

"They're a pain in the ass," Müller pronounced loudly.

Gasquet squinted at him. "They are the only way we can be safe from each other."

"What do you mean?" he asked before he saw Norwin's stone-hard expression.

Too late not to embarrass your leash-holder, Müller, Gasquet exulted silently. "I mean," he said in a languorous tone that left enough space for everyone to mentally insert the implicit addition of "you dolt" after the first two words, "the same puppetmaster is pulling our respective strings through different channels. And since he is getting reports on each of us from the other, he will know—immediately—if either of our groups fails to obey orders and follow the plan. If it was just one of us in contact with a controller, how could Rome be sure of knowing if we were betrayed from within, or discovered and eliminated? Hell, the opposition could then use our codes to tell our puppetmaster just what he wants to hear, while nothing of the kind would actually be going on. But with two of us, reporting on each other to the same puppetmaster, he has independent confirmation of our obedience."

Klaus had only blinked twice during the explanation. Gasquet had expected more. Perhaps the big Swiss was not so much stupid as impatient. "Still don't like it," he grumbled. "It would be easier if we were all one group, with one set of orders."

Norwin jumped in before Gasquet could, evidently determined to end what was, for his side, an exchange which featured the mental capabilites of his underling in a most unflattering light. "Klaus, there are seven men in this room. Add our seven, then maybe some more. Much more likely that such a large collection of men, without apparent employment, would be noticed quickly. Besides, one team had to prepare the ground here, and the other had to contact the choir boy and push him to get moving in this direction."

Gasquet nodded, determined to keep any hint of admiration out of his voice or face. "And you were that push?"

Norwin shrugged. "It had to be someone who knew the cantons, who knew where to find and how to poke old grievances."

Gasquet nodded indifferently, determined not to show any of his curiosity. How had Norwin been recruited? How had Borja been made aware of his existence? Gasquet would never know, any more than Norwin would ever be allowed to discover how Borja had come to retain Gasquet. Or how Borja had known, even before the actual mission was revealed, that Gasquet was familiar with Franche-Comté, fair with a pistol, good with a sword, and quite capable of leading men who would have to be retained and constrained during a long preliminary period of inactivity. Which was finally—*finally*—coming to an end.

"And you," Norwin Eischoll asked with a jut of his chin, "How many more do you have stashed away in the city?"

"Enough," Gasquet answered, wishing the answer was *more than enough*. "Several of whom you're going to encounter tomorrow if you got the invitation you were supposed to get for St. John's cathedral."

Norwin sat up slightly. "So you're going to be there, too?"

"Not exactly, but four men I've been controlling will be. One word of caution: for the first few seconds, keep a firm hold on your choir boy's collar. Don't let him run and play with the grown-ups until you have some targets."

"That sounds ominous."

"It won't be for you, not if you keep your own men back."

"Anything else?"

"No."

Norwin rose. "We need to have a contingency in case one of our two groups, or their controllers, are compromised."

Gasquet nodded. "Sensible. Here's what we do: every day we hang a different garment out to dry. Tomorrow a sock, Wednesday a hat, Thursday one glove, Friday a shirt, Saturday pants, Sunday a cape. We each send someone walking by our lodgings—and we'll know yours soon after you move in—every morning. If any other garments are seen, or if a garment is seen on the wrong day, or there is no garment hung out at all, it means that group is not able to comply and must be considered compromised. The first order of business will be to drop a message to any controller we have left. They'll pass along new instructions, including if and when we reapproach the compromised team. After that"—Gasquet shrugged—"we'll have to react based on the circumstances."

Eischoll nodded. "We need to be getting back."

"Yeah," Klaus muttered, "to report our failure at finding lodgings. Freiherr Ignaz von Meggen will be most disappointed with us."

Without offering or receiving a wave of farewell, the two descended the stairs.

Donat crossed his arms. "Well, that was interesting."

Gasquet was already scribbling a message in code. "I suppose. I just wish we knew more about them."

"I'm sure they feel the same way. And with good reason. They have no idea where we're from or who we know here."

"True. But other than our basic weapons"—Gasquet glanced at the loose pile of swords, wheel-locks, and daggers under a leak-proof table in the center of the room—"it's us who are waiting for *them* to deliver." He held the message out to Chimo. "Run to the drop with this, and bring back the one that Peyre saw there already."

Returning from his evening constitutional, Javier de Requesens y Ercilla tossed his hat on the waiting hook, was delighted to see it alight as he meant (which happened about two out of every five times, but that was only an incentive to further practice!), and congratulated himself on the elegant simplicity of the drop points he had arranged. In the course of his walk, he always made sure to step in some mud (at least, he always *hoped* it was mud), which necessitated him to stop and use his walking stick to dislodge the worst of it from the sole of his shoe. He always did so by leaning against one of three shingled buildings. There, while ferociously jabbing at the sole of his shoe with the walking stick in his right hand, he sneaked a finger beneath the edge of one of the shingles. Thus he would detect—and if so, remove—a narrow reed of just enough girth to hold a coded message from the operatives that Borja had presumably seeded here shortly after learning that Urban had taken refuge in Besançon. Each day of the week meant a different shingle to check and of course, most of the time, there was nothing to be found. But this day, although he had not expected any reply to his message until the next morning, he found a message tube already waiting for him.

His own, earlier message had also been picked up, albeit at a different location: a tavern whose name advertised its illicit backroom services with suitably obvious subtlety: *L'Anguille Vernie*, or "The Varnished Eel." Javier had, in his earliest days in Besançon, made this establishment a regular stop on his tours of the wharfside precincts. After a few predictable and tiresome intimations about the special menu available in the back rooms, the owner had mostly ignored him, accepting that he was simply another regular, although an odd one: why would a gentleman of means spend his time in a place frequented by wharf-hands and river-boat crews?

The answer was that Javier had learned long ago that places such as *L'Anguille Vernie* were precisely where men of middle station pursued whatever vices they found most irresistible. And, with little to accomplish in what was then a new town to him, Javier de Requesens y Ercilla had the luxury to unobtrusively and patiently observe the habits and peccadilloes of its clientele.

Usually, it only took a few visits to discern the men whose vices put them in potentially compromising situations. Usually, they were superficially upstanding persons who resorted to such shady environs to conduct discreet affairs. This was almost a sure sign of a jealous wife at home, one who would not accept the dalliances to which so many others consigned themselves. And therefore, a source of leverage. Better still if the man had married above his station and the wife possessed the majority of their property or funds. And best of all if she was homely, a hellion, or both. In short, best if her likely response to adultery was not to kick her husband to the curb and dispossess him of both means and good name, but rather, to hang on to him and her proud reputation and fragile self-respect with the tenacity of a bulldog.

Such men were remarkably easy to suborn if approached correctly. In order to maintain their mistresses without also alerting their wives to their indiscretions, they could hardly devote huge sums to their illicit enterprise. In families of great wealth, this was rarely much of a concern, but where resources were tight and pretensions were high, there tended to be necessarily close accountings of those resources, leaving the reprobate husband with meager coin to pursue his amorous adventures.

Enter the well-funded and mild-mannered stranger, Javier de Requesens y Ercilla, who began by commiserating with the husband, then lending a small sum, then larger ones. In short order, the drinking companions became debtor and creditor.

In such circumstances, Javier rarely needed to reinforce the carrot of his generosity with the stick of implicit social ruin. The adulterous husbands perceived readily enough that, if they refused to do this foreign gentleman a few simple and mostly legal favors, then he might stop providing them with the funds to pursue their affairs. Worse yet, he might, in person or by factotum, show up on their doorstep, on a day of his choosing, and ask for repayment of just a small portion of what had been extended in good faith to the man of the house. Who would, in the wake of such a revelation, be unlikely to remain the man of that house very much longer.

So it had been at *L'Anguille Vernie*. The one surprise had been the identity of the man Javier suborned: the owner himself. Strangely, men who ran such discreet dens of licentiousness behind the facades of legitimate businesses were often married to forceful women who helped manage the illict activities, and thereby, kept an eye on their husbands. After all, if it fell to a husband to strike up and then oversee cooperative relationships with those ladies whose backroom activities made the establishment so profitable, there was every likelihood that he might be inveigled into receiving recompense in something other than the coin of the realm. Trade in kind, as some called it. Conversely, wives were, as a rule, invulnerable to the special charms and talents of such ladies and kept the business relationships truly business.

Except, in the case of Jules, proprietor of *L'Anguille Vernie*. He had taken a headlong suicidal plunge into a relationship with one of the ladies who less frequently served his back room clientele. His wife, probably lulled into a false sense of security by having overseen the less savory aspects of his business for almost twenty-five years, missed the subtle cues of affection—genuine affection—between the two. She would surely have detected a woman of salacious proclivities, but Jules' *inamorata* was shy, almost retiring, possibly pushed into this means of securing coin as a bitter last resort.

And so Javier secured not only a willing and fully cooperative pipeline to a great deal of the town gossip and waterfront contraband, but a perfect overseer for the message drops he left for Borja's operatives. After all, only amateurs and fools used the same location for both ingoing and outgoing messages; why double the traffic to a single site when trying to remain unnoticed? So, once he had Jules under his thumb, Javier no longer sullied himself by visiting *L'Anguille Vernie*

in person, but sent runners—young lads, usually—to
deliver tubes, packages, bottles: anything that could hide
a coded message. Within hours, Jules would deposit
the container in the overgrown window-box shaded by
the sizable roof overhang at the rear of the tavern.
It was a gathering place for drunks and vagrants, a
melange of desperate and odorous humanity that the
town watch never bothered, so long as they kept to
their own private sewer of despair.

Turning up the wick on the lamp that had been
lit when the innkeeper had left his meal ten minutes
earlier, Javier at last studied the note he had found
under the Monday shingle.

A minute later, he frowned and pushed his dinner
aside, annoyed that it was getting cold and would get
colder still before he was done. He carefully set up
his radio, checked how much charge was left in its
cumbersome batteries, and commenced tapping the
emergency code to alert Rome to the fact that he
needed to make an unscheduled transmission and
that they should signal their readiness to receive it.
He used this protocol very rarely, reasoning that it
was all too easy to become the boy who cried wolf.
But this night, he was sure that Cardinal Borja would
want the news that had come to him.

Immediately.

Chapter 7

With the sun burnishing its rippled surface, the Tevere River seemed to move more slowly, like a flow of indolent, cooling lava that was not in a particular rush to go anywhere or do anything.

At least that's how it appeared to Cardinal Gaspar de Borja y Velasco from his window on the highest floor of the Palazzo Borghese. Everything in Rome seemed to move slowly, from its resentful population to the sluggish tempo of trade, to the rebuilding of those parts of the Holy City that could, in fact, be rebuilt at all.

As to the lethargy of the population, that was no mystery to Borja. He had been in Italy long enough to recognize the signs of decadence and hedonism when he saw it. How else could it be that the direct inheritors of the glories of Rome were now unable to rise up as an equal to any modern nation, were unable to establish even one colony in the New World, were incapable of perceiving his own ascension as but their own first step on the road to new prestige and power? Granted, those heights would be dictated and groomed by Spain, but with the proper coordination between the secular capital of the Christian World—Madrid—and its spiritual citadel—Rome—what could such an alliance not accomplish? Perhaps the Italians did not wholly lack vision, but in their current, debauched state, they had lost all the vigor of their Roman forebears.

The slowing of trade was indicative of the greater, more expansive rot abroad in the world: namely, the so-called Reformation of the Protestants. And their mortal sin was infinitely worse than the venal sloth and venery which afflicted Italy: it was blasphemy and heresy, aimed like another spear at the side of the crucified Christ. Lacking only horns and tails, the fallen princes of Germany and Scandinavia had conspired with the perfidious Jews to ensure that commerce to and from Rome had all but ground to a halt. And leave it to the carping town fathers of the so-called Eternal City to repeatedly and obsequiously maintain that the drought of goods and capital in their streets was not due to a Protestant conspiracy, but rather, fear over the "uncertain conditions and laws" which now prevailed.

As if there was anything uncertain about Rome under the redoubtable hand of Cardinal Gaspar de Borja y Velasco! All could rely upon his swift and decisive—if need be, brutal—enforcement of not merely secular law, but holy writ. When push came to shove, he did not leave such matters solely to the bribable magistrates who were likely buggering young boys beneath their robes of office. No, the next pope, Gaspar de Borja y Velasco himself, occasionally made the time to ensure that justice was done throughout his city, no matter the cost; of this, they could be sure.

And of the delays in rebuilding the Holy City? Well, that was simply an effect brought about by the confluence of the first two causes: Italian sloth amplified by the Protestant embargos that made it difficult to pay local workers. Who, in typically decadent fashion, refused to work for credit and the promise of bread in the meantime. Similarly, the masons and architects complained of the lack of necessary stone, mortar, tools, and manpower to rebuild or create new edifices approximating the shattered grandeur of the Castel St. Angelo and Hadrian's Tomb. So of course they all had to be forced to do their jobs, often with firm prodding from Spanish halberds. And if the workers and stone were both weak, and the latter often collapsed and crushed the former, well, was that his fault or problem? All creatures had their appointed place in God's creation. His was to propose; theirs, to dispose. His, to rule; theirs, to obey. It was astounding that they were such dull creatures, unable to see even that simple and inevitable hierarchy in the order of things. Hard to believe that their ancestors built aqueducts, invented wonders, and conquered almost the entirety of the known world. Oh, Borja lamented silently as he took another sip of rioja and contemplated the apathetic and insolent river of fading fire, how the mighty have fallen. *Sic transit gloria mundi*, indeed.

"Your Eminence," a familiar voice called from the entry.

Borja did not bother to turn, simply raised a hand and curled his fingers inward. "Come, Maculani. Share a glass of wine with me."

"I thank Your Eminence for the kind offer, but may not partake. Not while we are still receiving transmissions from Besançon."

Borja closed his eyes to gather both strength and

patience, then turned. "They are still tapping away at each other over the Alps, then?"

Maculani, a solid body surmounted by a square face with intense, bright eyes, nodded. "They are, Your Eminence. We have received word that the assassins our agents solicited in Luzern have, as hoped, arrived in the company of this fellow von Meggen."

Borja leaned forward eagerly. "Excellent. When will they act?"

."There is no word on that yet."

"Well, have you pressed them, Vincenzo?"

Maculani bowed slightly. "Even now, the radio operator is conveying your desire for the swift finalization and execution of our plan. We should have the answer within the hour, if the transmitting conditions hold that long."

"They had better hold that long," Borja grumbled, before realizing that what the radio operators called "atmospheric conditions" were not variables subject to human control, and that God might take a dim view of a cardinal—even a favored one!—railing, no matter how indirectly and unintentionally, against acts of divine will. But blast it, why could that will not have delivered the functionally apostate Urban into Borja's righteous and eager hands by now? Why did the Lord Himself seem intent on making the campaign to save his own Church on Earth so convoluted and filled with frustrations? Borja reflected that if one broke apart the letters of his own surname, one could spell "Job" and still have an "r" and an "a" left over. Perhaps, he thought, putting down his wine, there was a lesson in that.

Maculani stepped closer. "Is there anything else I may do for Your Eminence?"

Borja rose. "Pray for favorable conditions between here and Besançon. Every day that Urban is able to sow his heretical dogma in both innocent and infernally-motivated ears, the more damage suffered by Mother Church." Borja stared at Maculani, who stared back, unafraid. The cardinal smiled. "Your father was a bricklayer, was he not?"

Maculani frowned. "Yes, my father laid brick, Your Eminence. Indeed, for a time, so did I."

Borja nodded. "An honest occupation. Would that more of the consistory who now support Urban had a similar background. Their nobility is simply a mistake of birth, rather than of character developed through labor and perseverance." It occurred to him that he, and his core supporters—the Spanish Cardinals, as they had been called for centuries—were as much, if not more, the scions of aristocratic privilege. In an attempt to leaven that nagging hint of irony, Borja added, "After all, our savior was a carpenter." But somehow, that didn't quite have the effect he had hoped for. The opposite, perhaps. No matter.

"Yes, Your Eminence," Maculani answered in a carefully neutral tone. Which was unlike him, but the bricklayer-become-bishop seemed perplexed by the profoundly philosophical direction of Borja's discourse.

The cardinal turned to look at the Tevere again. "You know, Vincenzo," he sighed, "it is a daily wound to me that I have not the power to make you a cardinal. Yet."

Maculani—with a surprisingly quiet, almost stealthy, tread—came to stand alongside him. "I am aware of and humbled by Your Eminence's kind opinion of this servant of Mother Church. But my lack of a biretta is but a small consequence of Urban's continued obstruction of your path to the *cathedra*. The great danger lies in his continuing ability to create what others still see as legitimate cardinals, and so, to reconstitute a consistory of those who are foolish enough to take his side. Thankfully, the radio gives us the ability to direct the means whereby that flow of new cardinals may be cut off."

Borja nodded, but found he was no longer seeing the Tevere's bronze glow. Now, rekindled memory repainted it a sullen gray-blue, flecked with ice: rare, even in early February. But the winter just past had been cold for Rome, and, on that particular day, Borja had chosen against continuing to look out through the large, expensive panes of the glass window. He had drawn the thick curtains against the chill.

Maculani had been there, as now, taking notes. The matter being discussed was too sensitive to entrust to mere scribes. Borja had learned that the hard way. Just last year his secretary Ferrigno had been caught passing information along to the so-called Lefferti: the revolutionists who had styled themselves after the up-time assassin and adventurer, Harry Lefferts. Happily, in the end, they had been slain in the hundreds, Lefferts himself nearly caught with them.

And the architect of those victories over the up-timers, as well as the sleuth who had uncovered Ferrigno's treachery, had stood before him, radiating no more warmth than the wintery Tevere: Pedro Dolor. Who had, but a moment before, brought news of Urban's new location and with it, a powerful argument for Borja to adopt a device he detested and instinctively distrusted: the radio.

"So, how is it that you happen to have an agent with a radio in Besançon, Señor Dolor—er, Don Pedro?" Borja did not approve of promoting commoners so easily to titles, but it was the fashion in which Olivares' increasingly rare letters to Borja referred to this operative, and there was no point in doing anything that might annoy the count-duke.

Dolor shook his head. "My agent is not in Besançon, Your Eminence."

"Then how can he make so confident a report of Urban's presence there?"

"My agent has been tracking various signs of activity involving movements by the elite forces with which the USE is likely to protect Urban. He was in Basel when he got word of this colloquium that Urban is convening in Besançon."

"A colloquium? What does this mean? Why does he not summon a Council of the Cardinals?" Borja idly wondered if a sufficiently large bomb could be fashioned to send Urban and all of his heretical red hats into the heavens for judgment and damnation, all at once. Of course, such a powerful device would also necessarily be imprecise. Many innocents would no doubt be killed. But they would also no doubt be received in heaven as martyrs whose lives had been sacrificed to ensure the continued safety of Mother Church.

Dolor did not so much as blink as he explained. "The colloquium is expressly ecumenical, Cardinal Borja. My agent in Basel learned of it because of an invitation that had gone out to a leading Calvinist theologian who was wintering there."

"A *C-Calvinist*?" Borja sputtered.

"We feared as much, Your Eminence," Maculani muttered darkly as he scratched at the paper before him.

Borja resisted the urge to put a hand to his forehead; such a pose was not consistent with the firm and resolute image he wished to convey. "So, at the same time that this parasite upon the Church is whelping litter after litter of new cardinals every time he touches his chest and murmurs, '*in pectore*,' he is traitorously inviting heretics to help him spin a wider, unholy web. It warrants a crusade!"

Maculani's restless scrawling ceased. "That would be a—a most difficult and provocative undertaking, Your Eminence." From his startled tone, the recently elevated bishop seemed unsure whether Borja was speaking figuratively or literally. Borja was not entirely sure himself.

Dolor folded his hands. "I have few details of this colloquium beyond the fact that Urban has sent inquiries far and wide. Judging from other reports, there is an intimation that the United States of Europe are facilitating this with their dirigibles."

Maculani's inquiry was swift. "Not radio?"

"No, Your Grace. From your change in expression, I suspect you see why."

"Yes. Radio transmissions give an adversary routine access to codes, since they are always free to be heard by all who know the correct—er, is the word 'frequency'?"

Dolor bowed his head. "Bishop Maculani's knowledge, and foresight, are most excellent."

Borja could not help a proud smile from curving his lips slightly. Vincenzo Maculani had been a rare find: a cleric with an excellent education, a willingness to get his hands dirty (what former head inquisitor could do otherwise?), and an early life that made him familiar with the cynicism and brutish reality of the streets. So far as stratagems and their execution were concerned, he was nearly Dolor's equal.

But then Maculani went and ruined it all: "Your Eminence, this news—what it portends, and how we vouchsafed it—compels me to renew my appeal that we retain the services of a radio operator."

Borja almost groaned aloud. "Not this again, Maculani."

"Please, Your Eminence, consider how Don Pedro's report demonstrates the indispensable nature of this technology. Not only did this intelligence reach us from distant, winter-locked Basel within a day of its acquisition, but it was conveyed by a roving agent. Two radio operators, moving with two guards could furnish us with urgent news weeks, even months, before standard couriers could bring it to us."

Borja shifted. Which must have let Maculani know that this was the moment to press home his decisive argument: "And if we wish to stop Urban from creating more cardinals to build his appearance of legitimacy and of Church dominance, we must be able to control—carefully and precisely *control*—the operations we have considered mounting to stop him."

Borja stared at him, half annoyed, half hoping that Maculani would somehow find a different path.

But the square-headed and square-chinned bishop—who would probably have made a formidable wrestler—only stared back and added, "The operations we have considered will be most delicate, Your Eminence. Indeed, it would be quite advantageous for the hands not to know precisely what the head is planning until just before they are set in motion."

Borja glanced at Dolor.

Who shrugged. "Your Eminence certainly knows my opinion on this matter. Last year, when pursuing Urban VIII, I was forced to communicate with our agents in Venetian territory via pigeons. And once events moved beyond the reach of the coops the pigeons knew, our agents were left to their own crude devices. If we had had a capable radio operator traveling with or near them—"

Borja flicked a sharp, irritated wave in Dolor's direction, even as he looked away. "Yes, yes, you have made it quite clear how the outcome could have been much different."

Dolor did not reply, simply nodded and looked at Maculani.

Who looked baleful. He was not comfortable with Dolor. Last September, shortly after the assassin-turned-intelligencer had returned from Spain with letters patent from none other than Olivares, he had paid a respectful visit to Borja, even though he no longer answered to the cardinal. Maculani, not a talkative man in his most extroverted moments, sat as still and silent as a graven image during that brief meeting. When Borja later asked him of his impressions of Dolor, Maculani's frown had deepened. "He makes it hard to form an impression; he reveals so little of himself. Which I do not trust."

But on this particular winter's day, Maculani's crucial and possibly only ally was this selfsame man he did not trust. He turned his eyes back to Borja. "Your Eminence, I understand that you wish to guard

Mother Church against infernal up-time devices. So do I. But it may be that we may not protect her adequately without making an exception in this case. You know that Don Pedro and I often have very different opinions on our strategies and their execution, but we are of one mind on this. I believe I speak for both of us when I beseech you to consider: is not the good to be done by retaining the services of a radio expert far greater than any danger it might pose?"

In fact, Borja was not convinced of that easy formulation. Something told him that the greased slide into a world dominated by the up-timers and their devices began with just such "exceptions" as this. Ultimately, such exceptions would become more routine, then plentiful, and then ubiquitous, until, finally, the up-timers had recast reality in the form that suited them and their inscrutable, but certainly nefarious, designs. But the cardinal also had to admit that instant communications had been a far, far more decisive factor than the weapons or airships the up-timers had used to best them the prior summer. And he could not allow Urban VIII to continue on his present, ruinous course—ruinous both for Mother Church and Gaspar de Borja y Velasco. Concepts which, in his mind, had begun to elide and merge into one.

"Very well." Borja sighed. "We shall take this step. Who must we consult to find a reliable operator and technician?"

Dolor cleared his throat. "In acquiring a radio for my own operations, I have encountered a number of operators who might serve your needs."

Borja nodded. "Very well. Who do you recommend most highly?"

Dolor seemed to reflect for a moment, which struck Borja as slightly odd; Dolor always seemed to know his intended path long before he was asked to reveal it. "Bruno Sartori, a Venetian."

"A Venetian?" Borja was gratified that Maculani's voice had joined his own in a chorus of dismay and aversion.

"A Venetian," Dolor persisted quietly, "who was disowned upon being revealed as one of our agents last summer. He has been living in Rome since September, and has been unable to find suitable work."

Maculani's frown became a scowl. "And if this Sartori is so accomplished, why have you not retained him yourself?"

Dolor shrugged. "By the time I knew he had fled to Rome, my needs were already met. He would not have fulfilled them, anyhow: he does not speak enough languages. Only Italian, German, and weak French. Much of my work involves monitoring USE transmissions, and many of their operators use English or Amideutsch. Furthermore, he is a functionary, not a man for field work. He will be happy to receive a good salary in Rome, where he may have his creature comforts."

"Could he be bribed by our enemies, do you think?" Maculani asked in a low mutter.

"Possibly, but for the same reason he would not be serviceable in the field, he should not pose a security risk. So long as his salary is sufficient, I estimate him to prize safety from retribution more than any additional funds he might realize by becoming a double agent. However, if you are looking for an upright pillar of the faith who would serve out of principle, I fear I

do not have any such candidates to recommend. My
duties rarely put me in touch with such persons—at
least not those who have the skills you require."

Borja huffed lightly. Hardly an ideal candidate,
this Sartori. On the other hand, a paragon of virtue
might not be what they needed in this case. Particularly not with the orders they inevitably would have
to send to their operatives in Besançon. Pontificide
would trouble the conscience—and perhaps loosen the
guilt-ridden tongue—of a more upright man. So, on
second thought, perhaps this Sartori was indeed the
ideal candidate, specifically because he was *not* the
ideal Catholic. "The Venetian should do. Send him to
us as soon as you may." And now the delicate part of
the meeting, which hopefully Dolor would not realize as the reason Borja granted him an audience so
swiftly. "I understand that you traveled a bit before
returning to Rome. Searching for radios and operators
to recruit for your own operations."

Dolor's nod was almost imperceptible. "Your Eminence is extremely well informed."

Hah. Dolor can be surprised! One of the frequent
weaknesses of spymasters was that they often believed
that they, and their immediate enemies, were the only
ones doing any spying. "Did your own travels take
you to Besançon?"

"I am sorry to disappoint Your Eminence, but no,
they did not. It was not needed."

"Not needed?" Maculani asked.

"Yes, Your Grace. As His Excellency Count-Duke
Olivares already had taken steps to have an agent
placed in Besançon to observe the changes wrought
there by Duke Bernhard, it was deemed extraneous

for me to go there myself. I merely needed to get an update from the agent."

Borja frowned. "I do not understand, Don Pedro. You did not visit this agent yet you received an update from him. How was that effected?"

"By radio, Your Eminence, when I passed through Basel. At that distance, and without a mountain range in between us, reception was very easy and reliable."

Borja felt the wheels of a plan spinning toward each other in his mind, mesh together. "So. Olivares' man in Besançon is already furnished with a radio."

"Yes," Dolor confirmed. "Although I do not know if I would call him specifically the count-duke's man. He was placed there on the count-duke's order. I do not know to whom he reports directly. However, given his broad mandate, I suppose he is providing diverse information to a number of the crown's factotums."

Carefully now, Borja thought, and could tell that Maculani was thinking the same thing. "And is this agent's employ strictly reserved for the crown's business?"

Dolor thought. "I do not know. I do not believe so. Some of the agent's information suggests he was also financing some trading ventures himself. Although he is descended of a grandee family, he is from a branch that has fallen upon lean times. I doubt he would be specifically constrained from doing business of his own while abroad. I cannot recall such restrictions ever being placed upon our foreign factotums."

Of course not, since Spain, from the king on down to the most impoverished hidalgo, runs on money. "And so I presume you would not be averse to telling us who this agent is and how to reach him?"

Dolor frowned slightly. "I suppose not. His name is Javier de Requesens y Ercilla. I shall give you the times of day and frequencies whereby I reached him."

Borja nodded toward Maculani, who provided Dolor with a sheet upon which to write the information. As he did, the bishop looked up at Borja. "Once we have the radio, Your Eminence, we might be able to get a better idea of who Urban is making cardinals *in pectore.*"

Borja frowned. "What do you mean by this, Maculani?"

The bishop spread his hands in what seemed half explanation, half appeal. "Well, we have reports that Urban is resorting to up-time documents to arrive at a list of likely candidates, using them to determine which men his up-time self raised to the biretta. With the Papal Library lost to us—"

—a nice euphemism for what had actually happened: Neapolitan troops running wild through the Holy City, carrying off everything that was, or looked like it might be, valuable, and burning much of the rest—

"—Urban's copies of the up-time records were either destroyed or are among the remaining documents that are still being sorted. However, if we were to furnish a confidential agent in Grantville with a radio, we might be able to access a copy of that list ourselves, and determine which of Urban's later-life allies he is now raising up to—"

Borja killed that notion with a guillotine chop of his hand. "Had we known to do so two, three months ago, that might have made a difference. Now, any of his intended *in pectore* cardinals that are not still hiding in their cellars are on the road to Besançon, beyond our reach." He drew himself up to his full height. "We shall know who the traitors are when they enter that city for his so-called colloquium, for now we shall have a contact there who may report their arrivals." He smiled at Dolor, who was stepping back from the table. "Thanks to you."

Dolor bowed. "I am gratified to have been of help, Your Eminence."

Borja held up a hand to detain him. "There is one further courtesy I ask of you, Don Pedro. Because you have been a confidante of mine and a friend to Mother Church's attempts to reestablish order and its own imperiled legitimacy, the bishop and I deemed it safe to speak frankly of the grave measures that we might still need to undertake, an inevitable continuation of your efforts last year. We therefore presume that now, as then, you will keep these discussions in strictest confidence, not even sharing them with secular authorities. These are, properly, Church matters and should remain within the Church." He paused, looked long into Dolor's hazel eyes. "I take it that I make myself clear?" Which the assassin could not possibly translate in any way other than, *If you tell Olivares, I will come after you.*

"I understand perfectly, Your Eminence."

Borja was certain that he did. "I appreciate your discretion, as our situation is most difficult. Particularly here."

"In Rome?" Dolor asked.

"Most certainly," Maculani said emphatically. "Let us presume that God graces us by removing the heretical Urban. Will his followers come back? Of course not. They have turned their backs on the Church's true mission, so they know what awaits them here. So what will they do? Why, appoint themselves as a consistory and elect one of their own number pope. It has happened before."

Dolor shrugged. "You have a consistory also."

"And that," Borja said with a sigh, "is the larger problem. Or, I should say, the large problem of our smaller numbers. At this moment, we count—how many, Maculani? Seventeen cardinals, all told?"

Maculani leaned his head to the side as he recalled the list. "There's Doria, di Savoia, Moscoso, Galamini, Bentivoglio—who had to be compelled to declare for His Eminence—Spínola, the other Spinola, Torres, Borghese, Albornoz, Pamphili, Pallotta, Trivulzio, Centini, Campori, Salamandri, Zacchia. Urban has at least twice as many in support of him. Perhaps three times. And many of those who are 'unreachable' are, in reality, keeping their heads down until this crisis has passed. You may be sure that they will then reemerge testifying that they were always ardent supporters of the pope—whoever that turns out to be." He glanced at Borja quickly. "A figure of speech, only, Your Eminence. If God pleases to see that justice in the Church Mundane be done in compliance with the writ of heaven, then you shall soon sit upon the *cathedra*."

Borja was pleased—and reassured—by Maculani's emendation, but only for a second: rather than nodding, Dolor's face seemed more grim than ever.

"I understand your concern, Your Eminence. For if Urban is not removed by divine or mundane means, you may well have to defend this place. If you can."

Borja refused to be rattled by this dire projection. "And what could overcome my forces?"

Dolor shrugged "The entirety of occupied Italy's enraged population. Probably swollen by the forces of the unoccupied or neutral states that would stand to gain from your loss." He bowed a slow farewell. "Your Eminence."

Once the door had closed behind Dolor, Maculani leaned forward, his hard, heavy hands knuckles-down upon the mahogany table before him. "I do not trust him."

Borja waved a dismissive hand. "That is wise, insofar as Dolor is under Olivares' control, not ours. But I have had Dolor under observation and see no cause for worry. He is not devout, but then again, there is no evidence that he cares for any faith or philosophy at all. He is a materialist, yet neither takes bribes nor lives hedonistically. If he were Greek, I would presume his ancestors were Spartans.

"But whereas Dolor lacks a theologically enlightened sense of duty to Our Savior in heaven, he understands the hard realities of this terrestrial vale of tears. He is a singularly useful tool and counselor within the limited scope of his expertise and interests. Beyond that, he demonstrates little affinity for anything else, and no perceptible passions which might be used to move him to treachery of any kind."

Maculani nodded. "And that is precisely why I do not trust him, Your Eminence."

Borja smiled at the Dominican whom he had made a bishop and had brought away from his duties as Rome's head inquisitor. Maculani's mind was too sharp and too practical to waste upon the usually futile task of attempting to redeem undeserving heretics and unbelievers. Before, that is, they succumbed to the tortures that destroyed their bodies in order to compel them to repent and so, save their souls. "You are a suspicious fellow, Vincenzo," Borja murmured. "I like that." *Because you are* my *suspicious fellow.*

Yet Cardinal Gaspar de Borja y Velasco had found himself still staring at the door through which Dolor had departed on that cold February day, filled with unease.

It was the same unease he felt now as the Tevere glimmered more faintly beneath the setting May sun while he waited for the radio report from Javier de Requesens y Ercilla in Besançon. A large part of what made Pedro Dolor so unnerving was his almost prophetic foresight. Yes, his assassins had failed to kill Urban last year, just as his jailors in Palma de Mallorca had failed to keep rescuers from spiriting away the young hostages Borja had meant to use as leverage against the up-timers. But in both cases, Dolor had made initial recommendations that others—even Borja himself—had denied or ignored. And, in both cases, had his advice and requests been heeded, it seemed likely that the outcome would have been quite different.

But Pedro Dolor's foresight was, in fact, not the primary trait that made him unnerving. The greater part resided in his silent acceptance of outcomes and almost mechanical reflex to simply address the new challenges that resulted—without overtly or obliquely calling attention to the fact that, had his superior comprehension and anticipation been heeded, there would have been no failure in the first place.

Borja took up his glass of rioja again and sipped at it, a bit more deeply than was his wont. It was a matter of course that some men had greater abilities than others. But for a man not to revel in the triumphs enabled thereby, to fail to call attention to his superior perspicacity in order to accelerate his own ascension while undercutting the rise of possible rivals?

That, Borja concluded with yet another worried sip at his glass, was not merely distressingly atypical; it was positively inhuman.

Chapter 8

Having completed the entry code, Pedro Dolor stepped back from the door to the rooms he had taken for a year's lease six months ago.

Laurin, whose underground infamy as an assassin ranged from Paris to the Pyrenees and beyond the Piedmont, smiled faintly around the corner of the door as he opened it precisely six seconds after Dolor had completed the complex pattern of taps and knocks. Dolor entered, checking to the opposite side as he did so.

Radulfus, a marksman from some god-forsaken high Alpine valley where even mountain goats refused to live and where the humans were still using names from the Middle Ages, swung his heavy double-barreled shotgun away, his finger carefully outside the trigger guard. He nodded solemnly. Which gesture Pedro returned. Radulfus, who offered no nickname and refused to be assigned one, took no joy in killing; he simply wasn't fainthearted about it, either. He was different from the others, being neither an assassin nor a mercenary, nor even an intelligencer. But his family needed money and had little use for the popes, kings, or other mortal men who hoarded coins and held themselves to be something more mighty and privileged than they were. He didn't speak much of any language other than some strange variety of Romansch that probably dated back to Roman times, but he nonetheless had made his simple philosophy quite clear when, during one fireside discussion on the road to Basel, he had pointed at the ground and said, "All men go there. So all should be same here." Even had Dolor been the kind of man disposed to debate, he admitted he could have found little to dispute in Radulfus' worldview.

The second floor of the building was entirely theirs and, in the rearmost of the three in-line rooms, Dolor heard the muffled stutter of the radio set. He moved in that direction, calling as he went, "Whose signal are you hearing, Rombaldo?"

His Bolognese lieutenant, who had overseen the pursuit of Urban the prior year, held up a hand as Dolor entered. "It's the Spanish dandy."

"Reporting to Rome or Spain?"

Rombaldo turned to face him. "Rome. Again."

Dolor nodded, quietly pleased with the local fruits of his planning. Even by the time Pedro Dolor had visited Besançon late last October, Javier de Requesens y Ercilla had evidently been all but forgotten by Olivares and the grandee intelligencers who had sent him here. Dolor had spent that first visit to Besançon using his own radio to monitor the young fop's communications, all made in the simple code typical of low-importance Spanish information gathering.

Today's transmissions were in a more complex code, but it was one that Dolor was quite familiar with.

After all, it was he who had all but put the operator in Rome—Bruno Sartoris—in front of Borja's radio. In his last visit to Rome, it had been child's play to present reports in such a way that they highlighted the cardinal's need for a radio operator. Maculani had long before come to understand the profound, indeed indispensable, advantages of nearly instant communications and had pressed for the adoption of the new technology, despite Borja's reluctance.

That had allowed Dolor to remain casual, almost detached in the ensuing debate. So, when Borja finally relented, he had no reason to suspect that this was precisely the outcome that Dolor had sought. More to the point, Borja had no reason to suspect that when he solicited Dolor's recommendation for a radio operator, Dolor's suggestion was shaped to be optimal to his own, rather than the cardinal's purposes.

Neither Borja nor Maculani had enough competence in the new technology to know what set of operational protocols would be most advisable nor, most pertinently, what codes were most likely to be secure. So of course they had to ask Bruno Sartori for his recommendations.

And Dolor, in his earlier contact with the Venetian (who he had heard was interested in employ and met strictly as a professional courtesy), had been sure to ask pointed questions about the young man's expertise and experience in ciphers, particularly in light of the proficiency of the USE's codebreakers. Sartori was, of course, flummoxed, then panicked, and Dolor could see the fear building in his eyes: fear that he would never again find work operating a radio.

But Dolor made sure to mention what codes he felt

were state of the art, and would be available to Sartori if he were fortunate enough to find himself in Spanish employ. And of course, sure enough, those were the codes that, months later, the professionally lethargic Venetian suggested to Borja and Maculani. Codes with which Dolor was so familiar that he suspected he might be able to transcribe them in his sleep.

Javier de Requesens y Ercilla was contacted soon after by Sartori, using the frequencies and times Dolor had provided to Borja. Who promptly retained Requesens at a handsome rate and told him to expect a gift which would facilitate their business relationship. A day later, Borja transmitted suitable instructions to Spanish agents in Basel, and, a day later, the necessary code book was wending its way to Besançon, where Rombaldo was already on site, ready to eavesdrop on the "secure" signals between the Spanish fop in Besançon and the Venetian reprobate in Rome. Dolor had now compiled almost two whole months of their transmissions. Which had been his objective from the start.

None of this had been too difficult to foresee or achieve once it was determined where Urban had gone, after his escape from the tiny thorpe of Molino last July. While Borja, Olivares, and others spent lavishly—and futilely—hiring agents to monitor suspicious activities in likely capitols and offer suitable bribes, Dolor had strolled into Besançon in October and, within a few hours, confirmed his largely aforegone conclusion that this was indeed where the renegade pope was hiding.

Predictably, the other searchers had allowed their deductive process to be unduly influenced by their own political presuppositions. Dolor, who was now sitting behind Rombaldo and listening absently to the continuing stream of clicker activity from Rome, could no longer count the number of times he had seen that particular brand of professional myopia undo otherwise sound operations. In this case, all the powers that had reason to locate Urban began with the assumption that, as a key political figure, he would seek shelter and alliance with one of his autocratic peers, and therefore, word of his arrival could be discovered in the court of the one he had selected, even if he was not physically ensconced there. Or, just as likely, that he would be sequestered under a false identity in some remote citadel controlled by the crown itself.

Dolor did not consider those conjectures implausible, but elected not to start from that basis. Rather, his investigation immediately went to the tactical forensics of the failed attempt to assassinate Urban.

The farmhouse-villa where Urban had been hidden was the only major establishment for miles around and difficult to reach. Untenanted for more than a year, local laborers stopped in every few weeks to make sure that nothing catastrophic had befallen the place. Consequently, in the wake of the failed assassination attempt, the wagons required to remove over eighty corpses had to be hired from farms as far as fifteen miles away. Similar arrangements had to be made for the wounded.

Consequently, even though the casualties had long since been removed when Dolor arrived under an assumed identity, the surrounding countryside was still a-buzz with talk and rumor of the battle at Molino. It was, after all, the most important and exciting regional event in living memory, perhaps ever. Dolor's quiet demeanor, complete self-assurance, omnipresent guards, and heavy purse loosened the lips of most of the region's worthies. None of their accounts agreed on all points, of course, but by patiently recording and examining the tales of each, a serviceable composite emerged.

Firstly, the after-action report of the conditions at the villa itself confirmed the accounts of the three surviving assassins who had been foolish enough to flee back to Rombaldo. The battle had been fierce, and at least fifty of the assassins had died or been mortally wounded in the attack. By process of elimination then, approximately thirty of the defenders had been lost also. And it was likely that most of their wounded had survived owing to preferential treatment, so that meant the wagons which bore casualties to sources of better care were carrying persons loyal to Urban.

Dolor simply followed the trail of reports inspired by the passing of the wagons. He was able to track them southward, all the way out of the mountains. Shortly afterward, most of the wagons turned back, and Dolor found the reason easily enough. In a deserted meadow, thirty one marked graves surrounded a makeshift shrine. Just beyond them and behind a tangled copse, a mass grave humped up as if the earth wanted to vomit back the fifty-odd assassins no doubt lying at the bottom of it. The remaining wagons—leased from an actual hostler, now, not hires from mountainfolk—pressed on toward Vicenza, just over thirty-five miles west of Venice. However, before reaching the city, the mounted and well-armed party that had been following the last of the wagons split off to the west.

Dolor followed both leads. As expected, the wagons that had entered Vincenza carried the wounded defenders, escorted by a few junior down-time members of the USE embassy staff. The mounted group had swung to the west and had ridden hard. More than a few stable owners fondly recalled the lack of haggling when they charged exorbitant prices for watering and feeding the horses, and for remaining at a distance from the main body of their customers.

That trail led him to the Berici hills, where other news strongly suggested that Urban had not, in desperation, fled to Venice, a city notorious for its resistance to, and occasional antipathy towards, pontiffs. Instead, in the early days of August, the locals witnessed a great manmade balloon, trailing smoke and moving slowly under its own power, as it passed overhead, heading toward a leading noble's estate. Within a day, the dirigible retraced its aerial path, but then disappeared into the west, rather than the northern haze out of which it had come. Approximately a week later, the same or another airship repeated the cycle of the first, arriving from the north but departing to the west. After that, a much reduced mounted party made its way to Venice and the embassy there. Given Spain's many sources in that city where bribery was not merely a way of life but an art form, it was simplicity itself to learn the identities of those persons: all USE Marines or other mere functionaries that had been attached to the USE's embassy to Rome.

So: of the two choices that Urban had open to him— to escape to Venice and from thence by sea, versus heading north over the Alps—the pope had chosen the latter. But he had also chosen to avoid the perils of the road, both coincidental and intentional. Instead, he had made his way north by balloon. Which meant he had enjoyed the continuing—and intensifying—help of the USE and its leader, Gustav Adolf of Sweden.

After that, it was fairly simple to deduce the ultimate terminus of Urban's journey. There was no way for him to travel without security forces. Those forces would surely be commanded by Ruy Sanchez de Casador y Ortiz. That, in turn, almost certainly meant they would be accompanied by the faux-hidalgo's wife, Sharon Nichols, the famous up-time surgeon who also happened to be of African descent and therefore was widely and readily recognized in all the cities large enough to boast an aerodrome in which a dirigible might land and be serviced.

Dolor had not even needed to travel to each city along the way. The small number of cities with aerodromes, the limited number of dirigibles traveling between them, and the small number of passengers they were able to carry had already made them routine objects of intelligence reporting. Accordingly, Spanish sources in each city along the only two possible paths over the Alps—either via Brescia and Chur or via Belluno and Innsbruck—were quickly able to eliminate one of the paths. No such unusual party descended at Belluno or Innsbruck, which made perfect sense with what had been observed: the inbound dirigibles had used those stations on their southbound route, but had not returned that way. Following their customary circuit, the airships had left Berici heading west to Brescia and then north to Chur, which did indeed report that the persons of interest had in fact landed there and their dirigible was rapidly serviced for the next flight. Of even greater significance, they were apparently escorted by one of the USE's fixed-wing aircraft.

The rest was child's play, so long as an investigator once again eschewed the political presupposition that northbound travel meant that Urban had thrown his lot in with the USE and its Lutheran monarch, Gustav. There was a slim possibility that Urban might have entertained the possibility of his seeking refuge with Fernando in the Spanish Lowlands (and it would have made more sense in a variety of both practical and political particulars), but a quick check of the dirigible's activity after descending from the Alps into Biberach put paid to that notion. The dirigible that landed there never did complete the rest of its circuit, but fell off its regular route for several weeks.

The answer why was quick in coming: Spain's intelligencers in Basel reported the development of an airfield well outside the city. Since the USE's airplanes had flown in there once or twice, it was presumed they were simply grooming the landing strip for more routine operations.

Dolor suspected, and discovered, differently. The USE had apparently expanded their lease of the airfield to include dirigible operations. The one that had carried Urban to Biberach had smartly refueled and quit the easily observed string of known aerodromes, arriving instead at Basel. After which it remained there for two weeks and departed in no particular hurry, and with no persons of interest, back toward Biberach. And so the trail was lost.

At that point, finally, political sensibilities became a serviceable compass. Why would Urban go to Basel? And where did he mean to go overland from there?

In regards to the second question, one generality was utterly certain: Urban did not intend to go far. He had shown the good sense to avoid traveling on the ground, where the chance of serendipitous sightings and hastily arranged enemy ambushes grew exponentially with every passing day.

Remaining in Basel itself was out of the question. Neither the USE nor any factions friendly to it had any real power there. Paris would require weeks of travel and was a politically dubious choice. Spanish Flanders remained a better choice but was much farther still. Bavaria, while Roman Catholic, was a state under siege by the very forces that had spirited Urban away from certain death on no less than three occasions, now. Austria was a Hapsburg stronghold, and although increasingly at odds with the dominant Spanish branch of the family, would logically be unwilling to shelter and thus, possibly go to war over, a pontiff that Philip wanted removed. And if Urban actually sheltered with any powerful Protestant king in any largely Protestant land, it was doubtful that he would be able to attract and retain the support he needed to ultimately restore himself to the *cathedra* or so demonize Borja that almost all of Roman Catholicism would raise a hue and a cry against him.

So, by process of political elimination and limited overland footprint, Dolor placed his bets on Burgundy and Besançon. An almost violently Roman Catholic city in an equally Roman Catholic region, the most Protestant thing about it was its newly self-appointed Grand Duke Bernhard, who wished to bring increased religious tolerance to his potentially restive population. That, of course, put him on a social path quite similar to that espoused by the up-timers, with whom he had various arm's-length dealings. Furthermore, he had just recently married the Catholic regent of Tyrol, Claudia de Medici, whose territories were now one of the provinces of the United States of Europe. If there was a polity of more serendipitously mixed demography, pedigree, and alliance, Dolor could not think of it.

And there was another benefit, of course. Bernhard's grasp on Burgundy, while not tenuous, was anything but assured. Consequently, he craved both safety and legitimacy—and what answered both those needs more than protecting a pope? When it came out—as it was always intended to—that he was sheltering the pontiff, he would become a pivotal political figure, one who could not be counterattacked too freely or fiercely for fear that it would be seen by other nations as an attempt to take hold of Urban's fate and so, wrest broader political leverage.

So without any undue haste, Dolor and Rombaldo had traveled by coach to the last post-stop outside Besançon, entered on foot, and within hours, saw signs that spoke volumes to those who knew what to look for. The small up-time presence had not grown overtly, but signs of their influence had: their elite troops—the Hibernian Mercenary Battalion—were not a prominent presence but were in all the places one would expect to maintain sufficient overwatch and security. A significant detachment of Irish Wild Geese were there also, and it was quickly confirmed that they were commanded by no other than Owen Roe O'Neill, who had been conclusively implicated in the first attempt to rescue Borja's young hostages last year, and was almost certainly involved in the successful second raid in Mallorca. Sharon Nichols, USE ambassador to Rome, and her husband, Ruy Sanchez, were personalities who could not easily stay hidden or out of marketplace or barroom conversation. So it was that all the expected and inevitable signifiers of Urban's presence were found within the first day.

The rattle of telegraphy ceased. Rombaldo turned with a smile. "Rome says—"

"That Borja's assassins are to make contact with a new provider here in Besançon: a second handler who is arranging for the 'tools' they shall require."

Rombaldo folded his arms, leaned back. "Sloppy. Well, inelegant, at least," he amended, seeing Dolor's slight frown. "Like you always say, if you're going to leave a trail, just leave one."

Dolor shrugged. "Yes, if most of your people are professionals. If they're not"—his glance roved quickly across his own men: Laurin, Radulfus, Martius, and Giulio—"sometimes it is better to keep the most sensitive matters in a second pair of hands, until the very last moment."

Rombaldo smiled ruefully. "So that's why you've kept the chest locked since we finished training south of Basel."

Dolor nodded, rose. "And now it is time for us to unlock it. When they act, we, too, must be ready." He walked to the chest closest to his own bed, palmed a small, flat skeleton key out of an almost invisible slot in his belt buckle, and opened the chest. The others in the room, hearing and seeing the motion, laid aside whatever they were doing and came to stand around as Dolor swung back the heavy lid.

They stood there gaping as Dolor knelt down, making sure that the contents were in proper order.

Martius, a thoroughly nondescript thug from the back streets of Zurich, giggled in what sounded like fetishistic anticipation.

The dozen grenades were still snug in their respective compartments. They were ovals, longer than the spherical designs typical amongst down-time armies. Although they were patterned after models seen in up-time books, they were filled with black powder, meaning that they could not generate the same high pressure explosions. However, the weaponsmiths that Dolor had set to the task had determined that the black powder would do its best work if more tightly contained inside a shell more robust than those used currently. Also, its surface was marked by a grid of deeply scored lines which, had one looked inside, were reprised on the interior of the weapon's body, as well: all so that it would fragment more evenly, generating a more predictable and lethal spray of shrapnel.

Dolor nodded to Rombaldo who reached in and lifted out the grenades like a crate of oversized eggs. Underneath were four black powder revolvers and three double-barreled shotguns, two of them matches for the one in Radulfus' hand. Those three were all copies of the fourth that lay in special, reinforced padding, away from the others. It was the weapon that had been lost by one of the up-time armed Wrecking Crew when two of them dropped through a hole they had blown in the roof of the Insula Mattei during the failed Roman rescue attempt. The heavy, overbuilt copies made from it had been difficult and expensive enough, but it was the ammunition that proved to be the almost insurmountable challenge.

Although several of the shells had been made from

the odd material that the up-timers called "plastic," most were down-time replicas in brass with crimped tops. Like the guns they were intended for, they were heavy and fabulously expensive, each fitted with a French-manufactured primer that had cost its weight in silver. Slightly more, actually. However, the first copies of this kind of shell—the up-timers dubbed it "buckshot"—did not function properly; the shot emerged with only a fraction of the force generated by the down-time reproduction cartridges. At which point, Dolor instructed the gunsmith to dissect one of the few, precious intact rounds of ammunition.

What they discovered both amazed and bemused them. They had presumed that, like all other up-time cartridges, wadding played little or no role. But in the shotgun shells, particularly the ones loaded with black powder, the wadding proved to be both comparatively extensive and subtly complex: without it, the individual projectiles did not exit the barrel in a reliable pattern or with optimal force.

The four Hockenjoss & Klott percussion cap revolvers, all from the original manufacturer, had been comparatively easy to procure. One had belonged to the young male hostage, Frank Stone, taken from him when he surrendered in Rome. Another had been snatched from a dead Marine by one of the few assassins who escaped the failed attempt on Urban's life in Molini. He had carried it back to Rombaldo along with his report, too naive or stupid to foresee that his faithful return would ultimately be rewarded with a garotte: one less trail that might lead back to the masterminds who had planned the attack. The last two revolvers had been acquired through careful and quiet negotiations with private owners, always conducted through intermediaries.

Dolor stood and moved back from the chest. "You know which weapons are yours. Clean them. Then practice loading and unloading until you may do so as swiftly as you did when we finished training south of Basel. Use the blanks we have for that purpose: do not handle the actual ammunition."

"When will we use them?" breathed Martius eagerly.

"Soon enough," Dolor replied and drifted back to the radio. Sitting, wondering if Javier de Requesens y Ercilla would send a reply, Dolor let his hand slip inside his dark charcoal-colored cloak and checked that his private weapon—the one that only Rombaldo knew he had—was situated properly under his armpit. He ran his finger over the top of where the shrouded hammer rested against the weapon's frame, the smooth up-time metal always a wonder to touch.

Some might have considered the weapon a battle trophy—he had come by it in the process of defeating the Wrecking Crew—but Dolor took no pride in possessing it. He had taken it from the body of one of the Crew's two female members: a heavy English-woman by the name of Juliet Sutherland. She had been shattered beneath his cavalry's hooves and would have died a long painful death. He had approached her with the one percussion revolver he'd had at the time—Frank Stone's—and, looking in the direction where Harry Lefferts was hidden with a sniper rifle, Pedro Dolor put a single bullet into the back of her bloody and partially crushed head.

He could have made it a second quicker, so that it could only have been read as a mercy killing, but that would have been leaving a tactical and mental advantage unused. He had wanted Lefferts to see what had become of his fine plan, what it had done to his followers. Lefferts, while skilled, was still an amateur then, and such a scene was likely to send him either into a killing rage that would have delivered him neatly into the hands of Dolor's waiting troops, or would have broken his spirit, which would have been almost as useful in the long run. However, there was evidence that Harry's reaction followed a third and far more dangerous course: he learned from it, and resolved to learn more, to become a true professional. Unfortunate, since Dolor was not in the habit of trying to improve his enemies. However, that was an occasional and inevitable consequence of the job, and at least if he ever faced Lefferts again, he had the advantage of knowing that the up-timer would be more careful and so, more formidable.

The pistol Dolor had later recovered from Juliet Sutherland's body was called a snub-nosed revolver. It had a perversely short barrel, upon which was engraved the legend "S&W .357 Magnum." However, the short barrel, like the shrouded hammer, meant that the weapon was very unlikely to snag on clothes when drawn from a concealed holster and its cartridges made it unusually powerful for so small a gun. Consequently, the reason Dolor kept it for himself was probably the same one that had led Juliet Sutherland to choose it. Because her role in the Wrecking Crew usually involved interacting with people at close ranges, she did not frequently use a gun, but when she needed a weapon, its effect had to be shatteringly decisive.

Once again, ammunition had presented a special

challenge. It was hard to find, even the down-time manufactured cartridges that were of distinctly diminished effectiveness. However, the quality of the reproductions turned out by the German gunsmiths was worth the two gold escudos he had paid for each shell. Fitted with a lead bullet scored by a cross-cut tip, even the black powder rounds were devastating when used against unarmored targets at point-blank range.

He turned. His associates were splitting up, each retreating to a separate corner or bed to commence cleaning their weapons, several of them lavishing more tender affection upon these tools of mayhem than he had ever seen them express toward any living creature. He had been right to deny them ready access to all but one of the weapons during the weeks of waiting; they were like children, unable to keep from fiddling and fussing over their new toys. The likelihood that one of their number would have cleaned a weapon too close to an open window or would have decided to carry one concealed, just once, out into the street, was too great to have risked over the past six weeks.

The telegraph began its muted chattering once again; Javier de Requesens y Ercilla was giving Borja his money's worth and more than, self-importantly reporting minutiae that could not conceivably have any bearing upon the tactical and operational concerns of Rome's newly arrived group of thugs-turned-assassins.

Dolor felt one urge to smile ruefully, another urge to smirk, but suppressed both. Instead, he looked out the window into the fading light, his eyes following the dusk-silhouetted steeples and roofs of Besançon. It was a pleasant enough view, actually: a second story vantage point with few obstructions despite being one of a tight cluster of buildings served by an equally tight tangle of narrow streets—alleys, really—that were nestled near and behind St. Peter's church. The rent was surprisingly low because the building backed on the parish's graveyard, with all but one of its windows looking out over that dismal view. The other—not much more than a shuttered slit bored out of the wall to provide a cross-draft—gave unto an almost lightless alley.

But Dolor had been particularly pleased by the space, not only because it was both central and yet comparatively inaccessible, but because if he and his men had to flee, he had a ready warren of small streets into which they might disappear. Or, if the night was moonless or overcast, they could also use the main windows to hop down onto the roof of a first story extension and then slip over the low cemetery wall to flee through the tombstones, as invisible as ghosts.

Dolor heard Rombaldo—it was his tread—leave the main room and enter the one where the telegraph kept up its fitful rattle. "So, the self-satisfied dandy is once again playing at being an intelligencer, at earning his coin."

Dolor nodded.

Rombaldo shifted uneasily, as he often did when Dolor did not take up a proffered entree to conversation. "Of course, we might have learned of the arrival of Borja's new assassins a little earlier, if we had ever figured out where Javier the Fop was leaving and getting his drops."

Pedro did not even sigh in disappointment at Rombaldo, who, try as he might, never quite got the hang of genuine intelligence work. "We did not need to know, before or now. Requesens sends everything of value to Rome and we have the codes. Obversely, shadowing Requesens to learn the locations of his drops would only have given him the chance to spot us, to learn that someone was already watching him."

Rombaldo's reply came after a pause and was pitched in a lower, stubborn tone. "Well, if we knew where he drops instructions to his sell-swords, we'd at least know about their plans ahead of time."

Dolor turned and looked at Rombaldo. "We already will. Unless you think Javier will show enough initiative and impertinence to issue any such orders himself." Rombaldo shook his head. "So whatever Borja's group might do, we will hear it first from Borja."

Rombaldo nodded, met Dolor's eyes for another moment, then looked away and walked back into the other room.

Leaving Dolor alone. As he preferred.

Part Two

Tuesday
May 6, 1636

Among the choirs of wind and wet and wing

Chapter 9

Estève Gasquet peered through the 4x Dutch telescope. The security cordon around the majestic doors leading into St. John's Cathedral had not visibly changed. General control of the crowd and a few lower-sensitivity access points to the building were being covered by a special detachment of army guards. Gasquet did not recognize any of them from the patrols he had observed at the city's walls, towers, or gates. These were apparently picked troops, now serving as living barriers.

Positioned back from them, and only half-seen, were three-man teams of the Wild Geese. And although it was a certainty that troops of the Hibernian Mercenary Battalion were someplace nearby, Gasquet hadn't been able to spot them. They were probably in similarly-sized groups, hidden in positions from which they could respond rapidly, or as individual marksmen in concealed perches.

Beside Gasquet, Klaus Müller grunted something about breakfast. Estève ignored him. It was a bother to have the big Swiss along at all, but it was unavoidable. Only one of the Swiss could reasonably claim to

be ill on the very day that Ignaz von Meggen meant
to present his scraggly band of hopefuls to Urban.
And of course Eischoll had to be there to control the
others' reactions in what might prove to be a situation
requiring both prudence and delicate timing.

Gasquet snugged the telescope's eyepiece tighter.
Müller was certainly not up to that job. He was about
as subtle as an irritable bull and was large enough
to look out of place among the other smaller and, in
some cases, teenaged hopefuls. So, leaving him out of
today's proceedings kept the group of would-be Swiss
Guards looking a bit puny, a bit impoverished, and
so, a bit pathetic. The less seriously they were taken,
the less scrutiny they were likely to attract.

"Do you see them yet?" Müller sounded eager, as
if this was some kind of parade.

"No." Gasquet watched the crowds pouring in through
the Porte Noire, filling the square that radiated out
from the cathedral's steps. This wasn't just any morning
mass; it was being offered by Urban himself, and the
faithful were emerging to get their extra bit of holiness.
He suppressed a sneer. As if a pampered, nepotistic,
noble-become-pontiff could confer extra holiness upon
anything. All just part of the pious charlatanry that
Estève Gasquet had left behind years ago, along with
the family and farm upon which he'd grown up.

If he had been a superstitious man, Gasquet might
have seen the sudden increase of morning light as a
deistic reply to his atheistic contempt: a golden beam
sent to seek out and reveal hidden assassins such as
himself and the Swiss oaf whose stomach was now
grumbling louder than he was. But no, it was just the
sun rising above the overlapping silhouettes of Mont

St. Stephen and Gran Bregille behind them. "Move back a bit," Gasquet muttered.

Müller wriggled to the rear, into the deeper shadow cast over them by the blank northwestern wall of the cathedral's impressive canon house. Lying on the flat roof of a shed built up against it, they were functionally invisible. Anyone looking in their direction would be staring almost directly into the rising sun, while they remained within the crisp-edged, ink-black shadow of the house's peaked roof.

Conversely, their vantage point, while not particularly high, gave them an unobstructed line of sight to the cathedral's open doors ninety-five yards to the west, and an almost complete view of the Porte Noire one-hundred twenty yards to the north.

The view from the small roof also confirmed that the windows of Le Boucle were overflowing with flags and pennants, as if in preparation to celebrate some festival. The new flag of Burgundy was particularly prominent, a reversion to the one that had existed before the French crown's fleur-de-lis and the Hapsburg white and red had been added to it. And the colors of the old flag—diagonal stripes that had originally been blue and gold—had been subtly reshaded into the teal and orange hues of Bernhard's own House of Wettin.

A minor commotion at the Porte Noire drew Gasquet's attention. A group of men bearing makeshift wooden crosses were struggling through the crowd there. Gasquet fixed his telescope upon that area and adjusted the focus; Ignaz von Meggen's face swam into view, his most ardent—which was to say, genuine—followers close behind him. Norwin Eischoll and the rest followed in their wake.

Whatever von Meggen was saying, the crowd grudgingly parted before him and the cross he held aloft. In surprisingly short order, he made it to the foot of the stairs and began calling up to the Irish Wild Geese. From a concealed position, another of their number stepped out: tall, slim, red hair glinting in the sun. Owen Roe O'Neill. He stared down, discovered the source of the commotion, and his shoulders slumped slightly, as if in resignation. He patiently listened to von Meggen, whose erect posture and visibly corded neck suggested a passionate appeal.

O'Neill looked away once or twice, nodded about as often; it was clear that he was not enjoying this part of his duty. At all. Eventually, von Meggen finished. O'Neill looked over his shoulder, exchanged quick words with some unseen party in the cathedral's narthex, then turned back, put his hands on his hips, and stared down at von Meggen.

The crowd had grown silent.

O'Neill hung his head and motioned with one hand for von Meggen to ascend the steps. But when the rest of the Swiss made to follow, O'Neill's stance changed instantly to one of readiness: the other Wild Geese snapped-to, as well. His command, "Hold!" was clearly audible despite the distance. The rest of his instructions were not, but their content was clear: the rest of the Swiss reversed their course and stopped in a knot at the base of the cathedral stairs. At which point, von Meggen was waved up. But before the young freiherr entered, O'Neill made him pause again. Two of the rank-and-file Hibernian Mercenaries emerged from the cathedral. They searched von Meggen's person in a brisk, efficient fashion that told

Gasquet that this simple act—checking for concealed weapons—had been strategized and trained, just like the rest of their actions.

Evidently the significance of that was not even lost on Müller. "If it comes to it, those soldiers will be men to be reckoned with."

"And that is one of the reasons we are watching them, studying them."

"So that we might better fight them when the time comes?"

Dolt. "No. So that maybe, we will not have to fight them at all. They are creatures of training and habit. That may show us ways to avoid, or trick, them." Gasquet ignored Müller's increasingly puzzled frown, raised a hand to mute the question that was struggling toward enough coherence to push past his lips. "Your idealistic von Meggen is being allowed inside."

"Yes, but he's the wrong man. He doesn't want to kill the pope; he wants to protect him."

If there was a just god or a useful devil, he would certainly have picked this moment to strike Müller down for stating the obvious, a habit that was just one step above buggering goats, in Gasquet's opinion. "The moment the guards intercepted your friends, it was clear there would be no killing of a pope today, no convenient shortcut. And frankly, we held out no real hope of doing so."

"Then why are we—?"

Gasquet did not have the patience to let Müller finish. "Von Meggen is getting a new, essential weapon for us. We call it 'trust.'" The vapid expression on the Swiss's face told him that explication was required. "If von Meggen seems genuine, they are likely to grant his request to consider making you all members of the Pontifical Guard. However, if your fellows aren't allowed to swear their service today—well, then our job becomes more difficult."

Müller nodded: possibly he comprehended, possibly he just wanted to act as though he did. "So when will we find out which it is?"

The doors to the cathedral began closing. Gasquet squinted at the shadows cast by the sundial in the enclosed gardens of the cloister just north of the cathedral. "About an hour now."

"And until then?"

Gasquet pulled a stick-mounted mirror and a whistle out of his satchel and laid them in ready reach. "Until then, we wait."

The choir began to sing, and the sun edged higher.

The sun dial was touching the nine-thirty mark when the last notes of the concluding hymn suddenly increased in volume: the cathedral doors had been opened once again.

Müller's head snapped up. "Now what?" He sounded groggy.

"Now you stay awake. Things should start moving pretty quickly."

Crowds were pouring out the doorway, quickly ushered aside to make a path for those who were following, and also for three sedan chairs approaching from the cloister.

"For the pope?" Müller wondered aloud.

"That's what our crossbowmen have been told."

"Crossbowmen? Where?" Müller rose slightly, head swiveling through the points of the compass.

Gasquet reached over, pulled him down. "Remain hidden, oaf. Our job is to observe, only."

As the crowd filed out, the army guards turned their heads slowly, dutifully, in a dumb-show of ostensibly scanning for suspicious characters or weapons. However, as the volume of the exiting faithful began to taper, one of the Wild Geese extracted a golden-haired man from the line: it was von Meggen. Again he was searched, thoroughly but without the same rehearsed precision demonstrated by the Hibernian Mercenaries, and then released. But as he went slowly down the steps, he cast an expectant gaze back up over his shoulder.

The *Prouvènço* swung his Dutch telescope up along the path of von Meggen's glance and discovered Ruy Sanchez himself staring down from between the shutters of a narrow window, probably on the staircase that led up to the rather alarmingly tilted belfry.

Müller's gaze had tracked along with the aim of Gasquet's telescope. The Swiss apparently had very keen eyes. "That's the Catalan, Sanchez."

"Yes."

"Well, what is he doing up there?"

"Looking for us."

"What?" It sounded as if Müller had swallowed his tongue. "Us?"

"Not you and I specifically, you dimwit. But persons like us."

"Like us? What do you mean?" If Müller was insulted by Gasquet's characterization, he gave no sign of it.

Gasquet was grateful that his impatient slip hadn't angered the Swiss, since there was little enough trust or amity between the two groups involved in the plot as it was. "I mean that they are clearly interested in watching whom von Meggen joins as he exits, or if someone is loitering around, watching over him. They—or at least the Catalan—are not entirely certain he is acting genuinely; they are prudent, watching any person who tries to get direct access to Urban. They cannot afford to simply accept any such overtures as innocent, not without being watchful for signs that it is part of a broader ploy."

Von Meggen had rejoined the rest of the prospective Swiss Guards at the base of the cathedral steps. After a few moments of conversation, those who truly shared his hopes began smiling and nodding; the others, led by Eischoll, evinced muted versions of similar interest. Some were markedly better actors than their fellow-conspirators.

Müller frowned. "So they—we're—all part of the Papal Guards, now?"

Gasquet looked sideways: it was hard to believe that he, a *Prouvènço*, knew more about the formalities of that process than a Swiss. "No. In a situation like this, there is usually a review of all prospective guards by a direct papal representative or the pope himself, since the old commander is dead. I suspect your young idealist's happy news is that the pope has agreed to his proposition in principle."

Müller nodded. "Okay. But will it happen in time?"

Gasquet shrugged. "As far as I can tell, we're not in any rush." Von Meggen's group started moving away from the steps of the cathedral. Gasquet looked back up toward where Sanchez had been watching; that window was empty, now. "Apparently the Catalan didn't see anything worth investigating." Which had probably not surprised him; only rank amateurs would have attempted to contact von Meggen immediately upon his exit from St. John's. But it would have been equally amateurish not to keep an eye out for such a suspiciously-timed meeting, and whatever else Sanchez was said to be, an amateur was not among the labels affixed to him.

It was also not the sign of an amateur that three draped sedan chairs were now nearing the cathedral steps to fetch the pope, rather than a single open one. Von Meggen saw the approaching procession, conferred quickly with Eischoll, who nodded vigorously and assisted him in not only stopping the rest of the Swiss, but arranging them in a rough cordon along the likely exit route of the pontiff. As they did so, the sedan chairs and their bearers made their way up the steps and into the cathedral, one after the other.

"A shell game?" Müller wondered with a frown.

Well, he wasn't completely dense. "It is how they move the pope around the town, on the rare occasions that they do." What Gasquet did not add was that, over his weeks of watching, he suspected that, on some occasions, and between certain locations, the sedan chairs were nothing more than a decoy. The last three hundred years of Besançon's history had been rife with changes in rulers, in laws, in tolerance for different faiths. It was rumored that hidey holes and secret passages had been constructed and then forgotten by generations of refugees, informers, spies, and heretics, only to be rediscovered by thieves, murderers, and black marketeers.

However, whatever truth there was to such tales, and whatever shadowy pathways might exist, that knowledge was now possessed almost solely by the less savory local elements, with whom Gasquet had minimized contact. After all, if they were willing to take coin to assist him, they'd be at least as likely to accept even more coin to betray him. So the possibility that the pope moved through unseen tunnels on occasion remained a tantalizing but unconfirmed suspicion.

The first of the sedan chairs emerged from the cathedral, surrounded by a mixture of Burgundian soldiers and Wild Geese. As it started down the stairs, the troops in the square started pushing back the crowd—including the Swiss, who seemed more than mildly affronted. But that was of no concern: Eischoll had competently shepherded von Meggen's group to the correct spot.

When the second sedan chair did not appear, Gasquet granted that he was dealing with true professionals and that his crossbowmen never had a chance to attack two targets at the same time. By returning to the safety of the cloister singly, no assassins could hope to have better than a one in three chance of attacking the correct chair—assuming the pope was in any of them. But no matter: the crowd was dense, the babble of voices loud, the potential for confusion greatest. Gasquet picked up the stick-mounted mirror, slipped it into the sunlight, tilted it in the direction of the top of the Porte Noire.

Müller, following the angled flash, tensed expectantly as a faint silhouette rose into view atop the ancient Roman gate. The outline was that of a kneeling man, training a crossbow down at the sedan chair. When it's string released, no sound rose above the general din of the faithful multitudes straining for a view of Urban, the incarnate link between God's divine and mundane kingdoms.

The quarrel ripped into the low-center of the sedan-chair's front drapery, made a tearing sound as it buried itself in whatever chair was behind it. The sudden agitated swirl of the pierced drapery and the panicked flinch of two of the bearers, triggered an immediate chorus of cries, shrieks, and gasps. Half of the crowd's heads and torsos began wrenching around in attempts to discover where the shot had come from.

The Wild Geese were far more focused. The tall dark one who had been leading the escort gestured high, beyond the front of the sedan chair. Two of his men quickly pointed toward the silhouetted attacker, who was clearly working to reload the crossbow. The leader leaned back toward the cathedral's doorway: probably calling out the location so it could be relayed to whatever Hibernian snipers were in the vicinity.

In that second, dozens of the crowd had rushed toward the sedan chair, some in an apparent reflex to help their possibly stricken pope, others with the wide eyes of those drawn by the anticipation of a ghoulish spectacle. They came up sharply against the Burgundians, several of whom seemed to misinterpret the crowd's reaction as an assault, or at least, a complete disregard of their authority. Weapons were raised; one or two fell. Shrieks of pain and howls of outrage added to the bedlam.

At that moment of perfect chaos, four men broke free of the crowd, two carrying crossbows, two more producing suddenly smoking containers. The crossbowmen kneeled, fired. One of the two Burgundians in the path of the pair of charging assassins fell limply; the other staggered back, dropping his sword to lock his hands around the quarrel protruding from his left leg.

The sudden attack caused a brief, stunned ebb in the uproar—but then it rushed back in, redoubled and horrified.

But not before the two lead assassins sprinted along the path that had been cut by the crossbowmen and reared back to heave their smoking jars up the stairs toward the cathedral's doorway.

Von Meggen and Eischoll charged in from the side, tackling them. One of the bombs simply fell and rolled away, the burning rag stoppering it flaring irregularly. The other one was just leaving its wielder's hand when von Meggen tackled him. The firebomb wobbled into the air, landed on the stairs between the sedan chair and the thinned cordon of Burgundian soldiers: flaming oil splashed out in every direction. One of the Burgundians' tabards began smoking and hissing; the rent drapery of the sedan-chair torched with a sharp, breathy *whoosh!*

As fire leaped along the frame of the sedan-chair as if it was seasoned kindling, the rest of von Meggen's Swiss caught the two crossbowmen, who, apparently startled by the swift response, dropped their recocked crossbows and tried to press back into the crowd to avoid capture. Before they could do so, the Swiss had pulled the assassins down and hands began rising and falling in the scrum beneath which they were buried. Two of those hands held knives.

As Eischoll performed similar, and quite practiced, execution upon the bomb throwers, von Meggen raced to the nearest crossbow, scooped up one of the quarrels that had been abandoned, fitted it, and raised the weapon toward the silhouette atop the Porte Noire. That attacker had already fled to the northern side of the gate, but then stopped as if surprised, as if he had prepared a method of escape there but now found it mysteriously gone. He began running back across the top of the Roman arch, making for a nearby roof.

Von Meggen gauged carefully, fired—and missed. As did the rifle that spoke from the cathedral's bell-tower at almost the same second; stone fragments spat out from the top of the arch. The assassin sprinted harder.

Von Meggen seemed to be so absorbed with cursing himself that it took a moment for him to realize that Eischoll was beside him, handing him the other crossbow: loaded. Ignaz von Meggen did not even smile; he grabbed the weapon, raised it, aimed, and fired.

The assassin let out a faint cry. Hit just below the hip, he staggered, and pitched over the far side of the arch. Eischoll shouted for the Swiss to follow him, and with blades out, they rushed toward the twitching body that was face down on the street cobbles. The ones who reached it first were the older impostors. Their knife work was every bit as swift and efficient as Eischoll's had been.

Müller was silent for a long moment, did not notice that Gasquet was already returning the telescope to its case and policing the area to make sure they had not left any spoor to mark their position. "Were they your men?" Müller asked in a voice of almost childlike uncertainty.

"They were. We must go. Now."

"Yes. But—did you really think they could succeed?"

"At killing Urban? It was possible, but unlikely."

"Then why—?"

Gasquet rounded on the Swiss. "To give young Freiherr von Meggen an opportunity to prove his and his men's loyalty to the pope. And now, they've demonstrated their eagerness to risk their lives in his service."

"So . . . so you meant to kill your own men?"

Gasquet sneered as they crept toward the edge of the roof that faced away from the cathedral. "If by 'my men' you mean those ill-trained cutthroats I retained a week ago with a few silver pennies and a few flagons of wine, then yes, I did. Now, hurry, or I may begin considering a similar fate for you."

As Müller complied hastily and Gasquet gauged the jump down to the ground, he thought, *As if I'm not already doing exactly that, you Swiss oaf.*

Chapter 10

"Maleït sigui!" cursed Chimo the Catalan. "I left my loaf in the privy!" He moved hastily toward the door.

Gasquet's lieutenant, Donat Faur, wasn't sure he had heard correctly. "You took your breakfast to the shitter?" Chimo shrugged. "Really?" Donat was not squeamish, but imagining that made him feel queasy for a second.

"I was hungry." Chimo sounded both defiant and abashed. "I still am."

"Get it. Quickly. You're supposed to be guarding the door."

"Okay, okay," Chimo called as he started down the stairs. "It's just out back. Not like anyone can come in the building and get up the stairs without me seeing."

"Just hurry up!" Donat shook his head. "Manel?"

The quieter of the two Catalans looked up. "You want me to watch the door until he comes back?"

"Yes."

"I was cleaning a gun in the workspace." He glanced toward the small, draped-off area to which they had moved all their weapons and the work table that shielded them from the roof's many leaks. Manel waited for a reply, wearing his typical hangdog look.

Christ in a whorehouse, are they all dullards? "Well, then go get it and bring it out here. Just be ready to hide it if someone comes."

Manel nodded, rose, and disappeared behind the drapes. "No one ever comes," he added softly.

Donat rolled his eyes, went into the small, curtained area that was Gasquet's room and office, the only place in the attic with a window that provided enough daylight to read comfortably. Only he and Gasquet had learned their letters, and Donat tried to improve his by reading over the messages their handler left in a window box languishing in the perpetual gloom behind *L'Anguille Vernie.*

Beyond the workspace drapery, Donat heard a thump and a sound like a small cascade of marbles. *Now what?* "Manel, what the devil did you—?"

"The balls for the pistols. I knocked them over."

"Well, leave them be. Watch the door." Donat muttered, after which he devoted himself fully to deciphering the tightly packed script with which their handler had covered a small sheet of paper.

Baudet Lamy retreated backward toward the door of the largest ground floor apartment. Although a landlord of some means, he was careful not to antagonize his better tenants, and the widow Coton was one such. Her lawyer husband dead (probably slain by the barbed darts launched by her tongue) and her only child carried off by fever some years later, she was alone in the world and as miserly a soul as had ever wanted redemption. And if her current indignant temper was any measure, her soul wanted redemption more than most.

"I do not know what they are doing up there!" she hissed so loudly that Baudet wondered why she did not just shout it. "But they are moving heavy objects and up at all hours! And constantly coming and going, keeping no schedule appropriate to tradesmen."

Baudet raised his hands in an attempt at humble placation. "They may not be fully settled in their livelihood, Madame Coton. Indeed, they may not be tradesmen at all, but common laborers, attracted by the new businesses that the pope's visit has spawned. They may be stockmen, working at all hours, according to the needs or whims of their employers."

The widow Coton drew up to her full, desiccated height and tried to stare down her nose at him, despite being half a foot shorter. "That is not my concern. Their hours are irregular, their habits repulsive, and their use of the latrine vile. I am not even sure they avail themselves of chamber pots, so often can they be found inconveniencing the rest of us by occupying the privy for extended periods. It is probably a result of their irregular hours and constant shuffling and banging: it would put any normal person off their digestion, of that I am quite certain."

I can think of another tenant's behavior far more likely to curdle the contents of my stomach, you old prune. "Madame, I shall go upstairs and inquire as to their habits and if they might show more consideration to their fellow tenants."

Widow Coton's expression became sly. "You do that, Monsieur Lamy, and while you're at it, you might count just how many tenants there are in that apartment."

Lamy forgot about Madame Coton's vinegary personality and expression. "You mean—their number has increased since they occupied their rooms?"

Madame Coton shrugged histrionically. "I am an old woman, with failing eyes. But I have seen new faces coming and going. Just yesterday, in fact. I would not be surprised if their numbers have increased in the past two weeks."

Baudet Lamy straightened. Now, this was serious. "I thank you, Madame Coton. I shall attend to the matter at once."

Her smile was a horrible thing to see. "I am sure you will." Her voice was a reedy, cynical coo.

Lamy opened the door to the hall, hearing the rear door to the privy close as he stepped out.

"There goes one of them now," Madame Coton hissed archly. "Did you not hear him come down the stairs?"

Ears like a bat and a face to match; no wonder Monsieur Coton had died an early death. "I did not. I was entirely focused on your concerns. Which I shall now address." He closed the door with a bow and walked briskly toward the stairs. If her observations were accurate, it was time to set things right, both in terms of the behavior and the additional rent he had a right to expect from the occupants of the attic.

However, he reflected as he began to climb the stairs, they were all ready and rugged men. It would not do to antagonize them. But after all, there was no need of that. Rooms were at a premium in le Boucle. If they refused to comply with his terms, he could simply shrug and point out that the town council had empowered select men of the watch and militia to intervene in the case of squatters. And then he would leave and let them stew in their own juices.

Winded at the top of the stairs, Lamy raised his hand to knock . . . but discovered the door ajar. While not in any way illegal—it was a tenant's right to tempt burglars, if he was willing to pay for the losses—an open door was undignified and created an appearance of carelessness, of disregard for safety and propriety. Well, perhaps a little surprise was in order to startle the occupants back into something like an awareness of civilized decorum—

Lamy pushed open the door enough so that it banged back against the wall.

"Monsieur Gasquet? You are present?"

The attic was so dark that Lamy could not be sure if the cheap bedframes were occupied or not. But it was not Gasquet's voice that answered him from behind a screened off area which allowed little of the main dormer's light to enter the room. "No, Monsieur Lamy. It is Donat Faur." The man sounded surprised. "I am coming."

On the other side of the room, a silhouette slowly rose from one of the beds.

"Please do and quickly," Lamy replied, noting another draped area, smaller, off to the right. "I am told that you have had many visitors recently. Perhaps some family who has come to stay with you? If that is the case, they are more than welcome, but we must also increase your rent. There is also the matter of noise and late activity that has disturbed some of your—"

Sudden movement rustled the drapes of the screened area on the right. The cloth panel closest to Lamy opened, revealing a small dark man he had seen only once before, cradling a wheel-lock pistol. There were several more on the table behind him. As well as swords, daggers, even what looked like some kind of small petard. What on Earth—?

Donat Faur emerged from the larger screened area at the back of the room, his gaze shooting quickly from the man with the gun to Lamy. He raised his hands slowly. "Monsieur Lamy, I see we will have to take you into our confidence. We are undisclosed agents of the pope's, here to watch for threats to his life which might arise among the criminal elements—"

Feet pounded on the stairs behind Lamy, who had finally recovered enough from his surprise to become terrified, cold sweat starting out all over his body. As he turned to face the stairs, he was trying to keep from stammering. "Y-yes, of c-course, Monsieur Faur. I am sorry to have incon-convenienced you and your—your men."

The smallest of the tenants—a little Catalan who, from prior encounters, seemed closer in wit to an idiot than an intelligencer—bounded to the top of the stairs. He frowned, reached behind his back as he glanced over Lamy's shoulder, in the direction of the man with the gun. His eyes widened slightly. His hand reappeared, clutching a dagger.

"No, no!" Faur was almost shouting from behind. From which direction, stealthy footfalls were approaching.

"No?" said the dagger-wielding fellow in surprise. "You mean, he's going to help us kill the pope, too?"

Shock—at the audacity of that statement—vaporized Lamy's fear, but only for a moment. Because, he realized, the little Catalan had just uttered his death sentence.

Even before the next wave of cold sweat could start from Baudet Lamy's pores, he was dead on his feet.

Donat Faur watched the inevitable transpire with a time-slowed exactitude that, until this moment, he had only experienced during combat.

The moment Chimo uttered the words, "kill the pope," Brenguier, who had risen from his bed to close in softly behind Lamy, leaped forward, a thin dagger thrust out like a comically short rapier. The couteaux-breche, usually used for slipping between links of mail or through joints in armor, disappeared into the thick folds of flesh where the landlord's head sat upon his neck: Lamy went limp.

Brenguier had to leave the blade in place in order to get his arms around the stout man's body, to keep it from crashing to the floor. But while he was still swinging wide his arms to make that catch, Chimo rushed in, slashing a quick figure eight with his knife, his face contorted in what looked like an orgasm of savage ferocity.

The last "no" died in Faur's suddenly dust-dry throat. He put his hand to his head as Brenguier caught the almost eviscerated man, staring contempt at Chimo. "Idiot," Brenquier snarled at the little Catalan.

"Idiot? Why?"

Brenguier huffed out a laugh that was anything but amused. "The idiot wants to know why he's an idiot. *Mon Dieu*, where do I start?"

Chimo's face began contorting back into a mask of animal fury. "Hey—" he began.

"Enough," Faur snapped. Prior experience took over and had him uttering orders almost as he conceived of them. "Manel, go get Peyre from his watch point at the head of the street. Close the door behind you and lock it. No, fool; put that damned gun away first! Brenguier, hold Lamy up, but at an angle—yes, leaned back like that. Chimo, pull down those drapes, get them under the body. And yes, Chimo, you are an idiot."

They worked quietly, getting Lamy's corpse on the ground, and then getting a small chest under his back; the dead man looked like he was being broken on the wheel by the time they were done.

Chimo, blood spattered on the front of his shirt and coating his arms all the way up to his elbows, sat back and stared. "Why do you have him bent that way?" Peyre came in with Manel, stared at the aftermath, shook his head, and headed toward the bucket they used to fetch water.

Donat sighed. "To keep as much of the blood from collecting near the damn trenches you cut into his chest. We don't want him to bleed out here."

Chimo shrugged. "Yeah, well . . . it's already a mess."

Donat leaned forward, hand on his own dagger. "And we don't need it any messier, you fool. Besides, we're going to have to plant his body somewhere else, and when we do, it would help for him to have a little blood left in him." Faur saw the puzzled scowl growing on Chimo's face and cut off the question before he had a chance to form it. "Wherever we put him, it's got to look like he was attacked—and died—there. That means blood— lots of blood, considering how you carved him up."

"Yeah, well—how was I to know that Brenguier had already snuffed him?"

"By taking half a second to look and think before slashing, you idiot," Brenquier muttered. "The man was already folding over when you started."

"Yeah, well—that's my job, you know?"

No one said anything. What, after all, could they say? Other than the obvious: that Chimo truly was an idiot. And that several of them were seriously considering the possibility of dumping two corpses, rather than one. Not out of anger—although that would have been sufficient— but out of self-preservation: given time, Chimo might do something equally stupid. And they might not be able to control the consequences that next time. Assuming they all survived the aftermath of this event.

Peyre, watching the street, said, "Gasquet and Huc are back. I'll open the door, let them in, head down to get some water."

"While you're at it, steal some bedsheets, if any are out drying along the way."

Peyre nodded, unlocked the door and began descending the stairs just as Donat heard Gasquet starting up. Sounds of downward progress met upward progress: both stopped. Silence, then a few fierce whispers, one muffled curse, and the downward progress resumed. Two seconds later, so did the ascending footfalls.

Gasquet slipped into the room, looked around, then looked away as his expression darkened.

Chimo carefully studied the dirt under his fingernails.

Gasquet gave a quiet order to Huc, who locked the door, stood ready beside it and drew his knife.

Gasquet walked over, looked at the body, at the blood on the drapes and floorboards.

Donat looked at him squarely. "Did Peyre tell you what happened?"

"He told me he wasn't here, but it's not hard to figure out. What I want to know is why."

Donat shook his head. "People weren't doing their jobs. The person who should have been guarding the door left it open when he went to the privy, and the person who was assigned as his relief didn't stand his post right away. He was too busy picking up pistol balls, it seems."

Chimo and Manel looked like they might fold into themselves and disappear. At least, it looked like that was their intent.

"And you?" Gasquet asked, staring at Faur.

"Reading the most recent messages. Memorizing them." Which was partially a lie; Donat read them simply to practice his reading. But in doing so, he usually wound up memorizing them, too.

Gasquet looked away. "You're my lieutenant. You've got to keep an eye on things. Personally. Until everyone is where they belong and doing what they're supposed to be doing. That's your job."

Brenguier shifted uncomfortably.

Gasquet's eyes snapped over to stare at him. "You have something to say?"

"Yes, I do. Donat just about had the situation in hand when the little idiot got knife-happy. Again."

Chimo darkened. "Listen, you Occitan dog, I should—"

"Shut up," Gasquet whispered. "All of you. If Donat had done his job more carefully, this wouldn't have happened."

Faur felt his brow and ears grow hot; if Gasquet was going to blame him—

But Gasquet was already moving on. "Neither I nor

Donat have the time to make sure you follow every little order. And if you can't follow simple orders, then I need you to tell me: why should I keep you? What good are you? Because it's plain to see how much trouble you are." He stared at Manel then shifted his eyes over to Chimo. His eyes became even harder. After two seconds of silence, he muttered, "I'm waiting. I asked a simple question and I want a simple answer: Why should I keep you?"

Manel cleared his throat. "Because I won't make that mistake again. I got distracted. By guns. And then I dropped all the bullets. Next time, I'll put the guns aside. Right away."

Gasquet leaned down toward the small, dark man. "You put aside anything and everything when you're ordered to. And you never, ever, get distracted. That could get all of us killed. What you did today might still do that. But I promise you this, Manel: you do it again, and it will get *you* killed, for sure. By my hand. Do you understand?"

He didn't wait for a reply; he turned toward Chimo. "So what about you, Chimo? No answer? Because if I don't get one in the next five seconds, you're going to the same place we're taking him later tonight." Gasquet gestured toward Lamy's corpse.

Chimo's answer came out as an angry, confused whine. "But I—I didn't do anything wrong! Yeah, I left the door open: I won't do that again. I promise—"

—which elicited eye-rolling from several of the group; even among thieves and cutthroats, Chimo's inability to remember, let alone keep, a promise was marked—

"—but Gasquet, you hired me to kill. And I did. Is it my fault Lamy was already dead?"

There was an uncomfortable silence in the room of hardened criminals. If Chimo couldn't see, or wouldn't admit to, his actual failures, then the next minute might be his last.

Gasquet looked away, closed his eyes. Donat knew he was deciding. Without opening his eyes, he asked, "Were you ordered to draw your knife?"

"N-no. I'm sorry about that. But I thought—"

"Don't think, Chimo. That's your problem, because you don't do it well. As a matter of fact, you do it so poorly that, if you're going to continue to work with us—"

Translation: "if we decide to let you live."

"—then you have to stop thinking. You just wait for orders. And you obey them. That's it. Understand?"

"Yes, but I—"

"Chimo." Gasquet opened eyes that were devoid of all emotion or expression. "Do you *understand*?"

He swallowed. "Yes, Gasquet. I understand."

"Good. Now, get the water and a brush. And the last of our soap. Scrub this floor clean."

Chimo looked around. "Just me?"

Gasquet turned back to stare at him. "Yes. Just you. You made the mess; you clean it up. Besides, it's the kind of job you can be trusted with."

Chimo's eyes widened, as did his nostrils, but he got up and fetched the bucket and brush.

Gasquet glanced around at the others. "The rest of you: start packing everything up. We're going to have to find new rooms."

"New rooms?" Peyre repeated. "How? There aren't any left in the Buckle, or even—"

Gasquet shook his head. "Doesn't matter. We can't

stay here. We've got to find a place and move. So we need to be packed and ready." He motioned for Donat to step behind the dropcloth that marked his private sleeping space.

Once there, he asked a string of practical questions: how much noise had been made? Exactly how long between the time Lamy entered and he was killed? Did he say why he had dropped by on them? Had he said anything suspicious? Acted oddly? Tried to stall for time? Seemed like he wasn't surprised when he was threatened?

When Gasquet had heard all Donat's answers, he nodded, rubbed his chin. "Sounds like it was just dumb luck. And all because Chimo left the door open. The idiot."

Donat looked sideways at him. "You really mean to keep him, or are you just reassuring him until we can dispose of him more—quietly."

Gasquet shrugged. "The thought did cross my mind, but no, we can't afford the possible exposure or the loss in manpower. As it is, there aren't a lot of us to carry out this plan. And any body that turns up in this city this week is going to be investigated. By up-timers, possibly, or at least with their help. So, for now, we keep Chimo on a leash until we can let him off it to kill the pope."

"And after that?"

Gasquet let a lopsided grin creep on to his face. "Then it will be time to get rid of our rabid dog. We might have to run pretty quickly and silently once we're done, and Chimo isn't clever enough to do either without being led by the hand."

Donat nodded. "We heard the noise up by the cathedral. Did everything go as planned?"

"Yes. Better. Von Meggen had a leading role in defeating the 'assassins.' Took one down with a pretty fair crossbow shot."

"So Eischoll wasn't lying about his marksmanship."

"Apparently not."

"Any evidence that the pope's officers find it suspicious that all five of the assassins were killed?"

Gasquet grimaced. "Not as though Sanchez sends me his intelligence reports. But I don't see why they would be suspicious. The four in the square were torn apart by the Swiss and the crowds. And the one on the Ponte Noire fell to the street when von Meggen shot him, and Eischoll and his men were first on the scene. With their knives. Understandable enthusiasm in protecting the person of the pope. And the crowd followed their example."

"So no suspicion that it was staged? Not even any investigation into how the crossbowman got atop the Pont Noire?"

"Why would there be? The ladder was still there, on the ground. I just had Huc tip it over." Gasquet smiled. "You should have seen that crossbowman when he saw that the ladder had fallen: stopped like he'd run into a wall. But as far as Sanchez and his minions are concerned, it was just a lucky mishap that prevented him from making good his escape."

"And now?"

Gasquet sighed. "And now we clean up the *real* mess that Chimo made."

"You mean, planting the body?"

"Yes."

"Are you sure we wouldn't be better off hiding it?"

"Sure we'd be better off, but where? We'd have to

be certain it wouldn't be discovered for a week, maybe more. Because if Urban's people find a carefully hidden body, they will treat it as a probably significant murder, something that was meant to be kept from their attention. At that point, it's only a matter of time before they check all three of Lamy's properties and interview all the tenants and examine all the rooms."

Donat nodded. "At which point, even if we left, they'll discover that this attic was abandoned about the time the murder might have occurred. Then they'll get descriptions of us and our accents. It might take them a few days but they'd find us."

Gasquet nodded back. "Right. Whereas if we plant the body in an alley, make it look like Lamy was drunk, got killed for his purse, they've got a much less suspicious crime. Murders aren't that frequent here, but right now the Buckle is packed with strangers. And where the streets are full of strangers, there's easy picking for thieves. If Lamy got unlucky or fought back"—he shrugged—"well, there's your crime. Anonymous and routine."

Donat frowned. "How long do we have, do you think?"

"Before he's missed? Well, his family will be worried tonight, unless they're a hateful bunch. But they won't be able to get an official search started until sometime tomorrow. So if we plant the body tonight, we should be fine. The real uncertainty is how quickly we'll be able to relocate."

Donat cocked an eyebrow higher. "If you're sure that they'll accept his murder as a common crime, then why relocate at all? What do we have to fear?"

Gasquet shrugged. "What if they decide that maybe

Lamy's murderer wasn't just any ordinary thief, but someone he had dealings with? If they put that kind of effort into investigating his death, they could wind up coming here, to interview us."

Donat rolled his eyes. "Yes. That wouldn't go well."

"Right. So, come on; we have to figure out where to plant the body."

Chapter 11

Ambassador Sharon Nichols entered the Palais Granvelle preceded by Marine Captain Taggart—a formality, really, since the place was practically crawling with the Wild Geese and no small number of the Hibernian Mercenaries. Of all the places in Besançon, none were more secure at this moment, because Pope Urban VIII was on the premises.

She made her way across the entry hall, toward the staircase at the far side. Ruy was standing at the center of the broad first landing, the place from which speakers usually made public announcements to gathered guests. He smiled warmly when he saw her, but kept at least half of his attention fixed upon the speech of two well-attired *besontsins* who were leaning in towards him conspiratorially: junior members of the town council, if Sharon remembered correctly.

Servants—long since vetted and selected from the palace's core staff—moved briskly to and fro, traversing the hard stone floors as loads from the main kitchen crisscrossed with furniture being reshuffled out of the great salon, which was the room selected for today's preliminary gathering of all the cardinals who had come to Besançon. Taggart made to block the traffic to facilitate Sharon's progress, but she stopped him with a small wave. For what seemed like the first time in a week, she was not in a rush and she wanted to savor that feeling. She was quite sure it would be over all too soon.

As she started up the steps, Ruy hastily nodded his thanks to the two *besontsins* and gestured toward his approaching wife. The young men turned, were quite surprised, then bowed and muttered respectful greetings to the USE ambassador before descending the stairs at a brisk pace.

Ruy moved closer, so that when she set foot on the landing, she was almost in contact with him. Well, part of her, anyway. Ruy's smile turned into a mischievous grin.

Sharon rolled her eyes. "You are incorrigible."

"Indeed I am! It is the greater part of my charm."

Sharon managed to restrict her reaction to a smile, rather than the snort of laughter that was her first reflex. "Then heaven help you."

"Heaven is my only help when it comes to retaining any decorum when so close to you, my love. And even heaven's power is not so great that I can be assured of remaining in control of my actions."

"You don't give up, do you?"

Ruy's frown was histrionic. "My heart, you married a soldier—a latter day conquistador! Surrender is not a concept we understand. And certainly not when the object of our desire—and yet also veneration—is so perfect. And so very close."

"Ruy, stop it. No, I mean it. Now, what were those two local politicos talking to you about?"

"Ah," he said, eyes averting in some mix of despair and disappointment, "these days you only come to me to discuss our duties. And at nights—at nights you do not come to me at all, anymore! What, then, is a conquistador to do?"

"Ruy, you were the one who put the security protocols in place. You're the one who put yourself in a windowless, subterranean cubicle next to the pope's. And put me in almost equally protected quarters. But at least I have a window."

"To which I would come every night, if I could, and serenade you."

"Why? To scare the stray cats out of the cloister?"

Ruy looked as if he might actually have taken some small part of that retort seriously. "Is it my fault that God chose to give me the arm of a swordsman rather than the voice of a courtier?"

"Not your fault at all, Ruy—and better still he gave you two hearts: a lion's for the times when you are fighting, and a lamb's for the times when you are just being my husband. Now, don't get all sentimental on me. Let's get through the business; it looked like those two were delivering a report."

"My wife is not merely a gentle-tongued poetess who extols my humble virtues, but also a hard taskmaster. Very well. Yes, it was a report. A preliminary report, to be precise."

Sharon lowered her voice. "On the assassins?"

"Yes. So far, we have little in the way of identification."

Sharon frowned. "That's a strange way to put it. Usually, someone is identified or not."

"Exactly. But this is a middle case. None of the

senior Burgundians recognized any of them from the weeks of security screening. But several militiamen think one or two of them look familiar."

Sharon felt her frown deepen. "Familiar how?"

Ruy leaned closer: for the sake of secrecy or salaciousness, she wasn't entirely sure. "Familiar in that they may have had run-ins with the local watch on prior occasions."

Sharon pursed her lips. "Not arrests, just run-ins? That would mean something like suspicious behavior, petty burglary, a bar-fight, right?"

"Yes. And I have the same reservations as it sounds you do, my love: it is a long step from petty crimes to assassinating a pope."

"So what are you doing?"

"I have charged the younger Valençay, Léonore, to gather senior members of the watch and militia to view the bodies. Hopefully, we shall find someone who recognizes them. That should produce a list of known associates. From there, we may hope for information on their recent activities, the places they habituate, where they dwell."

Sharon frowned. "This is not what I was expecting to hear."

Ruy nodded slowly. "Nor I. Common rogues, such as these seem to be, are not typically proficient with crossbows, and would hardly think to improvise firebombs."

"Or to have such a sophisticated plan. They must have observed how we've used the sedan chairs like a shell game. The way they hit the first one with the crossbow, and then cleared the way to bomb the second: not amateur hour."

One of Ruy's eyebrows rose in response to the unfamiliar up-time colloquialism. "As do you, my love, I find some elements of the attack suspicious. Or at least worrisome."

Sharon's eyebrows went the opposite direction: they lowered. "Like what?"

"Let us consider the two reasons for them to conduct the attack. The first is money. If so, then why did their employer not pay for better or more assassins? Anyone who truly wishes to slay the pope knows they must have deeper pockets than this. The second reason: personal motivation. But where is the sign of that? Those who kill to make a statement usually bring something to leave behind, a token or manifesto or some other suggestion of the grievances that compelled them to act. Lastly, the crossbowman on the Black Gate should have escaped."

"Yes, but his ladder fell."

"Indeed it did, my love. And ladders do indeed fall from time to time. More frequently if they are used by careless workers. But when ladders fall, they make a noise. And if it is a crowd that knocks them over, then there is usually a shout of alarm." Ruy stroked one mustachio slowly. "So where was the sound, either of the fall or of the crowd?"

"Are you saying you think someone deliberately removed the ladder so the crossbowman couldn't get off the top of the gate?"

Ruy shrugged. "It would solve the conundrum. But if so, it begs other questions, such as: why would anyone involved in the assassination want to strand the man up there? To make sure he could not get away, could not become a loose end?"

Sharon shook her head. "No, because there was

no way to be sure that he would be killed simply because he was unable to get down. He might have been captured instead."

"Precisely."

"So what are you saying, Ruy? That the one who killed him was in on the plot, to make sure it was covered up?" She started. "Von Meggen? Really?"

Ruy shook his head. "No, my wife, I cannot envision it either; your incredulity is well placed. I spoke to that boy—well, young freiherr, I suppose—and he is as true and ardent a fellow as I've ever met. The kind who get themselves killed for their ideals too soon to learn to temper their fine beliefs."

"And so become safely jaded like some hidalgo I'm acquainted with?" Sharon made sure her smile was as private and warm as a touch to his arm.

Ruy nodded. "You chide me for fun, my love, and yet, what you say is true: Ignaz von Meggen's head is still full of tales of noble deeds and high-minded sacrifice. He would cut his own throat before he would become part of a plot against the pope."

"Then maybe the ladder was just removed by some mistaken workman, or your own security?"

Ruy sighed. "Not my security. I have made the inquiry of them all. So a workman? But during the mass, while the waiting crowds would have hemmed in any bystanders? And I cannot imagine it to be a random act: why would a passing person take it upon himself or herself to remove a ladder when there might indeed be someone atop the gate?"

"I don't know; you tell me."

"I wish I could, my lustrous love, but I cannot. And that is what I find worrisome about the attack.

No matter what hypothetical plot I construct, I can find none that explain all the facts as we have them. Hopefully, we shall identify the corpses of the attackers and find new paths to new answers. And now, I believe your duties are about to commence."

"What do you mean?"

Ruy glanced meaningfully behind her, toward the entrance. "Bedmar has just entered with his retinue."

"Bedmar? The gathering of the cardinals is not due to start for another half hour."

"That is correct, dear heart. And that is as His Holiness wishes. They have matters to discuss, these two."

"And so Urban asked me here to do what? Serve as a referee?"

"I suspect much more than that. After all, the might of the United States of Europe figures crucially in both their strategies, I'm sure. And by bringing you to be part of this meeting, they make you party to whatever plans they might agree upon." His smile almost became sad. "You are not here to be a referee, my love. You are here to complete their intended troika."

A familiar voice hailed them from the left hand of the split staircase. "Ambassadora Nichols, you must promise to cease distracting your husband. I require his full attention upon the safety of my person!" Urban descended, two Wild Geese in front of him. His nephew Antonio and the Jesuit father general, Muzio Vitelleschi, followed close behind the pope. After them came Larry Mazzare.

Ruy bowed. "Your Holiness, my wife is as blameless as she is peerless. It is I—still a weak-willed swain at heart—who cannot restrain myself."

"Now that is plain truth, plainly told," announced

another voice from across the entry hall. Sharon turned: Bedmar was approaching, flanked by Achille d'Estampes de Valençay and Giancarlo de Medici.

Sharon bowed to Bedmar and the two tigerish cardinals accompanying him, reflecting that all three of them were certainly more reminiscent of the lion than the lamb. "Your Eminences," she said slowly.

Bedmar's answering smile was mild. The other two looked at each other in good-natured surprise, as if uncertain to receive the title as genuine or a jest. "We are still *in pectore*, Ambassadora Nichols," murmured Giancarlo, "and so, remain incognito." There was a twinkle in his eye as he said it, nothing flirtatious, but she did wonder how his rumored proclivities as a womanizer would fit with his new position as a cardinal. Well, it's not as though it seemed to constrain the behaviors of the others very much, so there was probably not much to worry about, there.

Urban arrived on the landing, received their devotions without ceremony, and led them all off to the side, leaving the center of the lower staircase unobstructed.

Bedmar looked around, raising an eyebrow. "I understand the amenities here are somewhat limited, but surely, a room with ten chairs can be arranged."

"Surely it can," Urban answered with a smile. "But surely the cardinals about to arrive will be as curious and jealous as ever. So I propose we have our meeting here."

Giancarlo frowned. "Here? On this landing?"

"Of course. Who would suspect us of having a sensitive conversation here? But we will not be interrupted because the rest will be escorted to the great salon."

Bedmar smiled. "And so there will be no sign that

we had a private meeting, the content of which would spawn endless conjecture, and the fact of which would spawn resentment."

"Resentment?" Achille d'Estampes de Valençay echoed.

"At not being included," Mazzare explained with a wry smile.

Achille stared at the up-time cardinal, then at the pope. "In truth?"

Bedmar put a hand on his shoulder. "You shall learn, my good fellow and soon, fellow-eminence, that if a church father is doomed to spend eternity in hell, it is most likely the sin of envy that shall send him there. Or vanity."

Sharon did not add "or venery," but would have liked to. Seeing the pinched expression on Vitelleschi's already wizened face, she suspected he might have been thinking the same thing.

Urban folded his hands so that they were hidden in the folds of his long-sleeved cassock. "I appreciate your coming to converse before our brethren arrive in their full number, Cardinal Bedmar."

Bedmar bowed slightly, slowly. "When the Holy Father calls, his flock attends."

Urban smiled. "Not so uniformly as one might hope, these days."

Bedmar sighed. "There is much confusion in Mother Church."

Vitelleschi's chin came up. "His Eminence will pardon my plain speech, but I perceive it is weakness, not confusion, that afflicts too many of our number."

Bedmar's eyes measured the old Jesuit. Although not a cardinal, as the father-general of his order,

Vitelleschi was a force to be reckoned with. "After the treachery and fratricide that struck at the very heart of Mother Church, it is only natural that there should be much fear, as well."

Vitelleschi's chin went higher. "That red biretta you wear, Your Eminence, is the same color that adorns much of your cassock. You know what it symbolizes, of course."

"The blood of Christ." Bedmar sounded as though he was growing impatient. Which was easy enough to understand; Sharon doubted she'd appreciate being lectured to by a wizened old Jesuit.

Vitelleschi's pause was just long enough to convey the swift impression that Bedmar had answered incorrectly and that the Black Pope was laboring to find a suitably tactful method of correction. "I am sure that too is intended to be part of the symbology. However, when Pope Gregory X dictated that scarlet should be the color of a cardinal's garments—at the Council of Lyon in 1274—he emphasized a different reason: that it symbolized the wearer's willingness to shed his *own* blood for the faith." Vitelleschi may have sniffed slightly. "Apparently, that interpretation—and expectation—is no longer uniform among the consistory."

"And yet," Urban murmured with a glance at the aging Jesuit who resembled a frail whippet with the disposition of a pit-bull, "Cardinal Bedmar's presence shows the opposite extreme: profound courage."

Bedmar's eyes fell at the comparison. "Your Holiness knows I was not in Rome; I was in no immediate danger."

"No immediate danger, no, but in your case, it continues to grow every day. In part, I asked you to come before the meeting to express my appreciation for the delicate nature of your position. You provided indirect aid to the ambassadora and other up-timers who were in Italy around the time of Galileo's trial. Indeed, you were generous enough to allow your longtime aide to marry that same ambassadora."

Bedmar's smile matched Urban's. "As if I have ever been able to stop that Catalan mule from doing anything he set his mind upon."

Ruy pushed back his moustaches, and Sharon discovered that she was smiling despite herself.

"And yet," Urban continued, "there is a serious side to those events. You, an intimate of Philip's court, a grandee, and former general of his tercios, have not only remained friends with a hidalgo who turned his back on Spain to marry an up-timer, but, by coming here, signal your loyalty to Prince Fernando, who has proclaimed himself king in the Lowlands. I imagined that you might anticipate a daily struggle to remain in Madrid's good graces. So I was not absolutely sure you would come."

Bedmar straightened his shoulders, folded his own hands, and looked up squarely into Urban's face. "His Holiness is considerate indeed to foresee and sympathize with the challenges of my position. However, he has overtroubled himself with that worry. Presently, Philip would find it inconvenient to press the matter of dominion over his brother."

Antonio Barberini shook his head. "It is a wonder that Philip tolerates Fernando's declarations and New World enterprises at all."

Urban smiled at his nephew. "Of the many things that kings and popes have in common, Antonio, this may be preeminent: never give a vassal an order that they will not obey. You will then either be forced to unseat the vassal, thereby weakening yourself both by loss of an ally and the resources needed to unseat him, or you will elect not to do so and thus appear weak. Which is even more costly, in the long run."

Antonio spread his hands. "But King Philip must certainly see the eventual trajectory of his brother toward the United States of Europe."

Urban nodded. "Unquestionably. But it is also true that Philip and Olivares have seen and made much history, are seasoned enough to know that events may so conspire to make a confrontation with Fernando unnecessary. What if his Dutch partners fall to bickering among themselves and weaken? What if Fernando's cooperative projects with them in the New World founder? What if the USE or Grantville are crippled in a possible war with the Ottomans? In each case, the present circumstances which make a rupture between Madrid and Brussels seem inevitable could suddenly be undone. And if that should come to pass, then Philip will be glad for not having warred upon his brother. Which would not only cost him dearly, but further isolate Spain and make his branch of the House of Hapsburg eternally loathed by the others."

Mazzare nodded. "Yes, Your Holiness. However, with every passing day, it seems that any change in the *likely* course of events would need to be increasingly dramatic if conflict between the brothers is to be averted."

Bedmar answered with a blithe smile. "I could not agree more, my dear Cardinal Mazzare. And so, here I am."

Giancarlo de Medici shook his head. "And openly, too? Are you so willing to annoy Philip?"

Bedmar shrugged. "It is a far better strategy to annoy Philip than alarm him. To explain: by coming here openly, I have no doubt annoyed him, but he will also not be particularly worried. He might wish that I had chosen not to attend at all, but he will neither be surprised that I did nor will he fail to understand it. However, if I were to begin skulking about, trying hide my attendance here, Philip would become alarmed. Kings, and particularly Spanish ones, operate from the assumption that the more highly placed one of their subjects is, and the more secretive they become, the more likely that they are trying to conceal treason. Besides, I must come when His Holiness summons me. I am, after all, the cardinal-protector of the Spanish Lowlands, and so, representing the faithful of Flanders is required by my first loyalty and oath: to God and His Church."

"A priority with which Philip might contend," Urban quipped with a smile. "Albeit silently."

"Silently before his courtiers and ambassadors, perhaps, Your Holiness. But not in privy council. From my own days at the Escorial, I may assure you of that."

Urban's smile dimmed somewhat. "With so many of your brothers here, it is also my intention to address urgent matters touching on the future of Mother Church, once the colloquium has ended and its other attendees have departed."

Bedmar's own smile actually widened. "Holy Father, it would be strange indeed if you did not also take this opportunity to hold a Council of the consistory. Given last year's events in Rome, it seems essential."

Urban's smile matched Bedmar's as he turned to glance at Vitelleschi. "As I predicted, even without the faintest intimation of our intent, Cardinal Bedmar would know we planned a Council."

Vitelleschi nodded.

"However," Bedmar added, "what I do not know—indeed, what none of us know—is how many cardinals have escaped Borja's agents and survived to attend?"

"And why is that important?" Vitelleschi asked archly.

Bedmar smiled patiently. "Father, the Jesuits have been an eminently practical order since their founding. Indeed, had they not been, they would not have had one tenth the success they have enjoyed around the globe. And so, I press the practicality of my question to His Holiness: how many of us are there? Enough to make a stand—or just enough to make for a memorable collection of martyrs?"

Chapter 12

Larry Mazzare managed not to flinch at the directness of Bedmar's question. He saw Urban's smile become melancholy. "It is a fair question," the pope mused, "but these days, I find that I dwell more upon the faces we shall never see again, rather than the ones who shall join us here."

"Perhaps," his nephew Antonio suggested, "I should begin with those we have lost? To put that unpleasantness out of the way first?"

Urban nodded, eyes downcast. Bedmar frowned; his associates shifted their feet. If Larry read Achille's expression correctly, he was less than pleased with the cardinal-protector's brusqueness, seeing how it had affected the pope.

Antonio's voice lowered. "We know that Borja attempted to assassinate twenty-one members of the consistory, most of whom were located in the Lazio. About eight weeks ago, we finally confirmed that he succeeded in killing sixteen."

Bedmar waited for a moment, then prompted quietly. "Who?"

Vitelleschi's voice was rough with what sounded like a witch's brew of quiet fury, bitterness, and raw grief. "Santacroce, Carpegna, Crescenzi, Savelli, Roma—even though he was Milanese—Scaglia, Biscia, Oreggi, and Rocci. The blackguards found Cesarini visiting his soon-to-be diocesan neighbor Muti in Viterbo, where they presented themselves as papal messengers. They cut their hosts' throats after being allowed to join them for a glass of wine on the veranda." Vitelleschi seemed about to resume the list, then faltered, looked down.

Achille waited, frowned. "That's only eleven," he murmured cautiously.

Vitelleschi looked away.

Urban raised his head. "The father general understandably elects not to name the last five, out of consideration for Antonio and me. You see, they were family. Lorenzo Magalotti, my secretary, was also my brother-in-law. Girolamo Colonna, who I understand died after hours on an impaler's stake, was Antonio's brother-in-law. And my brother Antonio, for whom my nephew was named, also fell that day, along with my nephew's brother Francesco. Borja was so very thorough that he even hunted down a more distant nephew of mine, Francesco Boncompagni, and killed him like a feral dog in the street. So you see," finished the pope with wet eyes, "these are the wages of nepotism: that in raising all my loved ones up, I only ensured that they would be struck down. Instead of myself."

Larry had a sudden impulse to push forward, to offer an arm to keep Urban upright; it seemed impossible that a man who sounded so hollow and wretched could remain standing on his own. But the pope who had been born Maffeo Barberini, one of a long line of forceful aristocrats, straightened. "Four escaped, besides my nephew and myself. Gessi was lucky; he was traveling and heard the news before they could catch him. Brancaccio was canny: he had packed by the time Borja was sending out his assassins and was long gone from his villa by the time they arrived. Marzio Ginnetti was returning from his legational duties in Austria, and would not have left the Alps alive were it not for the intervention of the ambassadora's countrymen, including her own father, at Chiavenna. And it is now common knowledge that were it not for the most resourceful Ruy Sanchez de Casador y Ortiz and still more up-timers, I would have been buried beneath Hadrian's Tomb as it came crashing down."

Ruy bowed, eyes half lidded. "His Holiness does not lie, but he wildly exaggerates my humble assistance that night."

Urban smiled. "Yes. Of course I do. That is why I made you my chief of security: to give substance to my groundless opinions of your ability."

"And what of those cardinals who were further removed?" Achille often sounded more like a general than a cardinal, and he certainly did so now. "How many have come? How loyal can we expect them to be?"

Antonio rubbed a finger at his eyes. "Well, any who have come as cardinals have put their titles and fortunes at stake. Many, particularly those from Italy, cannot safely return to their dioceses, and the rest must be wary. So their loyalty is assured by vested self-interest. Of course, not all of them sped to join us. Some came later."

"Measuring their options?"

"In some cases. But for others, it was a matter of difficult travel and confused news of just what transpired in Rome."

Giancarlo stroked his beard. "And in the case of some, they could not move until they were certain they were unwatched. Such was the case with my uncle, Carlo."

"As well as Ubaldi, Lante, and di Bagno," Vitelleschi added. "And even though Franciotti is still *in pectore tacite*, he had to exercise the same care. The pope's high regard for him was well known, and his status as *in pectore* was obviously suspected. Those who were at greater distance from Rome journeyed more readily. Pázmány of Hungary came quickly enough, as did almost all of the French: de la Valette, La Rochefoucauld, Le Clerc, and Richelieu's older brother, Alphonse-Louis."

Bedmar frowned. "And Mazarin and Richelieu himself?"

Larry folded his arms, inserting each hand in the opposite sleeve. "They will not be present for the colloquium, but have signaled their intent to attend the Council that follows."

Noting the raised eyebrows in Bedmar's group, Achille added, "You may have heard that political matters in France are...at a delicate point, just now. If they do not attend personally, they have arranged for radio updates and already have proxies in place." He nodded somberly. "They have made their support of the pope manifestly clear."

"Well," temporized Urban, "that may be too strong a statement. But they have certainly signaled their opinion of Borja."

Achille nodded slowly but the expression on his face was that of a concerned bulldog. "Your Holiness, I would know the names of those that were not as swift in flocking to your standard. So that I may better protect you."

Urban smiled again. "Truly, my good de Valençay, you must practice thinking like a cardinal. Before this day is out, you will be a cardinal in fact."

"May it please the Holy Father, I have been a soldier my whole life, and while I love the cross, I will yet trust the sword as the best service I may offer you."

"Very well, my son. And I will share the names of those who came or replied later, but you must bear this in mind: in only a few cases might it indicate a reluctance to commit to me. The distances were great and communication frequently difficult. Any delay is more likely to be attributable to those causes."

"I shall listen with the ear of charity that the Holy Father commands."

"Very well. So: Aldobrandini, Bichi, Sachetti, and Spada came later, as did Caetani, who narrowly escaped the destruction of St. Angelo. His tale of flight and arrival here would be worthy of an epic poem."

Antonio looked up. "To be honest, several of those who came later have little love for my uncle but detest what Borja has done and become. Cornaro and Durazzo are both sons of Venetian doges, so it is not surprising that they were in no great haste to support *any* pope. Similarly, von Harrach of Bohemia may be an old friend of some of the Spanish cardinals and the Borghese, but he has denounced Borja as a monster. The same is true of von Dietrichstein of Austria."

"It was the same with Luigi Capponi," Larry added.

"A friend of Tuscany, he's borne a grudge against the Barberinis ever since the Duchy of Urbino defaulted into papal control. But he cannot accept Borja's actions. Besides, he's friendly with Father Luke Wadding, another of the new cardinals. They share bibliophilic interests, and Wadding's support for His Holiness apparently decided him."

Bedmar was nodding, eyes narrowed. Larry had watched him through the recitation of the attending cardinals and could imagine him putting mental checkmarks next to the names on the roster of the consistory. "Evidently some of our brothers remain undecided."

Vitelleschi nodded crisply. "Ginnasi is no longer in Rome: I can hardly blame him for going back to visit, or shelter, with his family in Bologna. He's eighty-six, after all. Pio is epileptic, so travel is always difficult for him. At this point, he may consider his affliction a godsend. Monit is a Milanese, and so should be in Borja's camp, but I suspect he disapproves. I also suspect he would not survive travel beyond his borders without openly declaring for the would-be usurper in Rome."

Giancarlo almost sounded amused. "And how many of us are scheduled to make the transition from cardinals *in pectore* to actual, this day?"

"No small number," Mazzare answered. "In addition to Father Wadding, and of course you and the lords de Valençay, there were a number of new *in pectore* notifications which had to be handled carefully since they were located in areas that Borja could reach quite easily. The cases of Filomarino and Giustiniani were particularly delicate, since their bishoprics were in Naples—and having come here, they can't return. It was easier to extract Sforza from Tuscany, and Grimaldi-Cavalleroni from Perugia, but their absences have already been noticed.

"Bragadin came from his bishopric in Venetian territory—Vicenza—and so was in no immediate danger, but we had to presume that Borja might be watching him, with an intent to intercept." Larry smiled. "And of course, as Cardinal Bedmar is aware, Falconieri, the nuncio to Flanders, was notified in just the past few months."

"And that is why I officially sent him south to consult with Cardinal Borja." Bedmar smiled back. "Strange how he decided to stop over here for these many weeks."

Mazzare nodded, smiled, thought, *Yes, and so convenient having your second-in-command here ahead of you, sniffing around to ensure that it wasn't a trap.* "There are a number of others that we would have asked, had their situations not been too precarious or sensitive."

Bedmar nodded. "Most prudent. However, I have it on good authority—Lelio Falconieri, to be precise— that there are more gathered here than that. Mostly Romans, I am told." He tilted his head toward Urban, his smile congenial but his eyes alert.

Mazzare had known this moment would come. Bedmar would of course be this well-informed, and would also want to know precisely with whom he was walking this risky path. But before Larry could begin a tactfully oblique approach to the issue, Urban raised a hand in his direction.

"Lawrence, I shall speak to this. After all, it is my

affair. I will not put you in the position of making excuses for me." He drew himself straighter and looked directly into Bedmar's eyes. "Over the years, I have identified men I trust, and whose faith and character commend them to the scarlet biretta far more than those who are senior to them in the Church. Some have been *in pectore* for years; more were made so within the last nine months. However, according to the up-time documents, all eventually did become cardinals. So although I chose men I knew, I also chose men who had been the beneficiaries of such a choice in that other world. I used those documents as a constraint upon my actions, and reasoned that if they were worthy there, they should be no less worthy here."

He folded his hands. "They are not all the most learned of our brothers. They have been my aids and assistants in the Pontifical Household: prefects, secretaries, superintendents, treasurers. One was even the tutor of my nephews. But at this point, I deem it more important that they are all clerics of conscience and character."

"And that they are of proven loyalty," added Bedmar.

Mazzare was ready to take offense—suddenly realizing how protective he'd become of Urban—but paused; Bedmar's tone had not been ironic or critical. No, Mazzare realized as he forced himself to lean back yet again, Bedmar the old general was acknowledging Urban's choices as prudent, appropriate to the dangerous reality that lay ahead.

Urban smiled faintly as he echoed Bedmar. "Yes. And that they are of proven loyalty. You may have met some of them on your visits to Rome: Poli, Cesi,

Panciroli, Ceva, Giori, and my nephew Antonio's cousin, Francesco Macchiavelli." Seeing Bedmar's look, Urban waved a negation. "Please spare me the clever quips; I assure you I have heard them all. And we are nearly out of time, so I shall speak bluntly. Were I in your shoes—or old war boots—my brother, I would be concerned about sharing so crucial an enterprise as this with men I had never met. So I have arranged for you to dine with them—privately—this evening."

Although Mazzare was sure that Bedmar would have made a fearsome poker player, Urban's comment caused his eyes to widen slightly. "I am honored, Your Holiness, but have the other cardinals had the same benefit of making their acquaintance?"

Urban shrugged. "Some have. I brought these six out of Rome as soon as possible, both for their safety and so that they would have the opportunity to meet the rest of our consistory as they arrived here in Besançon. But it would be disingenuous to keep playing at a charade which presumes that your presence here is no more significant than any other cardinal's." Urban stepped closer. "Your presence is the harbinger and proof of the coming schism in the Hapsburg line, and so, the next set of battlelines that shall be drawn in Europe. Yes, we are here to do God's work, to attempt to heal the wounds that have split the family of Christ into bitterly warring camps. But that same split threatens the world itself. It must be repaired or at least bridged before sectarian and secular strifes multiply each other and become so legion that they may consume the entirety of our species." Urban's voice was tense as he finished, his eyes searching Bedmar's urgently.

The cardinal-protector of the Spanish Lowlands actually took a slight step backward. "Your Holiness, I am—am struck by the singular compassion of your concern." His voice became careful. "But you have ever been a defender of the faith, and in that role, accepted that there was no way to achieve God's will without prevailing over those who no longer recognized His authority in the form of Mother Church. Yet now, your urgency suggests that this colloquium is more than mere political expedience—"

"It is. Much more," Urban interrupted, stepping into the space that Bedmar had vacated. "I know you have seen war, Cardinal Bedmar, have been on battlefields, but tell me this: have you ever been trapped in a house of desperate men and women, with ravaged bodies falling about you like red leaves in autumn? Where the only way to escape is to kill your attackers? And the only reason the attackers are present—and the men, and women, and children are dying—is because the killers are after you? You, personally?"

Urban blinked, collected himself, stepped back. "I am not a good man, Cardinal Bedmar. Few of us are. But last year showed me my failings—and their costs to others. Others who died for me, Protestants who died so that Mother Church would not fall into the hands of a butcher who would like nothing better than to have the scarlet of his robes come from the spattered blood of those he deems heretics, whoever and wherever they might be." Urban drew up his cassock tightly, as if recoiling from that future path. "Our Father in Heaven knows that I am anything but Christlike, but at this late hour, I have finally heard His Son's words. And among them were these:

'If a man has a hundred sheep, and one of them has gone astray, does he not leave the ninety-nine on the mountains. and go in search of the one that went astray? And if he finds it, truly, I say to you, he rejoices over it more than over the ninety-nine that never went astray.'"

Urban's eyes had wandered slightly, as if, looking inward, they had become momentarily blind to the world around him. Now their focus returned with sudden force. "Are we to slay the lost sheep? Or are we to accept Christ's teaching: that it is greater to love the wayward of the flock, and to preserve them? And their children, in all their multitudes. This, *this*, is why we are gathered here in the name of ecumenicism: to stop the slaughter of the sheep. To call them back, that they might come as close as they can."

Bedmar glanced at Vitelleschi, who would not meet his eyes. "Your Holiness"—and he emphasized the title with a tone of surprised reverence—"I hear and attend your wisdom, but—can a shepherd remain a shepherd if he does not insist upon obedience?"

Urban smiled sadly. "Do you know, Bedmar, until I was forced to flee Rome and save my sinful life, I had never watched shepherds at work. Have you?"

Bedmar actually blinked. "No, Your Holiness."

"Well, I have, just a week before the assassins came for me, while we rode higher into the Dolomiti. Do you know what I learned? The sheep do not follow the shepherd out of fear of reprimands or a blow from his staff. They follow because he is their source of nourishment, of safety, and, in the case of the best shepherds, because he sits among them with love as Christ sat among the children during the Sermon on the Mount." He put a hand on Bedmar's shoulder. "After Eden, the sword has always had a place in this world. But not in our hands, Bedmar. Not any longer." Urban VIII patted the stunned cleric's shoulder. "Come now; we are keeping our brothers waiting."

Chapter 13

As Cardinal von Dietrichstein rose to his feet yet again—almost as painful a process for others to watch as for him to carry out—Larry Mazzare chided himself for the most unchristian envy he felt toward Sharon and Ruy. They had an ironclad excuse for not shar- ing in the tedium of sitting patiently in the Palais Granvelle's grand salon, listening to every cardinal in Besançon discourse at length upon their opinions of the gathering, its purpose, its inadequacies, and so forth. Sharon and Ruy were not merely exempt: they were, by definition, excluded from the gathering. Convened as a preliminary session of the Cardinal's Council that would follow the ecumenical colloquium, the doors were sealed and guarded from the outside. What transpired within was Church business and was only for the ears of the consistory.

Atypically, Urban had begun by revealing—or "pub- lishing," thanks to the recording secretary—all the various *in pectore* cardinals in attendance, thereby bringing the attending numbers of the consistory from twenty-five to forty. It was not only a prudent step (one never knew what casualties fate or assassination might wreak upon the group with each passing month or even hour), but also a profound, if subtle, boost to the gathering's morale and intrinsic sense of legitimacy. They might not be convening in Rome, but they had almost three times the number of cardinals that Borja could scrape together for a consistory of his own, should he attempt to claim the right of sitting upon the *cathedra*.

So far, Borja had not attempted to formally claim the pontificate, which was not surprising; the current situation did not provide him with a precedent for him to do so. This time, the papacy's leadership crisis had not been brought about by competing claims during an interregnum, but by a failed attempt to kill the Church's duly-selected and long-sitting pope. Only once Urban was dead, could Borja begin to move toward succession.

Once the *in pectore* cardinals had been named and confirmed, Urban had outlined, in broadest terms, the ecumenical ruminations that had been fostered by his reading of the up-time circulars and proclamations collectively known as Vatican II. He wisely avoided translating those inspirations directly into statements of Church policy, thereby giving the cardinals nothing to argue with or against; he was merely reporting the ways in which they stimulated his deeper contemplation upon God's will, and how that involved putting an end to the internecine strife that had so bloodily riven Christianity for over a century.

These opening acts and remarks had all proceeded smoothly and fairly briskly. There was no disagreement over the heinousness of Borja's actions or the dire circumstances in which they placed Mother Church.

Consequently, there was little debate over the obvious need to reconstitute the consistory's diminished ranks, and to do so with numbers that dwarfed the comparative handful of cardinals who had remained in Rome, but who had, three weeks ago, been notified of the gathering in Besançon. Of course, most of them had heard murmurs about it weeks before, but Urban had been in no rush to provide Borja's minions with any concrete information any sooner than he had to. Unsurprisingly, none of the Roman cardinals expressed a willingness to journey to Besançon—and thereby attract the homicidal ire of their overlord.

So it was that history would record that a papal council had been convened in Besançon on Tuesday, May 6, 1636, at approximately two PM, and then went immediately into a five-day recess, the first four days of which would be dedicated to the Besançon Colloquium.

About which Cardinal Dietrichstein of Austria had more than a little to say. Standing with the aid of a gnarled cane, the formidable soldier of the Counter-Reformation had made it quite clear that he had little enthusiasm for the ecumenical spirit that Urban was trying to foster. On the other hand, he had declared Borja's actions monstrous, the man an abomination, and had been gratified when Ferdinand of Austria had encouraged him—with funds from the Imperial Treasury—to travel to Besançon to make it clear that Vienna could not and would not abide pontificide. But that did not mean that Dietrichstein was any more enamored of the legitimate pontiff than he had been before the terror in Rome, nor had he warmed to the notion of religious toleration.

Dietrichstein's tone came as close to sarcasm as a cardinal might safely assay with a pontiff. "Your Holiness, as I understand it then, we shall postpone the Papal Council to chat with heretics, having no definitive aim or purpose, and that we shall then resume the Council to confirm our willingness to accept them as our beloved brothers ... along with whatever Orthodox-rite rabble and Jews have deigned to attend?"

Vitelleschi's assistant, a genial Jesuit by the name of von Spee who had served Larry in a similar role, leaned forward at a glance from his order's father general. "Your Eminence, it is difficult to differentiate the serious from the sardonic in your statements, when all your utterances are made in such a tone."

"You may take all my statements and queries as serious. And as for my tone, that is my affair. And you would do well to watch your own, Father." Dietrichstein emphasized von Spee's humble title.

Von Spee nodded patiently, even smiled slightly. No one in the room, including Dietrichstein, could honestly think that the Jesuit's tone had been anything but deferential. But since the old Austrian cardinal could not strike directly at Vitelleschi, who was clearly the one Urban had assigned to chase the staunch anti-Protestant back into the narrow doctrinal burrow he had dug from the rock of his own inflexible bigotries, he had to satisfy himself by gnawing on the Black Pope's mild-mannered courser: von Spee.

But von Spee—a choirmaster who had been given the thankless and daunting job of overseeing the selection and performance of sacred music that would suit all the gathered faiths—proved to be up to the task of mollifying the rheumy old Counter-Reformationist.

"Well then, Your Eminence, let me reassure you that, as per His Holiness' initial remarks, the reason that we are suspending the Council during the colloquium is specifically so that you may all converse with those of other faiths in a completely unofficial capacity. The label 'colloquium' was chosen with great care and intent, signaling that the gathering is for discourse and deliberation, not decisions and decrees. It is for us to convey the change in Mother Church's heart without committing Her to any specific policies, and for those of other faiths to reflect on what they have heard. That way, we may later move more easily toward mutually acceptable agreements that shall settle the religious strife that exists and create an understanding that shall prevent its recurrence."

Dietrichstein raised his chin. "When I was given the privilege to wear the scarlet biretta, that was also the last day I could, in good conscience, speak of faith in an 'unofficial' capacity. We do not have the liberty to put aside our responsibilities as the fathers of the Church, von Spee, not for one second, let alone for four days."

Von Spee spread his hands in response—so quickly that Mazzare realized that Vitelleschi must have coached him to expect this reply, and to have a ready response of his own. "Your Eminence, His Holiness has said nothing to constrain how any of us are to feel about our Reformationist guests, nor about altering our perspective or sense of duty while interacting with them. Such decisions lie within the compass of one's own conscience. The only constraint is that, for the next four days, the members of this consistory may not presume to speak with the authority of the council that has been convened, particularly since it has not yet heard and decided upon the encyclical on ecumenicism that shall come under consideration when this consistory reconvenes on the twelfth. You speak as individuals. And His Holiness encourages you to listen as individuals as well. And please note: he *encourages*, not *enjoins*, you to follow these recommendations."

Mazzare folded his arms slowly. Von Spee was good, and surprisingly iron-spined for a man with so mild a demeanor. He did a good job of keeping that spine both well-hidden and flexible, which was why Larry had recommended him to Vitelleschi.

Dietrichstein seemed on the verge of making another retort. Then he grimaced as if he'd bitten into a lemon seed and lowered himself back into his chair. Once seated, he grumbled, "I fail to see why, if we must come together with heretics to settle upon some accords, that we do not simply do so in the next four days. Why not get it all done now, rather than forcing us to make two trips to two councils?"

Von Spee was about to reply, but it was Cardinal Luke Wadding who leaned forward from where he sat beside his new and improbable friend Muzio Vitelleschi; the Irishman was as charming, poetic and Franciscan as the Roman was aloof, austere and Jesuit. "Brother Dietrichstein, would you choose to share your house with a man on the very day you first met him? Would you not wish to know him longer, engage him in conversation, get the measure of his character and temperament? And so, once he was known to you, *then* consider making him your housemate?"

Dietrichstein irritably waved the analogy aside. "We

know who these Reformationists are. They are men who left the house their Savior built and have done their best to burn it down. If they occasionally follow the will of God, or do one of us a service, well—it is said that even a broken clock tells the correct time twice a day."

Wadding leaned forward, preventing Vitelleschi from uttering the ready retort that had probably brought him quickly upright. "Your Eminence, when you meet these men tomorrow, I would ask you to observe them carefully. Watch and listen from a distance if you like, or if you must. Because at the end of the day, I will wish to ask you if, in your heart of hearts, you feel them to be any less sincere, any less eager to see the face of God, than those of us in this room. And if you cannot continue to maintain, in good conscience, that they are nothing but frauds playing at charades, then can we not also agree that we have the greatest of all possible common ground from which to work, and from which to rebuild a bond: a hunger to stand, adoring and loved, before our Savior Jesus Christ?"

Dietrichstein tried to stare down Wadding, but the Franciscan's sky-blue eyes were as unchallenging as a kitten's. The Austrian looked away. "I will watch them as I always have: carefully. As a soldier ready to fight for the sovereignty and supremacy of Our Savior's Word."

If Dietrichstein had meant to end on a tone of truculent defiance, it was either of no importance to, or missed by, Luke Wadding; he simply nodded, smiled, and leaned back.

The next query came from an unexpected source: Cardinal Cornaro, who did not bother to stand. "My brother Cardinal Dietrichstein indirectly raises a point about the colloquium that has not been adequately addressed: why only seventy representatives of other faiths? Although I have no particular desire to be up to my armpits in even more heretics and usurers"—a few chortles arose—"I fear that seventy representatives will be considered too small a selection of those who would wish to hear what His Holiness has to say. In which case, we may find ourselves back here—or, God willing, in some more suitable city—simply to revisit all that we shall discuss here."

Larry felt eyes—Urban's, Vitelleschi's, Wadding's—on him as he stood. "Although I am determined not to intrude upon your deliberations and discussions, I must answer this, since the size and structure of the colloquium was forced upon us by practical limits. Specifically, by the practical limits of the technology that was used to gather such a convocation so quickly.

"You are all certainly aware that, despite the rapid proliferation of the USE's more basic model of airship, there were only a limited number at our disposal. Similarly, the number of passengers is also small: usually less than a dozen per flight. You are also aware that, although radios are proliferating even more rapidly, there is no organized relay network outside the borders of the USE as yet, and worse yet, the content of our transmissions cannot be secret unless the same code is in use by both sides.

"Consequently, we faced two challenges: limited ability to communicate swiftly, and limited ability to arrange equally swift transport. And you will all appreciate our need for speed: not only must we consider and prepare steps against Borja's usurpation of the Holy See with all possible alacrity, but we had to remain mindful of his assassins, who went far abroad in their effort to reduce the numbers of us gathered here today.

"Necessity compelled us to cap the non-Catholic representatives to the colloquium at seventy. We arrived at that number by assessing how many sects needed representation, where their most respected theologians or authorities were located, how long it would take to contact them all, get a reply, and then fetch the farther ones here using airships.

"I must also point out that, excluding a few exceptional cases, our invitations were not to individuals but to the different communities of faith. Obviously, had His Holiness or any other Church representative selected specific members from faiths which do not have their own clear hierarchies, our process would have been open to—and would have deserved—accusations of picking those attendees we felt would be serviceable to our agenda."

Caetani of Rome looked up. "We have an agenda? Have I missed something?"

There were a few laughs; Mazzare smiled. "You have missed nothing, Your Eminence. In this case"—*and it may be a first in Church history, up-time or down-time*—"the agenda is no more and no less than has been declared openly: the building of an ecumenical bridge, hopefully in the direction of a more peaceful future."

Dietrichstein tapped the head of his cane testily. "I am surprised that any of the Reformationists are attending at all."

Caetani looked at him, frowning. "Why? Because they are so suspicious?"

"No. Because they are so quarrelsome. *They* had to decide whom to send? I am surprised they have been able to conclude those deliberations within the decade, let alone within the year."

Mazzare was grateful for the low, but pervasive, rumble of laughter in the salon. Because the joke had come from Dietrichstein, it had extra power to clear the lingering miasma of intolerance. Now, before the miasma came back—"His Holiness had a similar reservation, but evidently, the Lord chose to work in mysterious ways on this occasion. That, and there may have been an extra level of urgency added by our stipulation that, if a group was unable to agree upon representatives, there could be no promise of admission to the later, determinative meetings. Still," Mazzare finished with a sigh, "I can tell you in all candor that, taken as a whole, getting everyone here was a most difficult undertaking."

"For which we thank you, Cardinal Mazzare," said von Harrach of Hungary with just enough formality to impart official appreciation, yet not enough to seem aloof.

Larry smiled. "I wish I could take the credit, Your Eminence, but most of the planning and all of the resources were provided by the USE in general, and the State of Thuringia-Franconia in particular."

That comment brought Péter Pázmány to his feet. Another elder statesman of the Counter-Reformation—a silver-tongued Cicero compared to Dietrichstein's bulldog—the other Hungarian took his time, arranged his cassock, folded his hands and looked around the room, before fixing his eyes on Larry Mazzare. "Cardinal Mazzare, why is it that you are unwilling to speak to us? Do you feel unwelcome?"

Mazzare shook his head. "No, Cardinal Pázmány. I feel that this council has welcomed me warmly and freely. But I fear that hindsight might make it wish it had not. Unless, that is, I restrain my participation."

Pázmány frowned. "Would you mind explaining that, Your Eminence?"

Larry nodded. "I have watched—carefully—how the people of this world have treated us up-timers. I will not say we are well, or even widely loved. Our ways are different, and we portend change that many people find profoundly, and understandably, unwelcome. Yet you have made me welcome in your world." He looked around the room. "I have never presumed that this is easily achieved, particularly given the troublesome perspectives and documents I brought with me from the twentieth century. Amongst which were the collective papal constitutions and declarations known as Vatican Two, which, ultimately, gave rise to this colloquium."

Larry spread his hands. "Even in my century, Vatican Two did not merely send ripples but quakes through the bedrock of the Church. It incited resistance, rejection, and talk of rebellion, of schisms within our community. All this, even though we had been making steady progress in that direction for over three hundred and fifty years. How, then, could such a document and its concepts fail to be still more titanically dislocating, and even terrifying, in this time?" A few murmurs of assent rose into the silence as Larry took a deep breath.

"It might seem to you that I am the natural voice to defend the value of Vatican Two, or at least its revelations into the deeper mind and intents of God, but I would argue that I am the last person who should do so." He saw the puzzled looks around the room. He smiled. "If I were to speak on behalf of the products of my century, you would all acknowledge my authority... but you would also rightly think, 'but he has the least understanding of how this will impact *our* world, how it seems to *our* minds, in this very different time and place.' And so, I recuse myself from any participation other than to answer your questions, as best I may, about the documents that have shaped His Holiness' ruminations upon this meeting and the encyclical he has been crafting. Which in no way, I must point out, resemble Vatican Two in any of their specifics. As His Holiness has already said, the up-time documents have served merely as an inspiration for the ecumenical discussions we shall have, not as a roadmap."

He swept all the faces with a steady gaze. "You have allowed me to exist and now serve among you, a visitor to your world. But this is *your* world. And I would do your welcome and trust a dishonor if I now tried to transfer the beliefs and reactions of my time into yours. It would not merely be a rude usurpation; it would be folly."

Pázmány's posture had changed from one of readiness to debate, to one of careful regard. "That is most empathetically considered, Cardinal Mazzare. You have certainly foreseen how your role in this could become problematic and have, I deem, taken all the steps you may to prevent that. But I wonder if your role is the only one which merits that measure of caution and scrutiny. I speak, of course, of the power that, by your own admission, has enabled almost every aspect of this gathering: the USE."

Mazzare had a notion of where Pázmány was going but wasn't going to lead him there on the off chance he had a different discursive destination in mind. "I'm not sure what you are referring to, Your Eminence."

Pázmány picked up a thick sheaf of papers. "I have read all the proceedings from Molino last year. And in it, Father Wadding made an excellent point: that we should not take steps that make us beholden to a power outside the Church, particularly one that arguably remains hostile. Interestingly, His Holiness agreed. Purportedly, that was why he has not dwelt in the USE, and has not convened either the council or the colloquium there. He wisely foresaw that the Vicar of Christ must not shelter in, as you put it last year, someone else's house. And if he speaks from such a place, particularly *ex cathedra*, he is weakening his words before they are uttered."

Larry nodded. "Which is why we have chosen Besançon, Your Eminence. There is an absolute insistence upon religious freedom and toleration, stemming from the relationship between the very highest persons in the land."

"Yes," Pázmány allowed, "akin to the religious toleration that enabled Gustav to proffer the offer of membership in the United States of Europe to Claudia de Medici, in her role as regent for her young sons. An offer which she readily accepted, and which therefore ultimately brings us back to the same concern: that even though these proceedings are not housed in the USE, their validity becomes questionable simply because they have been financed and effectuated by a Lutheran emperor and are being held in a land where the sovereign is not a son of the Church, and his spouse has vassal-like ties to that same Lutheran Emperor. Indeed, I would argue that the up-time councils invoked during your debate in Molino, Cardinal Mazzare, show that even those almost unthinkably liberal Church fathers of your time still understood and obeyed the basic principle of speaking from a position—a physical position—of strength.

"Specifically, I refer to the convocation of Vatican Two. Why does it have that name? Because of its location. It was in the Holy See. Within a Catholic country. Protected by allies that were overwhelmingly Catholic and had proven themselves the Vatican's friends—and never its enemies." Pázmány shook his head. "Even in that up-time world, where the Church was in no immediate danger of extinction, those popes nonetheless understood that *where* one makes one's decisions sends a message as well. In short, if you are promulgating doctrine, you do it from the very seat of your power.

"It is impossible to overstate how much more pertinent that strategy is here, in a world so riddled by self-proclaimed arch-foes of the Church. The location of this council sends a clear signal that Mother Church is homeless. The fact that it has to rely upon the money and resources of a Lutheran sovereign further proves that it is reduced to beggary."

Pázmány crossed his arms. "And so one must wonder if, in this position of singular vulnerability, we can afford not to ask how, in fact, the Church's reliance upon Good Samaritans for support and shelter influences *how* it makes decisions, and therefore, *what* decisions are actually made. To carry forward one of the analogies invoked at Molino, how much freedom does one have when speaking beneath a host's roof? For instance, can a guest, but particularly a weak one, afford to assert that his host does not possess his own house, but rather, that it rightly belongs to you? Because that is the case here: the keys to the kingdom of heaven were entrusted to the Prelate of Rome and to him alone.

"Can you call your host to account for the injustices and atrocities he has heaped upon your family, or in this case Catholics, from one end of Europe to the other? And more to the point, even if you could ask these questions beneath your host's roof, should you be there to do so?"

His tone became more intimate, as if he were talking to a friend over mulled wine on a winter evening. "In our own home, we set our own schedule, are secure in our own walls and with our own provisioning. There, we are strong: strong enough to decide and do whatever we must. Outside such a place, not all of us may frankly and boldly speak and act as God's grace would guide us. And if we cannot be sure of that, then by what right do we lead his flock, that for fear of offending a host, we refrain from speaking truth as bluntly as we might? Or that we resign ourselves to a comfortable middle course when our conscience tells us we must follow a harder, holy path? Why should the Church continue to exist, if we have been lulled by good manners into playing the part of Judas, of buying our shelter here not with thirty pieces of silver, but by betraying the Truth and the Word that is Christ our Savior?

"So, in summary, I ask you, is it right—or safe—to accept the hospitality of a host knowing that your honesty will offend him?" Pázmány drew up to his full height. "I say no. Do not go to his house. And so, preserve both your honor and his." He turned his head slowly toward Larry.

And he waited.

Chapter 14

Larry suppressed a sigh as he prepared to ease into an unavoidable rebuttal, and thereby, unavoidably become the other side of a rift in the council: a rift which might widen dangerously over the ensuing days.

But before he could speak, Luke Wadding leaned forward again. "Cardinal Pázmány, I am flattered."

Pázmány's composure may have faltered an iota. "Flattered?"

"Why yes, Your Eminence, because you have clearly made a close study—a *very* close study—of the similar reservations I voiced at Molino. Although not at such length."

Speaking quickly to drown out a few low chortles, Pázmány nodded. "I did study your arguments quite closely. I wish they had been better heeded, Cardinal Wadding."

The Franciscan smiled and shook his head. "Well, that is where I am afraid we must differ. I feel they were heeded quite well. As you no doubt conjecture, I was involved in the organization of this council. Were you not interested in why I did not resist its location

192

here? I would have been happy to discuss the matter with you." Wadding's tone was as mild as a May day, but his words put Pázmány in an awkward position: either he had to invite the Irish cardinal to explain why even he was satisfied with the current arrangements, or the Hungarian had to dismiss the opinion of the very man whose arguments had informed his own.

But Pázmány did not appear rattled, merely calculating. "I would welcome your insight into this matter, Cardinal Wadding." By which, he avoided appearing dismissive or disrespectful of his peer, while also keeping his options open: either Wadding would make a convincing argument and the Cardinal's Council of Besançon would go ahead without any lasting dissent, or Wadding would stumble and make Pázmány's point for him.

But the Irish cardinal's easy, confident tone left little hope for the latter outcome. "Approximately nine months ago, I stood in a far humbler home in the Dolomiti, making the same arguments against His Holiness sheltering in the United States of Europe. And as you recount, I won that argument. But I will now share with you the first thought that popped, unbidden, into my mind upon learning that we were not to take refuge in the USE: 'then where may we find safety?' Where may the Living Church survive, alienated from ready access to its flock, treasury, stout walls, loyal armies? Yes, my argument to avoid the USE had been one with, and won by, the Grace of God, but now I was faced with the terrible consequences of moving forward from it.

"For what would occur if the prince of our church did not find a safe haven from which to right the wrongs done to the *cathedra* and to his flock? And make no mistake: among those many wrongs, it is imperative that we restore the Papal Court to Rome as swiftly as possible. A Holy See that answers to Borja is the devil's delight. His use of its administrative and monetary traffic to further his savage policies ensure that the Church will become the agency of its own downfall, even among the most ardent Catholics.

"And so, I considered where we might establish a temporary papal court. But as I reviewed the natural alternatives—nations with Catholic monarchs—my heart sank. Spain tacitly supports Borja, as do Poland and Bavaria. To seek refuge in Austria is to pit one part of the House of Hapsburg against the other. The same is true of the Spanish Lowlands."

"And France?" Dietrichstein crowed. "We live in strange days indeed that I hear myself suggest such a thing, but it *is* a Catholic nation."

Cardinal La Rochefoucauld exchanged glances with Richelieu's brother, as well as the de Valençay brothers. He cleared his throat. "At the present time, we would not deem France a prudent choice. This is our unanimous position."

The great salon was utterly soundless. The only thing more astounding than France rejecting an opportunity to become the seat of the Papacy was that all her cardinals were in agreement. On anything.

Wadding broke the silence by completing his review of the unpromising options for establishing a temporary papal court. "The Doges of Venice have already had a taste of how willing and able Borja is to carry out an assassination plot in their lands and are rightly concerned about the Spanish tercios in Rome, Naples, and Milan. The small Papal States that once dotted the Holy Roman Empire have either been eliminated, reduced, or are indefensible islands in the midst of the state whose aid gives us such pause: the USE. And as for Ireland"—he waved a hand dismissively—"to bring the pontiff to my homeland would be equivalent to delivering him to Charles in London."

Wadding folded his hands and collected his thoughts. *And is letting the anticipation build, the canny old fox,* Mazzare thought approvingly, just before the Franciscan looked around the chamber again. "So I trust that it is clear that I find no fault with Cardinal Pázmány's resolve to assume the worst of the Church's current hosts and supporters in the USE. I understand his reasons quite well, and I concur that we would be foolish to simply accept that aid and assume the best.

"But similarly, we cannot waste time arguing over absolutes in a world which, as usual, is unfolding before us in shades of gray. Let us not allow our intense desire to protect the purity of Mother Church to lead us into that classic logical fallacy where we simplify the choices before us into polarized opposites when, in fact, they are not. Let us therefore also remember that we are gathered here, freely debating the wisdom of these steps in a city where Catholics and Protestants live side by side, and that the USE has provided us with the means and security to do so without any expectations or tacit agreements.

"And so, just as it is unwise to assume the best of these apparent benefactors, it would be equally unreasonable, and churlish, to assume the worst. Indeed, our faith tells us that good acts possess the power of redemption. Perhaps, then, the help we have received here in Besançon should tell us that the first concrete steps toward ecumenicism have already been taken—but not by us, for we lacked the resources to take them. Consequently, when we gather to give the imprimatur of Sacred Magisterium to a canonical embrace of broader toleration of our estranged brethren in Christ, we should perhaps be mindful of this: that what we put forth as ideas, as doctrine, follows after what *Protestant* Good Samaritans have already made manifest through *deeds*: this very council."

Wadding nodded to the council, smiled, and sat. As did Pázmány.

Von Spee leaned forward. "Are there are other matters or concerns to be addressed before we recess the Council for four days?"

La Rochefoucauld steepled his long fingers. "Just one."

Von Spee nodded his recognition of the French cardinal's desire to speak; the room settled in their seats. La Rochefoucauld was less political than most, just as he was more philosophical. When he proposed to speak, it was invariably on a matter of substance.

The Frenchman folded his fingers together. "Since my arrival, I have read the *ex cathedra* decree concerning those persons we now call up-timers." He nodded toward Larry, who nodded back. "While the determination and reasoning was in agreement with my own—that they are not the tools of Satan—I remain concerned that, to many minds of our time, your finding sounds far more absurd than what you rejected."

Von Spee smiled. "You mean that not only did Grantville's residents truly arrive here from the future, but that, by traveling back in time, they have now undone the events that produced the world they knew?"

"Yes, and so, have undone their own history." Le Rochefoucauld rolled his eyes. "What could be more simple?" He indulged in a small grin before his brow restraightened and serious lines marked his face. "Happily, we are well versed in the convolutions of theology and cosmology. And again, happily, once we have put Borja aside, our flock will hear our determination and place their trust in us, as their catechisms and traditions teach them.

"But what of the guests with whom we shall begin our conversations tomorrow? Have the Reformationists been apprised of the Church's position on these travelers in time?"

Von Spee glanced at Urban, who shook his head and replied. "No, my friend. For various reasons, we elected to withhold any pronouncement on the matter. Suffice it to say that such a decree should not be followed by silence. However, it was imperative that, after our deliverance from Italy, that we remain unseen and unheard until we could convene a council here. And we feared that Borja would take an aggressively, even violently, oppositional stance, which could have caused all manner of new suffering in Rome and the other places within reach of his army or decrees. Many Italian communities have adopted the machines, the entertainments, even the styles, brought by the up-timers. They could all have become targets of persecution, or worse still, targets for his growing body of inquisitors."

La Rochefoucauld inclined his head. "I suspected as much, Your Holiness. But I also suspected that many of our Reformationist . . . er, colleagues . . . would be equally unaware of the Church's positions on

Grantville and its people. So I wonder: will we have to begin by reprising our position, and the reasoning whereby we came to it?"

Vitelleschi's eyes reminded Larry of those of a hawk: sharp, focused, devoid of sentiment when in pursuit. "The Protestants were generally less likely to see it as a sign of demonic mischief than our clergy, Your Eminence. However, you seem to fear that this could arise as a serious impediment in our ecumenical conversation with them. Why?"

Le Rochefoucauld shrugged. "Because the origins of that conversation are to be found in Vatican Two: a document which has miraculously arrived here across vast gulfs of time. And because its primary advocate in Molino was the one who came back in time with it." Le Rochefoucauld's eyes shifted to Larry. "My apologies, Cardinal Mazzare. These concerns are in no way my own. But if they arise tomorrow, we would be well served by having considered them, and our responses, in advance."

"Most prudent," Larry answered, "and no need to apologize, Your Eminence. What you speak is simple truth."

Le Rochefoucauld gave a playful pout. "Well, not so simple perhaps, this traveling across time. But in all seriousness, even if they are willing to accept our position on the matter, I wonder if they shall prove willing to be equally tolerant of disagreement within their own ranks."

Pázmány stroked his beard thoughtfully. "I am not sure I understand your concern."

Le Rochefoucauld raised a didactic finger. "Let us for a moment presume that there may be those among them who will grasp at any argumentative straw which would save them from what might be worse than death, or even damnation: coming to any point of agreement with us. A sentiment which no small number of us might share, albeit in reverse."

The laughter in the salon was a low, genial rumble.

"What then if some arch-anti-Catholics catch upon this as the foundation of their contention to reject engaging us in discourse: that our ecumenical inspiration and initiative is akin to the apple Eve offered Adam? That it is, in fact, a poison fruit of the future, conveyed to us by the satanic spawn of Grantville?"

"They would be arguing athwart their own contention that the age of miracles is over," Vitelleschi pronounced.

"So they would. And that is my greatest misgiving. Can we not imagine the theological brawl that would ensue among them? The rationalists will try to point to exactly that inconsistency. That, in turn, will compel the more provincial minds among them to insist that even the most enlightened sects still acknowledge the reality of witchcraft. And so their representatives may all devolve into a veritable froth of many-sided debates concerning whether the supernatural power of Satan may manifest in this world if indeed the age of miracles is past. They may even work in a few trenchant inquiries into the number of angels that may dance on the head of a pin. But, whatever the particulars of their theological imbroglio, we will be unable to converse with them once they have retreated to their respective corners, staring doctrinal daggers at each other." Le Rochefoucauld rested his head in his hand. "It wearies me just to think of it."

Mazzare thought, and not for the first time, that had the Frenchman not been called to a life in the Church, he might have had some modest success upon the stage.

Bedmar stared around the grand salon, genuinely surprised. "Do any sane men still harbor such ridiculous convictions regarding Grantville? Either Catholic or Protestant?" The cardinal's nature as both a pragmatist and a materialist was not just in his words, but in his incredulous and almost contemptuous tone. Mazzare still wondered if his faith went much deeper than the inner lining of his vestments. If that far.

Von Spee provided the answer almost sheepishly. "We know quite a number of our own priests who still do hold the belief that Grantville is an infernal intrusion unto our world, Your Eminence. And if that opinion is held by some of the sons of Mother Church, we must conjecture that it will be present to some degree in all the sects with whom we will converse tomorrow. However, I suspect we may be able to curtail any significant disturbance over this question."

Urban leaned out to look at von Spee. "Please share it."

Von Spee shrugged. "Well, Your Holiness, as Cardinal La Rochefoucauld points out, it would be consistent with Reformationist doctrine to assert that the age of miracles is over, and that such a flagrant violation of that principle would be contrary to their teachings."

Vitelleschi stared down at his assistant. "Yes. And so?"

"And so, we introduce the topic by simply remarking that our determination on the matter of Grantville matches with what we presume to be their own: that to characterize such a phenomenon to be an act of either

God or Satan is also inconsistent with Mother Church's position regarding the post-Apostolic diminishment of miracles. We may not wholly deny the possibility of smaller, individual miracles such as stigmata, but, in the matter of Grantville, given the size and global impact of its appearance, we may honestly point to how our deliberations followed the same theological paths articulated by their own doctrine."

Vitelleschi looked at Bedmar. Who looked at Mazzare. Who looked at La Rochefoucauld. Who looked at Urban.

Who leaned back with a smile. "I think we may safely call that matter resolved, and this council in recess until after the colloquium. Thanks to you, Father von Spee." Whose eyes were now as round as saucers.

Mazzare suppressed a smile as he rose with the rest to honor the departure of the pope. *Well, von Spee, you just came to Urban's attention by solving a problem for him. Congratulations and commiserations; you're in the big leagues, now.*

Chapter 15

Larry stopped along the side of the dusk-dim street and held up a hand to pause Urban.

The pope tried peering over his shoulder. "What is . . . ?"

"Silence, please, Your Holiness."

Up ahead, the three sedan chairs entered the gate of the cloister slightly north of St. John's cathedral. As soon as the third had entered, a tall figure at the gate—Turlough Eubank of the Wild Geese—waved them forward. Those following on foot forced themselves to stroll toward the same entrance.

In front of Larry, Anthony Grogan, one of the older members of the Wild Geese, set the pace, his posture relaxed. But he always kept his cloak spread wide with his elbows, thereby ensuring swift access to both his sword and pepperbox revolver.

On either side of the pope, two tall, heavily cloaked cardinals walked with heads bowed—mostly to reduce profiling just how tall they really were. But that was difficult for the fully armored Achille d'Estampes de Valençay and Giancarlo Medici. Then came Cardinals

Mattei and Sforza, who were younger and still fit enough to run quickly if required. Two more Wild Geese and Léonore d'Estampes de Valençay brought up the rear.

Larry could sense the anxiety building in all of them as they neared the gates. Even the cardinals understood that if there was going to be another assassination attempt during the short walk from the Palais Granvelle to the cloister, the odds that it would commence at any particular second were growing...simply because there weren't that many more seconds left.

A window shutter creaked on the second floor of a nearby house—

Giancarlo swiftly hustled the pope behind Achille. The disguised papal escort started drawing their weapons—

A pair of hands emerged from the window in question, upending a bucket of washwater.

As it splashed down onto the cobbles of the street, a few muttered curses combined relief with sharp annoyance as everyone resumed the correct, apparently casual formation.

Twelve more paces—Larry was counting—brought them through the gate and into the grassy courtyard that fronted the cloister's garden. He realized that his armpits were very wet and that he could smell his own sweat, not something he had experienced since his twenties, even when exerting himself. But this was the sharp, sour stink of fear. And it wasn't just coming off him. Unless he was much mistaken, most of his companions were exuding a similar odor, especially Urban himself.

Granted, the vestments were hot, and the cloaks long enough to completely obscure both the person and equipment that were beneath it. The earlier midday showers had left behind a haze of mild humidity. In addition, the cardinals had all just come from the close seating in the unventilated grand salon, so it was probable that their sweat had been accruing for the last several hours. But the tension of walking exposed, surrounded by two- and even three-story buildings had activated the accumulated scents in a pungent mix.

Sforza and Mattei were called over to the group that had gathered on the diagonal path bisecting the garden. Matching "Tone" Grogan's brisk pace, the rest turned to walk beneath the covered walkway. As they did, they passed Ruy Sanchez and Owen Roe O'Neill, the two of whom were pressing an urgent point upon Dorfmann, one of the junior radio operators for the Hibernians.

"We realize," Ruy was muttering, "that it is difficult to maintain all the general overwatch posts while drawing enough for a covering force, but there was no other choice this evening."

Dorfmann started to make some reply, but O'Neill cut him off, annoyed, and pointing a long finger at the mercenary's chest. "And I don't give a tinker's damn what Lieutenant Hastings advised, but using the tunnel from the Palais Granvelle to the Carmelite Monastery is out of the question. Use of that is being reserved for a crisis situation, one where we can't safely evacuate the pope—"

Which was the last Mazzare heard of the Irish colonel's annoyed explanation; the sound of boots on wet flagstones drowned out his voice and whatever reply Dorfmann attempted next.

Urban leaned over toward Larry. "What was that all about?"

Larry shrugged. "Difference of opinion about the route we took back. Seems like the CO—uh, commander—of the Hibernians wanted us to take the secret tunnel from the palace to the monastery."

"Was the danger so great?"

"No. Sounds more like he's worried about adding irregular route security to his unit's responsibility, that it's stretching his men too thin. But Ruy and Owen are right: we've got to save the tunnel for emergencies. If other assassins are watching, and not enough of us come out the regular entrances of the Palais Granvelle, they're going to put two and two together and figure we have another way out."

As they reached the end of that arm of the cloister and the collonade angled off to the left, Giancarlo and Achille both murmured their respects and followed the walkway. The remaining Wild Geese closed around Larry and Urban as, ahead, two more of the Irish soldiers opened the door into the monastery itself.

As they passed within and handed their cloaks to a mix of monks and junior clerics, Urban asked, "And still nothing about the five assassins killed this morning?"

"Nothing, Your Holiness."

"Is that not...unusual?"

"Somewhat." Larry Mazzare wondered if downplaying the moribund state of the investigation qualified as wishful thinking or a minor lie. Well, if on reflection it turned out to be the latter, there was always the confessional.

Grogan led the two of them into a room where large wine casks lined the walls. He approached one on the far wall, grabbed the spigot on either side, and turned the whole assembly counter clockwise. A muted thump punctuated the end of his effort. He swung open the cask's false front and waved them both into the musty wooden tunnel that was revealed, murmuring his respects as they passed.

They emerged into a subterranean passage, where three more Wild Geese were waiting to escort them: two fell in behind them, one to the front, but all at a respectful distance.

Urban leaned in toward Larry. "Tell me: how do you think the presentation to the Council went?"

"Quite well," Larry replied. Hmm . . . was that more optimism or more prevarication? At this rate, he was going to spend a long time in that confessional . . .

Urban smiled as the long thin tunnel pushed their shoulders together. "You are too politic—and too fretful, Lawrence. I think it was a great success, and I should know: I have seen some very lively ones in my day. The inevitable niggling over details and procedures was brief, the serious obstacles to advancing a genuine ecumenical agenda small, and, for the first time I was able to plausibly report that the Holy See has no hidden agenda." He smiled. "You know, I almost believed it myself."

Larry grinned. "So did I. Do you think *they* did?"

"Lawrence, despite your cleverness, you retain a peculiarly naive optimism. No, no, do not pout: I mean no insult. I just find it refreshing—maybe reassuring—that you can remain so comparatively innocent, given how full of power and portents of doom your own world was. Indeed, you are living proof that the Church can persevere without holding the reins of that power. She did not contaminate you with the stain of bloody wars and deceitful statecraft. Would I could say the same for our Church here.

"But because the agenda will not be a surprise to them, they will not be angered, Lawrence. They will balk and quibble a bit when I reveal the specific resolutions that I shall make canonical, but they have all seen the general outlines of my thought. Had most of them found any of it intolerable, we would have encountered a groundswell of that resistance today."

"You anticipate no resistance at all?"

Urban shrugged as they ducked under a low Roman archway and entered a more finished tunnel; they were now in the stretch that led from the cloister to the secret chambers that had been built under St. John's. "Oh, there must always be some resistance, even though the resolutions I put forward will be few in number and reassuringly simple in their wording."

"Could their resistance become sharp enough to push any of them into Borja's camp?"

Urban frowned. "The great majority of them: no. They are either loyal to me, petrified of him, or both. Any others will follow the lead of the strongest who resists."

"Dietrichstein?"

Urban smiled and shook his head. "The one to watch is Pázmány. He is more respected, and has been a true son of the Church." The lead guard stood aside as they entered a small room furnished with what looked like a small portcullis. Addressing them by their titles, he gestured to several chairs. "Do you know," Urban continued as soon as he was seated, "that less than half a year after you arrived, Pázmány marched to Rome with a military procession in an attempt to convince me to initiate a crusade against the Ottomans?"

The guard pulled a handle next to the portcullis. Far away, through the thick timbers of the door, a dull bell rung.

Mazzare frowned and leaned against the backrest. "Great. So Pázmány wanted to start another war. As if there weren't enough of them going on in the world, just then."

Urban shook his head and his finger. "Now, now, Lawrence. Understand what lies behind that action: he has long been concerned with conditions in what you call Transylvania. Ottoman attacks have been a blight there for centuries. And, more to the point, he saw the signs of another of their campaigns mounting even then. You might call him a student of the ebbs and flows that mark the change in Turkish political and military tides, and he saw a wave rising beyond the Balkans. And, so far as we may see now, he was correct."

"Then what made you turn him away?"

"The papacy is hardly in any condition to lead a crusade to Constantinople. Until your arrival essentially ended the major religious wars in Germany, each half of Christendom was thoroughly obsessed with exterminating the other half. And besides, even if we had been unified, with fresh armies, history has proven that our numbers are insufficient for a durable victory. We may win early battles, take key objectives, but if we cannot occupy Ottoman lands and undo what their conquest has done, we effect no lasting change." He frowned. "And now—is such a change truly worth the tides of blood that would have to be shed beneath banners of both the cross and the crescent?" Urban shook his head; he seemed to be shaking off foul memories and bad dreams. "No: there must be another way. And we start it here, by unifying. Once Christendom stands together, genuinely and vigorously, the Turk will not ever make it out of the Balkans. And I can hope, eventually, that he will no longer wish to."

"A further agenda?"

Urban smiled as the portcullis began cranking and creaking open. "You know me too well. Yes, but peace with Islam remains the furthest objective of that agenda. Indeed, you had not yet accomplished it in your time, if I recall correctly."

Mazzare nodded sadly. "No, although we had thought so, for a time. Secularization of Islam arrived late, very unevenly, and finally began to weaken. What happened after we departed in the year 2000—who can tell?"

Urban shrugged. "And so I know I will not see such a *modus vivendi* achieved in my lifetime. Perhaps not in the lifetime of any babe yet born, but one day. One day. However, significant progress might be made on other objectives: an end to the persecution of the Jews, for instance." The portcullis was locked open with a sharp clack. The lead guard moved through, then asked them to follow.

Mazzare frowned. "It is hard to envision the current population of any European nation according equal status to the Jewish community."

Urban wagged a finger. "I did not say that, Lawrence. I simply wish to ensure that they may expect to live safely, and with tolerance—even if grudging—for their right to practice their rites without fear of violence. I am far too much a realist to believe that any one colloquium could cause a full reversal of more than a dozen centuries of arch prejudice. Simply influencing the religious leadership in Europe to take a consistent stand against their persecution would be a major victory. And it will take time for that opinion to wear down the ingrained prejudices of the monarchs whose ears they have.

"I suspect that further, more distant faiths, will actually be easier to reconcile with than Islam. But frankly, I do not spend much time considering the likelihood, or methods, of achieving such ends. One must begin with a small set of more readily attainable goals. Then, we shall expand from what we have learned, and achieved, in that process."

Mazzare did his best not to sound incredulous. "That is certainly quite an ambitious agenda, Your Holiness. Several lifetimes' worth, I suspect."

"I freely allow that, Lawrence. And my hopes for this colloquium are modest. I will be happy—elated, even—if, by the end, the Protestants and Orthodox merely believe that we are genuinely changing our position regarding other faiths. They will naturally be uncertain as long as the change remains a broad concept rather than a specific policy, and will still have reservations until we take action that is suited to those words."

As the corridor widened and doors became visible ahead, Mazzare raised an eyebrow. "I suspect that will be easier for them to believe than the further consequence of the Church turning its back upon the influence and tithes it enjoyed when it was the sole seat of global Christianity."

Urban squinted: far ahead the hallway was lit by lanterns, not torches in cressets. Urban headed toward those lights. "Before you arrived, we in Rome ardently believed two things: that we could still regather the entirety of Christianity to the Papal Rood, and that if we failed to do so, Mother Church would perish. But your history showed me that those absolute outcomes were both folly. No amount of killing or leverage will cause the Reformationists to renounce their beliefs. And we only make ourselves more hateful by continuing on such a course. So it is not merely idealism that moves me to this decision; it is pragmatism." The guard stopped in front of the pope's door and opened it with an ancient, rusty key.

Larry smiled. "I think you just might get the cooperation you want with that sales pitch, Your Holiness. And you just might become the most famous pope who ever lived. Even though you won't live to see all you set in motion."

Urban's quick sideways smile was histrionic. "Well, I may be remembered as the most infamous, at least. But I have reconciled myself to initiating changes and legacies that shall not only outlive me, but be only tangentially, if at all, associated with my name." He smiled. "That prideful concern, of being a figure whose fame lives on in posterity, was one of the sins of Maffeo Barberini." Urban's smile became impish as he glanced into his chambers. "I am Urban VIII now. And accordingly, I have new sins, new vices. Such as one last glass of wine, this night. Would you care to join me, Lawrence?"

Larry thought about the softness of his pillows, then about the unsolved problems of the day, and so, settled on a compromise between the contending possibilities of weariness or trouble-fueled insomnia.

A single glass of wine might be a good idea, after all.

•

Ruy Sanchez de Casador y Ortiz waited until the men who had escorted Urban from the palace to the cloister dispersed to their various quarters, and the first night watch had replaced the troops standing the last shift of the day. That job was actually his lieutenants', but he had learned a long time ago that the most ready and attentive troops are those who know their commander will occasionally watch them perform even their most mundane duties. Such as this one.

Satisfied that the guards and their officers were at their posts and adequately attentive, Ruy began walking toward the monastery—and saw, coming his way, the faint outline of a woman. A most dramatically proportioned woman. "Even in this light, I know when you approach, my love."

Sharon sounded amused. "Oh? And how do you manage that? I can barely see you."

"It is the light around you, the glow given off by your halo."

Sharon was close enough now that he could make out her face; he saw her slanted smile as she emitted a single burble of laughter. "My halo? Yeah, sure: I'll bet."

As they approached each other, he returned her smile. "I suppose other features are also visible at a distance."

She stopped a yard away from him. "Yeah?" Her voice was playful. "Like what?"

Ruy sadly eyed the distance between them. It was what they had agreed to because it was deemed the minimal acceptable restraint while they were within the walls of the monastery. "The magnitude of your many virtues and charms."

She resumed walking, but moved to his side. "Let's walk," she suggested. "And keep your hands off my 'charms.'"

Ruy smiled as he fell in beside her. "It is not in keeping with either Christian charity or compassion to torture a man so."

"Well, that is a shame." Her smile said that she didn't really think it was. At all.

His steps veered slightly closer to her.

"Hey! Watch it, Ruy! You heard what I said."

"Yes. Your charms are forbidden fruit. But I am also most worshipful of your virtue—"

"Ruy! You're supposed to be an officer. And a gentleman."

"I am both. I am a very tired officer. And a very desperate gentleman."

"Well, I'd think that being tired would make you feel a little less desperate."

"Alas, my beauteous wife, you perceive in reverse; it is enduring my desperation that makes me so tired."

Sharon rolled her eyes. "You are impossible."

"Yes. But you love me. Which is why you possess that halo."

She seemed to forget herself, started to reach out to touch him, then snatched her hand back. "You sly, silver-tongued fox."

"I am guilty of all your worst accusations, my heart. But in my defense, I must assert that it is your beauty that has driven me to these many sins. If only you could absolve them with a kiss—"

She stepped a little farther away . . . but not very much farther. "Ruy. Seriously." Her voice became genuinely regretful. "If we keep this up—look; why don't we switch topics?"

"I am yours to command," he said morosely. And he didn't have to act much to produce that tone.

Which was the key to his next gambit: to play upon her sympathy.

She didn't take the bait. "You're mine to command? Well, that's a nice change. So, I command you to tell me if you've managed to convince Urban not to celebrate Pentecost in St. John's."

Ruy did not like reexperiencing, or reporting, failure, but now he was compelled to do both. "Alas, I have not changed His Holiness' mind. His new demeanor may be more mild, but his will remains a thing of steel."

"Yeah, well, if his body were made of it, I'd be a lot less worried."

"You and me both, my heart. But he is adamant. Instead of being more cautious, he seems to be emboldened by the increasing number of physicians eager to flutter around him. As if you and Dr. Connal were not enough."

"Who now?"

"Father Leo Allatius. A Greek, born on Chios, I believe. A physician and translator, it seems."

"Translator?"

"Yes. Naturally, his Greek is excellent and his Russian and Turkish quite good. And he seems quite familiar with the Eastern rite. He's become something of a liaison to that contingent, unless I am much mistaken."

Sharon seemed lost in thought for a moment. "You know, I think I know a way to get him off your back. Although I'm the primary physician for Urban, and Sean Connal is my assistant and first physician for the Council of Cardinals, we should have a Physician in Residence for the other guests of the colloquium. And being a translator, Allatius is an excellent choice: he will understand their complaints directly."

"Shall I ask Father von Spee's permission to so task him?" Von Spee had also become something like a chief of staff for Urban.

"Yes, do, with my strong recommendation." She stopped. They had reached the corner of the cloister. The door in front of them would lead Ruy to the tunnel complex that Bernhard had expanded. The walkway that bent to the left would ultimately bring Sharon to her room at the far end of the monastery. "Time to say good night."

Ruy sighed. He raised a hand. "I am your obedient servant. I am bound for the cell next to what His Holiness calls his Hermit's Cave." Which was quite a misnomer: it was a large, comfortable room that the pope shared with two dedicated guards from the Wild Geese, much to Urban's annoyance. "I shall see you tomorrow, as desperate and fatigued as ever, I fear."

"Well," Sharon said, "we can't have that." Before Ruy could react—which was saying quite a lot—Sharon leaned in, gave him a quick, light kiss on the lips, and then turned and walked briskly away, her figure silhouetted against the dim, early moonlight.

Ruy watched her go, smiled, put his index finger to his lips, sighed, and reflected that now the cell next to the Hermit's Cave wouldn't seem quite so cold or lonely. The long walk there would be more tolerable.

Nevertheless, he watched her distinctive silhouette until she disappeared into the darkened archway that fronted the monastery.

Part Three

Wednesday
May 7, 1636

Of what, like skulls, comes rotting back to ground

Part Three

Chapter 16

Sharon Nichols stifled a yawn that brought tears to her eyes, through which she squinted ahead into the darkness of the Besançon's back streets.

"I'm sorry to have awakened you, Ambassador, but we really must hurry." Finan, her assistant and mobile radioman, sounded both genuinely sorry and genuinely agitated. That was unusual in itself; diminutive Finan was usually as imperturbably good-natured as he was efficient. Taken together, those traits were probably why he'd been chosen for his third, unofficial job: Sharon's bodyguard. Because like Mary's little lamb, everywhere that she went, he was sure to follow. Indeed, Finan had never done anything but simply trail after her until this morning. He had come banging on her door, softly at first, but finally so loudly that even Sharon Nichols, who took a perverse pride in how deeply she slept, could no longer ignore it.

She glanced up at the roofs that constituted the Palais Grenville's rear compound; there might be a faint lightening of the sky, of false dawn, there, but she could not be sure. "Why are we staying off the high street?" she asked.

Finan raised his left index finger so that it lay across his lips. "Quiet, please, Ambassador. We're stayin' off the high street for the same reason we must remain silent: so that no one will see us."

They drew abreast of the palace to their right, and the Carmelite monastery to their left. "Won't you at least explain *why* Ruy needs me?" When Sharon had first stumbled out of bed, she had been half convinced that Ruy had coerced Finan into playing the part of Cupid, to escort her along to some surreal tryst with her husband. She became fully convinced when, predictably, Finan had woven his apologies into his explanation that she must get dressed and join Ruy. His insistence that she bring her medical kit had been a clever touch: made it sound like a genuine emergency. She had resolved to conk her sex-obsessed husband with her physician's bag the moment she saw him. If she didn't, she admitted it was all too likely that she would succumb to his wildly inappropriate and yet wildly flattering wooing.

But now, as Finan slowed, checking left and right before they emerged into the far more open high street, she became increasingly tense. She had initially expected to be led into some forgotten corner of the cloister. Then, after they exited the monastery's gate, she suspected that they would turn into some small house, where Ruy would be waiting for her. But as they had continued courting the shadows of the smaller street that paralleled the main road, she began to have her doubts that this was, in fact, all part of some libidinous scheme. They were going too far, too stealthily, and Finan's rifle—a Soviet SKS that was special issue among the Hibernians—remained in his hands the whole time.

Instead of answering her question about the cause of Ruy's summons—had he even heard it?—he gestured for her to follow him closely. Slightly bent at the waist, he trotted across the high street, making for the slightly darker shadows cast by and hiding the facades of the buildings on the opposite side. Those shadows told Sharon that false dawn was edging over the eastern horizon, but just barely. Which made it just a little after four AM.

As they hastened on within the margin of those shadows, Sharon felt a slight sweat moistening her back, but not from exertion: it was from a sudden pulse of fear that ran up her spine. Clearly, Ruy's summons was not salacious but deadly serious—so serious that he was willing to wake her before four AM to travel in the company of her suddenly grave, almost grim, assistant, whose presence belied the notion that he was anything other than her bodyguard.

Somewhere far to the north, probably in one of the small greens that ran up to the walls just north of St. Paul's, an overzealous cock crowed his impatience at the laggard sun. Behind them, from the cluster of small houses gathered skirtlike about St. Maurice's, was a distant, sharp splash: probably a chamberpot being emptied into the dark streets in violation of the ill-enforced municipal order against doing so.

Finan led them west along the northern side of the high street, straightening only when they could clearly make out the facade of St. Peter's. A single dark figure loitered there, affecting a casual stance. Very poorly. With a sharp gesture, Finan indicated that Sharon should stay right at his heels as, once again, he broke into a trot. Slightly faster this time, and without hunching.

Finan exchanged a wave with the figure, which soon

resolved into the form of one of the younger Wild Geese, Danny O'Dee, who waved them farther west, toward a cluster of ruder, more tightly packed one- and two-story houses and shops. Finan plunged into one of the narrow streets leading into darker shadows. Sharon, simultaneously fearful and curious, followed.

Finan slowed to a quick walk; looking back at her when, after about one hundred feet into the tangle of tilting, aged buildings, he turned sharply into an alley, just beyond a public house with a high foundation. Its short flight of steps was almost hidden by a mass of mangy cats that eyed her indifferently as she passed. Sharon slipped into the alley mouth that had swallowed Finan—and came to a sudden, involuntary stop.

Ruy was there, as was Owen Roe O'Neill and one of the older Wild Geese—"Tone" Grogan, she thought his name was. They were gathered around a man—no, a corpse—sitting with its back up against the wall of the tavern. Even at this range, she could see that the front of his tunic was rent by a huge, lopsided "X."

"Ambassador," Finan's voice said a few inches from her ear. Startled, she flinched a step in the other direction and discovered where the young Hibernian had almost disappeared into the shadows at the mouth of the alley. "It's safer if you join the others."

Sharon nodded and walked quickly over to Ruy, even as her eyes went back to the body—

Male. Middle-aged. Overweight but not obese. A primarily sedentary occupation, she projected: even in the almost nonexistent light, she could see that his hands were not calloused or dirty. His clothes were not suited for heavy work, either, and while they were worn, they were not of particularly cheap manufacture.

Her mind spun through images, looking for an up-time parallel: they reminded Sharon of her old sweatshirts. Clothing past its prime, but still useful to run around in, particularly if you were about to do something that could make you a little dirty or sweaty.

"Sharon?" It was Ruy's voice.

She looked up. "Yes?" His eyes were sad, his expression almost—what? Sheepish? *Who, Ruy!?*

"My love, I am sorry for having disturbed your sleep, but—"

She shook her head. "No, I understand." She allowed herself a small smile. "I thought you were just trying to"—she suddenly remembered the other men standing close by—"were up to your usual tricks."

Ruy stepped closer, kept his voice very low. "As you can see, my summons was a matter of seriousness, not satyriasis." When she smiled at that, he frowned. "My wife, are you quite well?"

Sharon blinked. "Huh? Yeah. Why?"

Ruy glanced at the body. "Does this not—upset you?"

"A corpse? Why? Should it? I saw enough at Molino, didn't I?"

Ruy's eyes widened slightly. "My peerless love, I— well, I allow I did not expect you to stiffen with fear. You are a doctor—a surgeon—after all. But to smile while within mere feet of—"

"—of an inanimate object, Ruy. Don't mistake me: I wish I could undo what was done to this man. But I know why you brought me here: you want me to examine the body. Professionally."

"Well, yes. But—"

She put a hand on his cheek. "Ruy, part of being a physician, man or woman, is the ability to put your emotions and your reflexes aside so you can do your job. If I hadn't been able to do that, I wouldn't have been able to operate on you in Rome. And I assure you, I am not indifferent to this person's fate. It's just that I can't do anything to help him anymore." She frowned, glancing back at the crisscross lacerations that marked the front of the corpse's torso. "Although I've got to be honest: I'm not sure I would have been able to do anything to help him even if I'd been there with a surgical team right after he was attacked."

Ruy nodded, stepped aside and glanced at the body, inviting her to look closer, almost.

Sharon did so. "Knife, I'd say."

Owen Roe's voice was low. "Our thought, too, Ambassador."

She looked up at him; his face was a dark smudge against the shadows. "Just when are you going to call me 'Sharon,' Owen?"

Owen glanced quickly at Ruy, who smiled, shrugged, looked away. "Well, ma'am, er, Doctor...er. Well, Judas be choked, I'm not accustomed to calling ladies of such accomplishments by their first names, like they were my sister."

"Owen Roe O'Neill, I assure you, beyond the slightest shred of doubt, that no one is going to take us for siblings."

Although she couldn't see his pale skin, blue eyes, or red beard, his teeth flashed in a fast smile. "True enough...Sharon. Although I hardly deserve the privilege of such familiarity: I'm the one who disturbed your sleep, brought you out here."

"You?"

Before Owen could answer, Ruy cut in. "The colonel

is being more gallant than accurate, my heart. He had me summoned; I summoned you."

"That's as may be," Owen emended doggedly, "but you know damned well, Ruy Sanchez, that the better part of my reason of calling for you was because of your wife. She is, after all, your better half." A brief pause. "Well, the better three-quarters. As you've told us. Over and over again."

Sharon frowned, baffled. "Ruy, just what are you telling other people about me?"

Ruy's answering grin was lopsided. "Dearest, I must confess that I have a terrible habit."

"Just one?" Sharon asked mildly.

The Irish guard behind Owen stifled a guffaw; Finan may have snickered.

Ruy's smile widened. "Allow me to rephrase: among my *many* bad habits, one in particular led to your summons. You see, I brag. Uncontrollably. About you."

Well, as flaws went, Sharon allowed, that wasn't a particularly bad one. Unless . . . "Wait a minute: brag *how*?"

"My love, I am the most ardent and vocal admirer of your many skills and uncommon interests. Including your enormous appetite for books, and vast library. Particularly those novels that are called . . . eh . . ."

She smiled. "Police procedurals," she finished for him.

"Yes. Exactly. Those. So between that interest and your peerless skills as a physician . . ."

She smiled. "Yeah, yeah. So now I'm the M.E., huh?"

"Emm Eee?" Ruy repeated uncertainly.

Owen sounded even more flummoxed. "Er, well . . . of course, you're you. Who else would you be, then?"

Sharon hoped that her giggle wouldn't be seen as further evidence that she was in fact ghoulishly dispassionate, given that they were all standing three feet away from a recently murdered man. "I'm not spelling out 'me,' Owen. M.E. is a title." He, like most other down-timers, did not readily "hear" acronyms as such, largely because they were not a part of down-time speech. They reflexively heard them as words, being spelled out. "It's an abbreviation for 'Medical Examiner.' A doctor who, among other things, analyzes bodies to determine the cause and time of death."

"Oh, that," Owen nodded. "Aye. As your braggart husband is fond of explaining."

Sharon made sure her face was composed as she turned back to the body. "Why did you want me to inspect this corpse, Owen?"

"Well, Ambass—er, Sharon—I've seen my fair share of dead bodies, and this one was odd."

She moved her head closer, tried to get a better look at the cuts, the corpse's staring eyes and clothes. "Odd in what way?"

"You'll forgive the blunt speech to a lady—"

"I won't forgive your speech if it *isn't* blunt, Colonel. Anything that keeps the facts vague or imprecise is likely to help the murderer. And we don't want that, do we?"

"No, ma'a—um, *Sharon*. Well, there's not as much blood as there should be, and what there is doesn't look right at all."

She scanned the corpse. "You had a light when you discovered him?"

Ruy nodded. "Still do. We hooded the lantern. Best not to draw any attention."

"Well, raise a few cloaks to shield it and uncover the light. I need to see better."

When the three men other than watchful Finan

had gathered around to shield the lantern, Grogan unhooded it. Sharon did not merely see more clearly; it felt as if her entire field of vision was expanding, a sensation that she experienced when she went into what she internally labeled as "rapid intake mode."

An empty wine bottle lay next to the corpse. Residue on it strongly suggested it had contained red wine, so, depending upon the color of the stains it left when oxidized, that could problematize distinguishing it from the blood, and so, determining the freshness of the latter.

The corpse's pockets were turned out. While broader crime-scene competence was not something to which she could lay any reasonable claim, she knew that was frequently observed in the victims of theft—particularly if the theft was carried out post mortem, or at least once the victim was unconscious or otherwise unable to resist.

The front of the man's tunic was stained with blood. Maybe wine, too, but Sharon doubted that. These stains were browner than any dried wine she'd ever seen. She scanned down, seeing less blood than she expected on his baggy trousers. A lot less, actually. If he had fallen against this wall immediately after being attacked, most of his blood should have drained downward from the wounds, to the bottom half of his tunic and the upper half of his pants. But in addition to the comparative paucity of blood, it hadn't saturated the clothes as uniformly as it should have.

Or, she realized, *the blood isn't uniform in its dryness*. Some of the blood on both the tunic and pants still gleamed faintly. Overcoming an initial instinct against touching anything at a crime scene, she laid the tip of her index finger in the blood, drew it back: moist, and still red. She glanced back at the loose tunic. The chest wounds were lustreless, encrusted with the distinctive sienna-brown of dried blood.

"Dear heart . . ." Ruy started.

"Shhh!" she commanded, before she was fully aware of doing so. She flashed an apologetic smile at him, then waved the men back so she could see the pattern of blood on the ground.

Unfortunately, their feet—and possibly those of the assailant—had made a mess of it. But even so, it was distinctive. It was a wide pattern, which was to be expected: the victim had not exsanguinated in a rapid gush, as from an arterial wound, but from the lacerations that crossed his torso. So, not a single, well-defined point source for the blood. But the farther edge of the bloodstains on the ground were not appreciatively wider than those closest to the victim. And most instructive of all was the shape of the individual droplets that speckled the edges of the stains. She pointed them out to Ruy and Owen. "See those?"

They nodded and exchanged looks, as if checking to see if the other had any idea what these small droplets were supposed to reveal.

"It's a setup," Sharon explained. "I'm pretty sure this man was not attacked here at all."

"Because of the blood drops?" Owen sounded skeptical.

"That alone is not conclusive. But it sure is looking that way." She nodded at the spatters on the ground. "Consider the shape of the farthest blood drops. They're round. That's the mark left by a drop falling more or less straight down. But the farthest blood from the victim would have been traveling in an arc, so when it landed—"

Ruy's eyes widened. "A teardrop shape."

Owen was looking at the spray pattern, nodding. "Aye. And look there."

Sharon saw where he was pointing, knew what he had seen. "Yes, that's the other clue that something is wrong with this scene. Whoever planted this blood here—dumped it to make it look like the victim's— didn't stop and think that when you drop a liquid, drops arc out in all directions." She laid her finger on one of the few teardrop-shaped blood spots close to the corpse. "The head of the teardrop shape always points from its source, so why is this one pointing *toward* the corpse?"

Ruy nodded. "Because that blood did not come from him; it was poured out here, where we're standing, and splashed in all directions. Including in the direction of the corpse. Which is to say, in exactly the wrong direction." He beamed at his wife, then turned toward Owen. "Logically, then, our next step must be—"

"Must be to get me a table with lots of light in a windowless room," Sharon interrupted. "Now."

Ruy started at his wife's hard tone. "My love?"

"Ruy, this body has more to tell us, some of it very important to any subsequent investigation." She tried moving the corpse's arms: they were almost as stiff as a mannequin's. "Primary rigor mortis. And look"—she poked an exposed forearm—"fixed lividity."

Owen blinked. "What?"

Sharon shook her head impatiently. "The blood has settled; there's no blanching of the skin when you push it. This man was killed at least eight hours ago. Probably more." She studied the forward drooping head closely, then pressed upward against the forehead. Although the neck tissues were every bit as stiff as she expected, the dip of the head was slightly skewed off the center-line, and there was less overall resistance than she had expected. She allowed the head to rest forward again and motioned for Grogan to bring the light closer as she worked to tilt the whole body forward and explore the rear of the neck. Sure enough, just beneath the hairline, centered on the spine, was an incision from which a small trickle of blood had emerged and dried. She pointed it out to the others. "This is what killed him, not the slashing from the front."

"So it was two attackers," Owen breathed.

"At least. But not here. If one of his attackers was behind him, he couldn't have fallen *backward* against the wall."

Ruy frowned. "So, whoever slew him wished to make it look like common thievery. And had the presence of mind to wait until night to move the body."

"Which means that this poor sod died somewhere they didn't want found, or searched," Owen conjectured. "Which means we need every clue we can get about who or where they might be."

Sharon nodded. "That's why I need that well-lit, windowless room and a table."

"And where might we find that?"

Sharon turned and looked at St. Peter's steeple just behind them, now outlined against the lightening sky. "I hear that the Hibernians keep an outpost in there." She glanced toward where she believed Finan to be lurking. "Do they have some kind of ready room?"

Finan's voice emerged from the shadows. "Would a basement do?"

Chapter 17

Somehow, Sharon thought, it hadn't sounded so bad when Finan had suggested "a basement." It certainly hadn't sounded gruesome when they had filed into St. Peter's, explaining the situation to the parish priest, and then asking for the use of a room below ground level. The priest had shook his head and explained that the church did not have a basement per se.

But it did have a crypt.

According to both Ruy and Owen during their descent of the musty stairs, every self-respecting church in France or Italy had one, and, unlike the up-time context, the word here had more congenial associations. Instead of invoking horror movie images of ghouls and other undead monsters, here it was typically the repository of relics and the remains of particularly holy persons, and was often furnished with a chapel. St. Peter's crypt did in fact have a small altar and provision for worshipers. But for Sharon, a crypt was still a crypt, and a damned creepy place to conduct an autopsy.

On the other hand, there had been plenty of room

to set up a makeshift autopsy table and surround it with all the lanterns and oil lamps they could find. By which time, Sharon was starting to strip the body, and in so doing, confirmed what she had suspected. Bending the corpse forward easily, she grumbled, "The only reason I can do this is because they already broke the rigor mortis at the waist. Which meant this corpse was laid out flat long enough for the rigor to become complete."

"And how long is that?" Owen asked.

Sharon pushed hair back from her scalp. "In hot weather, maybe eight hours. At these latitudes and temperatures, probably at least ten or eleven. But I can probably refine that guess in a few moments."

Having carefully cut the clothes off, with Grogan lifting and moving limbs when necessary, she stood back, and took a look at the corpse. The upper half was uncommonly pale, but the flesh on the lower flank and particularly the back was dark and blotchy. "Yep. Fixed lividity." The faces around her were both attentive and expectant. "You must have seen it before, on battlefields. The blood pools in response to gravity. Whatever part of the body was uppermost drains down to the lowest. And at this point, it won't shift or respond when you press it." She demonstrated. Finan suddenly became more pale. "See? Fixed. That means at least eight hours, which confirms the time of death suggested by the rigor mortis. It also means that when he died, they laid him on his back, probably to clean the blood and try to keep some of it in him for later, when they propped him up. Not a very effective technique."

"And the wound to the rear of the neck?" Ruy asked softly.

"I'm working on it," Sharon mumbled as she gestured Grogan to roll the corpse on its side. She peered at the wound, frowned, reached into the padded compartment containing her largest magnifying glass, and peered again. She spoke as she observed: "Blade went almost straight in, partially severing the spinal cord. That's why the hang of the head didn't look quite right. Slight, ragged deformation at the top of the wound; probably the attacker was pulling the weapon out as the body was slumping. An internal exam might show corroborating kerf marks—"

"Whut marks?" Grogan echoed.

"Kerf marks. Where bones are nicked or cut by weapons." She stopped, thought. "Please lay the corpse out again, Sergeant Grogan," she asked. Waiting for him to finish, Sharon answered the questions she assumed Ruy and Owen were most interested in. "Progress of the wound channel is downward from the point of entry at the back of the neck. If I had to guess, I'd say the attacker was considerably taller than the victim. That would put his shoulder in line with the base of the victim's skull."

Owen frowned. "That's only a guess?"

Sharon nodded, opened the corpse's mouth, asked for Grogan to bring one of the lanterns closer. "Under the best of conditions, Owen, forensics is never entirely an exact science." She looked up as she pried open the victim's mouth. "And these are far from the best of conditions. However, I can tell you that the blade's cross section was an elongated trapezoid—a skinny diamond shape—that it was less than half an inch wide at its broadest point, and that its edges were quite sharp."

Ruy nodded at Owen. "A thin rondel dagger or a northern stiletto."

Owen nodded back. "An assassin's weapon. And used in that fashion: from the rear and to inflict a single, mortal blow."

Ruy stared down at the corpse. "So, as you feared: not a simple act of thievery."

Sharon nodded. "Nothing simple about this at all," she agreed. "The point of the weapon did not emerge from the roof of the mouth, so far as I can see. That angle further implies that the attacker is indeed as tall as we suspect."

"Why?"

Sharon shrugged. "Again, all conjecture, but visualize the attack. A shorter man would have to be striking overhand to hit that point at the back of the skull, or would have been aiming upward—and the entry wound is not consistent with anything other than a perpendicular angle of attack. But if the attack had been overhand, that means the attacker's move is not a thrust—not straight in and out—but an arc. And even if the entry wound looks precisely perpendicular, some of that angular momentum would have been imparted to the blade—meaning there's a good chance it would have curved down a bit inside the tissue and emerged from the roof of the mouth. But there's no sign of that.

"There's also no sign that the victim was drinking, and red wine in particular should have left signs. However, the tongue is not darkened, and there are no characteristic fresh stains on the teeth or at the gum line." She paused, hands on hips, frowning. "But I'd like to be sure."

Ruy nodded. "Of course. How is that done?"

She looked up at him.

He raised an eyebrow. "Here?"

She nodded. Where else could they do it?

Resigned, and probably thinking the same thing, he turned to Finan. "You must requisition some old bedclothes from the good father upstairs."

Finan frowned. "What for?"

"To keep the mess from spreading when we examine the contents of this fellow's stomach."

Finan followed his orders with uncommon alacrity.

By the time Finan arrived with the bedsheets and they had been spread, Sharon was finishing her external survey of the body. Since beginning, she had remained silent, not wanting to distract herself with updating Ruy and Owen with the details as they came up: better to give a single report at the end. She was feeling the effects of her abruptly foreshortened sleep, and, since a cup of coffee was not readily at hand, she was concerned that she might start getting drowsy, sloppy. So while she still had the concentration to do it—

Examining the contents of a stomach is never a pleasant business, and, done without proper gloves, can present some risks to the examiner as well. Which reflection made Sharon chuckle: since when had she become an examiner? The other voice in her head provided the answer with a healthy dose of snark: *ever since you arrived here in the seventeenth century, fool. Hell, you were able to surgeon your way through unpacking Ruy's intestines in the process of repairing what would otherwise have been a mortal gut wound, so you can sure as hell accept the title of medical examiner as well.* Because the simple fact was, in this time and place, she was pretty much the closest equivalent.

"You found something... amusing?" Ruy's voice asked from the end of a very long tunnel.

Poor Ruy! She must have been smiling as one part of her had scolded the other. Must be unnerving for her hidalgo husband—strider of continents and peerless armsman—to watch his time-traveler wife grinning and giggling as she poked around in a corpse's guts. Might make him rethink his conviction that she, and the rest of Grantville, were not demons in disguise. Because her present activity, and casual smiles while doing it, was not exactly powerful contrary evidence...

Sometime later, Sharon emerged from the trance of sorting through and peering into the dead man's stomach. Particularly given the poor light, it required complete focus while searching for clues. It was like a hunter trying to find rabbits in an overgrown meadow: the slightest bit of inattention is all it would take to miss the prey, to pass it by and never realize she'd done so. Sharon blinked, straightened, saw her hands and arms were stained most of the way up to her elbows. "I'd be grateful for some water."

Finan was there with a pitcher and a basin; although it was purely a literary device to say that someone's complexion turned green, he was doing as good an imitation of it as she'd ever seen.

When she had finished washing her hands and arms and had patted them dry methodically, she turned to face Ruy and Owen. "There was no trace of wine in the stomach. There are some small food remains, but they were heavily denatured by the stomach's acid.

If I had to guess, it was bread and cheese. A typical light lunch for the locals.

"The whole body exam confirmed my initial time of death estimates. The eyes, specifically the corneas, are cloudy and slightly sunken or 'flattened.' That's consistent with a minimum of eight hours since expiration.

"The one finding which may simplify the task of establishing the victim's identity is that there was a small amount of ink under the second and fourth fingernails of his right hand." Sharon saw eager optimism grow in Ruy's eyes; she hated having to squash it. "Unfortunately, I doubt he's a scribe. He's not dressed correctly, and he has none of the finger callouses that would be consistent with holding a pen for long hours. However, it still narrows the search: he is not only educated, but at least occasionally worked with writing, possibly keeping accounts or making notations of some kind. As such, he's likely to be known among other workers or guilds that require similar skills. He's approximately forty-five, has no major scars or signs of other physical trauma. Dermal aging is moderate; if he ever works outdoors, I suspect that is relatively rare."

Owen leaned forward into her pause. "And the attackers?"

Sharon sighed. "Obviously, any conclusions concerning them is the sheerest guesswork. But I think the following conjectures are reasonable.

"I suspect that the crime was committed wherever they live. They not only took all these precautions to make it look like he was killed here, but were able to wait for at least eight hours before moving the body. And frankly, given the quality of the rigor mortis and the progression of all the other signs, I think it's more like twelve hours. I saw the first signs of larval activity in the oral mucosa: the first place that the common fly goes to lay its eggs.

"Next guess: his attackers live uphill from where we found him, or they live fairly close. Carrying this body was not a simple job. The victim was heavy enough that it would have been hard work for two relatively fit men to tote him here, particularly if they had to travel a long distance or uphill to do so."

"So the attackers are not from the riverfront or the Battant," Ruy mumbled.

Sharon shook her head. "And here's another complicating factor: in order to sit him up and make him look like a drunk who got rolled by a knife-happy thief, they had to break all the rigor that would prevent his body from bending at the waist. That is not an easy job. Doing it after they brought him to the alley would not only be dangerous in terms of attracting attention, it would entail a considerable risk: what if the men carrying him couldn't do it on their own? But to avoid that, they would have had to break the rigor where they lived, which means that carrying the body was going to be that much more awkward: he was no longer conveniently stiff as a board."

Owen nodded, his blue eyes narrowed. "And carry him they did. Which means that, to them, the risk was worth it. So that has me wondering what it is they had to conceal."

Ruy rubbed his chin. "And what this poor fellow stumbled across."

Owen frowned. "Looks like there might be a few more assassins here in the Buckle, after all." He glanced at Sharon. "Anything more you might be guessing about the killers?"

She frowned. "Not much. I can tell you that the man who attacked from the front was strong, but probably not much taller than the victim, judging from the angle of the wounds. There were a few kerf marks on the ribs of the deceased: definitely a dagger but much heavier than the one which struck him from behind. I would tentatively say it was double-edged, but I'm basing that on observations that could have other explanations. However, I believe the frontal attacker was right-handed."

Ruy's left eyebrow quirked upward. "Indeed? Why?"

"Well, let's recreate the moment of the attack." Sharon began using her hands to depict the scenario in midair. "There's one man behind the victim, the one who actually kills him. This means that what we are presuming to be frontally inflicted wounds are, in fact, just that. Under certain circumstances, they could actually be inflicted by unusual attacks from the side or even behind; believe me, such weird things do happen. But in this case, there's already an attacker behind him who's using an entirely different weapon.

"So the shorter man in front with the bigger knife starts slashing at the victim. And the angle at which his blade pierced the skin pretty conclusively suggests that the two were at roughly the same height. This wasn't a case where a standing attacker was striking down at a sitting man."

"Now this is the point where I make a logical, but admittedly large, conjecture: that when the frontal attacker struck, the victim is dying or already dead on his feet, due to the wound inflicted to the base of his skull. So he's starting to fall. That means that the first front laceration is likely to occur higher on his torso, because the second slash would be made when the victim was falling back."

She pointed at the body. "The higher, and deeper slash is the one that runs from his upper left clavicle all the way down to his right abdomen, where it really does a lot of exit damage. Because the laceration is deeper, it suggests that this is a stronger, overhand strike. It also left very strong kerf marks; the blade ran powerfully, and very directly, against his collarbone and several ribs. So, since the two men are facing each other, a slash that starts high on the victim's left side, suggests an overhand attack by the attacker's right arm."

"Now look at the other slash. It starts much lower on the right-hand side of the victim's torso, at the nipple line. It is markedly less deep and the kerf marks are not only more faint, but at more of an angle, as if the knife was glancing over them. And since this slash starts on the right side of the victim's torso, it makes sense that the attack came from the left side of the attacker.

"So if we add all that up, the higher strike is the one that was stronger, more effective, and was apparently conducted when the men were both fully upright while facing each other; that's why the blade dug so deep and left such strong kerf marks. The second slash was more glancing—which would suggest it was a backhand cut, made while the victim was falling away from the attacker and his knife."

Ruy nodded. "So, yes: apparently a right-handed attacker." He smiled ruefully. "That, unfortunately, does not narrow the list of potential suspects very much."

"No," Sharon allowed, "but he's probably no more than an inch taller than the victim. If that. And he may be working with a much taller and fairly strong person: the one who attacked from the rear. And they used two very different knives to make their attack." She yawned, glad she hadn't had any coffee available; if she'd had a cup she wouldn't be able to get back to sleep before this morning's gathering at the Palais Granvelle. As it was, she knew she'd still be tired and probably look like hell. And this on the long-awaited day when Catholics and Protestants would finally come together, with her on hand as the benign, if silent, representative of their sponsor: the USE. She began repacking her bag. "Ruy, gentlemen, if you don't mind, I'd like to get right back to the cloister. I need to get a few more hours of sleep before I have to be present for the convening of the colloquium." When no one answered, she looked up.

Ruy and Owen were exchanging baleful glances.

She looked from one face to the other. "What?"

Ruy's face almost drooped along with his sympathetic tone. "Wonderful wife, I believe you have lost track of time. You have little more than two hours left."

Two hours. Just about enough time to wash off the various corpse smells, re-dress, choke down a small meal, and play her part at what might prove to be the most important interfaith meeting this world had ever known. *Sure, Sharon, you've got this: no pressure.*

She doubled the speed with which she was repacking her medical bag.

Chapter 18

Sharon wondered if her eyes were as bloodshot as they felt—itchy and rough—during the walk from Palais Granvelle's great salon to its even larger great hall. Fortunately, her modest role in the proceedings, to offer a brief word of welcome along with Besançon's mayor, was over, and she only had to stay long enough to hear Urban declare that the colloquium had begun. Then she could surreptitiously flee back to the shelter of the cloister and the comfort of her bed.

Wild Geese lined the final approach to the chamber, and what they lacked in parade finery they made up for in daunting readiness. Unlike typical honor guards, their hands were on their weapons, their eyes alert and always cycling from one doorway or window to the next.

Beside her, Larry Mazzare winked as they passed into the long high chamber, banked with seats on crude risers for the occasion. "Show time," he murmured.

Sharon smiled, despite herself.

As they were shown to their seats by a priest operating under the watchful eye of von Spee, she took a quick count: seating for just about one hundred and twenty persons. Close to the room's limit, from the look of it.

Situated several places to the left of the pope's slightly larger chair, she and Larry had the equivalent of box seats. Which was appropriate and flattering, of course, but that was not uppermost in her thoughts. Wishing they didn't have to stand until the pope entered and seated himself, she leaned sideways toward Larry, whispered out of the corner of her mouth, "So how long is this supposed to take?"

Mazzare shrugged. "You mean the official opening of the colloquium? Maybe five minutes. It's just a formality, really. The rest of the day is pretty much a bull session with catered meals. The real work begins tomorrow. Why?" he asked with an impish grin. "You in a hurry to go somewhere?"

"Yes," she muttered back at him.

"Where?"

"Anyplace but here. I mean, look at these guys"— she used her eyes to indicate the solemn-faced procession of middle aged to ancient clerics filing into the room—"They look like they're going to a funeral. Their own, some of them."

Larry nodded. "Can't really blame them. The two sides have been at each other's throats for more than a century. Plenty from both sides would probably rather stick a knife in each other than be in the same room. The last time something like this was tried, that pope had to issue promises of safe passages to those few Protestants who were willing to attend. And even that wasn't enough to reassure the few who were invited."

"So how do I know when it's time to leave?"

"You'll know. Von Spee will thank the lay persons in the room on behalf of the pope, with an assurance that the colloquium's collective gratitude will remain undiminished in their absence. That's the cue for von Spee's platoon of priests to usher you out."

Sharon wondered how much longer she was going to have to stand shifting her weight from one weary foot to the other when Urban entered, went directly to his seat, and before he had fully sunk into it, waved the gathering down with a casual smile.

Sharon saw surprised glances exchanged around the room. She surmised that popes, or at least this one, were not known for such informality.

As soon as everyone in the room had seated themselves, Urban rose, his downward gesturing palm keeping them in their seats. Several of the more conservative cardinals, who were seated in the gallery to his right, started. Dietrichstein looked like he might be on the verge of apoplexy.

If Urban noticed, he paid no mind to their reactions. He looked around the chamber, took his time doing so. "At long last," he said with a smile, "over many months and across many miles, we meet together. I thank all of you, both personally and on behalf of Mother Church, for undertaking the arduous, and in many cases dangerous, journeys that have brought you here, so that we might join in the name of the One God in Heaven."

The room remained silent. *Tough crowd*, thought Sharon.

"I have had the chance to meet with most of you individually, and in the case of those whose acquaintance I have not yet had the pleasure of making, I look forward to correcting that this day and those that shall follow. And so, in the name of our Heavenly Father above and the ties of faith that we all share in common—"

One of the figures seated to the left rose to his feet. "Before this colloquium is declared open, and therefore before any of us may be counted as party to it, I must ask this question: how do you define 'ties of faith that we all share in common?' Because truly, I cannot in conscience remain in this chamber or as a participant in this colloquium, until I know whether or not the Romish conception of these 'ties of faith' precludes my own perception of them."

Sharon sighed: *well, so much for the pro forma five minute opening.* She leaned toward Mazzare, who seemed every bit as surprised as the rest of the cardinals in the room, including the Orthodox contingent that was seated farther down from the cardinals on the right side. "So who's this guy?"

"Jiří Třanovský," Larry muttered. "Hungarian."

"Hussite?"

"No, Lutheran, but he's lost a lot of family to the Catholic armies. Grew up watching Hussites persecuted, too."

Sharon opened her mouth to ask if what Třanovský was doing was permitted when Urban, whose only response so far had been a slow, sage nodding, straightened. "Your question is prudent, Reverend Třanovský." The mischievous smile that was Urban's trademark flickered at the corners of his mouth. "And even fortuitous. If there are such questions to be asked, indeed, they should be answered before we gather together. So here is my answer: I have my own definitions for 'ties of faith.' I presume that you, and everyone else in this room, has their own conception, as well. I presume that, were we able to read what is in the hearts of men, just as we read what is written in a book, we would find that no two of us would define 'ties of faith' in exactly the same fashion."

Třanovský's chin came up. "That could have been said a year ago, or a century ago, and it would have made no difference to the atrocities perpetrated in the name of the 'true faith.' And yet here we are, the hopeful, lured by promises of tolerance for us poor heretics."

Vitelleschi, sitting to Urban's immediate right, came forward, his whiskers bristling like a hedgehog's. But Urban gestured him to remain calm as he replied. "Regarding this word, 'heretic': here is a promise to which you may bear witness, and of which I encourage you to make wide report. You will not hear that word emerge from my mouth this day, or any following, for as long as I shall live. And as regards the 'ties of faith' we share: I not only presume that they are different; I presume that we are entitled to those differences. They are the manifestations of the free will with which our Creator has endued us, and it is no man's place to compel another to change what is in another's heart. For Christ told us, 'judge not, lest ye be judged.'"

Třanovský's brow lowered in what appeared to be a mix of caution and suspicion. "It is said that Urban VIII is a most politic pontiff. It is also widely held that he is most patient in the pursuit of his true agendas. So a cautious man might wonder, 'perhaps Urban VIII will not speak the word heretic aloud, but might still have it in his heart, as he deals with us.'"

Urban smiled again. "If I could open my heart to you as we open the pages of a book, I would, Reverend Třanovský. I have given my word in lieu of that, and I can understand if you cannot bring yourself to trust it. So that is why this is merely an ecumenical *colloquium*, not an ecumenical council: that you—all of you—may take the measure of me, of us, freely." Urban's gaze moved slowly around the room. "We are here to converse, to consider, to break bread together: nothing more. There are no resolutions to be passed or commitments to be made, except those we might make in our hearts. There is but one objective: that we may spend time with and listen to each other, so that, should you be willing to meet us again, you may be certain of our intents and our commitment to this ecumenical initiative." His eyes came to rest once more on Třanovský, who had resumed his seat. "Does this answer your question, Reverend?"

The Hungarian's voice was less challenging, this time. "It answers my question, but does not settle the matter."

"Of course not," Urban said, smiling. "That is why we have these days together. It is in the knowing of each other that the matter will be settled, whatever the outcome."

Sharon was just starting to relax, to ready herself to acknowledge the anticipated words of both thanks and dismissal, and to walk out with a gait more composed and steady than her aching feet really wanted to effect, when a figure rose far down the right-hand bank of seats. *Oh, for the love of—*

Cyril Lucaris, the leader of the Greek Orthodox delegation, spread wide his arms to take in the whole of the chamber. "The Prelate of Rome speaks the wisdom of Christ with the Savior's mildness. Indeed, let us know each other as persons before we come together as representatives of our respective branches of the Christian family. However"—Sharon could have groaned: when a cleric said "however" it usually meant another ten-minute debate or discourse—"this wisdom, in addition to being welcome, is also in sharp contrast with much of what has gone before. So, in the interest of better understanding our hosts' new words and attitudes, I would like to ask: from whence comes this change?"

Urban nodded. "A question that may be asked quickly but would be long in the answering, and I have no wish to encumber this gathering with a recitation of my own recent journey to cleave closer to the Grace that is Christ's True Word. But if I were to put a metaphor upon it, let us say that about a year ago, I began realizing that my life was beginning to parallel Jonah's. But whereas Jonah's faith was tested and trued by being swallowed by a whale, mine was tried by being spat out of the Leviathan that is the mundane apparatus of Holy Mother Church. For the first time in long, long years, I was not buried deep within the belly of the Holy See's immense body of officials, administrators, scribes, and guards. I was about in the world, with little between me and my Maker but a handful of unlikely Good Samaritans"—he glanced at Sharon and Larry—"and in such times, a man has both the freedom and the need to reflect on what he has said and done." He raised his palms, as if invoking the assembly. "And here we are, gathered in the name of shared theological roots and a shared hope that this colloquium may pave the way to peace after each of you have consulted with others in your respective communities of faith. Only then might a later meeting be convened, by which I time I hope that my own situation is somewhat more—settled."

A new voice arose from the left. Sharon recognized the speaker: Johann Gerhard, one of the two Protestants who had arrived on the same day as Bedmar and the aspiring Swiss Guards. She settled back in her chair, wondered how long this unexpected question and answer session was going to go on, and doubted she'd stay awake for all of it.

Gerhard folded his hands. "I would touch upon the matter of, as you put it, your situation as the Prelate of Rome. Now, I know something of the number of cardinals in the Romish Church, and even many of their names." He scanned the faces on the opposite side of the chamber and seemed to count the red birettas as he did. "However, I now see many faces, and have heard many names, which do not match the roster with which I am familiar."

"Because they were made, and held, *in pectore*. Until yesterday."

Gerhard nodded. "So I conjectured. And it is reassuring to see so many replacements of the recent, tragic losses. However, that raises a ticklish matter: how is it that Europe's various Catholic monarchs stood by and watched so many cardinals be slaughtered? Why do those monarchs not right the many wrongs that have been done, most particularly in Italy itself? Most pertinently, if Philip of Spain were to declare Borja's seizure of the Vatican an abomination and a personal affront against God, the usurper could not last a day."

Next to Sharon, Larry was frowning: in the discussions leading up to this week, he and Urban had both presumed that Gerhard would be one of the more supportive Lutherans. They had also anticipated that he might begin with a harder line so that he could be seen as "coming around" to a true ecumenical relationship, rather than having been too cooperative too early and so, seem servile or even a prearranged collaborator. But this obliquely confrontational rhetoric sounded like the real thing, not a sham.

Vitelleschi was stirring in his chair, apparently readying himself for battle should Urban give the sign. But into the silence rose a calm, almost dispassionate voice from a most unexpected quarter: another member of the Lutheran group. Namely, Georg Calixtus, about whom Sharon knew very little. "To restore the proper Prelate of Rome to his seat in the Vatican is, unfortunately, a thornier matter than might at first be supposed."

Gerhard seemed surprised. "How so, learned friend? Spanish orders sent Spanish troops to put Borja on the *cathedra*. It was the doing of a Romish monarch; it should be theirs to undo, as well."

Calixtus nodded as his fellow Lutheran spoke, but Sharon could tell it was merely patient acknowledgement, not agreement. She learned toward Larry. "Okay, I'm in the dark here. Why is a Lutheran debating a Lutheran?"

One half of Larry's mouth bent upward. "Because they are more likely to listen to, and believe, each other than a Catholic."

Calixtus let a few seconds of silence pass before he replied. "Firstly, Johann, the matter is complicated by

Philip of Spain's refusal to either avow or disavow the orders which sent Count Oruna's Neapolitan tercios to Rome. Oruna himself has remained vague on the matter, saying only that when the most prominent of the Spanish cardinals requested troops, he complied without undue questioning. Obedience to God seems to have become obedience to Borja, insofar as the Viceroy of Naples is concerned. At any rate, no Catholic monarch or vassal thereof has taken responsibility for the unseating of our host, Urban VIII. And secondly, there is no historical precedent against which potential solutions may be measured."

Gerhard blew out his moustaches impatiently. "Come now, Georg. The history of the Church is littered with antipopes, the most notable being those who sat at Avignon."

Calixtus was nodding again. "Inarguably, that is true. But if we consider that analogy more carefully, we may find it lacks essential congruence to the current crisis. And so, it is a false analogy. Unintentionally so, of course," he amended quickly, "but false nonetheless."

Sharon leaned toward Larry again. "So why is Calixtus defending the Catholics?"

Larry replied in a mutter from the corner of his mouth. "He's arguably the original ecumenicist. Worked on creating a 'unifying theology' that would be acceptable to all branches of Christianity. Up-time, about five years from now, he was accused of being a syncretist."

"A what?" muttered Sharon.

Larry's response was a sibilant, "Shhhh . . ."

Calixtus took a few more moments to collect his thoughts. Then: "Firstly, Borja has not claimed himself to be pope. And there has been no movement in his vastly diminished—and many say, unenthusiastic—consistory to encourage him to take such a step. Which is actually sound advice, since in almost all prior cases of antipopes, they arose at a time when the cardinals of Rome elected a new pope, or very shortly thereafter. That is most dramatically not the case presently. Our host, Urban VIII, has been the Bishop of Rome for almost thirteen years. There was never the slightest question regarding the legitimacy of his election. He has not repudiated the Church, nor has a Council of the Consistory ever convened to compel him to renounce his title. Not even the establishment of the Avignon Papacy offers a useful parallel, nor does its eventual dissolution.

"And just as it was not built in a day, so it was not torn down any more quickly. The process of reunification under the Roman popes took almost fifty years. Many small wars were ostensibly waged over the rightful seat of the papacy but were, in fact, callously opportunistic struggles for material gain."

Calixtus sighed. "It is much more difficult now, two hundred years later with our entire continent bitterly divided by the greater and more ferocious wars of the Reformation. In no prior situation did any of the papal claimants kill a huge portion of the standing consistory, nor was the House of Hapsburg divided, nor was there an immense and unified Protestant power holding dominion where the factious Holy Roman Empire used to be.

"And as if that was not enough to paralyze a just resolution, in this case, the legitimate pope was twice an assassination target who was rescued by free thinking persons from the future, operating with the support and tacit approval of Rome's most staunch opponent: Gustav Adolf of Sweden." Calixtus smoothed his robes. "It is said that Philip believes he must rid the world of the up-timers and their influence, which means eliminating the pope who accepted both. He is equally compelled to avoid another papal schism and remain aloof from charges of pontificide. He and the cardinals that answer to him are thus on the horns of a most unpleasant dilemma."

"That's as may be, Reverend Calixtus," John Dury said, sitting at the forefront of the small knot of Calvinists who had attended. "But whether Spain or Italy, I don't see as it makes a great deal of difference to us. Both nations have been comparable in their ardor for our extermination."

"I do not debate that, Reverend Dury. But do you dispute that this colloquium is a very new situation, and that this is therefore a very new day? By which I must admit I am asking this pointed question: do you doubt that the olive branch offered from this pope is genuine?"

Dury, either unsure of his answer or unwilling to share it, murmured and sat. But before the moment had elapsed, a new voice came from much farther down that bank of seats. "Let us presume that the gesture that brought us here is genuine. However, let us also admit that it is extremely expedient." The speaker was Jan Komensky, more commonly known as Comenius: a Hussite theologian more famous for his focus on popular education and discourse than ecumenicism.

Before Urban could reply, a high, clear voice from the end of that same left-hand bank of seats offered a counterpoint. "An expedient action does not necessarily suggest that it is, de facto, ingenuine. It is, perhaps, merely doubly wise." Sharon knew this speaker for his provocative presence if nothing else: Menasseh ben Israel, an outstanding young scholar from the Jewish community and with ties to the Abrabanels, had risen slowly to his feet. Few of the faces in the great hall were welcoming; most seemed to be laboring mightily to maintain an expression of benign indifference. *Old prejudices die hard, just like Dad always told me. Or maybe he was telling himself so he didn't kill someone.*

Ben Israel had not finished. "However, whether expedient, genuine, or both, all actions, all decisions must always be suspected of being impermanent. So, when the present danger to the Church is past, will the ecumenical gestures made today continue to be expedient? And if not, what then?" He sat as an approving murmur rose up from the rest of the left-hand seats.

Urban leaned forward. "I cannot speak for those popes who may come after me, but I may say this about the encyclicals I mean to put before the Council of Cardinals in the coming days, and, I hope, the Apostolic Constitutions which will come after and become inviolable dogma. Canon law shall no longer be silent upon, or easily interpreted to allow, waging war upon fellow Christians, or killing persons simply because their faith does not make them, by our definition, 'believers.'"

As ben Israel nodded slowly, Třanovský jumped up. "So does this mean an end to the persecution, the torture? May we tell our communities that the burnings are over, that even Spanish streets will no longer be lit by *auto-de-fe*?"

Sharon flinched at that word. She remembered first hearing it when she was quite young. Not knowing how to spell it and look it up for herself, she asked her father what it meant. He frowned in a way he seldom did and answered, "A lynching. Conducted by priests."

But, young as she was, Sharon explained that she did not know what the word "lynching" meant, either. Her father's frown was quickly replaced by surprise and then the deep, sympathetic sadness that she only saw there when one of his patients died. He had risen from the kitchen table, reached down a hand. She took it, and by the time James Nichols reached his study, he was grim-lipped, as if determined to do something he very much did not want to do.

He sat her down in front of the wall that served as their library, peered along a shelf with books whose spines proclaimed names such as Baldwin, Du Bois, Wright, Morrison, Angelou, Ellison, and finally extracted a slim volume that was, in effect, an extended photographic essay. He sat beside her and held her hand as she turned through the pages; even at age ten, she was capable of clinical detachment, noting the details of how the atrocities had been committed even while compartmentalizing the slow, building rage that she never released, nor ever fully resolved.

And which she felt again now. Larry looked sideways at her. "You okay?"

"I'll be fine. Thanks," she murmured and understood— deep in her gut, not high in her head—why, despite all the deference and consideration shown the Protestants who had decided to attend the colloquium, so many were still filled with suspicion and anger. And why some of their communities had resorted to the same tactics, ultimately.

Urban was sadly shaking his head when Georg Calixtus' voice rose once again from the Protestant bench. "My friend, now it is you who is guilty of being a tormentor—and of your host, no less. Think of where you are. Are we seated in the gilt finery of the Vatican? Have we been dining on rare delicacies? How can you ask this of a pope who truly possesses his title, but little else besides? How is he to disseminate his decrees, much less enforce them? Rather, let us simply ask: is he sincere? I for one believe he is. And that is a start."

Urban suddenly seemed very old, and very, very tired. "These are indeed the circumstances in which I, and the legitimate Church, find ourselves. And I thank you, Reverend Calixtus, for your willingness to perceive and accept that our ecumenical gesture is in earnest."

Georg Calixtus smiled. "I have never doubted it. The speed with which you have taken the steps to bring us here marks that clearly. But you will forgive me if I am not completely convinced that although earnest, your reasons might not be *entirely* spiritual in nature." And he paused for the silence in the room to grow in the wake of his course change. He had been Urban's defender a moment ago, but was now poised to function as his inquisitor.

Larry folded his hands in the long sleeves of his cassock, and Sharon translated the look on his face: *Here it comes.*

But Urban simply nodded. "So, let us speak of the practicalities, then. And let us do so frankly, that they do not remain undescribed shadows between us. Let us bring them into the light."

Georg Calixtus' face might have been about to fold into a frown, but if so, he immediately pasted a mask of genial impassivity over it. "Agreed. But I am hesitant: from either one of us, direct speech could also be perceived as tactless speech."

"And that warning tells me you will not mean it to be so, Reverend Calixtus. So please feel free to share your concerns. I would have many, if I was in your shoes, and not all of them would sound pretty."

The great room of Palais Granvelle seemed to echo with silence, if such a thing were possible.

Calixtus cleared his throat. "At your urging, then. The far-flung administrators of papal lands and cities continue to communicate exclusively with the Church's Roman bureaucracy by dint of habit, under fear of bloody punishment, and lack of any reasonable alternative. Obversely, what few resources you have are here in Besançon with you, and it is quite clear that this cannot become a new Avignon, a second Holy See."

Urban nodded. "All true and concisely presented."

Georg Calixtus nodded back in acknowledgement of the compliment—and very possibly, buying a moment in which to buttress his composure. A gracious consideration of practical reservations, stated so frankly, was hardly what he and the other non-Catholics would have planned upon. Consequently, being in uncharted and unexpected discursive terrain, they were no longer working according to a plan, but improvising.

Which, as Larry had explained weeks before, was exactly what Urban had wanted, and which Wadding had urged, earning the old Irish priest arch stares and frustrated objections from Vitelleschi. But so far, the strategy seemed to be working, particularly since the objective was not to counter the Protestant arguments. Rather, like the willow in the wind, the purpose was to acknowledge their validity and so, move past them—and the danger of increased sectarian rancor—with all possible speed.

Calixtus spread his hands in an appeal. "So you can understand why there are many who wonder if, as Rabbi ben Israel said, your sudden interest in building bridges between us might be motivated more by the terrible crises of the moment than by the ecumenical words you have read from the future. If so, this apparent gesture of brotherhood in faith could also be the precursor to approaching us for the help required to retake your legitimate seat in Rome, and so, recover your power. Power which, I must add, has heretofore been exerted most vigorously against our various communities."

Urban rose. "Which, therefore, is power that it would be in your best interests to see diminished or eliminated." Urban's eyes remained direct upon Calixtus'. "Am I correct?"

Chapter 19

Larry Mazzare discovered he was holding his breath. The pope's Machiavellian summary had literally caused jaws to drop amongst Catholics, Protestants, and Orthodox alike. Such candor had little precedent in interfaith gatherings, and particularly not where the objective was to discover and attain some shared ground upon which an olive tree of enduring peace might be planted.

Urban stood waiting, and when Calixtus did not reply, he asked, "This is the logical conclusion to your line of inquiry and concern, is it not?"

It was Cyril Lucaris who rose to that question and implicit challenge. "It is."

Urban smiled. "Very well. Frankly, I am glad to have such direct speech now. Your presentation of the Church's situation, and your assessment of how it may bear upon the future of your own communities is, to my mind, without logical flaw. And although I may foresee somewhat different outcomes and draw somewhat different conclusions from the scenario before us, I do not intend to denigrate your projections in the process of presenting my own. Rather, I offer an alternative view based on one fundamental difference of perception. Indeed, we might call that difference the fulcrum point upon which the issues before us are balanced: whether, in fact, the Roman Catholic Church has come here to truly embrace your many faiths or not."

Urban paused. Again, the room was silent. But now, almost half of the gathering was discernibly leaning forward, if only slightly, waiting on his next words.

Urban did not keep them waiting for long. "Firstly, it would be ludicrous for the Catholics gathered here to argue against the obvious: that the true papacy of the Roman Catholic Church is in desperate need of friends and allies. Not since the days of the Apostles has our plight been so great, our future so uncertain.

"However, despite the immensity of our need, we cannot use the help you fear we eventually intend to solicit: specifically, the military might needed to restore the papacy to the Holy See in Rome." Many faces were surprised, many dubious, several openly untrusting. Urban seemed to take no notice of any of them. "This is both a moral and a practical resolution. However, on the possibility that you still doubt our morality, I shall explain the practical folly of recruiting Protestant arms in support of our cause.

"Imagine how Italy, which has never known any significant Protestant populations or incursion, would react to the presence of an army that has, for sake of argument, significant numbers of Lutheran soldiers. They would be deemed invaders, no matter how much their Catholic comrades attempted to reassure each city they approached.

"But even if these attempts at reassurance were successful, would that not simply play into Borja's hands? The rhetoric by which he justified the procurement and use of force with which he seized the Holy See was that I had become a tool of Protestants and up-timers. That I was plotting with them to destroy the Church from within. And so, if Protestant forces were to enter Italy with the stated intent of restoring me to the *cathedra*, would that not suggest that Borja had been right all along? And so, I would lose even the quiet support of the people of Italy.

"And lastly, from whence would these Protestant forces be drawn and how would they reach Rome? Yes, armies have crossed the Alps before, but it is a costly, long, and arduous undertaking. And the forces which survived the passage would no doubt be met before they could march as far as Milan. Or, if their objective was but to pass through neutral Venetian territory, that would be a reasonable and sufficient pretext for Borja to claim that Spain's traditional antagonists meant not only to place their own puppet pope back upon the *cathedra*, but to expel the Empire's forces from Naples and Milan as well, and so, control the entire Italian peninsula."

Urban's voice lowered. "But even if none of these complications existed, Europe still cannot afford to send forces into Italy at this time. The Ottomans stir toward us, according to all reliable reports and projections. What forces Christendom has left after twenty years of religious war may well be needed there, to prevent the banners of the Crescent from reaching further into Europe."

Urban folded his hands. "Consequently, although we

do not yet have a plan to restore the papacy to the Holy See, we do know that Protestant forces cannot be a part of it. And our natural allies, the Catholic nations of Europe, are either in disarray or are arrayed against us, supporting the brutal deeds—and beliefs—of Borja. After all, it is precisely as Reverend Komensky said earlier: if Spain, the greatest power in Europe, were so minded, it could have swept him from the *cathedra* at any moment it chose."

It was Komenský himself who responded, apparently bewildered. "So, if all those who might offer assistance either may not be recruited, or are unable to help, how do you hope your papacy to prevail?"

Urban smiled sadly. "An excellent question. If only I had an excellent answer. Alas, I have no answer at all. Options may arise, but none are evident presently, nor are they likely to be in the near future."

Joasaphus I rose, spoke loudly. Larry could not make out the Greek, particularly filtered through the thick Russian accent. Evidently, that impediment to understanding had been anticipated; Mêtrophanês Kritopoulos, bishop of Alexandria and a scholar and linguist of broad talents, stood to translate. "Then, with all respect for your precarious circumstances, how does this colloquium matter? Whatever decisions might be made here, and whatever you might decree later, you have no power to enforce or even promulgate them as dogma or canon law, either now or in the foreseeable future. Instead, it is increasingly likely that, without a powerful patron to shield you, it is only a matter of time before more assassins find you and, crawling over the bodies of your overmatched retainers, end your life. And then we shall be dealing with Borja, anyway."

Urban nodded solemnly. "Everything that you say is possible. However, I would offer these additional points to bear in mind. Firstly, although my retainers, as you call them, are few in number, they are most formidable and extremely professional. They have already proven that it is not so easy to send assassins against me as you may think.

"Furthermore, though the Church's resolutions in this matter may be articulated by me today, they do not end with me. If they did, I would not have put you to the inconvenience of joining us here. As was observed at the outset, mine is a large consistory, and if I fall, one of my brothers will replace me." Urban smiled. "Indeed, I think there are far more of us to eliminate than there are bands of assassins willing to engage in that risky task."

"Lastly, I suspect that, before long, our exodus will at last become stationary enough to be relabeled an exile. And by that time, I suspect things may have changed in the Catholic country most likely to be instrumental in restoring me to the *cathedra*."

Mêtrophanês Kritopoulos' next question was his own, and his voice betrayed genuine perplexity. "Which country is that?"

"Why, Italy, of course. Borja's rule is hard and not yet two years old. And I will tell you this about my countrymen: they are plotting. Of this you may be certain." He shrugged. "It is in our blood, even in the best of times." Smiles answered Urban's own. "But in times such as these, the oldest rivals find common cause in the losses they have shared, in the memory of sons and fathers and brothers slain by Borja's men, and of the daughters and sisters and mothers who have been—"

He stopped, his face suddenly red. "You understand my meaning. Sometimes, Italy's many polities can barely agree upon the spelling of Caesar's name, let alone settle their long-standing feuds. But after what has happened in Rome, they will agree on one thing: a resolve to throw off Borja's yoke. That will also embolden the rebels who have suffered under Oruna in Naples. Soon enough, they will all make their displeasure known."

"In short," John Dury concluded, "all you have are hopes built upon low-comic stereotypes of your countrymen."

The room hushed. Even in a room full of anti-papists, those were harsh words when used against a man now as patient and mild as the much-changed Urban.

The pope was slow to respond; Larry could not tell if he was having to control his temper or was simply choosing his words carefully. "I understand how it might seem that way. But I know my people, Reverend Dury, and I maintain that there is much more substance to these projections than you might expect. However, if my hopes prove bootless, it does not change the conviction and faith which prompted me to gather you here."

Urban folded his hands. "I come before you having completed a long journey, one which began when I received the up-time documents which detailed not merely what lay before our Roman Church, but we individuals who serve it." He paused. "I saw history's judgment of me. It was as unequivocal as it was awful. Worse yet, it was accurate. No amount of denying and rationalizing the reasons for which I had done things in my life changed the truth behind the deeds: that I had allowed the exigencies of this world—of material power—to completely push the hunger for His Grace from my soul. How was I to pass through the eye of the needle, when my every waking thought was upon ensuring success against rivals, rather than attaining worthiness in the eyes of God?

"I did not accept this judgment upon myself immediately. The habits of a lifetime are not easily or swiftly overcome. But the more I read, the more inescapable my new self-judgment became, and so, the more inevitable that I either fully and consciously turn my back upon God or turn back toward him, arms outstretched and on my knees. And in seeking for a way to do so, I discovered that the answer was there in front of me, every day, all the time. In fact, it resided in one of my titles: Pontifex—the builder of bridges.

"What the up-time documents not only reminded me, but showed by example, was that the responsibility to commence building those bridges is upon our Roman Church—and specifically, upon the Pontifex. The significance and onus of that title is not simply an historical inheritance from those ancient pontiffs who spread Christ's Word far and wide in the world. The meaning, and the duty it imposes, lives on today, perhaps more urgently than ever. For just as the early popes were often martyrs who had to surrender life itself to build a bridge, then today, it may be that a pope must sacrifice his pride. And what the up-time Church taught us—reminded us—was that this pride was one and the same with the sin of that name. Humility is easily lost in the Holy See, where unceasing efforts to build power and project doctrine with silver and swords pushes it to the side, causes it to wither.

"But the acts of the up-time popes, who steadily divested the Church of such power, showed me another way. It is not just a path to greater Grace, and it exists not just to save lives in these days. It is an inoculation against the opiating impulse to presume and claim that God is on our side, and that a war becomes just when we invoke His name."

Urban paused, looked around the room. "It was the up-timer who stands beside me now"—Larry felt a flush run from his head all the way down to his thighs—"who kept asking this simple question of me, and in doing so, was the voice of those popes who shall never be: 'when did God ever command us to kill for him?' And Cardinal Mazzare was not distracted or deterred from that inquiry when he encountered the sophistries which his down-time brothers attempted to offer as exceptions or caveats. He stuck to that simple question—and so, reopened my heart and eyes to God's Word: not a mystery, but simple exhortations, without need of explication or exegesis."

Urban moved his eyes across the audience. "Instead of instructing us to kill, or persecute, or torture, what did Our Savior teach us? To turn the other cheek. To wash the feet of those society deems our inferiors. To love others as ourselves. To bear in mind that the last shall be first and the first shall be last. And to love one another in honor and imitation of the way God loves us. How can even the most tortuous of exegeses of those teachings extract any validation for an exhortation to kill our neighbor, to persecute him in the name of righteousness, and to torture—torture!—his body so that a recantation of heresy might be extracted by pain?"

Urban lowered and shook his head. "No. These things—these earthly horrors—we must reject." He raised his head; if the liquid shine of his eyes was the result of stagecraft, Mazzare felt himself wholly taken in. He discovered that, once again, he was holding his breath.

Urban's voice may have quavered for one thin moment. "You may doubt my sincerity. I might do no differently in your place. My mortal failings are well enough known to all. But despite that, God chose me to bear the title of Pontifex, of bridge-builder. It has fallen upon me to take up that role meaningfully, to set aside my prior life and embrace this new one, however humbling or terrifying it might be. Because now I perceive the greater terror before us all: that if I cannot convince you to help me build this bridge, then nothing I say will have the power to change the distrust and destruction that has obtained between our communities for over a century.

"Yet, I am only a renegade pope, with nothing more than legitimacy and these friends to help me on this new path. And I understand that you can hardly convince your followers that the Roman Church has truly changed, because so long as it remains under Borja's command, it will become more imperious and inhumane than ever. Until I, or some other who follows me in spirit and conviction, sits upon the *cathedra* once more, how can we spread and enforce the Word, the new canon law, we shall decree here in Besançon?"

It was Menasseh ben Israel who broke the long silence that followed Urban's words. "So, if and when you return to power, you will disband your Inquisitions and your armies?"

Urban sighed. "Those are two very different questions, Rabbi ben Israel. Insofar as the armies are concerned, I would wish that Mother Church need never defend herself from aggression ever again. I also wish that the lion shall one day lie down with the lamb. But this day is not that day, as the growing threat in the Balkans reminds us.

"However, as concerns the Inquisitions"—Larry could not tell whether Urban had shaken his head vigorously or shuddered—"their license to exact confession or recantation through torment shall not stand. Their continuing existence as purely investigatory bodies is likely, for there will always be questions of whether given actions are consistent with, or contrary to, a life in the Church. But torture? Threats? Torch-carrying thugs pulling mothers and fathers from their homes in the night, their children screaming after them?" Urban closed his eyes. "No. That is at an end the moment I am seated in the *cathedra* again. And thanks to the up-time invention of the radio, I may send that word around the globe faster than the winds which gust along its equator."

Cyril Lucaris stood; he glanced shrewdly down the line of cardinals who sat on his side of the great hall. "And if your consistory here does not agree?"

Urban closed his eyes, and a faint smile bent his lips. "Theophilestatos Lucaris, do you honestly believe me so unskilled and naive that I would gather a consistory about which I had doctrinal doubts?"

There were smiles among the cardinals facing Lucaris. A few of the smiles were smug, several were downright wolfish.

And checkmate, thought Larry, who made sure his

expression did not change as a visibly surprised Lucaris reseated himself. Urban had indeed left nothing to chance. He had met with each cardinal individually, shortly after they arrived, to impress upon them the need for the council to work toward a definitively ecumenical proclamation, no matter how vague its wording might be. Anything less would probably mean that Borja and his brutality would define the work and perception of the Church for decades to come. And this was the moment where all that preparation finally paid off: the moment he revealed that his consistory had already accepted the broad outlines he had put before them.

Georg Calixtus rose, a smile on his face. "You see? As I said, this is indeed a new day. Let us greet it and resolve to sow seeds of peace we shall harvest later." He looked around the chamber. "Has everyone asked all the questions in their hearts? May we at last proceed to become acquainted with each other, and even our Catholic peers?"

The murmured assent was not particularly enthusiastic, but it was nearly unanimous.

Von Spee rose as Urban sat, and began presenting the rather formulaic list of thanks that would end with the official opening of the colloquium.

Sharon Nichols leaned over, clearly more than ready to leave. "So, after all that, do you guys have anything left to talk about?"

Larry smiled ruefully. "We haven't even scratched the surface." *But*, he added silently, *at least we are going to talk—and that's half the battle*.

Chapter 20

Although the tunnel was no longer as musty as when they had first uncovered it weeks ago, it was still unpleasantly cramped: two men could barely walk abreast and had to duck their heads while doing so.

Ruy, however, found it less constraining than Owen Roe O'Neill, whose height topped his by almost three inches. Behind them, Finan and three of the Wild Geese followed at a distance. Farther back, the door connecting the tunnel to the Carmelite convent creaked shut. The dim light decreased further, eliciting grumbles.

Ruy smiled. "Your men do not seem to be enjoying the tour, Owen."

"Can't say I blame them. Or feel differently."

Ruy nodded. "Such close quarters do take some getting used to."

"Oh, we're used to them. My lads and I have fought sappers in more than one hole such as this. Not a pleasant experience. Disinclines a man to similar surroundings, you might say."

Ruy, who held the lantern, raised it a bit higher. "I am not unfamiliar with such engagements. But I am glad to learn that your men have fought in such conditions. They will be more prepared, should the need arise here."

Owen ducked his head beneath a support beam. "Not likely to come to that. Assassins would have to know about this tunnel. Then they'd have to take the convent without our knowing and locate the entrance on that side. And, at exactly that same time, we'd have to be entering the tunnel from the palace end, evacuating the pope." He clucked his tongue. "Hard to see all those events lining up, Ruy."

The Catalan smiled. "I allow it is unlikely. But in war, unlikely events become almost routine, no?"

O'Neill's single chuckle came out closer to a grunt. "Now there's truth, plain and simple." He eyed the close walls. "Unless they're armed with pistols similar to our pepperboxes, I think we'd clear a pretty fair path through any assassins who tried to engage us down here. But it would still make for rough footing, having to step over bodies in this tight space."

"Begging the Colonel's pardon, but for us to have a set-to with assassins here would require that someone forgets to lock one of the tunnel's doors, don' it, sir?"

Owen shook his head. "No, McGillicuddy. The tunnel's got to be kept unlatched if we're to be sure to have the use of it in an emergency. Of course, none of the sisters other than the prioress know of it, and so, won't lock it by mistake. And the prioress checks it every morning to make sure that it's still open."

The door on the Palais Granvelle end of the tunnel loomed out of the darkness before them. O'Neill went forward and rapped the simple code.

The door opened, revealing the muzzles of two pepperbox revolvers.

"Fitzgerald, Jeffrey, swing away those pistols; y'can see it's us, right enough," complained Finan from over Ruy's shoulder.

"Can barely make you out at all, Finan. Maybe if you'd be standing on your toes—"

"You've had your foolish fun," Owen muttered gruffly as he exited the tunnel, stifling another round of jibes at the Hibernian radio operator's size. "Seems you eejits have forgotten how handy a smaller man can be in tunnels. And how they usually make better soldiers."

By the time O'Neill had finished chastening his men, Ruy and Finan had emerged into the small cellar just a half flight of stairs down from the palace's music room: one of the areas that they'd closed off in order to restrict the square footage that had to be patrolled by the Wild Geese. Ruy's steady gaze had the desired effect: the men exiting the tunnel stayed close and quiet. "Now that you have seen the passage, you will show it to the others in your units. In small groups. You will do the same when it comes to the evacuation routes we have established from all points where the pope might tarry for any amount of time."

Owen looked up, surprised, but said nothing.

Tone Grogan did, however. "Sir, with all this perambulation yer assignin', well, that's a great deal of time during which our posts will be understaffed."

Ruy nodded. "Quite true. But it is preferable to the alternative: that you walk all the routes in groups of ten or twenty, during which time our defenses would be critically understrength. And in the process, you give our enemies far too much information."

Owen raised his chin. "Colonel Sanchez is right. A few of you out for a stroll won't cause a stir. If the lot of you go out on what looks like a treasure hunt, anyone watching will know it's training, for sure. They'd be fools not to follow you and deduce that we mean these as escape and redeployment routes. And they will plan accordingly. We can't have that. We have to keep them in the dark as much as we can."

Turlough Eubank nodded. "Understood, sirs. We'll keep our pace and behavior as casual as we might."

Owen nodded his appreciation, but added a cautionary note. "That's a fine plan as long as you don't take it too far."

"Sir?"

"Turlough, just let the men *be* casual; don't tell them to *act* as though they are. The balance of them are not great thespians, if you take my meaning."

Turlough smiled. "Taken to heart, sir."

"That's a good lad." O'Neill started to mount the stairs to the palace's main level. "Now get on with the lot of you, and start the next group on the circuit."

Ruy let the group exit, before he brought up the rear slowly. "My apologies, Colonel. I had meant to brief you on the orders for our men to walk the various tactical routes earlier this morning, but last night's activities have disrupted what we planned today. Such as our ten o'clock meeting...which neither of us was able to attend."

Owen nodded as they mounted the stairs. "Damned if I don't share some of my men's concerns, though. I'm not keen on walking the routes in broad daylight. Why not wait for dark, send larger groups, get it done while the pope is in his hermit's cell, behind a triple layer of guards?"

Ruy shrugged. "Because, ultimately, we would draw

even more attention at night. As it is, our men are already moving from one post to another throughout the day, as they relieve each other and relay messages. They have become part of the daily traffic upon the streets of Besançon. A small increase in activity has an excellent chance of going unnoticed.

"But at night? They might not be detected immediately, true, but once they are, they will stand out like bulls in an empty paddock." They had exited the music room and were now in the broad corridor that ran like an artery through the part of the palace designed for public functions: the great hall (which also served as the ballroom), the grand salon, the immense entry hall, and the kitchen and storage areas from which the staff mounted each event. "And if our men become conspicuous, then so will the route they walk. And so our adversary will be able to reason out our contingencies."

Owen was nodding, but his chin was still thrust forward a bit: an expression Ruy had come to identify as signifying a measure of intractability. "Well, that's well-reasoned, but then I wonder: might it be better still if we just have the officers and the sergeants walk it? They'll be the ones seeing to the execution of the different contingencies."

As they descended a short flight of stairs into the entry hall, they looked left to return the salutes of the guards at either side of the wide staircase. Ruy replied once they had turned right to pass through the kitchens. "I deem it insufficient that we only acquaint the commanders with the various routes. For if we have need of any of the escape routes, it means that our primary defenses have been breached and we may have already lost officers. Our units may be disrupted. Under such conditions, there will be no time to organize unrehearsed contingencies." He stopped in front of the door to the servant's section. "So, as the pope's chief of security, I am afraid I must insist upon having all our men walk the routes themselves."

Owen shrugged. "I like prudence in the officers both above me and below me, so you'll not find me complaining. My only concern is that we'll spend the next two days a bit understaffed, with more watches to stand and more posts to man than we've got bodies to go around."

Ruy smiled. "I have an affinity for prudent officers as well, and I appreciate—and share—your misgivings. We simply differ on which is the lesser of two evils."

O'Neill looked at the door leading to the servants' refectory. "Well, neither are so evil as this part of the job."

Ruy cocked one eyebrow high. "You find interviewing the palace staff bothersome?"

O'Neill cast a hand sideways, as if indicating the fault lay with the world at large, not any one specific part of it. "It's this nosing about in people's business that irks me. I'm still a soldier, Ruy; I hope to be until my Maker calls. You've been one, too, and it's a simpler job than this trying to sniff out a rat among the staff. Me? I'd rather this palace be off limits to everyone but our units and the Benedictines from down the street at Notre Dame. Not really a chance of a traitor amongst that lot."

Ruy smiled. "Frankly, I agree with you. But the sensitive palates and aristocratic expectations—not to say pretenses—among many of the attendees make that quite impossible. And only one of pope's inner circle sympathized with our desire to temporarily dismiss the staff and prohibit all other external contact."

"Who? Mazzare?"

Ruy shook his head. "Cardinal Mazzare has largely recused himself to keep the proceedings 'free from up-time influence,' as he put it."

"Then who was it who was willing to do without all the folderol?"

Ruy smiled wider. "Father Vitelleschi."

O'Neill's grin matched Ruy's. "Good on that tough old bird. He's halfway to an ascetic himself, and he'd not be willing to increase risk for the sake of high-born sensibilities."

"That is true enough," Ruy agreed. "Unfortunately, he also lacks the sensibilities of a diplomat, which are sorely needed at this colloquium." Ruy put his hand on the door to the kitchen. "So: have you readied yourself?"

"Let's get it over with."

After meeting and briefly conversing with a seeming infinitude of porters, servers, cooks, butchers, victualers, footmen, and bookkeepers, Ruy was ready to convert to Owen's perspective and seek a place back in the ranks of the tercios—anyone's tercios—just to be freed from interviewing servants and workers. On the one hand, it was blindingly tedious; one lifestory bled into the next like a canvas made up of multiple, sequential watercolors, all painted from the same color. On the other hand, it was persistently unsettling. Ruy knew, from personal experience, what it was like to be at another human being's beck and call. He had started out life that way, had ultimately made his fortune and accrued a title (or at least no one challenged its authenticity), but had wound up a servitor once again at the end, as Bedmar's armsman and confidante. No matter that the service had been extremely profitable, that he had lived nearly as well as his employer, that he had dabbled in the skills and habits of a courtier in his own right. It did not change the simple, inescapable fact that he had not been, in the final analysis, his own man. When Bedmar beckoned, he came; when given an errand, he went. And now, here he was, put in the detestable position of having to dig into the private affairs of persons who were already hostage to the will of others, who got their coin, their bread, their survival, by learning how to bow a little lower, to mumble apologies with a little more deference.

He suspected that Don Owen Roe O'Neill, coming from a nation that existed for centuries under a similar yoke, had the same sensibilities. As they waited for the major domo and his assistant, the senior victualer, to arrive for their interview, Ruy said as much to the colonel.

Owen Roe smiled sadly. "I've spent almost no time in Ireland, but when I have, it's been to hire young cultchies to take foreign coin as mercenaries, as Wild Geese. Who are, you might say, the most trapped of all servitors."

Ruy frowned. "You may sell your sword to any."

Owen Roe's smile became brittle. "That's the theory, but that's not how it works out, my friend. Firstly, none but Infanta Isabella's court treats us as anything other than fodder for enemy cannon. Under every other banner, we're given the dirtiest jobs, which is to say, the ones most likely to cut your life very short. And good luck to the mum or sister back in Ireland to ever see a farthing of the pay you bought with your life."

He shook his head. "So, that leaves most of the young mercenaries of Ireland with one option: to serve under Isabella—and now, Fernando—in the Spanish Lowlands. But doing so means we'll never see our homeland again, except to go and hire more of our young lads away from where they might make trouble for the Sassenach occupiers. Which is the only reason they let the likes of me back home at all... and never for very long."

Ruy found himself at a loss for words of cheer—or words at all, which was a most unaccustomed and uncomfortable feeling. So it was a positive relief when, a mere moment later, Jean LaVey, the major domo, arrived with his spindly second in tow. Ruy had spoken to LaVey before, but that discussion was essentially a pro forma exercise in which the Frenchman recited his bona fides, indicated the various town fathers who would vouch for their authenticity, and gave a general accounting of his actions and whereabouts for the last three months. Throughout, LaVey demonstrated the unctious palaver with which he had secured his rise to major domo; by all accounts, he was markedly better at flattery than organizing a noble's household. But, due to current conditions, and much of the regular staff being off with Duke Bernhard and about to commence campaigning, he had been given additional powers and further trust with the keys and other means of access to the valuables in the house. Upon hearing this, O'Neill began questioning him in earnest, and far more closely. Several times, LaVey glanced toward Ruy, as if seeking deliverance or at least some measure of intercession. Ruy only smiled.

Throughout the ebb and flow of the interview, LaVey's assistant sat in a farther chair, watching with the fatalistic fascination of a cornered mouse witnessing a cat tearing apart one of his rodent kin. When O'Neill asked his final question—"And does anyone else have the same kind of access to the house and its contents?"—and LaVey gestured at his spindly assistant, that spare man seemed ready to jump out of his skin, so profoundly did he start.

O'Neill turned toward the suddenly terrified assistant to the major domo. "You: what's your name?"

"Claude. Claude Delgado, Your Excellency."

O'Neill raised an eyebrow. "Monsieur Delgado, is it? Hmmm . . . Spanish name, that."

Claude blinked several times before he was aware that a reply was expected of him. "Yes, sir, Spanish, sir. A common name here in town. *Besontsins* all of us, after the family moved from Barcelona about a century ago."

"And since then, *bousbots*, every one of them," the major domo added dismissively.

"*Bousbots*?" echoed O'Neill. "'Toad shooters'?"

Ruy sat forward. "The local term for inhabitants of the Battant. From the Protestant campaign against the city in the 1570s; the Catholic winemakers who lived over the Doub, near the vineyards, impaled a horde of toads on small stakes as a warning to the Reformationists. It was not effective; battle was joined even so."

LaVey was nodding. "And once a *bousbot*, always a *bousbot*, eh, Claude?"

Claude nodded nervously, unwillingly, looking as if he might somehow fold into himself and disappear.

Ruy did not know what he found more irritating: LaVey's superciliousness or Claude's cowed timidity. He leaned forward toward the latter. "Well, you know why we are here, Monsieur Delgado. We wish to know your activities and whereabouts for the past few months."

Delgado simply stared at him, looking as if he might soil himself any moment.

"Your superior says you have access equal to his. Is this true?"

Delgado's head wobbled in what could have been either a shake or a nod.

Ruy felt himself on the verge of losing composure; he decided to see how Delgado would react, what he might reveal. "Well, man, speak up: what do you have to say for yourself?"

"N-nothing, my lords," Claude almost whined. "I am innocent!"

"Of what?"

"Of . . . of whatever crime you are investigating!"

"And why do you think we are investigating a crime?"

"What else, with such seriousness? And with weapons at hand?" He glanced nervously at their belts. O'Neill leaned back in but started asking simpler, more finite questions in a quiet tone.

Ruy almost rolled his eyes. *So, once again, we play what my peerless Sharon would call "good cop, bad cop."* Although this time Ruy felt as though he needed to wash off; whether from LaVey's obsequious attempts at familiarity or Claude's trembling cowardice, he could not say.

O'Neill managed to get the bare facts out of the

still quivering Delgado quietly and quickly. Ruy and the Irishman exchanged glances, then shrugs. Delgado's life sounded about as uninteresting and narrow as any human could conceivably endure. It felt wrong to have made him testify to the particulars of it, as if it were somehow akin to a public shaming.

"Very well," announced Ruy, rising. "We are done for the day. If we have further questions, we shall seek you out."

LaVey's protestations of fulsome cooperation were the counterpoint to Delgado's trembling stillness.

No sooner had the door back into kitchen closed behind them, than LaVey came out upon their heels. "I must say, sirs, that Monsieur Delgado is a disturbing man, at times. Yes, I must say that."

You must *say it?* Ruy thought as O'Neill asked, "Disturbing in what way?"

LaVey seemed momentarily flustered, as if his assertion hardly needed explication. "Well, because he keeps very much to himself. Too much. If you take my meaning."

Ruy stopped, turned to face LaVey. "I'm afraid I don't take your meaning. Please make it more clear."

LaVey halted so suddenly that he almost tripped over his own feet. "Delgado is . . . well, he is unwilling to socialize with the rest of us." He leaned closer, his voice lower. "And it is said he has . . . untoward affairs."

"Untoward? You mean, of a criminal nature?"

LaVey blinked, surprised. "Well, no . . . but maybe?"

Ruy knew a reaching tone, an attempt to seem important, when he heard one. "We will keep an eye on him." *And even more on you, LaVey, since you seem so eager to implicate your coworker.*

Ruy turned and strode quickly toward the doorway
that led back to the entry hall and, beyond that, to
fresh air.

O'Neill was pacing him. There was a slight smile
on his face. "So, I'm guessing we're done here?"

"Very much so," Ruy breathed. "Let us get outside.
Quickly."

Chapter 21

As they descended the steps of the Palais Granvelle, Ruy peered up at the sun. He had about an hour before reviewing the watchposts and then receiving the investigatory update on the fellow they had found murdered in the alley the night before. Enough time for his intent, then. Ruy set off toward the Carmelite convent, just across the street.

"Half a second, Sanchez," O'Neill called from behind him. "We've the circuit to walk."

"There's something we must do first, Owen." Over O'Neill's unusually square shoulder, Ruy saw one of the double doors of the Palais Grenville open; Sharon stepped out into the sun, blinking down at them.

"Well, gentlemen, out for a stroll?"

"Nothing would please me more, my heart of hearts, but alas, we are still on business."

"On mysterious business," added O'Neill. "Well, mysterious for me."

Sharon smiled. "Well, I do love a good mystery."

Ruy raised an exasperated eyebrow. "I should think the one you already have is sufficiently absorbing, my dear."

"I'm an overachiever. Now, demystify the new mystery, Ruy."

He shrugged. "Owen exaggerates at my expense. There is no mystery; there is only something I did not have time to explain to him before you distracted me with your riveting presence."

"Nice try, Ruy. 'Splain."

Ruy sighed. "The 'mystery,' as you would style it, is that I believe we must visit the Carmelites yet again. Specifically, Prioress Thérèse."

O'Neill was frowning. "Why?"

Ruy shrugged. "Because I am not sure the questions I have put to her thus far are either far-reaching or specific enough."

"You mean about the escape tunnel that links the convent and the palace?" Sharon asked. She suddenly seemed as energized as if she had had two cups of coffee.

"Not exactly," Ruy explained. "On reflection, there may also be tunnels that we have overlooked."

Sharon frowned. "You think the prioress would intentionally withhold that kind of information?"

Ruy shrugged. "I do not think so, but I cannot be sure. Furthermore, she might have heard rumors to which she gives no credence, but might be of keen interest to us."

Sharon edged closer. Which made Ruy very happy. "What kind of rumors?"

He was so fixated on his wife that he forgot to answer for one very long, very embarrassing second. "Firstly, when we arrived, you may remember I had several very long conversations with Archbishop de Rye. Not only has he been in Besançon his entire life, but he takes pride in being the city's de facto historian. And, having been archbishop for forty-nine years now, he has had direct access to information which is often sealed to others.

"Among the most intriguing details he shared with me is how much of Le Boucle is built upon earlier ruins. Consequently, tunnels and connections were often not so much mined as they were cunning connections between buried buildings and basements, shored up to be serviceable."

Sharon looked at the ground between her feet. "So we could be standing right over a labyrinth of old passages."

Ruy nodded. "As is the case with St. John's and the cloister. So I must ask the prioress if she knows, or has heard rumors, of such tunnels and chambers under the convent."

"What about Palais Granvelle itself?" asked Owen.

Ruy shook his head. "Construction commenced in 1534, concluded in 1547, and the process began with a specially excavated foundation for basements and cellars. So the only connection between it and any other building is the one which was put in earlier this century, to the building which occupied the ground that the convent does today."

Sharon frowned. "So if they knocked that earlier building down, how is it that the tunnel still connects them?"

"That is where this morning's brief conversation with the prioress became most intriguing. Just before she closed the tunnel door behind us, she remarked that the convent is not, in fact, an entirely new construction. A considerable part of it was retained from the original, older building which was refurbished, altered, and expanded. And as we learned this morning, the part which connected it to the palace tunnel was purposefully left intact. However, the parts of the convent that are even older could still be connected to other buildings by preextant tunnels and partially collapsed rooms of buried buildings."

O'Neill put a palm to his forehead. "So our secure fallback position for the pope—the Carmelite convent— might not be so secure, after all. And it's sure as grass is green that the prioress isn't going to let us go poking around every room looking for hidden passages."

Ruy shook his head. "Nor do we have the time or the manpower to do so now. So we must make appropriate inquiries of the prioress. If she has never heard such rumors regarding the convent, then it may indeed be secure. On the other hand, if she believes there may be other connections, we must reassess our plans."

"You mean, not use the tunnel as an emergency escape passage?" For the first time, Sharon sounded more worried than intrigued.

"No, my love; we cannot afford to wholly reject that option. But whereas we believed that the pope would be secure once within the convent, we can no longer assume that. He will require a much stronger guard contingent to accompany him there, and we must anticipate the need to evacuate him from the convent itself shortly after he arrives."

Once again, the palace's doors opened. Lieutenant Hastings, senior officer of the Hibernians, and his shortest trooper, Finan, strode out, caught sight of the group and moved quickly in their direction.

Ruy suppressed a sigh: *will we never get across this street?* But what he said was: "Lieutenant, I trust all is well?"

Hastings remained as impassive as ever. "I hope so, sir. Finan?"

The Irishman—ironically, the only one among the rank-and-file Hibernians—nodded and turned toward Sharon. "Ma'am, it might be nothing but—"

"Go ahead," Sharon ordered. She and Ruy had come to know Finan well enough to implicitly trust not only his discretion, but his instincts.

"We're picking up extra radio traffic in town. And if Odo is right, lots of it."

Ruy stepped closer. "Explain."

"Yes, sir. You're familiar with our basic activity: comm check all stations twice a day, one coded transmission to Grantville, usually one in reply. Anything above that is a matter of tactical urgency."

"Yes, yes," Ruy agreed, although he hadn't been the one to set up the radio protocols. That had been Grantville's new Mallorcan intelligence chief, Miro.

"Well, sir, over the past few days, the ambassador's radioman Odo has picked up a couple of other transmissions that we believe are originating either from within Besançon or very nearby."

"Could it be radio traffic from airships?" Sharon asked.

Finan shook his head. "That's what we thought at first, ma'am, particularly since the blimp that brought Cardinal Bedmar only departed yesterday. But in the last twenty-four hours, the rate of traffic has increased and the signal has been strong enough that Odo has heard and recorded long messages. Except those messages aren't from any of our stations or airships and they're in a code we don't know."

Ruy heard the lack of conclusion in Finan's tone. "What more?"

"Odo thinks that some of the intermittent traffic we've heard before now may have been in the same code. He had presumed that most of the signals didn't make sense because they were coming from a great distance and were either fragmentary or unclear. Now, he's half convinced that what he heard were snippets of a completely different set of code characters."

Owen turned toward Sharon, also frowning. "Is there any chance that your friends in Grantville have devised new codes for special purposes. For signaling among the airships, for instance?"

Finan looked at her and shook his head; Sharon gestured for him to speak. "The airships communicate without code, sir—what radio operators call, 'in the clear.' The reason being, if they run into trouble and only get to send a fraction of a message, there's no time lost trying to determine which code it is. And with respect sir, although we Hibernians are not officially soldiers of the USE, we'd be among the first to know if there was a new cypher being used for intelligence or special operations—because it's likely some of our lads would be involved."

Ruy glanced at Sharon. "What is to be done? How may we determine the source of the transmissions? How shall we decipher their code—or codes?"

Sharon nodded, thought for a moment before looking up sharply at Hastings. "Lieutenant, I'm going to need access to both of your portable ratio sets—with fresh batteries—at all times."

"Ma'am, I don't have enough men to keep recharging the—"

"Then get one of the Benedictine monks or a
trustworthy *besontsint* to turn the cranks or pedal the
machine or however it is you recharge your batteries.
But I need mobile radio support, twenty-four/seven,
do you understand?"

Hastings glanced at Ruy, who raised his eyebrows
in reply. Hastings sighed. "Yes, ma'am. Right away."

She turned to Finan. "I need you to keep in touch
with Odo."

Finan frowned. "Ma'am, that will drain the batteries very quic—"

"I am aware of the battery drain. That's why we're
going to have someone constantly recharging them.
But the only way we're going to find the location and
identity of the person transmitting in this code is if
you are available to coordinate with Odo the next
time he detects one of these bursts of radio activity."

Ruy leaned towards his wife. "I do not understand,
my love: how will two radios help?"

Sharon smiled. "There's a game played by radio
enthusiasts: 'fox and hounds,' I think it was called.
The fox is the transmitter and sends short, occasional signals. The 'hounds' are the receivers, who
triangulate on the position of the fox by determining
the directionality and the strength of the signal it's
sending. The object is to close in on and find the fox,
wherever it's hiding."

"And so—?"

Sharon's smiled widened. "And so, Odo is at a fixed
radio set. He doesn't have the same power supply worries. He can keep actively scanning the dial for radio

transmissions, assuming the unknown transmitter—our 'fox'—isn't always using the same frequency. When he detects it, he alerts Finan, who will then tune his radio to the 'fox's' frequency and, along with the other mobile radio operator, will try to close in on it."

Finan's question was as much confused babble as it was speech. "H-how...how the fe—how the divil am I supposed to do *that*?"

Sharon turned her winning smile upon him. "Well, finding that out is job one. Have Odo send a high priority message to Grantville: we need all the info they can scrape together about 'fox and hounds.' If I recall correctly, some of the folks there have actually played it."

Hastings nodded. "Another question, Finan: did Odo keep records of those unusual intercepts?"

"Don't know, sir."

"Well, find out. If he did, he's to relay them to Grantville at once, routed to Mr. Miro."

Sharon shook her head. "I don't know if it's the right term for the army, but 'belay that order, Mr. Finan.'" She met Hastings' stare. "Think it through, Lieutenant. If we know to listen to them, it stands to reason they know to listen to us. And if they do, and they hear snippets of their own code embedded in our transmission—"

"Then they know we're on to them."

"And will change their code," finished Owen admiringly. "Ambassador, if I haven't said it before, I'm glad you're on our side!" He winked at Ruy. "Well, I guess we know who's the brains in *your* family, eh?"

Ruy smiled, taking in the radiance that was Sharon. "I have always said so, and now you see for yourself that it is not an exaggeration."

Hastings snapped a salute. "Sirs, madame, I presume I'm no longer needed. Any orders to pass along, sirs?"

Ruy shook his head, but O'Neill spoke up. "Word to my men and yours, Lieutenant: all evening liberty is suspended until Monday, earliest. Officers of the watch need to be made aware that there will be no leaving billets on private matters, any hour of the day or night."

Hastings looked worried. "Sir, with all due respect, a flagon or a pint of an evening is all the men have to look forward to."

O'Neill nodded sourly. "Yes, and a wee bit of tickle and peck with unwilling barmaids, unless life in the army has improved its moral character in the last few days. So the consolation must be that the good fathers of the canon house will provide extra wine in reasonable measure for as long as the men are to remain in their billet when not on duty. We can't afford to have them on the town, talking about where they've been strolling of late, can we?"

Ruy nodded slowly. "I appreciate your precaution, Colonel. Hastings, add this to Colonel O'Neill's orders. Until Monday, any man discovered fraternizing with locals in any fashion, in any place, will be subject to military discipline."

"The lash, sir?" asked Hastings.

Ruy shook his head. "Better they don't know; it puts more fear in them."

Hastings' smile was small but genuine. "That it does, sir. I shall pass on your orders, sir."

Ruy and O'Neill saluted; Sharon turned to look at them. "Ruy. Lashes? Really?"

Ruy could not cover his puzzlement fast enough

to keep his eyebrows from raising. "Yes, of course, my dear." Seeing her surprise contract into anger, he suddenly wished that O'Neill and Finan were far, far away. "My love, I do not understand your consternation. Surely, you are familiar with the habits of military discipline."

"Yes—of *civilized* military discipline. Not torture." She turned to Finan. "Let's go see if there's any news about the identity of the murder victim."

Ruy stood looking after her; O'Neill stood looking at him. "She's a—a woman of strong convictions," the Irish nobleman muttered after several moments.

Ruy could not help but smile. "She is all that and more, my friend." He put a hand on O'Neill's shoulder, turning them both in the direction of the Carmelite convent. "Come, then; let us pay a visit to the prioress."

Chapter 22

Mulling over which apple he might have bought, had he intended to purchase any at all, Pedro Dolor watched the gathering of his enemies at the base of the Palais Granvelle's stairs break up after an urgent discussion... about what?

Dressed in local garb and a dirty workman's smock, Dolor noticed the impatient produce vendor, who started to roll his eyes at the indecision of his only potential customer. However, noticing that customer's direct and unblinking gaze, he apparently decided it was much more important to rearrange the asparagus that had just come in from the countryside beyond the Battant.

Dolor felt a pang of frustration as Sharon Nichols went one direction with a small Hibernian—the one who usually bore a portable radio—Hastings went back up the stairs toward the palace's wide doorway, and Sanchez and O'Neill resumed crossing the street. A pity, he thought. All gathered together in one place, at one time. Had he been able to anticipate their chance meeting, and place a hand-cart with a bomb nearby, he could have killed or at least incapacitated the opposition's security cadre and the USE's ambassador, all in one fell swoop. Of course, that would not necessarily have translated into a successful attack upon the pope, but in the ensuing chaos of such a loss, there would have been sure to be miscommunications and mistakes that he could have capitalized upon...

Dolor backed away from the apples; enough daydreaming about what might have been. He had been lucky enough to see the five of them gathered together as he emerged from the cellar he rented in a nearby building. The urgency of their discussion suggested that they were dealing with an unexpected development of some kind. He watched as Sanchez and O'Neill walked past the fountain of Neptune, the god nude and astride a dolphin—a rather provocative statue to leave embedded in the facade of a convent—and then as they passed quickly into that same building. According to his reports, they had already visited it: Sanchez on his own several months ago, and the pair of them again early last week. And now they were entering it again, with a marked sense of purpose.

Perhaps when he returned to his rooms near St. Peter's, there would be news that might hint at the source of his foes' sense of urgency—and therefore, furnish some intimation of how he might take advantage of it.

Upon entering the second story apartment that had been his home for the better part of three months, Dolor didn't even have time to ask if there was any interesting to report: Rombaldo fairly charged from where he was hovering over their radio. "There is news!" he almost shouted.

"I gather as much. And you may lower your voice. I am in the same room, not down the street."

"Yes, yes . . . but this is urgent. I almost sent a runner after you but . . ."

"You did well not to, as per my instructions." Dolor made for his own room. "If anyone was to stumble upon our preparations by following one of our less gifted associates, we should be lost."

"Yes, but this *does* bear upon our preparations—or at least those of Borja's thugs."

Dolor seated himself. "Indeed? Have they been found out?"

"No, but they could be." Although they were now in a separate room, Rombaldo inexplicably chose this moment to lower his voice. "They killed their landlord."

Dolor came as close to laughing as he ever did. "You jest."

"Do I ever?" Actually, Rombaldo did jest, albeit rarely.

"When did the murder come to light?"

"Depends who you ask. It just became general knowledge within the hour. But there were rumors making the rounds on the docks this morning."

"And how did those rumors start?"

"Apparently, one of our informers saw some of the Wild Geese carrying a body through the side entrance of St. Peter's."

Dolor sat up. "The Wild Geese? How many? Was anyone with them?"

"A few, but one stood out: the ambassadora."

Dolor nodded. So that might explain the hasty and unprecedented gathering he had noticed outside the palace: a quick conference on the state of the investigation into the body they had found. Which they might have identified either shortly before or after they dispersed, since the word was already spreading. It also explained why Sanchez and O'Neill had been late to begin the morning circuit of their watchposts. The discovery of the body had no doubt turned them out of bed early, and the subsequent investigation had probably run roughshod over their normal itinerary.

But the ambassador . . . Why had she been called out into the predawn streets? The answer came as quickly as the question: perhaps the victim had still been alive when discovered. Or perhaps her medical background might offer some insight into how he had been attacked. Or maybe they had reason to hope that her insights might be more astute, more precise, than that . . .

A thin thread of memory tickled Dolor. He vaguely recalled that there had been an oddity in the dossier he had compiled on Sharon Nichols, a fact that eluded him now, except that he felt sure it was anomalous and yet somehow relevant. But what was it? One way to find out: "Rombaldo, I need you to send a radio message to my confidential agent in Madrid."

"The one in Olivares' office?"

"He does not report directly to Olivares, nor is he in the same office, although he is part of the count-duke's intelligence apparatus." In fact, he was nothing more than a glorified file clerk, but one who was very propitiously placed. "Once you have contacted him, send him this message." Dolor hastily scratched out a request and handed it to Rombaldo.

Who looked at it quizzically. "I do not recognize this code."

"You are not meant to. Just enter it as written. And wait for a reply. When you have finished that, send Giulio out to observe and gather what further rumors are spreading on the street."

Rombaldo frowned, then shrugged and shuffled off glumly to do as he was bid. Dolor almost closed his eyes in frustration; the man touted himself as a "professional intelligencer" but, when shut out of confidences, occasionally sulked like a schoolboy. A very spoiled schoolboy, at that.

Behind, Dolor heard the faint hiss of the radio being activated. "Rombaldo, is there any speculation where the murder took place?"

"Word is the body—Baudet Lamy—was found up against the wall of the *Trois Frères* tavern."

Dolor shook his head. "No. That was not where he was killed."

Rombaldo started tapping out his request, which he would repeat until the radio operator in Spain signaled that the message had been received in full. "Why are you so certain the body was moved?"

"Because we have observed Borja's men. They almost never go out, except to get their food. We've never once seen them visit a tavern or a brothel."

"Damned dull, if you ask me." Rombaldo's voice suggested that he sympathized; it wasn't too different from the discipline that Dolor had imposed upon their own group.

"Dull but prudent, Rombaldo. Because they were not often seen, there will be few people who will remember their faces. But now that the corpse has been identified, it will only be a matter of time before they are visited by soldiers, or the Wild Geese."

Rombaldo took a second to respond. "That's only if they suspect that he wasn't killed in the street."

Dolor took out the three blades he routinely carried—a poignard, a throwing knife, and a razor-edged stiletto—and considered which he should sharpen and clean first. "They will certainly suspect that he was not killed there."

Rombaldo's reply was immediate, intrigued. "Why do you say so?"

Dolor shook his head. "Just listen for a reply from Madrid. We may not have much time to save this operation."

Twenty minutes later, the radio started chattering in response to Dolor's query. Rombaldo had to listen to three full iterations of the message until he could confidently send the cypher that indicated the transmission had been received in full.

Rombaldo's heavy tread approached from behind. "Yet another code that I don't recognize."

Dolor turned and took the transcription from his assistant. "That's excellent news."

"Why?"

"Because it is a code of my own design, and to my knowledge, it has not yet been cracked." *Of course, for all I know, no one has yet tried.*

Rombaldo remained standing as Dolor began to skim the contents of the message. "What's the use of having a code that no other person understands?"

Dolor did not look up. "A promising intelligencer ought to be able to reason that out."

In fact, a decidedly mediocre one should have been able to arrive at the answer. Despite a prodigious memory, Dolor had always found it irksome when, in the course of an operation, he had need of information that he could no longer recall. On several occasions, that failure had cost lives—and very nearly his own, once. So he had retained a clerk in Olivares' bloated intelligence-gathering apparatus to maintain a separate set of files, to which Dolor weekly sent a considerable volume of data. In the early days, organizing it for easy retrieval had been challenging, but then, in the process of arranging for an intelligence pipeline from inside the Grantville High School library, he had happened upon what was, to his mind, one of the most extraordinary and useful innovations that had come back into the past with the up-timers: the Dewey decimal system.

He adopted its orderly organization of ideas by topic and source to his own purposes and so, by memorizing only that data directory, he was able to both submit coded updates to his archive and call reports from it with ease. And, since only he understood the encoding, his proprietary information was doubly safe: a tiny and indecipherable needle lost in the vast haystack that was the sum total of Olivares' intelligence files.

Dolor was so familiar with his own cypher that he did not need to decode it; he read it with the facility of a familiar second language. He skipped the biographical summary of Sharon Nichols, as well as the chronology of her movement and actions: he was already well-acquainted with those particulars. Instead, he concentrated on the footnotes, seeking the entry that might have created the shard of memory that refused to either dissolve or resolve into something definitive.

The luxury of having dossiers on his probable opponents was something he had long wanted, and had finally been able to actualize after last year's dual debacles in Molino and Mallorca. Dolor had made a compelling case that lack of detailed information on the up-timers had been why they had repeatedly surprised Philip's best troops and intelligencers over the last two years, and had thwarted almost all attempts at preemption, prediction, or containment. Dolor had also proposed a simple solution: suborn a person who worked in Grantville and have them collect all available information on a list of particular topics or persons. Olivares was ambivalent, objecting that if the up-timers' counterintelligence service detected this ploy, they could use it to feed Madrid disinformation. Dolor had shaken his head, clarifying that he did not propose overtly recruiting an agent for Spain. Rather his approach was to solicit the person's services on behalf of an anonymous consortium of merchants who wanted a detailed understanding of the present and future needs of the phenomenal community, so that they might anticipate and thus dominate trade with its unusual and influential population as time went on. The data collected for this purpose would then be picked up by a wholly uninvolved (but surreptitiously shadowed) courier who would deliver it to actual Spanish agents who would, in turn, radio it back to Madrid.

Olivares was delighted by this strategy of using what the up-timers called a "cut-out," so that the person gathering the information was wholly misled as to why they were being tasked to do so. He approved the operation and then promptly forgot about it.

Several months after it had been running, Dolor added a further dimension to it, explaining to the source in Grantville that several of the firms in the consortium had come to feel that it would be advantageous to monitor the tastes and interests of one hundred of Grantville's leading citizens. It stood to reason, after all, that as Europe continued to explore all things up-time, there would be an increasing interest in the pastimes and preferences of the community's leading figures. Fashion always followed the famous, after all. So it would be very worthwhile if the data gatherer could perhaps contact a friend or acquaintance in Grantville's library to learn the reading lists of the town's leading personalities—for a reasonable fee, of course.

Within three weeks, Dolor's enterprising and highly motivated data-gatherer had located a willing library worker. The level of illegality involved was insignificant compared to most down-time crimes, and the reward was evidently made sweeter by the thrill of imagining oneself involved in trend setting.

From there, it was a simple step to determine all the books that had been bought, loaned, or leased to copy, either from the reprint publishers, the library, or private collections. Tastes and trends among both buyers and borrowers were self-evident, particularly among those who were devotees of some particular topic.

Dolor was quite certain that Sharon had been just such a devotee; he remembered her spending considerable sums to collect the reprints of a certain category of book. But he could not recall precisely what that category was. But ultimately, he found the footnote he was searching for on the last page of her dossier.

Sharon Nichols, having been a visitor to Grantville,

had only the scant possessions she was carrying in her luggage when the town made its fateful transition backward in time. Consequently, while she and her father set about acquiring the necessities of life in their new community, they resorted to withdrawing books from the library for their entertainment. And Sharon's loan record, along with her subsequent reprint purchases, combined to reveal a secret passion:

Forensics. She had taken out every mystery novel that focused on what the up-timers called a medical examiner, as well as several nonfiction books on the topic. She had apparently devoured the five available books in what was called the "Kay Scarpetta" series as soon as the library's services normalized. She then read similar novels, all of which featured titles comprised of contorted, even tortured, metaphors and idioms, such as *Déjà Dead*. To their discredit, even factual books followed this trend toward unintentional self-parody, one of the more memorable being *Unnatural Death: Confessions of a Medical Examiner*. It never failed to strike Dolor how, although the up-time world had been a place of extraordinary plenty, it had become wretchedly impoverished in matters of refinement and taste.

Dolor put down the dossier and spoke loud enough for Rombaldo to hear. "The ambassador is not merely a doctor. She has studied what the up-timers call forensics."

"What is that?"

"The study of how best to examine bodies and crime scenes to find evidence that reveals the identities of murderers."

Rombaldo sat down across from Dolor. "That sounds worrisome."

"It would be disastrous if she had access to even ten percent of the technology used in their up-time investigations. Happily, she does not."

"Still, you seem concerned."

"I am. Even without that technology, she has imbibed a method of investigation which could prove dangerous to us. In addition to examining bodies to determine how and when crimes were performed, she is accustomed to looking for patterns in events. So you may be sure that she is quite aware that Lamy was not killed in the street in the middle of the night. You may also be sure that she shall quickly attempt to reconstruct how he spent the hours of his last day and where he might have been when he died."

Rombaldo swallowed. "She will visit all his properties."

Dolor nodded. "Among the other routine stops he might make. However, most murders are committed by a person who knows the victim; her method will compel her to start there. Then, it is largely a matter of chance how she prioritizes the list of sites at which he may have been killed. A landlord contracts many services, and Lamy owned three widely separated properties. Nichols, or rather, those persons she can recruit as investigators, will not be able to visit them all this day. But they certainly will have by the end of tomorrow."

"Then what are we to do? Accept Borja's men as already dead?" Rombaldo sounded as though that alternative pleased him.

Dolor shook his head. "We cannot. We haven't the numbers to be certain of assassinating the pope on our own. We need Borja's men to drive him into our trap. So we must preserve them."

"If we are lucky, that is."

"No: if we are smart. Here is what must be done. Laurin must go to the butcher's and get several pints of beef blood—"

"What? Just like that?"

Dolor stared at Rombaldo, who looked away quickly. "Your tone wants correction. Laurin will get the blood for making blutwurst. He will take it to whichever of Lamy's properties is furthest from the one occupied by Borja's men. He is to spatter drops on the stairs, leave a large stain on the path out to the privy, then smear it as though something was dragged through it."

Rombaldo nodded. "To keep them busy."

"Yes. I suspect that they will not be distracted by that lure for long. But once seen and reported to the investigators, it will fix activity on that site, at least until the ambassadora sees it personally. By that time, it should be dark."

"But what good is that? They'll continue looking." Rombaldo saw Dolor's look. "No?"

"No. Firstly, if they go around this city knocking on doors and conducting searches throughout the night, that will both annoy and frighten the tenants at every one of Lamy's properties. That kind of disturbance could create a panic at the very moment when Urban and his allies most want calm and confidence.

"Secondly, I do not believe Sanchez and O'Neill would agree to dedicate their own security forces to this search. They are spread thin enough as it is, and if they are active all through the night, they will not be effective come daylight. So it is likely that Bernhard's soldiers, or even the watch, will be given this duty. And they will not be eager or effective in carrying out this task in daylight, even less so in the dark. If they have not found Borja's men by dusk today, I believe they will not resume the search until tomorrow morning."

Rombaldo shrugged. "And that is very fine, but then what? If, as you seem to suspect, Borja's men killed their landlord in their own flat—the morons—then they will be found some time tomorrow, will no doubt panic, and ultimately be slain. Of course, they might drop a message for the fop tonight, who might then update his master immediately, but that could have the same effect, in the long run. Who knows what outrageous orders Borja may give them?"

Dolor rose. "All true. And so our focus must be on what we need to accomplish next, not on what we fear could occur. And we have two distinct objectives. Firstly, we must relocate Borja's men. This requires ensuring that there are other lodgings that they may flee to, and then making them aware of that fact."

"Easier said than done. There's not a room to be had for miles."

Dolor ignored Rombaldo's remark. "Secondly, we must ensure that they are not given orders which will cause them to reveal themselves or strike before the time is right."

Rombaldo considered that for a long second. "I don't see how that is something we could gain control over."

"Happily, Borja himself has provided us with an answer to that quandary, as well as a solution to the problem of relocating his men."

Rombaldo simply shook his head. "Because you say so, I'll believe it. But I cannot foresee how it could be done." He rubbed his hands together. "There is potentially a more—direct approach."

"Which is?"

"Recruit some locals and assassinate Urban our-selves. We could find half a dozen among the riverboat smugglers, at least."

"And how would you secure their loyalty? And how would you craft a plan that would not obviously use them as cannon fodder—a job which no amount of pay will entice a man to take? But even those are not the most urgent reasons against such a scheme. There is the matter of accountability." He leaned forward. "We need to kill the pope, yes, but the bloody dagger must be directly and unequivocally traceable to Borja's own hand. If his assassins are neutralized before they may strike, how are we to achieve that?"

Rombaldo shrugged. "I never have liked that part of this job. It's hard enough to kill a pope; it's damn near impossible to make sure that someone else takes the blame."

"It is difficult, but not impossible." *But while on the topic of who shall take the blame . . .* "You have observed Borja's men more than any of us. Do you recall if any of them are left-handed?"

Rombaldo started at the sudden change in topic. "No, not to my knowledge."

Then, for the time being, I shall be. Every once in a while, ambidexterity proved to be an advantage in Dolor's line of work.

"Why is it important if any of them are left-handed?" Rombaldo asked.

"Tactical considerations." Dolor lied. "No detail is too small to consider. As you say, this is a very dif-ficult job, made more so by the two prior attempts that have failed. Each time, our opponents learned from the mistakes that almost cost Urban his life. Each time, therefore, we were the whetstone upon which they have sharpened their abilities. Today, I watched them walk what I presume to be multiple escape routes."

"Then we have them, if they try that."

"Do we? They have marksmen with repeating rifles in all the bell towers. And they will never move Urban in such a way that he can be immediately be picked out: there will be decoys, or shrouded conveyances such as the sedan chairs. Our hope lies in surprising them again and again so that all their fine planning breaks down. Then, and only then, will we have a clear opportunity to complete our mission."

Dolor reached into his traveling chest, pulled out a long dark cloak that was not entirely dissimilar from the kind worn by lesser officers of the watch, and laid it across the bed.

Rombaldo stared at it. "You are leaving?"

"Yes, to capitalize upon the solution Borja has put before us. Which requires that I must be in the Battant and back again before the bridge closes for the night."

Chapter 23

Pedro Dolor had visited *L'Auberge de Boucle d'Argent* before, careful to do so when Javier de Requesens y Ercilla was out on one of his drop-gathering constitutionals. So he had had ample prior opportunity to examine the latches and locks on those doors that had them. De Requesens' suite of rooms on the top floor had a better lock than most, but it was easily bypassed. Dolor wondered why a throw-bolt had not been installed; de Requesens had certainly paid a high enough rate, and for long enough, to exert that kind of leverage over the owner. But the Spanish dandy had not done so, probably telling himself that doing so would only attract undue attention. Such were the mistakes of amateurs.

Dolor eased the door open a crack. Requesens was sitting near the window, angled so that he could take in the view. More amateurism. A professional stayed away from windows and would at least have hung a bell on the door when engaged in any activity that was significantly distracting. Instead, the young Spaniard was finishing his meal while reading what was either a book or a code manual: Dolor could not tell from the distance.

He waited until Requesens lifted another forkful of food to his mouth and started chewing, then slipped in sideways, moving swiftly to put himself more directly behind the dandy. As the fellow continued to eat and read, Dolor shifted more attention to his peripheral vision: no weapon near the oblivious Spaniard's hand, nor anywhere else in the room. The radio was also located near the window, and a wire ran from it to the opposite wall, up to a rafter, and out under the eaves: an aerial. There was a strongbox against the far wall, which probably held the records of prior communications and a variety of codebooks. The room was relatively tidy, and not just because a menial came in to clean every day. Requesens' books and clothes were arranged with angular care: the longest plane of every object was either parallel or perpendicular to all the others.

When it became evident that the young "intelligencer" was not going to scan his surroundings or otherwise detect Dolor's presence, Pedro cleared his throat softly.

Requesens paused in his thorough chewing, looked up, tilted his head as if listening more carefully—and then tucked into his meal again.

Dolor suppressed a sigh; he cleared his throat more loudly.

Javier started, glanced left, then right, then turned— and, seeing Dolor at last, uttered a gasp that rapidly turned into a throaty cough. A half-masticated chunk of pheasant flew out of his mouth and hit the floor with a wet splat. "Who are you? How did you get in?"

Dolor nodded a greeting. "A gentleman in the service of Spain should take greater care to remain watchful. I would recommend you take your meals facing but not in line with the door, and with a weapon at hand. It would also be better to do so away from the window."

Requesens sputtered out what sounded like the beginning of a question, then another, then just swallowed. He stepped back, fetched up against the edge of the table. That seemed to restart his paralyzed brain. "What do you mean, 'a gentleman in the service of Spain?' I am Spanish, yes, but am merely a commercial factor, providing market and other information for various clients."

Dolor shook his head. "You are Javier de Requesens y Ercilla and you are kept here by Count-Duke Olivares. Although you do have other clients, that is true."

De Requesens swallowed again, this time audibly. He scanned Dolor's cloak carefully. "You are not from the watch."

"I am not. I am sent by a common friend. One with whom you have just recently established contact, here in the Buckle."

It took Javier a moment to parse out the exact meaning of Dolor's carefully oblique statement. "You—you are from the other contact, the other handler."

Dolor nodded. "I am. But you should have made me work harder before you uttered the words yourself. I could have been from the other side, a counter intelligence agent, making an educated guess, seeing if I could get you to implicate yourself. As you just did. You must be more careful."

De Requesens regained some of his composure, and with that, his wits. "And who are you, that you should know all this and lecture me at my craft?"

Your craft? Dolor ignored the question, afraid derision might creep into his tone. Instead, he walked around the room and peered into the others beyond. Outwardly, he affected an appreciative demeanor; in actuality, he was busy cataloging everything he saw. "Olivares is a generous taskmaster, I see."

"See here: I will know your business with me."

"I bear a word from your master."

"And how do you speak to Spain, sirrah?"

"You are not the only man with a radio in this town. And I am not speaking of your master in Spain. I am speaking of the other one."

That rattled the dandy. "But—how are you here? I was assured by Rome I had sole knowledge of both groups—"

"Yes, well, you will appreciate that we are in a business where lies and misdirection are the stock in trade. We know of you; you know of us. Gasquet's men know the Swiss and vice versa. However, Gasquet only knows how to contact you; the Swiss only know how to contact us." The last claim was conjecture, but it was typical of multicell operations and de Requesens accepted it without reaction. "If any group is compromised, it would show in their communications with the others. And so Rome would know and take appropriate steps."

"Yes, but you should not be aware of my identity or where I am located. That, too, is crucial the security of the operation."

Dolor nodded sadly. "Normally, yes. But we caught wind of a developing situation. It seems that Gasquet's group has taken a misstep."

De Requesens wiped a thin sheen of sweat from his brow line. "A misstep? What? When?"

"We don't know much about it, but the word is that one of his group killed their landlord."

"What? And they did not report it?"

"You will have to take that up with them. However, Urban's security has taken an interest in the murder and is following all possible leads. That will lead them, ultimately, to visit all the landlord's properties. We had no way to communicate with you, but we were able to alert Rome. They gave us the information needed to contact you."

De Requesens sat heavily. "This is a disaster." Then he frowned. "Why did Rome not contact me?"

Dolor shrugged. "They didn't say. But I suspect it's because you are working alone. We have enough people to take the necessary steps."

"What steps?"

"To contact you. To prepare Gasquet's men to be moved. To keep an eye on the investigation." It even sounded plausible to Dolor.

De Requesens nodded. "Yes, of course. I shall compose messages for Gasquet, and—"

Dolor shook his head. "No time for that. We'll do it."

"*You* will do it? How? You do not even know the drop points."

Dolor shrugged. "Tell me and we'll take care of it."

De Requesens recoiled. "Tell you my drop points? No, that is expressly against the control protocols. Just as you have set and kept secret the drop points for the Swiss, so I have with Gasquet."

Dolor had known this would be the hardest argument to finesse, so he sidestepped it. "If you want to argue the point, then please do annoy Cardinal Borja in Rome so that he can confirm the orders he gave us. On the other hand, take a moment to think calmly. Once you move across the river, and once Gasquet and his men are relocated, would it still be safe to use your current drop points?"

De Requesens looked away. "It would not be . . . optimal," he admitted.

"It would be inviting disaster," Dolor exaggerated. "So you will need to set up new ones as soon as you and Gasquet are both relocated. Which means that the drop points you reveal to me will be defunct within the next twelve hours. And practically speaking, you don't have the time to write a message and send it to them, not if we're going to relocate you in time."

As Dolor had hoped, the new wrinkle—relocation—pulled de Requesens' attention away from giving up Gasquet's drop locations. "I am to be relocated? Why?"

Dolor stared at Javier. "This town has almost no space left in it, certainly not for seven men." He gestured at the rooms in which they stood. "Of course, if this suite were to become available—"

"And then where do *I* go?"

"We have a contact over the river. He owns a small inn. The rooms are very modest, but at least there's no increased security over there. In fact, the watch is lighter than usual; it's all been concentrated here in the Buckle. The innkeeper has already been paid through next week. We kept the room there just in case we ran into unexpected problems here in town."

"So I'm to stay in the Battant?" De Requesens said it as if the word was a synonym for *sewer*. "But I will be unable to come back to the Buckle—and I must, to set up new drop points for Gasquet and his idiots."

"That is not correct. You can get back across the Doub; you have identity papers. It will just be much more inconvenient."

"It will be harder to maintain a low profile." De Requesens' complaint ended on an almost petulant whine.

Dolor shrugged. "Well, that's all part of 'your craft.' Besides, things will move quickly now. With any luck, there will be but one more message from Rome, and but one more drop to make." He looked around. "Write down your drop locations for me and then gather what you need. The bridge closes shortly after dark and I need to be back across the river by then."

De Requesens stared around hastily; he turned a full circle without taking any action, his eyes wide.

Dolor adopted a tone of voice not unlike the one he used to calm skittish horses. "First things first. The radio. The codebooks. Your correspondence. Anything else that, if found by the authorities, would betray your identity."

Emerging from his paralyzing state of distraction, the young hidalgo set about gathering all the items, emptying the contents of the heavy lockbox into a leather traveling bag that was soon bulging. Nodding approvingly, Dolor said, "Choose only the clothes you can carry. You can replace your toilet once in the Battant. I shall check for any documents or other items you might have left about."

There was almost nothing, as Dolor had suspected, but he did find a bill on the table: a small charge for a better grade of wine that had been sent up with his dinner. He scanned it, found what he had hoped to: an obsequiously appreciative closing line from the hotel's owner. Dolor pocketed it, then remarked that de Requesens had best write a note to the innkeeper, announcing his departure.

"Yes," he agreed. "That's only proper. I shall take it to him just before we—"

"I will give it to him," Dolor stated. "It is possible, if unlikely, that I have been followed. If so, that suggests that Urban's men are looking for you. So we must make haste. Then, after you are safely across the Doub, I will return and deliver your note to the innkeeper, as well as to put a deposit on the suite to hold it for Gasquet and his men."

The Spaniard shrugged, wrote the note, and handed it to Dolor, who also volunteered to carry de Requesens' clothes and toilet, which had been rolled together into a traveling bag. Javier, on the other hand, insisted on keeping hold of the radio, its batteries, and his papers, which slowed him to a stooped, stumbling walk as they left the suite.

Dolor put up a hand as they neared the bottom of the stairs. "I will go ahead, see if the way out back is clear."

It was a narrow hallway, mostly used by kitchen staff to take deliveries and carry out rubbish, and it took a few moments of patient lurking next to the stairs before there was an untrafficked moment. Dolor leaned back into the staircase, waved for de Requesens to follow, and moved briskly to the door. He held it while the young Spaniard tilted dangerously toward the wall as he came off the stairs, almost dropping the radio and papers. He swayed upright, lurched into the passage and slipped out the back door . . . just as an oblivious serving maid exited the kitchen, laden with plates for the common room.

The one redeeming aspect of the walk to the Pont Battant and beyond it to a small, tilting inn was that de Requesens was too breathless to talk much. Dolor offered once to help share more of the burden, but the hidalgo refused, and while it would have been better to complete the journey more quickly, it was more important to leave him in possession of what he felt were his most secret materials. To do otherwise might have kindled some suspicion in de Requesens that this was part of some plot to deceive him into compromising the confidential nature of his work and present burden. Which was, of course, precisely what was occurring.

As they were crossing the Pont Battant, however, and de Requesens stopped to adjust the load on his shoulders, the span was deserted enough that he hazarded in a low voice, "Since you know my name, it seems only fair that I should learn yours."

"Fair? Perhaps. But if I answered, would you not then fear for your life?" De Requesens stared in shock. "Think on it. Given what we are about to put in motion, our only safety is in anonymity. So if I were to disclose my identity, it stands to reason that I had no intent of letting you live to reveal it."

That silenced the young intelligencer until they came in sight of the age-darkened shingling of the inn. Dolor paused. His companion looked up, staring ahead, squinting. "What is it? What do you see?"

"Nothing."

"Well, that's good, isn't it?"

Dolor shrugged. "It might be. But it would also be what we'd see if Urban's men learned that this was where we might be headed. They might be waiting inside. Or nearby." He turned toward the stables, gesturing for Javier to follow.

Once they were inside, Dolor laid down his burden. "Stay within. Best remain hidden in that empty stall."

"And what are you going to do?"

"There's a small chute that goes through to the side sheds, for receiving hay. I shall slip through there, walk the perimeter of the inn, make sure that it is unobserved. I shall make a quick pass through the common room as well, just to be sure. Then I shall come back and fetch you." He looked at the burden that was bowing the younger man's back. "You might wish to put that down; I will be a few minutes."

De Requesens stubbornly held on to it. Dolor shrugged and, pulling his cloak closer about himself, slipped across the barn to the chute. Crouching, he was through it in a single step.

Once outside the barn, he paced quickly about the inn, not bothering to conceal himself. No cooks or maids were loitering out back, no tipplers were tarrying on the stairs up to the commons room. He slowed his pace, straightening his cloak carefully and making sure that his garments were not twisted in each other. When he was sure that he had full freedom of motion, he slipped back to the barn and entered with a stealthy, shadow-courting sidestep.

"Hsst," he breathed at the stall where he'd left de Requesens.

The Spaniard gasped slightly. "*Mierda*, I did not hear you coming!"

Dolor shook his head. "Be quiet."

"Very well. But are we safe?"

"We were not followed," Dolor replied truthfully. "The way seems clear but it is always possible that our adversaries are more cleverly hidden than our senses can detect. Are you ready?"

De Requesens nodded.

"Then pick up your bags and let us go quickly."

The Spaniard bent to comply. As he did, Dolor's left hand went into his cloak and came straight out in one smooth motion. His poignard entered de Requesens' chest a thumb's width to the left of the sternum.

The young intelligencer did not even get out a complete gasp as Dolor stepped closer with the grace of a dancer. He slipped his right arm behind the falling body. Stunned brown eyes looked up into his own. They had lost focus by the time he eased de Requesens down into the hay.

Dolor glanced quickly about, listening intently: no one was approaching. Staying wide of the rapidly expanding pool of blood, he removed his poignard and wiped it clean on the hidalgo's elegant pants leg: it would soon be sodden, anyway. Slipping the blade into the scabbard under his right arm, Dolor used his left hand to plant the wine bill from *L'Auberge de Boucle d'Argent* in the Spaniard's coat pocket. He easily gathered up the bags the young man had carried with considerable distress, snagged a finger through the strap that held his clothes and toilet bound together, and started back toward the Pont Battant at a leisurely pace.

And all the way there, even after he let de Requesens' personal effects drag off his finger and into the Doub, the heavier elements of the toilet forcing them toward the bottom, Pedro Dolor recited silently, in time with the cadence of his steps: *left hand strike, left hand strike, left hand strike . . .*

The door was not yet closed behind Dolor before he started issuing orders. "Rombaldo, break down our radio and set this one up in its place."

"Why? Is it better?"

"No. But it is the one that de Requesens used, and in my experience, all complex machines have their own strange quirks and characteristics. When Rome receives messages from us, masquerading as de Requesens, it must resemble his communications in every particular. For the same reason, examine this satchel of his transmission records."

"That will take—"

"Be silent. Read as much of it as you can. We must familiarize ourself with de Requesens' compositional habits: his idioms, his sentence structure, his word choices. All of it. We will compose our replies to match those of the vast compendium he has so thoughtfully provided, along with his codebooks."

"Do you think Borja would really notice a few small differences?"

"Borja, no, but Maculani might. And we can take no chances." He raised his voice. "Giulio."

"Yes, Pedro?"

"You are to put on the monk's robes we acquired. Keep your hood up, find two street messengers. The younger the lads the better."

"What are they to deliver and where?"

"The first messenger is to hand-deliver this letter to the innkeeper. In person." He handed a single, wax-sealed sheet to Giulio. "This is a note from de Requesens to the innkeeper, indicating that he has vacated his suite."

"And what is the second messenger to deliver?"

Dolor reached into his own deal-wood desk, pulled out a larger, carefully sealed packet that he had prepared before leaving for *L'Auberge de Boucle d'Argent*. "This is also to be hand-delivered to the innkeeper. It is a week's rent on the suite that de Requesens has just vacated, and a note explaining that the young Spaniard mentioned his intention of relocating yesterday. Send the messenger with this half an hour after you send the first." Giulio bobbed compliance and went to find the monk's robe. "Laurin."

The strangler sidled closer. "What is needed?"

"You know the house where Gasquet and his men are staying?"

"Ought to. Have watched it enough."

"And they have never seen you?"

"Señor Dolor, do you mean to insult me?"

"No, I ask a serious question, and you must be absolutely certain about the answer."

"They have never seen me."

"Good, because your life and our operation could depend upon it. You are to go as a crier to their street, announcing that there are rooms for rent at the *L'Auberge de Boucle d'Argent* at only twice the normal rate."

"'Only' twice the rate?" Laurin repeated sceptically.

"Exactly."

"No one will take rooms at that rate."

"That's the idea—no one but Gasquet, that is. By now, he will know, or should at least suspect, that he must vacate his current rooms. He'll be ready to pay that rate—or at least ask you if it is negotiable. Which you will confirm on the sly. Like everyone that Borja has sent here, Gasquet has been provided with ample funds, and he will spend it; it's their necks if they do not relocate."

Laurin nodded and moved off.

Rombaldo frowned. "If they find de Requesens too

soon, they'll go investigate where he last lived. And they'll walk in on Gasquet."

Dolor shook his head. "Quite the contrary. We want them to find the corpse as quickly as possible."

Rombaldo's frown deepened. "That would be disaster."

"No, it will be an elegant solution. I made sure the body will be found swiftly. It probably has been by now. When they check the pockets, they will find a bill that identifies de Requesens and indicates that he was very recently staying at the *de Boucle d'Argent*."

Rombaldo's frown gave way to surprise, and then a wide grin. "And so Urban's investigators will be there first thing in the morning. Before Gasquet and his crew."

"Precisely. By the time he and his men turn up, Ambassador Nichols and anyone assisting her will have visited the suite and scoured it for anything that promises to be a clue. And they will have no reason to return. I have also left the investigators another small conundrum."

"And what is that?"

"I killed de Requesens very professionally, and with a left-hand strike."

Rombaldo's raised an eyebrow. "But you are right-handed."

"Yes, I am. However, since I was a boy, I have practiced everything I do with my left hand also. Forced ambidexterity."

Rombaldo's only reply was a puzzled look.

Dolor began drafting a very small note using the drop code with which de Requesens had communicated with Gasquet. "Firstly, by killing de Requesens with a blow that I made sure to be obviously from a left-handed attacker, it introduces a new variable into their investigations. They have only seen right-handed attacks. Now they have a left-handed murderer to look for, one who did not bother to hide the body of a man who will be a puzzlement to them. He clearly had a radio in his room, since an aerial was left behind. But no documentation was to be found, and his employment is unclear. Also, since he has been in Besançon since 1634, there will logically be uncertainty whether he could reasonably be connected with an assassination plot that cannot have been more than three months in the making."

"But what will all that accomplish?" Rombaldo asked finally.

Dolor shrugged. "Wasted energy and uncertainty. Which are our friends. Every clue or conjecture that might connect de Requesens' murder to Lamy's or a potential assassination plot is now countered and complicated by another that seems to point in the opposite direction." He finished the note and began rolling it tightly enough to fit into one of the reedlike tubes that de Requesens had used for his drops. "All plots are made up of intentional acts, arrayed purposefully around an objective. But what if one or two such acts do not fit into any given pattern? And what occurs if an outsider must reconstruct the actual plot?"

Rombaldo smiled. "They're stymied. They try to make all the pieces fit. But they can't."

"Exactly. And even if such an outsider was shrewd enough to speculate that some of the clues were spurious, motivated by an intent to mislead, how would they know which pieces those are? The best they can do is construct multiple hypothetical plots, but they remain unable to determine which is accurate. If any. And so they waste precious time not only trying to choose among the many plots, but also come up with countermeasures or responses that can be adapted to all of them. Which are ultimately inferior compromises, compared to what they would have devised if they had been able to discern the one strategy by which they will be attacked." Dolor rose and put on a shorter cloak that looked nothing like the ones used by the watch.

Rombaldo looked up at him. "Where are you going?"

Dolor held up the message tube. "To put this where Gasquet will find it."

"And what does it say?"

"What you might expect. That there are rooms waiting for them at *L'Auberge de Boucle d'Argent*, paid in advance, and that they should not arrive there until after noon, tomorrow. Also, that this is the last message drop in either direction, that Rome fears we have used them too long, and that the chance of detection is too great, now that we are nearing the actual assassination attempt. Instead, the attack plan will either arrive via a messenger I send, or be relayed by whoever is controlling the Swiss. And even though Gasquet is to remain the leader for the attack, he is to accept the plan that he receives, no matter the source."

"And you are depositing it in the drop site yourself?"

"I am."

"Because it's particularly dangerous?"

Dolor stared. "No. Because I wish to take in the evening air."

Part Four

Thursday
May 8, 1636

Downward to darkness, on extended wings

Chapter 24

The sun glinting off his helmet, Achille d'Estampes de Valençay's armor creaked as he approached and muttered: "I hope this day finds you well, Colonels."

Ruy did his best to affect complete composure, despite having run all the way from the waterfront just minutes before. "I am quite well, Lord de—er, Your Eminence."

Owen Roe O'Neill smiled. "Indeed, we're doing better'n your good self, from the sound of your voice, Cardinal de Valençay."

"I suspect you are correct, Colonel O'Neill." Achille turned to glance toward the approaching procession of covered sedan chairs.

"A taxing march from the cloister?" Ruy inquired.

Achille shook his heavy head. "The march, as you call it, is my one respite. His Holiness, though, feared insulting me by requesting that I don my armor this day. 'Will you forbear this conceit?' he asked me. Forbear! Is this what I am come to, now that I am a cardinal before I am a soldier? This 'conceit' is what I truly am, and this is where I belong: in the air, wearing a cuirass, in the vanguard, and ready to defend my pope. But after the 'conceit' of today's process is concluded"—he stared down the street toward the Palais Granvelle—"then I must put all that aside and sit in a stuffy room, high-ceilinged to facilitate a greater collection of dust. And I will sit there closeted all day, and tomorrow as well, with the stink of old and infirm men rising up about me, while they do the only thing that they still may: talk." He stared balefully at Ruy and O'Neill. "Have you ever listened to churchmen, no matter the faith, talk for nine hours?"

"Can't say I have," Owen murmured, with a poorly hidden grin and a scratch at his ear.

"I have not had that singular privilege," Ruy said, with an attempt at gravity.

"Then you have not had a foretaste of hell." Achille looked over his shoulder. The reshuffled papal procession was drawing closer. "I have fought Turks and Algerines, Englishmen and Huguenots, and I will tell you this: war is but a human hell, a condition of mundane suffering and terror. But the actual Hell, being the creation and domain of beings beyond our ken, must likewise contain horrors and tortures more profound, more exquisite, than any human may divine—except, perhaps those who devote their lives to the contemplation of what lies beyond." He set his helmet's visor back in place; his voice was as muffled as if he had fallen into the Pit which he was describing. "And so, the clerics of this colloquium have managed to import some of that infernal agony into our material world—by talking. Endlessly, pointlessly talking."

O'Neill's eyes may have twinkled. "God knows, you're a stronger man than I am, Achille."

Somber gray eyes looked out the narrow vision slit of the helmet. "I am not given to boasting, but, yes, I may be. Wish me well."

"*Bon chance!*" Ruy called after his broad, receding back, and not without some genuine sympathy.

Achille raised a gauntleted hand in a rueful farewell.

Ruy and Owen looked after him as he rejoined the procession.

"Suddenly, security detail doesn't seem quite so tiresome," O'Neill said slowly.

"Not even after running half a mile uphill without a bite of breakfast to sustain me," Ruy answered. He assessed the Frenchman's dejectedly slumped shoulders, then whispered so that Owen's men could not hear. "I'll wager a flagon of red that he will not finish the day without breaking a chair or a chin."

Owen looked sideways, disbelieving. "Is it an eejit you're takin' me for, Sanchez? I wouldn't chance that bet for the change in a tinker's trousers."

Which, Ruy hypothesized from the Irishman's tone, must typically be a small or nonexistent sum. "I fear that the noble Achille shall find the life of a cardinal very dull, even if the title is little more than a convenient formality."

"Seems a certainty." O'Neill glanced at Ruy's dusty boots and trousers. "And where were you coming from just before, hasty and heaving great breaths?"

Ruy only realized how truly comfortable he had become with the Irish nobleman when he discovered himself rolling his eyes in exasperation. "I was interviewing the prospective Swiss Guards."

Owen nodded. "It's a good sign that Urban is taking care to see that they are all trustworthy."

Ruy watched the first of the sedan chairs draw closer. "Our good pontiff was not the source of the caution: I was. Again."

Owen glanced sideways at him. "Oh-ho. And for your loyalty and troubles, you got the job of vetting them, didn't yeh?"

"This is, in fact, the grisly truth."

When Ruy did not add anything, O'Neill looked at him, frowning. "Any of them look...suspicious?"

Ruy shrugged. "One or two seem rougher types. They are in it for the money only, I suspect. Although it is hard enough to blame them for that."

"And the rest?"

"A few who are more quiet, but that may simply be a product of their advanced years—which is to say, over twenty. The others?" Ruy heaved a great sigh. "There are four whose lips may still be wet from their mother's milk, are enthusiastic and idealistic as only the very young may be. I see little good coming of this, but Father Vitelleschi is uncharacteristically optimistic. He considers their appearance here, and in time for the proper date of induction, a providential sign." He shook his head. "He should know better."

Owen clucked his tongue softly. "Mayhap he does, Ruy. He may not mean that providence is showing itself in their might, but rather, in what they symbolize to others. That unbidden, the true sons of the Pontifical Guard instinctively seek and find the true pontiff, like the three Magi journeyed to Christ. Besides, we intemperate Irish brutes can't remain the pope's guard forever, any more than the pope can remain out of Rome. Neither one makes for a respectable situation, you understand." He grinned crookedly.

Ruy nodded. "And you suspect those two 'situations' will end at roughly the same time?"

Owen nodded, squinting at the second sedan chair as it approached. "Once the pope is on the *cathedra*, our job will be done. Or as soon as a proper guard is trained up. Then it will be time for the Wild Geese to fly back to Brussels. At least, those of us who are left."

Ruy had served with many noblemen in Philip's tercios. He had also served with many frank and plainspoken soldiers. But he had rarely encountered the two qualities in the same person. He reached up to put a hand on Owen's shoulder. "I, for one, shall be sad to see the day when you Geese alight. The pope has never had guards more true."

Owen smiled. "Or soldiers so needed by their own homeland." His shoulder stiffened slightly. "Here they come." As the second sedan chair drew abreast, he scanned the procession immediately behind it with narrowed eyes, but was careful not to move his head, and so reveal that he was seeking something.

Ruy smiled. "I know which one he is, of course."

"Well, of course you do, y'damned Spaniard. You set the order. Bah. I can't tell where he is. Glad I didn't take your wager on this bit of silliness, either."

Ruy tried to keep a triumphant tone out of his voice. "Look behind the third sedan chair. The hooded clerk on the right. And I am a Catalan, not a Spaniard."

"Well, by God's own gravy—didn't His Holiness squawk about that?"

Ruy stroked his impeccably groomed beard. "Not in the least. In some ways, I believe he welcomed his role, today."

"Welcomed it? Why? Meaning no offense, but to

look at him, I wouldn't have thought a stiff hike to be among the pope's daily disciplines and devotions."

Ruy's answering smile was genuine but faint. "No, you may rest assured of that. But you did not know him before last year, before he had been driven from the Holy See. He is a changed man."

"I'm thinking you are not referring to a sudden affinity for vigorous exercise."

"I am not." Ruy's voice was serious. "He is a man who has been very close to death, and whose great power was stripped from him by those who claimed to be among his closest counselors."

"So he enjoys the simple things of life more, now?"

"That, too. But this, I think, he does more out of an instinct for penance."

"Penance? For what? For surviving the poisoned tongues and knives of the devil's minions, those who'd kill a pope?" The heat in O'Neill's voice was personal, and Ruy suspected he knew the source: the same Spanish cardinals, captains, and king who had been ready to dispatch Urban VIII in this world had proven faithless to their Irish servitors in the other. In the up-time history, four more years would see almost all the Wild Geese dead in hopeless wars, and the promise to furnish them with the means to retake their homeland from the English conveniently buried along with them.

Ruy put his palm atop the pommel of the rapier riding at his left hip. "Urban VIII did not live a particularly Spartan existence before Borja ejected him from Rome and sought his blood. Nor was His Holiness a man who always put merit before family when he chose who to promote within the Church, or whose petitions he most favored from among its many lay princes."

O'Neill let his gaze wander away from Ruy's eyes. Although no stranger to the realities of politics, the Irishman still seemed unwilling to accept that popes were as fallible as Ruy's experience—and centuries of history—has proven them to be. "So you're saying he walks his own wee Via Dolorosa when he can—to remind him to keep moving away from the life of a Pharisee and more toward that of his Creator's Son."

Ruy smiled. "I suspect that says it very well."

Tone Grogan came trotting up. "The ambassadora will be here presently, sirs."

"My poor wife," Ruy lamented, turning to look in all directions. "Once again, she was roused before I was."

O'Neill nodded but kept watching the procession, or more accurately the alleys and roofs that overlooked it. "The corpse they found over in the Battant?"

"The same."

"Any news from her so far?"

"Nothing except that papers on the body pointed to *L'Auberge de Boucle d'Argent* as his residence. At last word, she was heading there to examine his rooms and interview any persons who might prove useful to the investigation."

As if summoned by the remark, Sharon came around the corner of the building they had been waiting in front of and glanced at the two Wild Geese blocking the entry. "So this is the place?"

"It is, mada—Sharon," O'Neill said, patching over his gaffe with an apologetic smile as Finan and two Burgundian soldiers caught up with her.

Ruy moved one solicitous step closer to her. "What of the fellow they found in the Battant, my love?"

Sharon puffed out her cheeks; whether from exhaustion

or a moment of reflection, Ruy could not be sure. "Hard to know where to begin. Most important fact first: I'm pretty sure he was a player here, but I don't know how, just yet."

"A 'player'?" echoed O'Neill uncertainly.

"Sorry: up-time slang. A person of interest; someone involved with whatever schemes are unfolding here in Besançon. We got to *L'Auberge de Boucle d'Argent* at about nine AM, and they had already cleaned his room."

Ruy frowned. "Could the innkeeper be implicated, trying to cover up evidence?"

Sharon shook her head. "I thought of that. We questioned him pretty closely, but he had a pretty straightforward reason: inquiries after rooms. Apparently the victim, a young hidalgo by the name of Javier de Requesens y Ercilla, had mentioned to some acquaintances that he was planning on moving over the river. Word spread quickly. The innkeeper already had inquiries, had taken a deposit. Probably made a killing, too."

O'Neill raised an eyebrow. "In what way?"

Sharon shrugged. "Requesens had been in his best suite, second floor, since sometime late in 1634. That had been great for the innkeeper; steady occupation of his most expensive rooms. Except, starting about two months ago, as the rates went up, he had to keep the price of his suite the same: Requesens had essentially committed to a quarterly lease. So the owner is now doubling or even tripling the old rate."

"Hmmm . . . so de Requesens is hardly a recent arrival."

"No," agreed Sharon, "but that doesn't make him any less interesting. I could go into all of his interesting habits, his ready supply of money and no evident employment other than checking prices on various commodities in town, and the fact that he got mail from various cities in southern France, the Swiss cantons, and Spain and was never seen to post a reply. But what really matters is what we found in his room: an aerial for a radio."

Ruy brushed at the left wing of his mustache. "By which you imply the radio itself was absent."

She nodded. "Along with its batteries, any transmission or reception notes, or any of the correspondence he received. However, other than his purse, toiletry kit and probably a few clothes, the rest of his wardrobe and personal items were still there. Well, had been taken from the room for 'safe keeping' by the innkeeper. He got pretty grumpy when I impounded all of it."

O'Neill smirked. "Yes, terrible state of affairs, that. Preventing him from personally traveling all the way to Spain—at his own expense, no less—to deliver all the dead fellow's effects to his grieving Ma and Da. Whereas a lesser innkeeper might have succumbed to the temptation of selling it out the back, and no one the wiser."

Sharon rolled her eyes. "Yeah, the owner of the *L'Auberge de Boucle* is certainly a stand-up guy."

"A what?"

"So honest that he wouldn't once think of selling de Requesens' possessions. Ten times in the first hour, maybe, but never just once."

Ruy put a hand on his wife's arm. "You have just defined the character of almost every innkeeper who has ever lived, beauteous wife. Now, what of the fellow's body? Did his demise resemble Lamy's in any way?"

That brought a frown to Sharon's face. "No. I can't say for sure, but I think this killer was a real pro: one thrust straight to the heart. The weapon used was quite a bit broader than a stiletto, but the blade was not as wide as the daggers most people carry. If I had to guess, I'd say it's like one of those I've seen you use in your left hand when you're fencing."

"Ah: a main gauche."

"Yeah: that. I also think the victim knew the attacker, at least enough to allow him to get very close. There weren't any defensive wounds, and, judging from the straw in the stall, there wasn't any struggle. The attacker was able to get within a foot or two, and then: bam. He was done. Probably dead or at least nonresponsive before he hit the ground." Sharon thought. "One other thing—and be warned, I'm not entirely sure of this. But I think this attacker was left-handed."

"How do you know?" Ruy asked, delighted by the prospect of hearing his wife demonstrate more of her extraordinary ability to read such details into scenes of murder.

"Ruy, I want to reemphasize that I don't *know*. But here's what I saw: the victim was not moved. There was no sign that anything had been dragged through the straw. Also, the blood loss was completely consistent with how and where he'd fallen. So I'm going to gamble and say that the scene was not modified in any way by the perpetrator. If that's true, then the place where the attacker's feet apparently brushed away the straw, in relation to where his victim was, strongly suggest that they were standing to each other's left. That's why the stab wound was so perpendicular to the ventral surface of the victim's torso."

Sharon looked up from her inwardly concentrated stare and evidently saw that the eyes looking at her were no longer filled with understanding. "Umm . . . the stab wound went straight in. If the knife had been in the attacker's right hand, given the apparent range and position of the two men, it would have gone in at an angle. The only way for the blade to enter parallel to the sternum if it was in his right hand would be some kind of weird backhanded strike where the attacker started with it drawn across his body from the left." She mimicked the position she was describing. It was not merely awkward; Ruy could think of no reason for a presumed professional to choose such a strike. "And see: there wasn't enough room between them for his arm to get in that position, not without alerting the victim to what was coming."

Ruy nodded. "I think you are correct, my love: the attacker was left-handed. And he made sure to stand to the left of his attacker so that he could thrust straight out and into the heart. Nothing else makes sense."

O'Neill kicked at a pebble. "Not bloody much about this whole bolloxed show does make sense. So we've got a corpse in the hay, killed by a thug who's not using the same hand or weapon as either of the two who we presume did in Lamy. So no apparent connection between the two murders. But your lady wife digs a wee bit deeper and it turns out that the corpse is, as she so aptly puts it, 'a person of interest.' He's got intelligencer written all over him. And yet all of his intelligencing equipment and records are gone. Strange, if he had been planning to leave as the innkeeper let on, that he made such a mess of his move. O' course, that pales aside the fact that rather than go straight away to the inn he apparently meant to stay in—wonder if he'd even arranged a room there?—he goes to the stables first, though he doesn't have a horse. And there he just happens to meet an old chum who does him in for sake of auld lang syne." O'Neill glanced from one to the other. "Sure an' it all makes fine, logical sense."

Ruy started rubbing at a throbbing which had just begun in his left temple. "I think I would prefer to change places with Achille, just now."

Sharon shook her head. "Look: first of all we don't know that the two murders are, in fact, connected. I know, the timing looks very suspicious, but it could be coincidence."

O'Neill nodded. "Yes—or, not to gainsay the lady—it could be the first murder which somehow made the second feller bolt from his rooms sooner than he intended."

Ruy started rubbing his other temple. "You mean, that de Requesens feared that our investigation of the first murder would somehow point to him."

O'Neill shrugged. "Seems as likely an explanation as coincidence."

Sharon shook her head harder. "We're wasting time. Your runner said that you'd found the house of the . . . er, master mason who was in charge of building the convent." She glanced at the building behind them. "Is this it?"

Ruy nodded. "It is."

"And what did he tell you?"

O'Neill looked at Ruy, then muttered. "Sharon, I'm thinking it's you as will do the best job at getting information from him."

"Why's that?"

Ruy extended a hand toward the door. "I believe you should see for yourself."

Chapter 25

The moment Ruy swung open the cramped door to the small cellar, Sharon Nichols knew why she was the one they were counting on for answers.

As she ducked in, her eyes confirmed what her nose had told her a few moments before. The foreman—a lifelong resident of Besançon by the improbable name of Parsifal Funker—sat tied in a chair. At first glance, there was no sign of what had killed him, but Sharon, moved partly by instinct, partly by deduction, went around to the rear of the chair-bound corpse and ran a finger along the base of his skull. Sure enough: there was a single, precise hole, upward-angled to slip under and past the occipital plate into the brain. "Instant death. No pain. Extremely professional. Any other sign of damage to the body?"

"Naught but a bit of old school convincing," muttered O'Neill darkly, gesturing toward the corpse's left hand. A splinter had been inserted under the nail of the index finger. It had gone in less than a quarter of an inch. If any blood had been spilled, it had been lapped up by the rats that had already dined extensively on the corpse's entrails.

Finan entered the room reluctantly, but without the same pallor that he had initially displayed when assisting her at the last crime scene. She gestured him over. "Light, please."

Having anticipated the need, he had already lit the lantern; he held it high.

Sharon began the methodical process of cataloging the stage of death with her eyes and her fingers. "He's been dead a while, but the rats have spoiled one of the best indicators: by chewing into his organs, they've released any trapped gases produced by decomposition. Tissue is desiccated, but hair, nails, and skin are not loose yet. Skin shows a lot of blistering, though—what parts the rats left—and it looks like fluid leaked from the nose and mouth, but I can't be sure."

Sharon stood back from the corpse. "Significantly more than three days, probably not as long as two weeks. Given the temperature of the season and the humidity in this room, I'd say a week to ten days. But that is more by guess and by golly than science. I just don't have the right tools to measure the cellular changes that might—*might*—give me a narrower time frame."

"Still," mused Ruy, bearded chin in muscle-corded hand, "he was killed before access to Besançon was restricted. When many of the later clerics were still arriving."

She looked up at him. "Why is that important, do you think?"

"It might not be. But consider what is coming to light with these last two corpses and *if* there are any connections to a greater plot. De Requesens lived here for almost a year and a half, so he was recruited to take part in—in whatever we are uncovering—opportunistically.

He was an *in situ* resource who was reassigned to, or even impressed into, some relevant role. And now, here before us, we have evidence that other persons have either been ahead of us in gathering information pertinent to the hidden ways of this city, or who took this grisly step of denying us access to it." Ruy stood in front of the corpse, hands on hips. "I think we may be sure that however the attack on the pope may be sprung, it will not be a surge of cutthroats attacking the procession from the mouth of a dark alley. This all bespeaks long and careful planning."

O'Neill was still looking at the dead man's shrunken left hand. "Yes, but does it tell us if the man who killed de Requesens is the same one who did in this poor fellow?"

Sharon shook her head. "No way of knowing. Not sure how he wound up in the chair, but there's no sign that he struggled. If there was bruising, I can no longer tell, but there are no defensive wounds on his arms and nothing under his fingernails—except that splinter."

Which is what O'Neill was staring at. "It's pure guesswork, but this killer might have been right-handed. But only if he was the same one who did the interrogating."

Sharon, who took considerable if unstated pride in her forensic acuity, was surprised and a bit annoyed that she had no idea what the Irishman was getting at. "Why do you think either might have been right-handed?"

O'Neill nodded at the splinter under the left index finger. "In days past, I was present when our Spanish employers used methods like this to get information from prisoners. In general, the interrogator sits directly in front of the prisoner, and conducts the work on the hand directly across from the one he'll use to do the business. So a right-handed interrogator tends to ply his trade on a prisoner's left hand, and vice versa. As I said, a completely unscientific bit of guesswork."

"But reasonable," Ruy said with a nod. "I have witnessed the same thing—and I have seen far more of Spain's interrogators at work than you have, my friend."

Sharon turned toward Ruy, whose voice had fallen at the end of his comment. His eyes did not seem to be seeing outward, but were rendered sightless, probably by looking inward at old scenes conjured up by his remark. She suddenly wondered if he was so fey and playful most of the time because he had always been so, or because he had turned to it as a means of remaining lighthearted and wholly engaged in each passing moment, lest dark memories overtake him from behind.

"Well," she said, "whether or not the man with the knife was also the man asking the questions, it's pretty clear he was a hardened killer."

Ruy seemed to rise back to the surface of the world around him, and then smiled sadly. "That phrase has far more emphatic meaning in your time, dear one. Here, most killers are, as you say, hardened. We see so much more death, after all. If I recall correctly, in your time, only a fraction of the people who consumed meat ever saw the animals slaughtered, let alone reared the creature from the moment it was born or hatched. Still, I take your meaning. This is a man who is well-practiced in killing, judging from the surety of the stroke."

Sharon frowned. "As sure as the stab to the heart that killed de Requesens. It's tempting to think that they were done by the same man."

"Tempting, yes, but if, as Owen points out, the interrogator was also the murderer, then there is some suggestion that the killer here was right- not left-handed. And if all this is evidence of a deeper plot, then it seems quite reasonable that there may be two professional killers plying their trade in Besançon. Or more."

O'Neill stepped away from the corpse briskly; his tone was sharp, annoyed: "Maybe. Possibly. Hypothetically. Seemingly. Suggestive of. The uncertainty of this work is enough to drive a man mad. Give me a battlefield any day."

Sharon suspected he wasn't speaking figuratively. "That's a shame, since I think you've got a gift for it. After all, the two of you tracked him down." She stared at the corpse. "By the way, how did you locate him?"

O'Neill almost spat. "Oh, yes, there was another jolly bit of sleuthing."

Ruy folded his hands. "Mother Thérèse of the Carmelites was the source of the information."

Sharon knew that evasive tone. "Doesn't sound like she shared it too gladly."

"Not initially, but we were very persuasive."

"'Very persuasive?'" O'Neill repeated. "So that's the new way we say 'bullying a nun' these days?" Owen seemed to be considering a punch at the stone-lined walls of the cellar.

Sharon left her eyebrows raised as she turned back to Ruy. "What kind of bullying are we talking about?"

Ruy smoothed his mustachios meticulously, so she knew there was some grade-A fast talk coming her way. "My Gaelic friend is succumbing to the poetic impulse of his people to embroider a humble tale into one of greater magnitude."

"Not by much," O'Neill grumbled.

"We simply wanted a detailed account of the construction of the convent."

"And that required bullying... for what reason?"

Ruy folded his hands in a philosopher's pose. "It seems that in the early years of the convent, before Mother Thérèse became the prioress, there were rumors of... laxity."

"Ruy, are you saying that the nuns... that they... well...?"

O'Neill's face was red as he interrupted. "Yes, that is exactly what he is saying."

Ruy glanced carefully at Sharon. "It is not *I* who said it, dearest of my heart. And understandably, the mother superior did not want to admit it. But Archbishop de Rey had intimated that such had been the case before her arrival."

"Ruy, I am waiting to hear what this has to do with a dead man." She gestured to the body in the chair.

It was O'Neill who answered, his voice bitter, his eyes aimed hard at the wall. "This poor sod was a master stonemason, and from 1619 on, was what you might call the foreman of the gang that was setting the interior stone. That would have included ensuring that the tunnel from Palais Granvelle remained functional, as well as seeing to the creation of any new passages. And it is rumored that one such was created to facilitate—access—between the convent and the Benedictines nearby."

Sharon nodded slowly, looked away. For all his

travels to many countries and familiarity with court politics, Owen Roe O'Neill had harbored a doggedly idealistic view of the men and women who had taken vows of chastity to devote themselves to the Church. But ever since going to Rome to rescue Urban last year, it had become increasingly difficult for him to cling to those notions, and he experienced each disappointment as if a scab was being torn off a just-healed wound. It reminded her of the crisis of conscience she had witnessed in some of her Catholic friends back up-time, when the pedophile accusations began accumulating in the Nineties. When it got to the point where no rational person could explain it away anymore, they became increasingly myopic and defensive, angry and bitter at the Church, and yet unwilling to hear anyone criticize it. Now, as then, Sharon resolved to give Owen his own space; there was really nothing else to be done.

Ruy's eyes were sad as he, too, looked away from his friend. "Naturally, the prioress was unwilling to talk of these ... irregularities in the early years of the convent. I think the only reason she agreed was because the mother superior who had overseen the work is now long deceased. Unfortunately for us, the current prioress arrived at the very end of the construction, and so had little knowledge of who had been in charge of it. Happily, she offered to contact the stonemasons guild, which did in fact keep records on the members who had been retained, at least those who were masters. Just before supper yesterday, she sent a list of names to us. A short list, since many have gone to their reward since then. And of all those names, this fellow was the only one who would have overseen the construction of more tunnels, or who would have been responsible for making safe and permanent passages through any buried rooms of earlier buildings. There was another fellow whose name they had not recorded, but whom they remembered: a local mute who never rose beyond journeyman but who was known for his ability with tight or hidden passages. And, being illiterate as well, he was as much prized for the assured confidentiality of his work.

"Owen and I resolved to come here together this morning, but I was called away to prepare the young Swiss for their induction into the Pontifical Guard on Saturday. By the time I got here, Owen had already tried knocking. He was told by the neighbors that poor Parsifal was something of a recluse, but given the urgency of the matter, he and his men forced the door and ultimately found this sad scene."

Sharon nodded. "So that's what you meant when you said that whoever killed this man was preventing us from getting necessary information. Because without him, we don't know the mute's name or where we might find him."

Ruy nodded. "That is part of it, certainly."

Sharon frowned. "Part of it?"

O'Neill nodded grimly toward the corpse's tortured hand again. "Whoever sent Parsifal Funker to his Maker didn't just walk into his house and kill him. They had a chat with him first. They wanted to learn something. Just like us."

Sharon felt a chill go down her back. "The mute."

Ruy nodded. "We cannot be certain, of course. Funker may have known other things of value to his killer. But if the apparent plot to attack the pope involves avoiding our security by moving through long forgotten tunnels, then those assassins would also have wanted to find the mute. First, to learn what hidden passages might best serve their needs, and second—"

"And second, to kill him," Sharon finished. "So, can we find other masons who may have worked with this mute, either on the convent, or elsewhere?"

O'Neill nodded. "We might. They might even admit to remembering him. And if we're very lucky, they might even know where we can find him. Which is why I sent for six runners, who should be waiting outside, by now."

Ruy smiled reassuringly at Sharon. "We shall provide each one with the name of a master or journeyman stonemason with whom Mr. Funker was long associated. They will search them out, inquire after the mute and any others that might have known him, and continue to follow the leads."

"Until they run out," O'Neill added darkly.

Sharon wiped her hands and moved toward the door. "Let's hope it doesn't come to that."

Chapter 26

Pedro Dolor had awakened with a most unfamiliar sensation: indecision. As he cleaned his weapons, and then laid them out—those he carried, those he kept concealed close at hand, those in the pack with which he would flee if all was lost—he continued to grapple with the question that had whispered to him in his usually dreamless sleep. Should he masquerade as de Requesens and contact Borja in an attempt to gain some insight into the attack plan, or at least the weapons and equipment that would be furnished to the Swiss?

It was a step Dolor had never envisioned taking, simply because if handled incorrectly, it could compromise Rome's assumption that it was still communicating with Javier de Requesens y Ercilla. In that event, it was possible that the attack upon the pope would be launched prematurely, or cancelled. And so Dolor would not only have failed to carry out Olivares' orders to ensure that Urban was killed and that the blame fell squarely upon Borja, but would have ruined his own plans to slowly but inexorably lead Madrid into a cascade of mounting international blunders.

Dolor had to understand Borja's attack plan so he could provide both the needed support and yet not get so enmeshed in the combat that he could not withdraw in a timely fashion, thereby leaving Borja's men to be captured, interrogated, and so, point fingers toward Rome.

But if Dolor did not gamble everything now, he might have insufficient information and time to achieve his delicately intertwined objectives later. He thought about it all the way through breakfast, chewing very slowly as he did. It was a most difficult choice.

Borja saved him the trouble of making the decision. The remains of breakfast were not yet cold when the radio began clacking interminably. Rome had learned from a radio-equipped Spanish agent in Basel that the colloquium had already commenced. A darkly imperious question followed: was this in fact true?

Dolor sighed as he sent his affirmative reply, dreading the deluge he was certain would follow.

Borja did not disappoint him. A torrent of complaint and near-abuse ensued, which, despite its many creative variations, all boiled down to this: why had de Requesens not thought to so inform Rome, or gather any pertinent information to send along?

After leading with the effusive and ornate apologies that were Javier's rather revolting habit, Dolor replied with a most reasonable explanation: Because, from the outset, those had never been an explicit or implicit part of his duties. Indeed, according to the transcripts of what he had been sent, Javier had been obliquely chastised on several occasions when his reports had become too detailed, or concerned matters that were mostly tangential to his mission. Dolor felt fairly sure that had been Maculani's contribution.

However, the answer was unquestionably all Borja. After several transmissions of extraordinary length in which the simmering cardinal implausibly explained how de Requesens' silence on other matters worthy of report had been a subtle and sadly failed test of his perspicacity and initiative, Borja began sending a series of one line transmissions that enumerated all the matters of interest which Javier might have reported upon, and which he now should.

The series continued to steadily accumulate over the course of the next two hours. The radio would clatter briefly, fall silent for a few minutes, and then sputter to life again. And again and again and again. Dolor watched it, and almost stopped paying attention to the text of each message in favor of perceiving the subtext of the growing list: it was a view into the mind of a man who could not admit that he was wrong. It was the inner voice of a megalomaniac who would go to any lengths, including explanations that were fatuous marvels of contorted and tortuous invention, to prove to a distant underling that Gaspar de Borja y Velasco was never in error. Because in doing so, and by recieving no rebuttals in reply, the cardinal secretly took comfort in believing he had even proved it to himself.

After a long day of intermittent and obsequious acknowledgements of Borja's utterly ridiculous demands for detailed information on the attendees of the colloquium, their activities, and the probable beginning of a Papal Council, Dolor sent Giulio out to gather a few of the facts that could be gleaned simply by listening to talk in any one of the taverns within a three-minute walk of the palace. Then, when he estimated that Borja's tone was beginning to suggest that the cardinal had not only fully vented his spleen, but had become bored by flogging his subordinate over the airwaves, Dolor slipped in his own crucial question, albeit indirectly. Gasquet, he sent, was becoming restless now that the Swiss had arrived yet remained uncooperative about informing him when the weapons and plan of attack might be forthcoming. Furthermore, the leaders among the Swiss were using Gasquet's dependence upon them to undermine his authority as the designated leader of the attack.

As Dolor suspected, this was all the stimulus that Borja needed to find renewed energy for putting his verbal whip to his subordinate's well-flayed ego. How sharp a disappointment it was to him, and to the hopes of Mother Church, that de Requesens could not even keep a small crew of shiftless murderers in line. Was this what passed for firm leadership in the spoiled younger generation of hidalgos, these days?

Which was the opening Dolor had been looking for. Using de Requesens' habitually meek tone when correcting his superiors, he pointed out that the separation between himself and the assassins made it functionally impossible to control them in any way. If he initiated that kind of contact with them, or attempted to give them orders on his own, he would be blatantly violating the most crucial directive that Borja had given him: to remain out of the decision-making loop.

The dramatic change in the tempo of the signals told Dolor that his explanation had had the desired effect: Borja was now finding the exchange not only tedious, but burdensome. The subsequent bursts of brief activity accumulated into what was essentially a concluding laundry list. Gasquet was impertinent and had to remain patient. The plan and the weapons were being withheld as long as possible to eliminate the possibility of betrayal—either out of greed or a guilty conscience—to Urban's servitors. There was no use trying to wheedle any details out of Rome because the controller of the Swiss would coordinate the delivery of the weapons and the plan, independent of further instructions. He had been retained due to his familiarity with not only the region and Besançon, but an intimate knowledge of the precise location where the assassination would be carried out. Gasquet would indeed be in command of the attackers, but would be required to follow the plan without alteration.

There was a long pause and then a single cypher: the one indicating that the exchange was concluded. Dolor leaned back.

Rombaldo sat down in the chair opposite. "I heard the last message. Not much to go on."

Dolor nodded. "Not much at all." He frowned. Deciding he had no choice left but to use the Swiss themselves to glean some of the necessary information, he peeled a piece of stationary off the pile that had been taken from de Requesens' suite, and began writing.

"To Gasquet?"

"Yes. Instructions that he contact the Swiss and inform them of his new address."

Rombaldo shrugged. "But how will that help us learn what attack is being planned?"

"I am instructing him to also ask them for a list of the weapons to be relayed, so that he, and therefore I, can be certain that all the ones intended for his men will be delivered as promised."

Rombaldo shook his head. "What makes you think the Swiss, or rather, their controller, will respond to that?"

"Because I will indicate that the request originates from our joint patron. Specifically, that Rome has tasked me to make sure that none of the weapons furnished, or funded, were liquidated ahead of time: not an uncommon practice with employees who decide to disappear if an operation looks too dangerous. Of course, the real reason is to learn the nature of the weapons. That may give us some clue as to where the attack will be carried out, or at least, the kinds of environment in which it will *not* be carried out."

Gasquet nodded. "Reasonable. I'd certainly be thinking of dodging away with a few extra ducats in my pocket if my employer didn't provide a convincing plan ahead of time."

Dolor nodded, but neglected to remark that Rombaldo was in very much the same situation. Until they learned about the attack at the last minute from the Swiss controller, Dolor's own group also remained without a plan. Instead, he handed Rombaldo the coded message and said, "Have Giulio go to *L'Auberge de Boucle* and hire a messenger to deliver it upstairs and wait for confirmation."

Rombaldo sighed. "He'll probably buy himself a drink while he waits, you know."

Dolor shrugged. "Of course he will. He's an amateur."

As are you all.

Chapter 27

Dusk was painting the west violet and peach when the cloister bell began to call the monks to dinner. Singly and in pairs, they began moving toward the refectory, hands in their joined sleeves, heads inclined. Although this was not an order that required a vow of silence, or even promoted it, their convergence upon the chapter house was as loud as the closing of a dove's eye.

As Sharon watched the last of them file in and the large double doors close, she sent a sideways smile at Finan. "Thank you, Corporal. That will be all."

"M'lady?"

Her smile widened. "You may go and see to your own meal and get a little extra sleep. For all we know, we could be called out in the middle of the night to look at yet another murder victim."

"I'm right as rain and ready as I am, Ambassador Nichols. I don't need to—"

Sharon turned towards him. "Finan. Thank you. Now, go away. You need some time to yourself." *And so do I.*

Finan took a step away, hesitated. "M'lady, guarding you is my duty. I'd not leave you to—"

Sharon laughed. "You will leave me, partly because I want you rested to do your duty properly tomorrow and partly because—well, because I say so." She gestured at the outward-looking sentries atop the watchpoints that ringed the cloister. "I am quite safe. And we are both quite tired. So, git!"

Finan, expressing his misgivings with a frown instead of words, did finally turn and move off.

Sharon sighed, staring after the bantam corporal, wondered what she'd do without him, turned to look back at the deepening dusk—and saw Ruy approaching on the walkway that traced a diagonal from one corner of the courtyard to the other. *Right on time.* She began to walk toward him, even though her first impulse was to run into his arms.

Because their jobs in Besançon had been pulling them subtly apart, and not just in terms of time. Ruy Sanchez de Casador y Ortiz was a perfect chief of security for the pope not merely because he was smart, tactful, shrewd and an experienced soldier, but because he had considerable familiarity with the way assassins thought and acted. More familiarity than Sharon would have guessed. And every once in a while, when his eyes grew distant while looking at a mutilated corpse or dissecting how an ambush could take place, she found herself asking, *Is my Ruy familiar with this because he's foiled it before, or because he's done it before?* She knew that the life of a Spanish soldier was not a pretty one, that the treatment of prisoners in his time often constituted what were called war crimes in hers, and that sometimes the distinction between an act of war and an assassination was more a matter of word choice than anything else. And so she wondered: how far down this road has he gone, and how often, and where, and why? And just as intently as she asked those questions of herself, she intensely wanted not to have them answered—for fear of what those answers would be.

So she wanted to run to him, to hold him close and feel and say to herself: *this is the Ruy I love. This is who he is now, and who he always wanted to be, no matter what he might have been forced to do and be before.* But she knew that if she did that, he would detect her desperation, if for no other reason than she was normally very circumspect about public displays of affection in the cloister. And if he felt her worry, he would not stop inquiring as to its cause until she answered. And when she did, then what?

So Sharon Nichols walked to Ruy, who was, as usual, beaming at her, and once they had drawn close enough together, he inclined his head as he asked, "And might fair lady mine wish to take a stroll on this fine night?"

And as her heart leaped up with love and dread, she managed to merely smile, offer her arm, and say, "I'll bet you say that to all the girls."

And they walked.

After they had taken a half turn around the cloister, Ruy murmured into her ear, "Alone at last."

"Yes, at last. But I have news."

"So do I. But you first, my love."

"No, mine can wait."

"As can mine, and besides, I would be a cur if I did not both insist and remind: ladies first."

"Hmm. Nice to know you think I'm a lady after some of the times we've shared. I remember the first night in that farmhouse in Lombardy..."

"The marvel of a true lady is that although her abilities and virtues approach the divine, she nonetheless has talents which are delightfully infernal."

"Ruy, stop it. Like I said, you go first. 'Cause, 'age before beauty.'"

"And so I am slain by my one love, pierced to the heart by the cruel truth of her insight!"

"Yeah, and when you're done dying from it, you start. Please."

"Ah, very well. Some disappointing news, first. To use the parlance common in the books of which you are so fond, the 'trail is cold' on landlord Lamy's attackers. An estranged stepbrother of his could not be questioned; he is just recently out of town. However, by all accounts, he is not capable of the crime himself. He is even less physically fit than was the victim, it seems. Of course, it is not beyond possibility that he retained the services of two or more thugs. At any rate, there is no precise information to be had regarding his whereabouts or probable date of return.

"Now, on the matter of canvassing Lamy's properties as possible sites where he was murdered, or where relevant clues might be found: three of his rented rooms were interesting, but none gave us any leads."

"Not even the one where they found some blood on the stairs and on the way to the outhouse?"

"No, and the watch spent a great deal of time speaking to all the tenants in that wretched place. Many of whom made savage accusations against each other, none of which proved to have merit."

"And the other two?"

"Both were flats vacated without warning. The smaller one was apparently an overcrowded room down on the water, whose changing denizens were perpetually behind in their rent. They disappeared a day or two before Lamy's body was found, owing a full week."

"Might he have gone there and got knifed instead of paid?"

"Possible, but I am told the place was a sty. And that to call it such was an insult to most pigs. Which means it had not been cleaned in some time, including any removal of incriminating bloodstains. At any rate, it yielded no evidence.

"The last property was the top floor of a house in the hospital district, rented by laborers. The watch found it emptied of all effects, and left as tidy as the other was filthy."

"Tidy as in 'freshly cleaned of evidence'?"

"Alas, the watch was uncertain on that point, or perhaps they simply lied to conceal the shoddiness of their observation."

"What about neighbors: did they report anything suspicious at either location?"

Ruy sighed. "At the smaller room, the 'neighbors' are mostly wedded to the bottle or other vices that would make them unlikely to notice or remember the apocalypse if it occurred in their own bed. As it might, on occasion. At the larger flat, there are only two other residents, one of whom makes his living on the river and was only rarely at home. The other was described as a woman of advanced years, poor hearing, powerful opinions, and questionable veracity.

She had much to say about the departed tenants' lack of consideration when using the privy, but would not budge from that topic—probably because she had no other reasonable source of vitriol against them."

So the search for leads that might connect the murder of Lamy to some larger plot against the pope had effectively fizzled. No real surprise there. If she or Ruy had had the time to be the first person on site in each location, to bring an experienced and dedicated eye to assess it before it was irrevocably spoiled, then maybe something might have turned up. But the limitations implicit in relying upon the town watch had been understood from the start and there was no other way to follow up on all the leads. Well, perhaps there had been better luck in the follow-up on this morning's murder victim.

"Any luck in locating people who worked with Parsifal Funker and also knew of the mute?"

Ruy shrugged. "Almost every stonemason in town worked with Funker at some point. Hardly surprising, given all the churches in so small a city. However, only two knew of the mute, and then, only from years ago. And neither of them were ever involved in any of the mute's—shall we say confidential?—interior work."

"So does this guy work alone?"

"Firstly, by their account, he is past the age of working safely with stone. But it may very well be as you say, that he worked alone. In addition to being mute and illiterate, he was always extremely reclusive, even secretive. And apparently, he has become even more so. Which is not uncommon, or a bad idea, when one has made a living installing hidden or secret constructions. All sorts of persons may wish to converse with you for all the wrong reasons. Better if they cannot find you."

Sharon nodded. "Did the prioress give you any information, even rumors, about other tunnels that might be connected to the convent?"

"No. She was unsure that any confidential work had ever been done. Her predecessor never elected to take her into confidence on the matter, which would be particularly understandable if she herself had somehow been involved in the laxity that the archbishop mentioned. However, the Carmelites have recently searched—as well as nuns can be expected to—for any possible points where the convent's lower areas might be connected to older structures. They found nothing."

"Do you think the search was, well, sufficiently detailed?"

"Admirably thorough, from the sound of it. They searched all sides of the lower levels, excepting the one that they know abuts on an adjoining cellar in the only building that is built up against their own."

"You mean that sad old flophouse?"

"The very same eyesore. And before you may ask, oh my brilliant and ingenious wife, no: that building is not built upon older ruins. It is as dull a construction as exists within this city's walls, I am afraid."

Sharon reflected that, in the books she favored, there was always a part where the investigators ran into nothing but dead ends. Except that usually happened early in the story. Here, with the colloquium almost over, it felt altogether too likely that whatever assassination plot might exist was probably entering its final, preparatory stages. Sharon was not a fan of how reality differed from the fictional worlds she so enjoyed, which were so intellectually satisfying. This just made her feel a bit panicked and very stupid. "Did anyone have any idea where the mute might live? Any at all?"

"Sadly, no. He often lived on the site where he worked. And his last jobs were not always well advertised, if you take my meaning. But we have recruited men of discretion, including some of St. John's canons, to make inquiries and visit likely sites." Ruy took her hand in his, squeezed it gently but firmly. "He will be found."

Sharon nodded agreement, but her thoughts were: *Yes, let's hope so. But I'm not holding my breath.* And: *you're breaking our rule about no PDA in the cloister, and damn it, that's just fine with me, tonight.*

The pressure of Ruy's hand pulsed slightly tighter. "And now you."

"'Now me' what?"

"You had news for me?"

Sharon grinned as she rolled her eyes at herself. "It's no fair, Ruy. You're twice as old as I am, but I have only half your memory."

"It pains me—in so many ways—to correct you, my love, but you are mistaken in two particulars. Firstly, your memory is quite remarkable. And secondly, I am, alas, more than twice as old as you are. Indeed, I am daily mystified and gratified beyond words to awaken into a world where, for reasons I cannot fathom, you see me as something other than an infirm old goat—"

"Now, stop right there, Ruy," she said with histrionic severity. "I don't know many twenty-five-year-olds who are half as fit as you are, and that's as far as I am willing to be lured into your ploy to have me flatter you. As regarding you being a goat—well, I suppose that's not all bad." She was afraid her sly smile might have veered over the line into an outright leer.

Whether it did or not, Ruy acted as though it had; swiping at his moustaches the way a rooster might preen, he smiled broadly, and then raised a remonstrative finger. "And while I will remember—and return to!—this delightfully audacious banter, I am no more easily distracted than you, my wondrous wife. I ask again: what news?"

Sharon was pleased—or was she?—that Ruy had so swiftly deflected her suggestive remark. "Whoever else is using a radio in Besançon was burning up the airwaves today. And we're pretty sure it was a single set, in a single location. And it was getting constant messages. They must have drained their batteries at least once."

"Was any of it decipherable?"

Sharon shook her head. "No. It's all in the same cypher, but we got a good, clean sample of it today. It's always being varied, of course, but there are some signal clusters that show up more often than can be explained by random combination. Odo, who's gotten pretty good at this stuff, insists that there are bigger patterns he can feel as we transcribe what's being sent."

One of Ruy's eyebrows raised very high. "Odo *feels* this?"

"Look, I don't pretend to understand, let alone be able to explain what he means. Damned if I understand half the things he *does* explain. But I trust him. And here's something that's a simple fact: there was more activity than I've ever heard here down-time.

Somebody had a lot to say. And given what's been going on here over the last few days, I don't think it's unreasonable to posit a connection."

"Nor do I. But I know that look. You have an idea, a plan of action."

"You bet. The signal from Besançon was so strong, and so close, that it has to be in the city."

"How do you know?"

"Because I had Finan take the mobile set for a short walk, and even then, we were able to get some directional results."

Ruy stared. "What do you mean, 'directional results'?"

"Remember what I told you about radio direction finding game called 'fox and hounds'?"

"Er...yes."

She wasn't entirely sure he did. "Okay, so here's how it works. The easy part is just simple distance. The farther away your receiver is, the fainter the transmission gets; the closer you get, the stronger."

"That stands to reason."

"So that's how you know you're moving farther away or closer. The trickier part is determining which direction on the compass the signal is coming from. For that, you get a special antenna—we've fashioned a simple round one—and you turn it in a circle. When the 'face' of the circle is facing the transmitter, the signal grows stronger, because more of the antenna is catching the signal. When you turn away and the circle is no longer facing the transmitter, only one side of it is really getting the signal, so it weakens. And since we'd be using two mobile sets, we can coordinate from two directions and narrow it down very quickly. In fact—"

Ruy held up a hand. "Two mobile radio sets?"

Sharon nodded, refused to be deterred. "Yes, two sets: Finan's and one other. As we agreed with Hastings."

"Sharon, my love: did you inform Hastings before you commandeered the second set?"

"There wasn't time," she mumbled, looking away. "But I doubt he'll be very annoyed."

"Why?"

"Because if we get signals tomorrow, we should be able to get a location very quickly. And at that point, I'm going to pull him and the reaction force in to take a look at who's sending these messages."

"My love! What if something should happen—such as an assassination attempt—while Lieutenant Hastings is performing this task?"

"Ruy, it won't take very long. It means walking a few blocks. And if this radio traffic isn't innocent, then we may catch the assassins before they can strike."

"My love, all that makes impeccable tactical sense, but *only* if your presumption—that the radios are being operated by the assassins or their handlers—is correct."

Sharon nodded. "Yes, that's true. And I think we should take that risk. The timing is too suspicious. The day the colloquium was called to session is the day the radio activity picked up both dramatically and inexplicably. And no one else in town who is known to own a radio has been using it these past few days: we've checked. So whoever it is, they're not openly declared owners. And what are the odds that they're just innocent hobbyists, communicating in a code we can't crack?"

Ruy thought. "If I were to play the part of the devil's advocate, they could be journalists who came in under false identities, reporting on any rumors emerging from the colloquium."

"Could be, but with the session being closed, what do they have to report? Particularly when tomorrow is another closed-session day. So if the airwaves are once again humming then, I don't think it's news. It's coordination or something like it. Ruy, this could be our only chance to stop an attack before it occurs."

Ruy's smile was sudden and very wide, and before the last words had left her lips, he had caught her around the waist with both arms. "My wife from the future is not just a surgeon and an investigator but a steel-eyed general! Your hypothesis is too plausible to ignore. We shall do as you say, wonderful wife."

Sharon eyed him narrowly. "Because you think it's the best plan or because you're trying to make me more . . . pliable?"

"Your question suggests that only one of those reasons could be true."

Sharon smiled. "You are terrible, Ruy Sanchez de Casador y Ortiz."

Ruy smiled back. "Now *that* is truth plainly spoken. And I shall prove it."

When he bent forward to kiss her, she whispered, "You always do."

Norwin entered the common room of *L'Auberge de Boucle d'Argent* in workman's clothes and a rough cap on his head. Estève Gasquet, sitting alone at a table, moved toward the bar, not looking at him.

Norwin drifted toward the bar as well and produced a pipe. When the barkeep stepped over, he shook his head. "On second thought, I'm going to have a smoke."

"Nice night for it," agreed the barman as Norwin left with a nod.

Gasquet pushed his empty flagon toward the barman, who looked at it. "More?"

"No. Finished for the night."

The barman nodded, and by the time Gasquet had leaned away and started toward the stairs, he was busy wiping out the flagon and talking to the next customer.

Just before Gasquet reached the stairs, he stepped slightly to the left, which put him in the short narrow corridor that led out the back. As he went through the already open door—the traffic from the hot kitchen was frequent enough that it made no sense to close it—he half turned his head to get a glimpse of the barman: his back was turned.

Gasquet slipped into the cool evening air and made for the side of the building.

Norwin was already there, his pipe lit. He did not look up but muttered. "Lee of the chimney: full shadow there. Person would bump into you before they see you."

"Thanks, but I've acquainted myself with the details of my flop." Gasquet hoped the bored tone concealed his annoyance. Norwin was a damned quick study with a damned sharp eye. He'd be a dangerous opponent, if it ever came to that.

The Swiss just shrugged. "What's so important that we should take the risk of being seen together?"

"My handler is getting pressure from Rome. About the weapons and the plans and why we don't have them yet."

Norwin took a long pull at his pipe "I don't like it either, but it was Rome's idea."

"Maybe, but they're nervous now."

Norwin nodded. "Ah. Afraid that our controller sold some and pocketed the money for himself, just in case we don't like the plan and decide to leave town?"

Gasquet smiled. "Something like that."

Norwin tapped around in the bowl of his pipe. "Wish I knew more than you do, but I don't. I suspect the most important feature of the plan is that it can be kept completely secret until the last second."

Gasquet nodded. "Yes, but we can probably make a few educated guesses." He couldn't be sure if Norwin was telling the truth, but his reactions to a few hypotheses might clear that up. If Eischoll started trying to redirect Gasquet, it probably meant that Norwin felt he was getting close to a truth the Swiss handler wasn't willing to share. "Clearly, it was important that you and the rest of your group became part of the pathetic Swiss Guard parade so that you'd gain the opposition's trust. That's why you were the ones who killed the pigeons I set up for you during the attack at St. John's."

"Yes, clearly the case. And nicely done."

Gasquet ignored the compliment. "It's equally clear that we are not going to get the plans or the weapons until right before the attack. And I don't like that."

Norwin shrugged. "When did it ever matter what those such as ourselves like? We are simply tools, to them."

Gasquet couldn't tell if Norwin's phlegmatic response was genuine or a very nicely underplayed attempt to steer away from the topic by suggesting that inquiry was futile. "Well, there'd better be a reasonable chance of surviving this."

Norwin inclined his head slightly. "If there isn't, I won't be a part of it."

His comment was so direct, and so indifferent in tone, that Gasquet found it difficult to believe it to be anything other than the simple, unadorned truth. "Well, I hope they know that. About all of us."

Norwin took a small draw on his pipe, which made a soft guttering sound. He spoke as he let the smoke drift out of his mouth. "I believe they must know that much. The way they've planned it thus far tells me this isn't the first assassination they've arranged. Which means they must also know that, if they want the job done, we have to consider the payment to be worth the risk." He tapped the ashes out of his pipe. "After all, no amount of silver is worth near-certain death." He stretched, still not looking back at Gasquet. "I'll send you word as soon as I get it. Enjoy your meals and beds; they're a damn sight better than ours."

He strolled away, fading quickly into the gathering darkness.

Part Five

Friday
May 9, 1636

In the high west there burns a furious star

Part VIII

Chapter 28

Rombaldo rolled his eyes when the radio started clattering again. "Damn, Borja is a tiresome bastard. He won't even let us finish breakfast." Actually, Rombaldo was the last one eating; he tended to linger over meals.

Pedro Dolor shrugged. "I suspect now that he's had a night to sleep on it, he has discerned further reasons why any problems with the unfolding of his plan are due to the late Señor de Requesens, not himself." He finished wrapping up their own radio and its batteries and fitting both tightly into an outsized rucksack. Rombaldo was already wearily copying the characters onto a long roll of paper; notepads had not yet been much produced down-time. Probably not cost effective, Dolor surmised, which was a shame. He had seen one or two left behind by fleeing up-time telegraphers and thought them an excellent invention.

His lieutenant looked away from his task balefully. "You know, I think I just might plead bad weather and request a resend. Maybe I'll send it twice." He smiled wickedly. "Or more."

Dolor shrugged. "It's a waste of our batteries, too.

So unless you want to do the recharging, conclude the task as rapidly as possible."

Rombaldo's smile soured. "Anything else?"

"Yes. Finish burning our notes. I suspect we'll be moving soon. The rooms need to be empty and clean before that. When we depart, it should be like any other day when we walk out the door. No large packages, no traveling cases. Just the clothes on our back and what's in our pockets."

Laurin looked up from where he was sharpening one of his knives. "You could let us help you move the gear, you know."

"I know that very well. It's more important that none of your faces are seen, none of your voices are heard."

Radulfus grunted. "You should not take all risk."

Dolor shook his head. "It is less risk this way. You are all proficient at your craft: killing. But you are unable to mask your accents, your nervous glances when you come out of the shadows. I am. That is part of what I have trained to do: to be innocuous and easily overlooked when I must be."

Rombaldo kept recording the steady flow of characters. "Should we burn de Requesens' papers, too? Surely we won't need them all."

"No, but our adversaries will, if they are to have a clear compass that points at Borja's men and takes any suspicion off us. When we leave here, we shall make sure to leave clues that point to this flat."

"But they will know he didn't operate from here. They will identify his body and know that he was killed soon after leaving *L'Auberge de Boucle d'Argent*."

"Oh, I am confident they already know that. But whoever killed him will be presumed to be Borja's agent, removing the dandy due to incompetence. Or they will prefer another narrative. It hardly matters: the evidence that de Requesens was the assassins' handler will be authentic. And once they find the code books, they will use them to decipher all the messages they have no doubt intercepted, including those from Rome. At that point, our adversaries will no longer be so determined to find the details of why de Requesens was removed. They will have a powerful indicator that Borja was the architect of whatever happens here. And we, and all sign of us, will be gone." Dolor shouldered the rucksack and began moving for the door.

Rombaldo held up a hand. "Wait a minute; did you hear that?" He pointed toward the radio.

Dolor shook his head.

"Borja—must be him—was going on again about not even he knows the attack plan. But here's an interesting comment: 'From the moment we chose where to strike the blow, it has been our intent to not merely rid ourselves of the current apostate pontiff, but of as many of the faithless cardinals and Reformationist heretics who now hang on his every treasonous word.'" Rombaldo looked up. "Do you think that is just figurative language and wishful thinking, or..."

Dolor shook his head. "No. Because he not only indicates that he knows the place where the attack will take place, but why it was chosen: to do damage to as many of Borja's enemies as possible.

"Which means he has just told us where the ambush will take place. And it is just where we thought." Pedro considered. "And I believe he has also told us roughly when the attack will occur."

"And when's that?"

Dolor shrugged "Before the colloquium concludes. How else can Borja hope to get both cardinals and 'Reformationist heretics'?" Dolor walked briskly toward the door. "There is no time to lose. When I return, I will take two more of the guns to our starting point."

"And the last two? Will you take them during the night?"

"No; too risky. With less traffic at night, there is a greater chance that entering the building with a load might attract notice. I will have to take them tomorrow morning. And hope that will not be too late."

Sharon frowned at Finan's report. "Are you sure?"

"Absolutely, ma'am. If I understood Rochus' runner aright, we're within three hundred yards, already."

Sharon checked the map again, and the points they'd plotted so far. Finan was turning the radio slightly again, looking for the direction that gave him the strongest signal. The two Burgundian soldiers glanced over and muttered something to each other in the almost impenetrable *besontsint* dialect that predominated over in the Battant. But the tone sounded rich with doubt and even superstition.

Sharon had her own doubt to deal with: specifically, that this could have been done so quickly. The signals had begun about seventy minutes ago, when Odo sent a runner down the hall to where she was handling the morning's correspondence. While she double-checked that her shoulderbag of plotting equipment—compasses, binoculars, map, pencils—was ready to go and did the same with her doctor's case, Finan sent a signal to the other Hibernian radio operator, Rochus Zehenter,

who had been left on call in the event that the signaling resumed.

Twenty minutes later, each radio team, furnished
with a battery carrier and three runners each, were
in their designated starting positions: Finan on the
steps of St. Vincent's and Zehenter in the shadow of
St. Paul's. Being on essentially opposite sides of the
city—St. Vincent's to the southeast, St. Paul's to the
northwest—they began the leapfrog process of moving, finding the new direction, waiting for the other
radio operator to do the same, and then starting all
over again.

Within thirty minutes it had become obvious that
the transmitter was between them and only slightly
to the south. Within another twenty minutes, the
two teams caught sight of each other, concluding that
Zehenter now needed to swing around to the other
side of the transmission point to increase the accuracy
of the search. Now Zehenter was located less than a
hundred yards away, between St. Peter's graveyard
and the clutter of houses that backed on it, whereas
Finan was on the street that marked the limit of
those houses in the other direction. The next runner
waited, eager: even he could tell that the hunters were
closing in on their quarry.

Sharon took a deep breath. "We stop here, for now."

"We stop?" Finan's voice ended on an almost comically high note.

The runner, understanding that much English, prepared to dart off, but Sharon held him with a look.
"Let's take a moment, take a deep breath, and start
moving more carefully. Let's not rush around. Let's
not make any overly sudden moves."

376 Eric Flint & Charles E. Gannon

Finan shook his head. "But why?"

Sharon looked sideways at him. "Because anyone can go to the Grantville library and read about radios. And about playing fox and hounds."

"So you think they might be watching for us?"

"No; I'm just saying let's be careful." Actually, Sharon had long ago conjectured that the transmitters did *not* know that they could be located, given enough time. Had they any awareness that extended transmissions could be studied for range and direction, they would have sharply limited the length of each exchange and their willingness to stay on the same frequency the whole time. "So we go slowly. You runners"—she nodded at the knot of them—"you walk now. Except you." She pointed to the eager one. "You run as if our lives depended on it." *And they very well might.*

"*Oui, madame.* And where I run?"

"To Lieutenant Hastings."

"The message?"

"Tell him where we are, that he should keep his men out of this area of the map"—she circled the densest part of the tangle of houses that framed one side of the St. Peter's graveyard—"and that he and my husband should join us here. Right away." She took a deep breath. "The hounds are about to corner the fox."

Pedro Dolor made sure that the boxes containing the guns and grenades were within easy reach, but closed and with a light tarp over them to keep out the dust and moisture. He looked around the low-ceilinged cellar, and, satisfied that all was in order and ready for use, he exited, locking the uneven door behind him. He walked slowly up the mostly earthen stairs, dusted his hands off, emerged into the building's sad excuse for a vestibule, and opened the door.

The late morning light smote his eyes. As he raised a hand to ward it off, he discovered that the vendors who congregated near the road separating two of the city's major inns from both the palace and the convent, were all turning in the same direction. He spared a glance to see what had attracted their attention.

A tall Hibernian—it was Hastings himself—was striding quickly toward the crossroads, barking orders to a group of soldiers with rifles at the ready. He then sent a runner—whom Dolor recognized as one frequently used by Urban's security chiefs—across the street to the Palais Granvelle. Whatever he told, threatened, or promised the boy was obviously a major incentive: he sprinted so hard that he left a trail of dust in his wake.

As Hastings walked toward the street that Dolor himself used to return to his abode, the Hibernian turned, pacing backwards while he stared up, up, and up—until he was signaling to his man in St. Peter's bell-tower. The highest in city center, it was also where the Hibernians had stationed one of their observation posts, as well as one of their snipers. Whatever hand codes they exchanged now—effected with the speed and surety of true professionals—were not ones that Dolor had seen before. But when they were done, the sniper rose and began moving around to the northern compass point of the tower.

The part that looked back across the graveyard at an angle, and ultimately, in the direction of Dolor's rooms.

Dolor slowed, keeping his face calm but moderately interested: the kind of expression that would be expected from a curious tradesman momentarily distracted from his business. The likelihood that this could have anything to do with his men, with his operation, was incalculably small. There had been no error, no oversight, no clues left that could lead Urban's security forces to him. Keeping on his original path, he crossed the street, well behind the half dozen Hibernians following in Hastings' wake.

More activity from the direction of the palace caught Dolor's attention; he was careful not to turn to observe it, but simply notice it peripherally once it came closer. Which it did, the sound of running feet growing until they seemed ready to cross his path . . .

Ruy Sanchez de Casador y Ortiz sprinted past, holding his scabbarded rapier tightly so that it did not bounce or tangle, moving far faster than the thirteen-year-old who had fetched him. Indeed, moving far faster than any man his age should logically be able to move. But Dolor saw what his incentive was soon enough.

Turning the corner into the street, he saw Sanchez heading toward a knot of individuals, perhaps one hundred yards down the street, not far short of where Dolor himself would turn off to head to his lodgings. After a moment, the heads and shoulders in that group moved enough to show a profile—and a complexion— that were unique in Besançon: Sharon Nichols. And right next to her, as always, was her short guard and radioman. Although currently, it seemed to be the latter role that occupied his attention. Holding one of their enviably portable wireless sets, the Hibernian—Finan: yes, that was his name—moved in a slow circle. And as the radio's unusual antenna—a hoop, not a simple wire—turned like a gaping mouth in the direction of Dolor's flat, the group became excited again, pointing in that same direction, and then to a map that Ambassador Nichols was holding as if all at once stunned, triumphant, and worried.

Dolor adopted the expression that would be most inconsistent with what he felt—resigned boredom—and shuffled away from the disturbance and into one of the smaller streets that wound its way into the collection of houses.

And would ultimately lead to the alleys he could follow to his house's back window.

He maintained his pace. And hastily contemplated contingencies he had never imagined needing.

Even when Ruy arrived at a full sprint, the sense of general anxiety that had been growing like a tight fist behind Sharon Nichols' sternum did not go away; it simply ceased getting any larger.

She looked around at the ring of strangely unemotional faces; Hastings, six of his Hibernians, six Burgundian soldiers, and even Finan all had reduced affect. Their eyes no longer revealed anything going on inside of them; they were unblinking visual intake organs and nothing more. It was not the look she associated with violence. That was often the reverse: wide nostrils and eyes, lips tight, often pulled back slightly, faces flushed. No; this was the look of war, of men resolving themselves to violence to come. *And*, she always thought, *of an emptying of their own humanity.*

It wasn't a criticism. Anything but: at least twice in the past year, men wearing that look had been instrumental in saving her life and those of her embassy staff. And she understood why they wore it, why they emptied themselves of humanity: because what soon followed was its opposite. No matter how precise the planning, how professional the conduct, war was always an encroachment of primeval savagery upon civilization. And the ease with which it did so was a horrifying reminder of just how thin a veneer of ritualized codes and courtesies civilization actually was.

Only Ruy's face was still truly human, but she could see that part of him—the part that knew how she felt about such situations, was concerned for her emotional well-being—was already hardening around the edges, chilled by the approach of cold, brutal necessity. Before she could stop it, she shivered—not out of personal fear, but visceral loathing for what was almost sure to come next.

A surge of concern momentarily thawed Ruy's stiffening expression. "Sharon, my—" He stopped and she could read the reason in his eyes: her rank and his role. In this particular place and time, there was no room for personal sentiment, for any expression of intimacy. Every gesture, every nuance, was now carefully circumscribed according to the terrible formalities, the final rituals of order, before the plunge into chaos. "How may I help you?" Ruy said with great gravity, his eyes caressing and soothing her as his hands and arms could not.

"I'm fine, Ruy. I'm just—well, this is the part I don't look forward to."

It was Finan who spoke through a rueful smile. "An' it please the Ambassador, none of us do."

Hastings nodded sharply. "All the more reason to get about it, and quickly."

Ruy's nod was deep and profound, rather than brusque. "What do we know?"

Sharon pointed to the map, letting her finger hover above a dense cluster of houses overlooking the graveyard—terribly fitting, she realized with a chill along her arms and spine. "We just got a final result from Zehenter, which places the transmission source here. Almost certainly this larger building."

Ruy nodded. "And where is Zehenter now?"

Keeping her finger on the graveyard-facing line of buildings, Sharon moved her finger forty yards farther away from St. Peter's. "About there."

"And who is with him?"

"A pair of Burgundian soldiers."

Ruy nodded. "Are you still using runners?"

"Yes."

Hastings nodded, in the annoying way that military men did when they began to understand the tactical importance of the questions another soldier was asking a civilian, foreseeing the operational intent through some combination of professional training and experience. Which, Sharon reminded herself, was a phenomenon even more prevalent among doctors. So she didn't have much room to complain.

Hastings pointed to where Zehenter's team was on the map. "We'll want them to stay in the shadows at this point. Ambassador, is there any further advantage to be gained from using the radios for—er, for—"

"Direction finding," Sharon supplied.

"Yes, thank you: any further use for that?"

Sharon shrugged. "I suppose we could narrow the source down a bit more. But I figured that, if we are on the trail of assassins, they might have a lookout. And if we got too close—"

Hastings nodded. "Ambassador, your instincts were

perfect. And if I understand you correctly, we are now free to move our radios to a different frequency to coordinate directly with Zehenter."

Sharon nodded. "Yes. If you think that's safe."

Hastings shrugged. "As long as we keep to our own code, I suspect we'll be fine." He looked around the rest of the group. "However, from here on, we must make any further approaches very carefully." He crooked a finger at the oldest of the runners they had retained. "Take this message to the observation post in St. Peter's: we need a telescope scan of these four buildings"—he pointed at the suspected tangle of houses on the map—"to see if any of them look suspicious in any way. Have the observer send the outpost's runner with the report." The adolescent lad looked stricken by this exclusion; Hastings explained. "Their runner won't be winded and we need the report as quickly as possible. Go."

As the young fellow dashed off, the lieutenant glanced at the remaining runners. "Have any of you been in any of these buildings?" One of the younger lads put up a hand. "Describe it."

This boy's English was very limited. "Room is one. Low roof. No clean."

"How long since you were there?"

The boy thought. "Four, five month, but no change."

Hastings rubbed his chin. "So a filthy, low-ceilinged single room. Apparently no new tenants recently. Not our target, I think."

"No," Ruy agreed, "but possibly a source of information on their neighbors. Particularly any relatively new neighbors." Hastings seemed ready to send a Burgundian to make inquiries, but Ruy put up a hand. "Let us wait until we receive the observer's report. In the meantime, let us send one of your Hibernians and one Burgundian to each of these street corners." Ruy ran his fingertip from point to point until he had essentially drawn a large box around the houses in question. "From these corners, our men can monitor significant or suspicious movement into or out of the area of interest without being visible to anyone inside it."

Hastings sent the men on their way. "Anything else?"

Ruy glanced at the two remaining Hibernians. "Send one of them to Zehenter, along with another local soldier."

Hastings frowned. "Should we split our forces so completely?"

Ruy smiled. "Have you ever hunted with hounds and riders, Lieutenant?"

Hastings' answer may have been a bit stiff; as an Englishman, he may have heard an oblique social denigration in the hidalgo's question. "I have not had that pleasure, Colonel."

Ruy's answer clearly put him at his ease. "Trust me, Hastings, you are not missing anything. However, think on it this way. Early in the hunt, particularly if the prey is potentially dangerous, you start by surrounding it. Without also alerting it, if that is at all possible. Once you have it contained in an area of your choosing, then you bring your forces back together." He smiled. "We are still hunting what may turn out to be a very dangerous bear. If so, then we will regather in such a way to ensure that it cannot escape. For you may trust that I am obedient to this one military axiom, Lieutenant: I will not allow my forces to be divided in the face of an enemy."

Lieutenant Hastings almost smiled back. "Very good, sir. Anything else?"

"Yes. Each of your squads carries a lantern that can be used as an Aldis lamp, do they not?"

"Correct, sir."

"Excellent. Who in the team is carrying it?"

"Our signals specialist, Feuchtwangen. I take it you wish him to be the man I send to Zehenter?" At Ruy's nod, Hastings leaned toward the man, murmured a frequency number, then turned to Sharon. "Ambassador, if you would be so kind as to instruct Finan to establish contact with—"

"Yes, with Zehenter on the new frequency, as soon as Feuchtwanger delivers it," interrupted Sharon, who was determined not to be pigeonholed as the token clueless civilian. "That way, Zehenter's group can work as our communications center; they'll be able to signal to the tower from the shadows with the Aldis lamp and relay to us via radio. That way, everyone stays on the same page. Is that about right?"

Sharon's grin was mostly patient, but she was just a bit peeved, too. She could tell that Hastings had been about to explain all that, but take twice as long while also making it sound far more difficult. She harbored a secret delight when she saw the tall Englishman's gaze falter uncertainly; *damn, just because I hate watching you zombies prepare for a battle doesn't mean I don't* understand *what you're doing*. She turned to Ruy, who was doing his best to hide a small grin. "Now what?"

"Now," Ruy said, folding his hands in his trademark philosophical pose, "we wait for news."

Chapter 29

Finan looked up from the radio. "I'm in contact with Zehenter."

Ruy nodded. "Very good. Send the following: 'Message begins. Remain in shadows against buildings. Stop. Establish Aldis light exchange with observer in St. Peter. Stop. Request reconnaissance updates from same. Stop. Signal when all achieved. End.' And here comes our preliminary report from the bell-tower." He gestured behind Sharon, who turned to see a runner raising a trail of dust as he came toward them. As she turned away, Ruy used that moment to adjust his shoulder holster, which always tended to ride up a little. Now the up-time revolver would come out without snagging on his buff-coat (more likely) or the armpit rim of his cuirass (much less likely).

He had his hand back in a casual position on his hip by the time Sharon turned back around, her eyes following the young man as he pattered to a panting halt in their midst. When he straightened up out of his post-sprint cramp, Ruy asked, "So, then: what message?"

"The gentleman—the observer—says . . . it must be . . . the middle house. The one . . . with two . . . stories."

Ruy nodded to Sharon, who held out the map. Ruy speared the building he had suspected from the start with his index finger. "This one?"

"*Oui*—yes. That is the one. All the windows. On the north side. Are shuttered. No other houses. Have windows. Shut like that. All the others have them. Open for the breeze." The fellow stopped wheezing. "The gentleman says that the second story windows of this house always appear this way, ever since they were given duty in the bell-tower. They thought that one of the upstairs flats was shut up, maybe—empty— during their first month. But the windows do open. Sometimes. Never for long."

"Did he report on seeing any people there?"

"Only once, twice. Four or five different men. Only men. Not much furniture. Nothing on the walls, not even a cross. At least not where he could see it. But it was clean."

Hastings frowned. "Come again?"

That idiom confused the young *besontsint* for a moment; then: "The walls that he can see, and the parts of the floor—are never dirty. They do not dry their laundry on lines. So they must do it in the rooms. But when they do, the shutters are not open."

Ruy nodded. "Not just simple bachelor laborers or tradesmen, from the sound of it. But before we decide we have found our target—tell me: were the other buildings all normal? Nothing unusual?"

The runner nodded. "Normal. Clothes drying, people shouting—men, women, children—all leaning out from the open windows to cool off when it was hot last week. Sometimes, when there was snow, chamber pots being emptied when they thought no one would see."

Hastings folded his arms. "The second story of that first building does sound a likely place to visit."

Ruy nodded, turned slowly to Sharon, hoping she would not become irate over what had to come next. "Sharon, without you, without your expertise and ideas, we would have missed these persons, whoever they turn out to be. But now, I must ask you to return, with one of the soldiers, to the Palais Granvelle. We must now move toward—"

"I know exactly what you're moving toward, Ruy Sanchez, and you're not going there without me."

Ruy smiled sadly—and he was genuinely sad; he hated disappointing his wife, but... "My peerless and irreplaceable wife, you are the USE's ambassador to this place. Not a soldier. It was madness risking you out on the streets with such scant protection in the first place."

"Yes, well, as the ambassador, I call the shots. Including this one. I'm coming."

"My dear," Ruy said, noticing he sounded as though he had an intolerable stomachache, "I cannot obey that order."

"Ruy, husband or no—"

"Sharon. My darling. I am not disobeying your order because I am your husband. I am disobeying your order because I must also answer to Pope Urban, Estuban Miro, and beyond him, Edward Piazza. And beyond him, Michael Stearns. They, too, have given me duties, and I feel certain that they would unanimously agree that I would be derelict in those duties if I was to allow the ambassador of the USE to remain so close to what might prove to be a hazardous area. So, my dear, must I repeat my entreaty that you leave?"

Sharon was staring at the ground, very hard, as if her gaze might crack it open and a new alternative might arise from it. When she looked up suddenly, Ruy had the terrible premonition that, figuratively speaking, that had just occurred. "Very well. I accept that there is no extenuating circumstance that requires me, as ambassador, to remain in this area. So I will not stay for that reason. Instead, I am staying because I am the only person capable of genuine forensics and adequate analysis of evidence. Whatever happens next, I am essential to a timely investigation of what you find in those rooms."

Ruy opened his mouth but nothing came out. He had assumed that a glib and reasonable counter would present itself almost immediately. But as his agile mind flitted over the various rebuttals that presented themselves, he rapidly found flaws in every one. And if he gave Sharon just one more second—

As it turned out, she didn't need another second. "Forget it, Ruy. You're not going to come up with a way to get rid of me. You can't know ahead of time that whatever you find in this building is going to be the whole assassination plot, tied up in a neat package, and fully resolved by your actions. And if it's not, then you need someone with skill in forensics and crime scene assessment to preserve the clues that might lead us to any further culprits that might still be lurking in Besançon once you're done playing *Miami Vice* in there."

"Playing what?"

"Cops and robbers—or terrorists, I guess. And look:

since I'm a surgeon, I might need to be on hand
to save the lives of any assassins you haven't killed
outright. If we're going to have anyone to talk to
after this, they might need patching up." She stared
around at the group. "And so might some of you. So,
in order to both carry out the best investigation we
can and to protect our own personnel"—she glared
at Ruy—"I've got to be close enough to do the jobs
that only I can do."

Hastings was looking back and forth between security chief husband and ambassador wife. "Sir? Ma'am?"
he said. He sounded like he was trying to swallow a
sideways chicken bone.

Ruy shrugged. "You will detail one of the soldiers
to assist Corporal Finan in protecting our ambassador. And our surgeon. And our forensic specialist."
He smiled at her. "Our own troublesome yet divine
trinity made into one flesh."

Sharon almost smiled as she flounced past him.
"And don't you forget it."

Pedro Dolor walked slowly, rather than stealthily,
toward the most secluded corner from which he could
see the entrance to the house in which he lodged—and
came to a soft, gradual halt; two men were already
at that corner. One was a Burgundian regular, who
was clearly following the lead of the Hibernian with
him. Both were peering around the corner as Dolor
himself had intended to do.

Instead, Dolor turned, almost lazily, to retrace his
last few steps as he thought through his options.

The front door was under observation, so he had no
direct access. Trying to open a hole in the surrounding

forces was the kind of tactic that only a novice or an idiot would consider. Even if he could take the two at the corner by surprise, it was unlikely he could do so without one of them making enough noise to attract the attention of the rest, whose numbers were completely against him. Hastings and six of his Hibernians had run past him. Then Sanchez had followed. The ambassador, while not a concern in and of herself, always had at least one Hibernian with her—Finan—and often a further small retinue of Burgundian soldiers. Furthermore, Hastings had been exchanging hand signals with a sniper and an observer in the bell tower of St. Peter's. If there was a feasible way to defeat that large a force without catching at least half of them asleep in their beds, Dolor didn't know of it—and this was the kind of scenario he pondered frequently, by way of a professional exercise.

Also, the significance of the sniper and observer added a further, very complicating dimension. The emergency escape route Dolor had always relied upon—out the back windows and through St. Peter's graveyard—was suddenly useless. It was a long shot—somewhere between 120 and 130 yards, Dolor estimated—but the Hibernians had the weapon, training, and scope to score hits at that range. And any hit from a .40-72 black powder cartridge was likely to be debilitating, at the very least. Worse still, unless someone in his collection of killers chose this day to start thinking professionally, they were likely to reflexively try the back windows—and thereby, almost certainly lose one or two of their number discovering that the team at St. Peter's was watching for exactly that attempt at flight.

Warning Rombaldo by radio had never been an

option, unfortunately; Dolor had known that the moment he saw the ambassador and others crowded intently around one of their mobile sets. It seemed that, somehow, they had been able to use their own radios to locate his. He remembered encountering mention of such a feat in one of the up-time books he had read: a military thriller depicting the almost surreal battles of their time. But he had been under the (admittedly, vague and indirect) impression that pinpointing the location of a radio transmitter required powerful sets specially designed for that purpose. Evidently, the task was vastly more simple than he'd imagined, which left him with yet another reason not to attempt to warn Rombaldo by radio: he might very well give away his own location. But primarily, he did not pursue that option simply because there wasn't the time. It would have taken close to a quarter hour to retrace his steps to the cellar, unpack their original radio, hook up the batteries. and then hope that its signal would not be crucially degraded by the stonework and dirt surrounding him.

If, therefore, he had any way to still act effectively, and potentially undetected by his opponents, it would be because of the suite's small back window. It took some skillful wriggling to get through it—Dolor was not convinced that Radulfus could make it through at all—and then required a stovepipe climb down for ten feet or so, at which point it was still a seven-foot jump to the ground. But the window actually looked like it belonged to an adjoining building, so unless someone knew the floorplan in advance, there would be nothing suggesting that it was another means of egress from the flat.

Of course, if Sanchez's men had come across that information, or if they were operating on information passed to them by one of Dolor's own men, then his only reasonable option was to leave the scene as quickly as possible. However, Dolor considered the first scenario implausible and the second one very unlikely. There were several reasons why he had sharply restricted the amount of time his men were allowed out of their rooms. The most important had been because, with the exception of Giulio, his handpicked crew were all far better at killing people than meeting or socializing with them. They had the kind of personalities that someone might remember, and not in a flattering fashion. So operational security had required that he minimize their contact with the outside world.

It had the secondary benefit of limiting any opportunities to betray Dolor and the others. None of them had any prior experience of, or contacts in, Besançon; that had been one of Dolor's selection criteria. As a result, even if they had contemplated shopping around to see if someone was willing to pay them an informer's wage, they had no place to start and little opportunity to find a way to begin.

So, hopefully, Sanchez was not aware of the small side window. And if he was . . .

. . . *I'll find out soon enough.*

Ruy waited until the last of the four pairs of "box watchers" they'd sent to monitor the approaches to the house slipped around the corner. "So, we are together now." Which meant five Hibernians (not counting Finan), five Burgundian swordsmen, Hastings, Sharon, Ruy himself, and three runners. He nodded to the youngest runner. "Can I trust you to deliver an important message?"

"Sir, you can!"

Ruy kept a smile off his face. "Very well. You must go to the Palais Granvelle. You must ask to speak to Don Owen Roe O'Neill. If he cannot be located, ask for Dr. Sean Connal. Inform them what you have seen here, that we shall be taking action soon, and that we do not presently require his help but wish him to be aware of what is transpiring. Go now."

As the fellow sprinted off, Ruy turned to the oldest. "How are you called, lad?"

"Simon, Colonel Sanchez."

"Simon, you will walk with this fellow"—Ruy pointed to the youngest of the Burgundian swordsmen—"to the house we have selected. You are to knock on the door of the family in the first floor rooms directly below those in which we are interested. If no one answers, you are to enter the rooms and inspect them; make sure no one remains in them when you leave. If someone is in those rooms, you are to inform them that the Archbishop Rey himself has had news from beyond Besançon that bears upon them and that he must communicate it to them in person—all of them and immediately. If they refuse to all accompany you, he"—another finger jab at the soldier—"shall persuade them to do otherwise. It is crucial that you leave no one in that apartment. Do you understand?"

The boy nodded.

"Off with you, then."

At which point the third and last messenger waited expectantly for a moment before asking, "And what of me, sir?"

"You," Ruy said solemnly, "have arguably the most important job of all."

"And what is that, sir?"

"You are to wait with the ambassadora and her radio-man. If our radios fail, or if we must send a quick, unexpected message to someone without ready access to a set, you will be entrusted with delivering it."

The boy stood very straight. "You may count on me, sir!"

Ruy believed the young fellow meant it. He turned to Finan. "Corporal, please send the following to Zehenter, for relay to St. Peter's by Aldis lamp. 'Message begins. Will enter soon. Stop. Expect attempted flight through rear windows. Stop. If windows open ring church bell once. Stop. If rooms appear strongly held ring again. Stop. Engage any defender holding a firearm. End.'"

Rolf, the corporal in charge of Hastings' reaction force, craned his neck to see down the street. "Runner and Burgundian returning from the house, sir. No one with them."

Ruy nodded, took a moment to put a gentle palm along Sharon's tense arm. "We have all the advantages, my love. It shall be over soon."

Sharon looked at him balefully. "No matter how many advantages you have, trying to arrest or fight people in buildings is never a sure thing."

"You are right. Which is why this is where you remain, with Corporal Finan and the runner. As soon as it is safe, we shall send for you." Sharon nodded, crossing her arms as if there was a chill in the warm air.

The runner and soldier who had been sent to the

house tucked around the corner. "No one home," the soldier explained. "And we think we have a good idea of the floorplan. Looks like the top is pretty much the same as the bottom, but we can't tell for sure: the house seems to share a few walls with adjoining buildings. You come in facing the stairs to the second floor. On your left, on both levels, are small rooms; might be enough for a single person. Might be storage. On the right are the doors into the two larger apartments. The ground floor is essentially two rooms, one in line with the other. Long and thin."

"Railroad flat," Sharon added, using what was apparently an up-time term for such an apartment. "One room after the other, no hallways."

The soldier nodded. "That's it. But the entry narrows a bit. If the top floor is like the bottom, there's an alcove to the left as you go in. Used for storage, mostly."

Hastings folded his arms. "We shouldn't wait too long. Every minute increases the chance that one of them will leave, or something will happen that gives us away."

Ruy nodded; he discovered he was not as ready to simply rush the house as he would have been in earlier times. Why? Was he getting old? Or was he unwilling to shock his wife? Sharon's reaction to what down-timers often saw as brute necessity was often to perceive it as callous indifference to human life.

Or...

...or was he adopting a bit of her view? He'd soldiered for Spain for more than four decades, all told. There were certainly times when the only prudent course of action was often ruthless, even cruel.

But there had been too many other times when he
had witnessed, had even been a reluctant abettor, of
brutality and savagery for its own sake. And if now, in
the October of his life, he felt that guilt more keenly,
perhaps it was not untoward that he repudiate it not
just with words, but with deeds: by changing the
measure of care exerted to protect innocent bystanders from what was, in all likelihood, about to occur.

Ruy looked up almost seven inches at Hastings. "We
will make haste slowly, Lieutenant. We shall advance
on the house—"

"—and then up the stairs and burst in?" Hastings
finished, almost eagerly.

"No. We shall move as quietly as we may into the
positions I indicate."

"And then what?"

"And then we will knock on the door."

"Knock on the door?" Hastings' frown was mighty.
"Sir, that's—that's giving away the advantage of surprise."

"Perhaps that is better than being surprised to find
out that we were wrong about the occupants being
assassins—after we rush in and slaughter innocents.
But if they are not innocents, they will not wish to
fight: they will wish to flee out their back windows.
And I am fairly sure they shall be surprised by what
they experience when they try."

Hastings' frown had almost transformed into a
smile. "The men are ready, sir."

Ruy undid the holster snap for his Smith & Wesson
.357 magnum. "Then let us not keep them—or the
inhabitants of the second floor—waiting."

Hastings glanced at Sanchez as he waited for the axe. He shifted to English, so that the Burgundians would have a harder time following their exchange. "This plan presumes much, Colonel."

"Not really, Hastings. The left-hand door up there"—he jutted a bearded chin up the staircase—"should give way. And it is unlikely that the occupants of the room across the hall will emerge with weapons at the ready. If they were no better disciplined than that, they would have given themselves away to the neighbors long before now. By the time they can even peek out, you should all be under cover near the target door, and we will have three more armed men waiting near the head of the stairs."

"And so, find ourselves in a standoff. We could just rush it, sir. The Burgundians have little appreciation of what they might encounter. They would open a wedge for us. A quick resolution." Hastings received the axe from the trooper who immediately returned to the room, Winchester at the ready and looking perplexed as he slid into the alcove to the left of the door.

Sanchez was shaking his head. "Unfortunately, that quick resolution would kill most of the Burgundians as well as the blackguards we will probably discover on the other side of the door. Whereas a standoff, Lieutenant, is another word for victory, insofar as we are concerned. They will realize that the stairs are passable for them. They will open the rear windows if the way is clear. It will appear so." Sanchez

"When they discover to their dismay that it is nothing but a safe escape route, they will stop considering their vastly diminished options. We shall consolidate our position. They will realize

---

Chapter 30

Lieutenant Marwin Hastings had to remind himself that being an officer meant no longer leading from the very front. Toward the front, yes: otherwise, you were not close enough to see the situation and give appropriate orders. But having spent many years as a sergeant—even before joining the misnamed Hibernians—his deepest instinct was to be the first to charge, to go up the ladders, to leave the trench. Or, in this case, go through the door.

But that job fell to the new sergeant, Rolf, who turned the crude handle and, pushing his shoulder against the door, first peered and then slipped through the widening crack. Percussion cap revolver in his right hand, he moved the door slowly into a full open position. He checked the doorway on the right, and then the left, before waving the rest forward with his left hand.

Hastings, third through the door, pointed at Rolf and the Hibernian who had followed him in and then aimed his finger up the stairway to the door on the left.

Rolf nodded, took a two-handed hold on his pistol,

and, staying close to the right-hand wall, began going up the stairs at a slightly slower than average pace, the second trooper right behind him. The fourth and fifth men, the two right behind Hastings, didn't need further instructions; moving as far to the left as they could, they aimed their lever-action rifles up the stairs at the right-hand door just visible beyond the edge of the second floor landing.

Hastings unholstered his own weapon: a nine-millimeter Glock 17 that had been gifted to him by the Wrecking Crew as a gesture of thanks for his actions at Molino. Which seemed very far away and very long ago at this particular moment.

From beyond the front door, two of the Burgundian swordsmen peeked in, both curious and cautious; they had busted into many houses in their time, but not as if they were playing hide-and-seek. Hastings held up a hand; they shrank back.

Rolf paused two steps below the landing, and, keeping his gun trained on the door to the right, moved diagonally up across the last two stairs and then as far as he could to the wall farthest away from the stairs. Hastings nodded, satisfied; if anyone came out of that door now, they'd be in a crossfire between Rolf's pistol and the rifles at the base of the stairs.

He pointed to the sixth and last Hibernian, then to the right-hand ground floor door. "Survey and report."

The man nodded, opened the door slowly, stopped when it creaked unexpectedly. So did everyone else. When there was no response from the suite on the second floor, he edged it open a few inches more and slipped in.

Hastings glanced up the stairs to the trooper who had

followed Rolf and indicated the door on the left-hand side of the landing. The trooper nodded. He followed the same diagonal path that Rolf had taken, but instead of crossing to the far side of the landing, he stopped just to the side of the left-hand door. He tried the flimsy knob, turned to face Hastings and shook his head.

Which was what Hastings had expected, and dreaded. He leaned toward the front door, put his hand outside, and made a waving motion. In less than two seconds, Colonel Sanchez was in and standing next to him. How could that old man move so quickly? And so quietly?

Before Hastings could update the Catalan, he had glanced up the stairs and nodded. "No way into the room to the left, then."

"Not without using force. As we discussed."

Sanchez nodded. "It is too valuable a position to forego. Proceed."

Hastings glanced toward the right-hand door as the trooper who had opened it slipped bac{ "Report. Quickly."

"Nothing of significance, Lieutenant."

"Is there an axe?"

"An axe, sir?"

"Yes. Quickly!"

"Er . . . yes, sir. A small one-handed trimming, even splitting, smaller pieces

"Excellent. Fetch it quickly. Ther up a position just there, in the alc

"You mean, the alcove of the r

"Am I mumbling, trooper? Y chez will give you instructions be ready to withdraw back h

"Yes, sir!"

that time is entirely on our side. And if they do not decide to surrender, they will ultimately resolve to make a suicidal rush. Of course, not all may be so bold as to follow that resolve. And so we shall have survivors to interrogate."

Sanchez shrugged. "Besides, if you send men charging through a door with the expectation that they will be immediately under attack, they will kill the first thing they see. It is only human nature. And should we be wrong about who is in that room—well, I am not prepared to have innocent lives on my conscience."

Hastings was not eager to add them to his long list of regrets, either, but he was even less eager to take the risks necessary to create the tactical situation that Sanchez had envisioned. However, for good or bad, the decision was not his, and it had been made. "Then, Colonel, if I may—?"

"Proceed, Lieutenant. And remind your men: speed is everything. They must not stop to look. They must carry out the plan and *then* assess."

"I have impressed that upon them, sir. You will give the necessary orders to Luton?"

"Who?"

Hastings nodded toward the trooper huddled in the alcove to the right.

Sanchez leaned, caught sight of the man, and nodded. "I shall coordinate from here." He smiled. "For now."

Hastings held in a sigh. Would this be the day when, finally, the legendary Ruy Sanchez would actually sit out a fight? For the sheer sake of keeping things straightforward and simple, Hastings hoped it would be. But he had his doubts. Axe in hand, he started up the stairs.

✧   ✧   ✧

Larry Mazzare got his trembling foot on the last step up to the top of St. Peter's bell-tower. The sniper and observer turned, stared. The sniper only looked at their unexpected visitor for a moment; shrugging, he huddled back down over his weapon, and arranged the sandbags upon which his weapon rested, making sure that the lever still had an unobstructed downward range of motion.

The observer, who had an Aldis lamp in one hand and a pair of excellent down-time Dutch binoculars in the other, tried to make a little bow. "Your Eminence, I wasn't—that is, we didn't expect—"

Panting for breath, Larry waved off the man's courtesies. "Didn't expect. To be. Here myself," he wheezed out. Damn, when was the last time he'd run? Or jogged? Or did anything other than worry? That had to change pronto. But for now—"We were breaking for lunch when I saw Ruy—er, Colonel Sanchez bolt out of the Palais like the hounds of hell were after him. Stopped the messenger before he could leave. Found out what was happening and where."

"And you knew to come here?" The observer sounded like he was poised between utter amazement on one side and utter disbelief on the other.

Larry shook his head. "Back in my world, I was a hunter, too. Priest or no priest, meat was expensive. I wasn't going to starve, but there were some families and shut-ins who needed that protein. So, sure I came up here; best hunter's stand in town, from what I can see. And I knew it would have a vantage point, given where the messenger said Sha—Ambassador Nichols had detected the radio transmissions."

The observer shrugged. "Can't say that I understand what's going on half as well as you seem to, Your Eminence. But—are you just here to watch?"

Larry shook his head. "More to help. If I can."

"Well," the observer mused, "we do need one more hand."

"For what?"

The observer pointed to an iron hammer lying beside the sniper's bench. "For that, Your Eminence."

"And what do I do with it?"

The observer smiled. "I'll tell you when the time comes. But for now, just stand next to the bell—"

Hastings reached the landing, handed the axe to Rolf, who was slightly shorter, but more heavily built, then crouched to the left of the target door.

Rolf signaled the other trooper to join him. Together they readied themselves in front of the door, Rolf prepared to unleash a kick just to the left of the knob, the other ready to shoulder it in.

Hastings raised his hand, three fingers up. He silently mouthed a countdown as he folded each finger back into his palm: "One. Two. Three—"

Rolf's kick broke the old lock easily, and the two of them were in the room before the door had finished swinging back on its hinges.

Hastings, Glock trained on the target door, spared a quick look. No personal effects: just a cot, ratty blankets, and happily, a much-stained and many-seamed table that was clearly used both for food preparation and eating.

By the time Hastings had taken that in, Rolf had pinned the door back, putting it—and him—out of sight from the target door. He brought the axe around swiftly at the top hinge and half split the wood in which it had been fixed. A moment later, the other trooper had worked the table around so that it faced the door. He tipped it forward with a crash; it was now cover for at least two kneeling men.

Hastings turned back to look at the target door, gave a thumbs-up down to Sanchez at the bottom of the stairs, and hoped to Jesus Christ Almighty that Rolf would be quick with that axe...

Rombaldo, sitting with Giulio in yet another attempt to teach his fellow Italian how to send and copy coded communications from the radio, started at the crash just beyond their door. "God's balls, what's that?"

Laurin, who was sitting in the alcove with the shotgun, glanced toward Radulfus, who was up in one smooth motion, his hand out for the weapon.

"Might be the neighbors—" Martius began.

A heavy blow followed by a splintering sound put aside any notion that this could be any typical domestic disturbance.

As Laurin handed off the shotgun to Radulfus and scooped up the Hackenjoss & Klott revolver from the top of an empty box next to entry, he waved toward Martius. "Take a look!"

"Me?" said Martius in a voice that was altogether too high and too loud.

Another splintering blow landed someplace just beyond the door: it sounded like something metal clattered away from the impact.

"Yes, you, idiot," Rombaldo hissed, running over the contingencies he and Dolor had worked out if the watch ever came knocking. Except, if that was the watch, why hadn't they just come busting in?

Martius was still delaying.

Another splintering blow. Radulfus, who had squatted down in the alcove and had lined up all the ready shotgun shells in front of him, nodded and mouthed the word "axe."

"Go open the door, damn you!" Rombaldo said in a low gutteral voice. "Now!"

Martius paced cautiously to the door, and, hand trembling, turned the knob and pulled it toward him.

At the same moment that Rolf brought down the axe a fourth time and the door to the small room sagged on its mostly separated hinge, the target door opened.

The trooper beside Rolf brought up his rifle, shouted, "Halt!"

The door across the landing immediately slammed shut.

Rolf grabbed his room's listing door, gave it a twist: a groan and a snap and it came free of the bottom hinge. As he maneuvered it into the narrow space between the door frame and the table, he pitched his head at the target door and grunted, "What did he look like?"

"Medium height, medium build, nervous as a witch at a bonfire."

Hastings nodded, whispered, "Tell them to come out without weapons. By order of the City Watch."

Which the trooper did. There was no response. However, it sounded as if people were scurrying around in the rooms beyond the target door.

❖   ❖   ❖

"You're sure?" asked Rombaldo.

"*Sard!* Of course, I'm sure," Martius almost whined. "Hibernians, two of 'em. In the room across the way. An' it's already blocked off by a table."

"How did they find us?" Giulio hissed, wringing his hands, and glancing at the shuttered rear windows.

"Doesn't matter," Rombaldo snapped. "They did."

"It matters if one of you is a betrayer," Radulfus observed evenly.

From beyond the door, came a youngish voice. "By order of the City Watch, you must come out, unarmed."

Laurin padded two steps away from his position near the door. "I saw them, too. These asslickers have rifles. Copied up-time rifles. Powerful. We can't fight our way out."

Rombaldo ignored Laurin, whose conclusion had been implicit before he'd opened his mouth. Of course they couldn't fight their way out: the Hibernians had clearly taken their time to formulate a plan. Which meant they had had time to gather sufficient numbers. And they probably had the watch—or the local soldiers, or both—here with them. Rombaldo sighed; even though he and the others had up-time equivalent weapons—and the shotguns were arguably much better suited for a shootout in such close quarters—there was no way they could fight their way out the door, down the stairs, and off to—

To where? They had to disappear. And there was only one way to do that. Well, two, actually, but there was no reason to share that detail at this particularly moment. "Giulio, take the escape rope and crawl out the back window."

"It's not night-time, and they could be out there!"

Rombaldo rolled his eyes, even as he thought, *yes, they most certainly could be out there.* "So open one and check first, dolt! And if it looks clear, shinny down with the rope. We'll follow. Martius, get the other shotgun and cover him." That addition had the effect of making Giulio a great deal less anxious.

"And what about us?" Radulfus gestured to Laurin and himself.

"Shoot them if they try to get in. Follow us down as soon as we're out the window."

Giulio, next to the window and about to undo the shutter latch, turned toward Rombaldo. "And what are you doing?"

Rombaldo was going into the other room that he and Dolor had divided between them. "What do you think? Getting the other revolver and the papers that we can't afford for them to find. Now go!"

Larry Mazzare decided that a cardinal's cassock had been designed to keep heat in, not let it out. Although the air was cool, particularly up here, his body felt like it was trapped in its own, mobile sauna—

"Middle window opening!" cried the observer, so loudly that Larry was afraid their enemies might hear. "Your Eminence, one ring of the bell, please."

Larry complied, striking the side of the bell with the hammer. It made an odd sound: sharper, less resonant. At the same time, the observer leaned back where he could no longer be seen from the building, but was visible to Zehenter's team, just twenty yards farther along the line of houses and hidden in their shadows. He turned up the wick of his Aldis lamp, aimed it, and began flicking out a message.

The sniper's voice was almost a bored monotone. "One man, slight build. Crawling out on the roof of the building beneath it."

Larry looked over his shoulder. Saw the spare fellow pulling something behind him. "Is he playing out a rope?"

"Your Eminence has keen eyes. He is indeed." The sniper adjusted the scope, then his rifle, tracking with the target. He leaned his head toward the observer. "What is Zehenter saying? Do we take the shot?"

The observer shook his head. "No. CO wants this guy as a prisoner. Let him get most of the way to the ground; the Burgundians will bag him when he's dangling on his rope."

Which the spare man was already doing as he went over the roof of the adjoining building, scrabbling down toward the ground just beyond the low graveyard wall. The observer triggered his Aldis lamp, then raised his binoculars.

A moment later, three Burgundian swordsmen came charging out of the shadows. Even up in the bell-tower, their shouted orders to surrender were audible, albeit faintly.

But Larry, who was not busy sending signals or lining up a shot through a scope, noticed what neither of the Hibernians did: a shadow moving near the window. "Movement at the window," he muttered.

The sniper cursed and twitched his rifle back in that direction.

But not before a figure there leaned out with something cradled in his hands. Something that looked very much like—

Two shotgun blasts split the dry afternoon air in

quick succession. Two of the Burgundians fell over, one writhing, the other going down heavy, limp, motionless. The other Burgundian fell in his haste to reverse his charge.

The sniper began firing rapidly at the man in the window, who had inadvisedly paused there to reload his weapon. The first bullet clipped the window sill. The lever clacked. The second shot was an overcorrection; plaster jetted out from the building's outer surface, just shy of the window. The smoke from the first two rounds, blowing up and back, went past Larry's face as a fast *blam!-krakchak; blam!-krakchak* sequence began, cleared just in time for him to see the fourth round hit: a slight puff of dark red. The fractionally seen form tumbled away from the window.

At the same moment that the one unwounded Burgundian finished stumbling and scampering back into the shadows that were out of the window's field of fire, the observer called out: "First target cutting across graveyard. Eleven o'clock, range increasing."

The sniper had paused to put two more rounds in the big Winchester's magazine, looked up to see the observer's finger tracking along with the slight man. He swung his weapon in that direction and laid it atop the sandbags in one smooth motion.

"Ten o'clock," continued the observer.

The sniper squeezed the trigger; a gnat's breath later, the top half of an old tombstone behind the fleeing man disintegrated in a small, angry explosion of talclike white smoke.

Larry held his breath. It was essential that none of the assassins escape, but to see one, probably unarmed, gunned down as he fled—

Before Larry Mazzare could decide what he should—what he *could*—say, the sniper had levered another round sharply into the Winchester's chamber, paused, exhaled, and squeezed the trigger—all in less than two seconds.

The tiny figure, the only one amidst the forest of stone death markers, went down, arms outstretched and tilted up, as if trying to break a fall and reach out to heaven, all in the same motion.

Larry hung his head.

"That's done," said the sniper, who immediately started reloading his weapon again.

"Your Eminence," asked the observer.

Larry looked up, hoped he wouldn't vomit.

"I've just seen another man moving, beyond the windows. He has a gun. You have to ring the bell. Again."

Larry, wondering bitterly if anyone in all of Besançon now doubted that the second floor of that house was "strongly defended," raised the hammer.

Chapter 31

The church bell—a distant and uncommonly flat sound—rang again.

"*Scheisse*," muttered Rolf.

Hastings simply nodded. It wasn't as if, given the two shotgun blasts from within, there was any doubt that the room would be strongly held against them. He gestured Rolf over to join him next to the target door, gave a hand sign that the first trooper on the stairs, Bruggeman, was to take his place. The next trooper advanced up the stairs, two of the Burgundians stepping up to wait just behind him.

Rolf gathered his equipment, vaulted the door-and-table barricade/parapet, and crouched down next to Hastings.

"*Scheisse*," he repeated vehemently, glaring at the door. "I'll bet you want me to splinter that lock."

Hastings patted him on the shoulder. "This is what they pay us for."

"But why always *us*, sir?"

"What do you mean?"

"First, there was that insane fight inside the farmhouse

in Molino, and now, here. Why do we always get the room-to-room situations?"

"Just lucky, I guess. But this time, I think we've improved the odds. Substantially." Hastings pointed to the two Hibernians sheltering in the right-hand room, their Winchester .40-72's laid atop the overturned table. "Bruggeman, Haaf: if we come under fire, return it. If you see a target, take it." He glanced at the trooper waiting on the top step. "Stand ready, Wachter." He turned back to Rolf. "You count it out."

Rolf nodded; he looked at Wachter until their eyes were locked on each other. Rolf drew back the axe and silently mouthed the count: "One. Two. Three . . ."

Rolf swung the axe—too hard. It bit into the door above the handle. "*Scheisse!*" he shouted.

The response from the room—two pistol shots—punched holes in the target door, then the door laid sideways in front of the table. But having penetrated two stiff surfaces, the bullets did not have enough energy to make any significant progress through the thick tabletop. Bruggeman and Haaf each put a round back through the door.

Rolf already had the axe in motion. This time, it landed just above the handle. A splintering crunch and the target door gapped. As Rolf hauled the axe back, Wachter leaned around from his position at the top of the stairs, struck the door with the butt of his gun, and tucked back again swiftly.

A shotgun blast erupted outward through the opening door. A pistol round punched through the wall alongside Rolf. Hastings reached up, grabbed the sergeant's belt, and pulled him down as Bruggeman and Haaf returned fire.

Hastings glared at Rolf. "At this range, walls are concealment, not cover." He glanced over at the barricade. "Layout like downstairs?"

"Yes, sir, and the alcove is where we expected it." Haaf answered from behind the table; it sounded as if he was reloading. A wise use of time, reflected Hastings as he raised his left hand—in the thumbs-up position—to where Sanchez would see it.

From the entryway downstairs, he heard the Catalan's reply. "Understood. Trooper Luton, stand ready."

Rombaldo had wasted a precious second debating whether he actually should remove a few of the other random papers near the radio. In that moment, the axe had crashed into the door a second time, splintered the lock, and more shots were traded. Well, no reason to wait.

Rombaldo went directly to the small, heavily shuttered window in the room he and Dolor shared, swung the latch away quietly, holstered the pistol he had scooped up, and swung his left leg out over the ledge.

It was about fifteen feet to the ground, which he would have simply risked jumping had the window not been so narrow that he had to exit sideways. But the walls on either side of the window came out from the building, hemming it into its own narrow channel. So, hanging onto the top of the frame with both hands, and bringing up his left leg so that his foot was braced hard against the wall to the right of the window, he moved his right leg out so that it was next to the other. Extending his knees slightly, he felt the left-hand wall grind into his back. Pushing hard with his legs, he removed his hands from the top of the window frame and began to shrug and shimmy his way down the channel.

It was exhausting work to lower himself even a foot. And there were another five to go. *A stovepipe climb*, he thought angrily, *I'm too damned old for this.*

But, he philosophized as he inched down the second foot, *I'd better hurry up if I want to get any older...*

Crouching behind the bed he had pushed closer to the now-breached door, Laurin considered reloading the two spent chambers in his revolver, but decided against it. The bastards could come through the door any second. If he was reloading when they did, he might as well have put his own pistol to his head and pulled the trigger.

But it was equally suicidal to lean out and fire, even though he could hear them muttering and moving less than twelve feet away, just beyond the door and in the room across the hall. What to do? Well, when in doubt—"What now, Rombaldo?"

Laurin waited for an answer. None came. "Rombaldo?" Shit! Had that shifty Bolognese actually—?

"Gone, I wager," Radulfus muttered from his position in the alcove just beyond the door. He finished reloading and closed the action quietly. He nodded at Laurin, then jerked his head toward the back: toward the narrow window through which Rombaldo must have fled. "You go out, too. I cover you. And follow."

Laurin gauged his chances. They were good, if he could survive a fast leap across the open area between himself and the rear framing wall of the alcove. Unfortunately, that leap exposed him to the two Hibernians sheltering behind their makeshift cover in the opposite room. But once behind that framing wall, he had enough cover to run all the way to the back of the flat and slip into the private room where Dolor and Rombaldo had slept—and where the narrow window was presumably already open and waiting for him. How Radulfus planned to follow him was difficult to foresee, but he didn't waste any time thinking about that. It was every man for himself now, and if the big Swiss didn't realize it, well, he should not have embarked upon the career of a professional killer.

Because abandoning your peers at judicious moments was just another, inevitable, part of the job.

Before Laurin could even finish that thought, before he could remember how terrified he was of exposing himself to the murderously powerful rifles of the Hibernians, he leapt.

Hastings, who had finally had the time to get out his corner mirror and check beyond the entry to the flat, started when a body flashed across his field of vision: a man with a pistol, diving from the right side of the room to the left, behind the rear wall of the alcove.

Haaf and Bruggeman both fired quickly, but not quickly enough: they heard the man roll to his feet and then begin running, sticking close to the back wall of the flat which they could not see.

But in the next moment, a spatter of distant rifle fire announced that the sniper had seen the movement through the open rear window. Rounds started cutting into the floorboards, blasting plumes of plaster through the walls. The running man, desperate to evade this sudden fusillade, evidently swerved away from that outer wall, because he emerged back into view, forgetting or misgauging where he would become visible to Haaf and Bruggeman.

The two Hibernians were already leaning over their rifles as the man reappeared in their field of vision, dancing and ducking away from the sniper's bullets. They fired simultaneously and began working their lever actions and blasting rounds at the man. He turned, raising his pistol as he was hit, faltered, and then was hit twice again. He fell his length upon the splintered floorboards, a long moan escaping from him as he did.

In the very next moment, a figure—dim through the smoke—leaned around the near corner of the alcove and discharged a shotgun straight at the Hibernians. Haaf, who was not as experienced but was both more cautious and more attentive to training, had not risen up to get a better look at the damage they had done to the man with the pistol. Bruggeman—larger, good-natured, and somewhat inattentive—had put his head up. Three single-aught balls punched bloody holes in the upper right side of his head; he slumped away from the overturned table, nerveless, blood welling up from the gaping wound that was located where his eye had been.

Hastings resisted his first impulse: to charge around the corner and kill Bruggeman's killer. Instead, he shouted: "Target confirmed. Start the music."

Ruy Sanchez turned to the trooper who'd been left standing in the matching alcove of the first floor room as if he was a truant boy. "Mr. Luton, fire upward. All the rounds in your rifle. And then step back. Quickly."

"But—"

"Do it."

Luton shrugged even as he shouldered the rifle, aimed straight up, and levered five rounds through the ceiling above him.

As bullets started jetting up geysers of splinters and dust around the assassin in the second floor alcove, Hastings pointed to the two Burgundians at the top of the stairs and made the combined hand signal for "wait" and "follow me."

Cursing, the gunman in the alcove—miraculously missed by all five bullets—fired his own weapon through the much-vented floor boards beneath him.

Ruy Sanchez was biting his lip as Luton paused a moment before beginning to step back out of the alcove—at the very moment a blast and downward spray of balls tore through the ceiling and pounded the floor where he had stood a fraction of a second before. As it was, splinters from the already savaged ceiling shot wider, several lodging in his buff coat, one cutting a long bloody gash along his left cheek.

Luton stumbled back into Sanchez, who steadied him.

Ruy sighed. "Next time, when you are warned to step back quickly, do so."

Hastings moved as soon as he heard the shotgun firing. Racing around the door, he went low for the near corner of the alcove. Rolf, a step behind him, went high.

They had thought to catch the assassin with an empty weapon. But the man—as tall as Hastings and as heavily built as Rolf—had already reloaded one chamber of his sawed-off shotgun, and was snapping it closed as they leaned around the corner.

Only three feet away.

The shotgun came up. Hastings yelled, "Halt!" Realizing that there was no time for that, he began squeezing the trigger of the Glock 17 at the same moment that Rolf's percussion cap revolver went off just a foot above his head.

The big assassin was hit a fraction of a second before he could bring the shotgun around, staggered as three nine-millimeter and two .44 caliber bullets hit him in the torso. The wrist holding the shotgun weakened, so that, at the moment it should have cleared the edge of the alcove, it was still lagging, wobbly—

It discharged.

The two Hibernians kept firing in a frenzy of self-preservation.

Splinters flew out from where the corner of the alcove had been. And in that very moment:

—Hastings felt a heavy, dull blow to the side of his head and a sharp pain in his lower thigh;

—Rolf barked out an urgent "*Scheisse!*"

—and the man slumped over, his shirt riddled and bloody.

As the assassin slid down the wall, leaving a trail of multiple blood smears, Hastings half-fell, half-pushed away from the site of the point-blank gun-battle. Rolf was clutching his left bicep; blood, but not a lot, was leaking out between his fingers. Before Hastings' rump hit the ground, the two Burgundians charged into the room, swords drawn, eyes wide and desperate and murderous. Dazed and partially deafened from all the discharges in such rapid sequence and in such close quarters, Hastings waved them on, put a hand to the side of his helmet, and felt a huge dent that had not been there before. Then, as he glanced down at the long splinter of ancient wood that was sticking out of his thigh, he heard a fierce, wild cry, deeper in the room. And as he looked up, he knew what it meant: the Burgundians had come across the man that Haaf and Bruggeman had taken down—and he was still alive.

Hastings, his voice muffled in his own years, yelled, "NOOO!!!"

But too late: the Burgundians' swords came down, almost in unison, and finished the job that the Hibernians' Winchesters had started.

From behind, Rombaldo heard a ferocious flurry of gunfire—shotguns and rifles—a pause, and then more of the same.

He forced himself to keep his pace casual, just as he had rehearsed with Dolor. He even yawned. Not that there was anyone here to see him; he'd chosen the most circuitous, shaded, and narrow alley that led away from the flat. And in the general direction of St. Peter's and the palace. Because—again, as Dolor had taught him—most people who either try to hide, or try to find those who do, are amateurs. And part of what an amateur does is to project what they would do in a given situation and then assume their quarry is following a similar plan of action.

It was not really a flaw, Dolor had explained: just an unavoidable limitation. Amateurs not only lacked the skill and methods of professionals, they lacked the correct habits of thought. Which included realizing that the course of action chosen by an expert adversary might bear no resemblance to what anyone else, even another expert, might choose. Contrary to a commonly held assumption, experts had less in common than amateurs; after all, they not only drew from a much more diverse array of tools and skills, but blended them in unique ways.

Another, longer spasm of gunfire: a good sign. If the attackers still hadn't secured the second story flat, then they had not yet commenced a broader search. Indeed, it would take them a while to sort out the aftermath of the shootout, giving Rombaldo all the time he needed to—

"Rombaldo."

He started at the sound of his name, uttered very near by, turned toward the narrower alley he had just passed, thought to draw his gun—

—and realized, with a rush of relief, that he knew that voice. "Dolor!" he whispered so emphatically that it was almost as loud as had he said it in a normal speaking tone. "Thank Christ and all His whores! They found—"

Dolor had emerged from the shadows of the alley. "I know. I saw. Are they close behind you? Where are the others?"

"Are they 'behind me'?" Rombaldo repeated dismissively. "I got out the side window. They're still fighting back there. As for the others . . ."—Rombaldo shrugged, looked away—"They are dead. Or as good as. Now, where do we go? The cellar?"

Dolor shook his head. "Too close. We will need to flee further than that. But before we do"—Dolor moved closer, looked up and down the alley, and dropped his voice one confidential octave—"I need you to carry this."

Rombaldo, following his employer's lead by checking up and down the alley too, experienced a sharp stab of pleasure as he realized that Dolor was entrusting him with something more important than ever before—and in that same moment, realized that the pleasure and the stabbing pain were not one and the same.

He looked at Dolor and then down. Suddenly light-headed, he saw his employer's poignard go in and out of his chest two more times. He looked back up—he'd started sliding down, one hand on Dolor to keep himself from falling—and realized that those calm eyes, those treacherous hazel eyes, were likely to be the last thing that he would ever—

Dolor stepped back as Rombaldo, or rather his corpse, fell over on the small, uneven cobbles like a broken doll, his legs folded under him at an awkward angle that only corpses can achieve. He checked himself quickly: no blood. Wounds to the heart do not spurt like arterial ones, but one could never be too careful.

Dolor switched his poignard out of his left hand, wiped it on Rombaldo's trousers, sheathed it, and faded back into the narrow alley from which he had emerged. Rombaldo's perception had been accurate in one regard: there would not be any pursuit yet. Indeed, they might not realize immediately that anyone had fled through the side window, given the tight fit and contorted position one had to adopt to use it, to say nothing of the fairly high level of athleticism required. And even once it was identified as an escape venue, they would be hard pressed to organize even a shorthanded search, distracted as they would no doubt be by the medical needs of their own wounded.

As Dolor emerged into a wider alley that backed on one of the major inns across from the Carmelite convent, he was further reassured by Rombaldo's grim assessment of the odds that any of the others had survived. They would certainly not surrender because they all knew what awaited them: torture and eventual execution, and if not for their murderous intents in Besançon, then for the dozens of murders they were known to have committed elsewhere.

And if they had not all been slain outright or mortally wounded? Well, there was nothing Pedro Dolor could do to rectify the situation. There was only hiding and, hopefully, surviving the first twenty-four hours. After that, the search would continue but begin losing both the attention and fervor necessary for it to be successful.

So the only loose end had been Rombaldo, whose elimination had been regrettable but necessary. If the security forces, but particularly Nichols and Sanchez, knew that even one assassin escaped, they would mount and maintain an intense search. It was also entirely possible that Rombaldo's face had been seen by either the sniper or the observer whom the Hibernians had prudently placed in St. Peter's belltower weeks ago. Armed with that kind of information, the ensuing manhunt would have been relentless and probably have led them to Pedro Dolor himself.

Dolor emerged from the alley that ran behind the inn, ambled casually into the small street that communicated with Besançon's main boulevard. Being caught now, at this middle stage of his grand scheme, was unacceptable. It would mean the end of Wilbur Craigson's lifelong ambition and objective: to rise up, to be proximal to the persons of the highest rank in the Escorial, those who had both the authority over—and responsibility for—the actions of the Spanish Empire and its many agents. And in order to preserve that objective, Rombaldo had had to perish.

Dolor waited for the traffic in the street to relent a bit. Apparently, the commotion and gunfire several hundred yards away had drawn all sorts of curiosity seekers. As he started across the street and headed for the door that led to the basement from which he had emerged less than half an hour ago, he thought of Rombaldo with one final tinge of regret. It had been an unfortunate necessity, and the deed had been decidedly inelegant. But the alternative would have been disastrous.

Both for Wilbur Craigson and the entirety of Europe.

Chapter 32

Not finding Ruy on the ground floor where she was told he'd be, Sharon panicked. She pounded up the stairs, pushing past one of the Burgundians so forcefully that he almost fell. Of course, Sharon was a big woman and a lot of the Burgundians were, well, to her way of thinking, a little on the runty side.

She arrived on the landing and saw two Hibernians in a small room beyond an overturned table. And peeking around the bloody corner of that table, she could see a pair of unfamiliar boots, toes up. But no Ruy. She turned to the doorway on the right—

—and she stopped. Not just moving, but breathing.

Carnage. The blood started just beyond the entry, and intermittent pools and spatters of it extended as far as she could see, to the rear wall of the room. And there, standing in the middle of it all, was Ruy Sanchez. Who looked up, smiled, then evidently saw something in her face which made him rush over. "Sharon, my love, you look—unwell."

Sharon shook her head. It was all she could do. She hadn't known she'd have this reaction. She knew that if shooting started, that there would be blood and bodies. But what she hadn't expected is that she would suddenly relive that terrible night last July when the assassins hunting Urban had attacked them by surprise at Molino. And suddenly, she was not just here in Besançon; she was there, too. It was the moment when she'd first emerged from the radio room, where Ruy had forced her to remain with Odo. It was the moment she came to the head of the stairs, the first time she'd seen the bodies strewn all across the greatroom, and then all through the house—right before she started operating on them. Dozens of them. Without benefit of anesthesia beyond whiskey, grappa, and then when that ran out, cheap wine which they were more likely to vomit up from the agony.

She closed her eyes. She wasn't there. She was...

Here. She opened her eyes, stared at Ruy. "Right," she assured him. "Just having a...moment. I'm—I'm better, now. Are there any surgical cases?"

"Only one that's serious. A Burgundian soldier was hit by one of their shotguns out the back window. He has one ball in the leg, one in the shoulder. Then there are a few minor wounds: Rolf was hit by a shotgun ball in the left arm, but it didn't do more than break the skin; he plucked it out with his own fingers. Which was foolish, since that set him bleeding more heavily. Lieutenant Hastings was stunned by a ball that hit his helmet after going through both sides of the alcove's coaming, and he has some splinters in his thigh. More splinters gashed Luton's cheek."

Sharon nodded. "Just give me a minute. To get someone to start boiling some water—"

Ruy's hand was on her arm. "Sharon. My love.

Breathe deeply. Again. There. Now, consider. This is what you have been training Dr. Connal to do: using up-time surgical methods. None of these wounds are life-threatening. In most armies, no one would even treat the splinters or a ball that did not lodge itself beyond the reach of simple fingers. So: allow Connal to practice the art in which you have mentored him."

Sharon nodded, both because Ruy was right and because she was relieved that she didn't need to rush right into surgery. "What kind of pop-guns were the bad guys using, that they couldn't even get a bullet through Rolf's buff coat?"

Ruy shook his head. "The projectile in question went through two walls at a corner, then encountered his buff coat. I conjecture that the bullet was so deformed and slowed by the time it hit his arm, that it hadn't enough energy left to do more than it did. Still, he was—we all were—very lucky. Only two of our number are dead: one of the swordsmen and one of the Hibernians."

The fact that this did seem very fortunate to Sharon told her just how much her perspective had adapted to the realities of 1636 CE. In this day and age, most similar scenarios would have been bloodbaths: men charging up stairs, a tangle of corpses at the doorway, bullets pounding through walls, killing civilians. What Ruy and Hastings had done—combing through adjoining apartments to clear them, and then the carefully sequenced preparations—were just not how room entries were conducted in this era.

"Okay," Sharon said, determined to keep her mind from veering to comparisons that made her at once nauseated and suddenly, unexpectedly homesick. "That leaves me free to put on my forensic investigator hat. Who was in here?"

Ruy took her to where she could see the three corpses. "A fourth is being recovered from St. Peter's graveyard," he murmured.

Sharon looked at the corpses. The causes of death were obvious and without investigatory value, so she focused on other features. Such as—"None of these guys are scruffy. Even their fingernails are clean, except for the smaller guy who got shot at the window." She scanned around until she discovered what she expected to find. "Look at those cakes of soap, those washbasins. Is that typical?"

Ruy frowned. "Not at all. Not even among elite units in a regular army."

Sharon nodded. "And like the observer said, the place is clean and totally without decoration. No trash, no distractions: all business."

Ruy nodded. "Their leader insisted on order, and inspired enough respect—or fear—to get it. Not common among men such as these."

Sharon nodded. "I thought not. No more common than up-time pattern weapons." She gestured toward them, then looked back at the corpses. "And not a left-hander among them, judging from where and how they've strapped on their daggers and small swords."

Ruy smiled. "You are very observant."

"Yeah? Well, I observe something else: no stiletto. Unless there's something you haven't shown me yet."

"Well, there is—but it is not a stiletto. There was no such weapon among them or their effects."

Sharon nodded, then started, glanced around. "Speaking of their effects... There's at most one change of clothes here. No coats. Not much in the way of toiletries. Did you find any food?"

Ruy shrugged. "A few loaves. A cheese. A knife."

"But they've been here for weeks, for as long as the Hibernians have had an outpost in the belltower."

Ruy brushed one mustache wing, then snapped his hand away self-consciously. "So, they were in the process of divesting themselves from this place. Which goes along with what we found regarding their weapons."

"Not enough of them?"

"Not enough ammunition. Had the engagement gone on for another half minute, they would have run out of cartridges. Which are disturbing in and of themselves: both are consistent with types we use."

Sharon looked again, then sucked in breath as her upper teeth came down gently on her lower lip. "Well, those are the same pistols our Marines use, that's for sure. But a sawed-off shotgun?"

One of Ruy's eyebrows lowered. "Not among your army, but several members of Harry Lefferts' old Wrecking Crew evinced a preference for such weapons."

Sharon frowned, nodding. "They sure did. I wonder . . . ?"

Ruy matched her nod. "So do I. But before you ponder too much on that, come see the last item of interest."

He led her into a small, semiprivate room at the far end of the flat. He waved a hand in the direction of the "item of interest." "*Voilà.*"

Sharon walked closer to the expected radio. It wasn't an up-time model, nor one of the better knockoffs. But what was most interesting—and even disturbing—were the neatly stacked codebooks, and beside the operator's chair, the carefully filed transcripts of messages received and transmitted. Dated. And signed. She looked back at Ruy. "Well, this should help find out who's behind all this." Then she looked at the orderly radio operator's station, the spartan surroundings, the number of beds. "One or more of this group is missing."

Ruy stood aside . . . revealing a window, less than eighteen inches wide, the shutters back. "I am in complete agreement with your conjecture."

Sharon walked over to it and looked at the unpromising pathway to the ground. "Something here doesn't add up," she murmured.

"What in particular? There are certainly many loose ends, including a man who almost certainly escaped. Perhaps with some of the records we'd find most useful."

Sharon nodded. "Yeah, but I mean something more general. This whole setup; it just feels wrong somehow, like we're missing something big, not something small." She frowned and shook her head. "It's just a hunch. I can't explain it any better than that."

One of the runners had entered, whispered a short message into Ruy's ears, and disappeared.

"What was that?"

"I believe one of our loose ends has just turned up."

"Oh? What kind of loose end?"

"A body. Found not more than eighty yards from where we are standing, in an alley that would be most swiftly reached by exiting through this window. And with another of the USE Marine pistols in his belt."

Sharon nodded. "So, that must be the head honcho— or at least the guy who was told to run. How did he die?"

"Would you be surprised if I told you he was

stabbed straight in the heart? At least three times? And from very, very close range?"

Sharon frowned. "Now that you mention it, that doesn't surprise me at all. I guess I'd better go have a look before they ruin the crime scene."

Larry Mazzare lingered longer over his meal in the chapter house because Ruy and Sharon did as well. When they rose to exit, so too did he. And, like them, he waved off his combination bodyguard and assistant.

When he emerged into the cooling air of dusk, thick with the fragrance of the garden, he discovered that the couple had already begun their evening walk but more slowly than usual. Larry followed their path with a slightly quicker step; he saw Ruy half turn his head and smile.

Thirty seconds later, Larry drew up behind them. They parted so that he could join their stroll, one on either side of him. "A busy day," he said quietly.

"Quite, Your Eminence," Ruy replied with a slight smile.

Sharon sighed. "Look, Larry: I get it. I know you have to get the latest news from us. So you don't have to beat around the bush. Just ask."

Larry sighed. "So it's true you found the body of another assassin who escaped?"

"It seems so," Ruy murmured.

"And is that all of them, do you think?" When neither of them answered, Mazzare looked at Sharon. "As the heroine of the hour, many people are particularly interested in your opinion."

Sharon frowned. "Firstly, Larry, I'm no hero. The heroes are the ones who went into that building. I just had an idea for how we could find the bad guys. As for having eliminated all of the assassins: what would you have me say? We certainly got *some* of them. And yes, I'm pretty sure that the one who got out the side window is the guy we found in the alley. But it's clear we're missing at least one, well, 'person of interest.' Maybe he's an assassin, maybe not. But either way, something doesn't feel right."

"What do you mean?"

Sharon put a hand to her head. "It's hard to explain. I mean, the place was too orderly. And there are indications that not too long before, they'd been burning the transcripts of messages they had transmitted and received. And the code books and everything else were set up the way Odo has them, so that the operator has everything needed within easy reach." She shook her head. "I just can't believe these are the guys who killed Baudet Lamy. Everything about that murder tells me the perpetrators there were undisciplined, even amateurish. So I'd expect their rooms to reflect that: that they'd be slobs, all living however they chose to individually. Kind of the way pirates are."

Ruy's voice was gentle. "Which means, Larry, as I keep telling my extraordinary wife, that it may be that the murder of Lamy was, as we also considered, not connected to any assassination plot."

Sharon shook her head sharply. "No, that doesn't wash either. Okay, so they might have had a reason to believe that moving Lamy's body was the right move. But that whole attempt to make it look like he bled out in that alley? And that bottle of wine they put in his hand? And his unemptied purse?" She shook her head. "They're amateurs. But what's more, they are amateurs who weren't out to steal his money, or even get away after they killed him. I mean, if it was just a couple of guys who decided to do in poor Lamy, then why move his body at all? Why wouldn't they just have left him where they killed him, even if it was in their own flat? Why not just get out of town?"

"But not those guys. They moved him in the middle of the night. Either they're too stupid to think of leaving Besançon, or they couldn't: they had to—*had to*—stay. So here's the question that keeps bothering me: why?" She shook her head again. "There's something funky about that crime. Sure, it could be a coincidence: a murder that the killers decide they have to try to cover up, occuring exactly at the same time as an assassination of Urban is being prepared. But as the saying has it, coincidence is a rare and endangered species. And I'm not buying it."

Ruy put his hands behind his back and his head down. "It turns out that these murderous dogs had the radio that belonged to the fellow killed in the stables, Javier de Requesens y Ercilla. It also appears that much or all of the code books and correspondence records we found in the rooms were his also."

Larry started. "But that means—" The implications were too odd and came too fast for him to articulate his perceptions before Ruy began again.

"Yes: the man who killed de Requesens also knew of and contacted the men who we killed today, passed on the equipment and information that they needed in order to continue preparing their attack on His Holiness. And the manner in which the one who went out the window was killed strongly suggests that the murderer was trusted by, or at least known to, the victim, as was the case in de Requesens' death."

"What do you mean, the manner in which he was killed?"

"At close range. And the blade's cross section, angle, and height of entry are, collectively, a match for what I found on de Requesens' body. An *exact* match."

"So—the left-handed killer?"

"It's only a guess, but the forensics suggest it."

Larry shook his head. "But it doesn't make sense. If the group you eliminated today was being supported by de Requesens' left-handed killer, then why wouldn't he also save the life of the only one of them who escaped? Why, instead, does he kill him in an alley?"

Sharon's voice was as glum as her face. "That's what I've been wondering. We're missing something."

"We sure are," agreed Larry. "And add this to the pile: how did this mystery killer know to kill the men he did, when he did? We've been spending almost all our effort wondering why he killed de Requesens, but this makes me think the more important question is *how* did he know to do so? Because today, once again, the killer was the right man in the right place at the right time—or did he just happen to be strolling along where he intercepted the guy fleeing in the alley? And even if he did, how did he know to kill a man he helped just a few days earlier?"

Sharon's breath caught suddenly. "He, the left-handed killer, must have a radio, too."

From over Larry's other shoulder, Ruy exclaimed, "Yet another one?"

"It's the logical conclusion, Ruy. Heck, is there any other explanation? Even if he was always watching de Requesens, what could he have *seen* that would have led him to believe that killing him was necessary? And it's the same mystery today: was the killer somewhere in the same neighborhood as the house we hit today, watching? Or, more likely, is he getting his orders—and information—from somewhere else, via his own radio?"

Ruy nodded slowly. "Yes, and probably from whatever figure of command was on the other end of the radio communicating with de Requesens or today's murderous dogs. But why would that figure of command have yet another agent, the left-handed killer, in town? De Requesens was clearly the handler; the group we eliminated today were clearly the assassins. Why a third party? What is his role?"

Larry, who had read his share of high-stakes political thrillers, felt a chill go up his spine. "He's a cleaner."

"A what?"

Sharon had turned to look at Larry with wide eyes. "So whoever is behind the assassination attempt, Borja or Philip or someone else, has their own personal angel of death hovering near all the other parts of their operation, to make sure that if anything goes wrong, it gets cleaned up before they can be implicated."

Larry nodded. "This left-handed killer is here to facilitate their operations, but also to make sure there is no 'blowback,' to use the term Estuban Miro has adopted."

Ruy frowned, dubious. "So, do you mean to propose that this 'cleaner's' decision to kill the last of the assassins in the alley indicates that we have accounted for all their assassins? That once they were compromised, the figure of command's highest priority became the need to clip any loose ends, and so, protect the identities of those who set these blackguards in motion?"

Sharon shook her head. "Not unless Lamy's murder is a coincidence. Because if it isn't, then there's another set of killers we haven't detected yet. Remember: one of them used a stiletto to kill him. But there wasn't a trace of that kind of weapon in the flat or on any of the bodies."

Larry frowned. "You're putting an awful lot of weight on whether a stiletto is present or absent, Sharon. They might have ditched, or even lost, it."

Sharon's chin came out. "Yeah, well, there are other indicators as well. Like the difference in discipline. I'll say it again: I just can't see today's group as also being the bunglers who killed and then planted Lamy's body."

Larry nodded. "So, when I finish this walk, and I have to update His Holiness and Father Vitelleschi, as well as Bedmar and the large, very protective cardinals he brought with him, do I tell them there is another group of assassins or not?"

Sharon shrugged. "Tell them we think there might be another group, but we can't be sure."

Larry shook his head. "They're not going to like that answer."

Ruy sounded a shade defensive. "Please convey our apologies to His Holiness and the Eminences, but it is the only one we may truthfully offer."

Larry waved a hand. "Oh, I understand that, but remember: there was an assassination attempt four days ago at St. John's. Now you found and eliminated another group. If you can't definitively say there is yet another group, I think they're going to start presuming otherwise."

"That would be—very foolish of them." Sharon sounded like her jaw had gotten stuck.

"Don't I know it. But, if my read of the personalities involved is accurate, they will start wondering if this is just a case of us up-timers, and our closest allies, starting at shadows. The one thing they all agree upon regarding us is that we're almost comically risk averse. If a thing *can* go wrong, we presume it *will* go wrong. Try talking to them sometime about the up-time concept of personal life insurance. First they think it's a joke. When they realize it's not, they laugh. Sometimes, bordering on hysterics."

Ruy nodded. He had smiled at the same tendency in up-timers, but he wasn't smiling now. "I understand your concern. And I fear you may be correct. However, we may not drop our vigilance. Even if they instruct us to do so. After all, they have little detailed knowledge of our plans and protocols. So we should be able to continue on as we have done."

Sharon nodded. "Yes. But I doubt they'll give us the same *carte blanche* when it comes to grabbing large numbers of the Burgundian soldiers or the city watch to mount searches or patrol suspect areas. In the meantime, we should try to come up with alternate scenarios that explain all the clues we have, answer all the mysteries we have yet to solve. That way, we might be a little more prepared for whichever situation turns out to be the correct one."

Ruy's voice was very gentle. "I agree we should continue to seek explanations for all that we have observed. But in my experience, there are always more feasible scenarios, as you call them, than we ever have the time to formulate. I can envision a dozen different logical explanations for what we have found thus far. The problem is that none of them commend themselves above the others."

Sharon was silent. "Yeah, okay. Just so long as we don't start getting lazy."

"Of that, my love, you may rest assured. Owen and I will keep our men alert, no matter what overconfident rumors they may hear in the street, or from the august company gathered in the palace." His tone changed. "About which: how do things proceed amongst the colloquialists, Your Eminence?"

"I wish you'd just call me Larry, Ruy."

"And I wish you would stop trying to compel me to do so, Your Eminence. It is how I was brought up. It would make me most uncomfortable to do otherwise."

Larry sighed and waved away the topic with a flap of his hand. "Okay, I give up."

Sharon leaned forward to look directly into Larry's face. "Now: the colloquium."

Larry nodded. "Yes. The colloquium. Some minor drama every day. Two days ago, it was a false security risk when someone was heard bumping around in a closet. Four of the Wild Geese responded with guns drawn...and let out a cat. Today, the major domo, LaVey, was relieved over a bribery scandal of some sort. He claims he was set up, although he has a history of having sticky fingers. Meanwhile, every head of the serving staff that reported to him—kitchen, grounds, stables, you name it—is now running their own show without any inclination to coordinate with any of the other heads. So tea is late, rooms don't get cleaned, and a good number of our participants are displaying their less spiritual side as they all but swoon over every substandard meal and undusted table."

Sharon stared at him. "Larry. You know what I'm asking about: the colloquium itself, not the sideshows."

Larry kicked peevishly at a small bit of mortar that had come loose from the rough bricks beneath their feet. "I just wish the colloquium was focused on its supposed purpose—but it's not."

"Now what does *that* mean?"

"It means that everyone is supposed to be here talking about starting an official ecumenical dialog."

"And they're not?"

"Well, yeah, to a point. And yes, they're making reasonable progress on it. But what really has their attention—what they can't wait to debate in the time between the sessions, in the corridors and in the corners—is the fate of the Catholic Church."

"You mean, whether it should be in Urban's hands or Borja's?"

Larry shook his head. "No. There's no difference of opinion on that point. But for most of the non-Catholics, that matter also doesn't have the most powerful political implications. What they're usually talking about—before I approach and they clam up—is what would happen if the endgame of the split Church played out as the second fall of a Roman Empire."

Sharon's eyebrows raised. "I could see the cardinals thinking the Church had that kind of power, but not the others."

Larry shook his head again. "That's not what I mean. What the more enlightened Protestants have realized is that, as did the fall of Imperial Rome, a fall of Catholic Rome would create much the same kind of power vacuum, albeit a much smaller one. But it could become the catalyst for a new round of wars all across the map of Europe."

Ruy frowned. "Religious wars?"

"No, plain old secular ones. Here's the short version: the more shortsighted Protestants and the secularists came here eager to see The Holy See implode and fragment. If that happened, then the Roman Catholic Church, bereft of her property and power, would be a religion like any other, no longer able to directly field her own armies and fund her own political initiatives. And no small number of Protestant rulers seemed to be dreaming of some kind of tidy aftermath in which they would watch that fall take place, and then calmly and benevolently apportion those many valuable fragments among themselves.

"However, the shrewder minds here saw that human nature predicted a different outcome. There would be no patient division of papal lands and cities, just a pack of royal wolves tussling over a continent-spanning carcass. And you can guess how that would wind up."

Ruy nodded. "Each state would fear to accept a smaller share of the scraps than the others, lest that smaller share should translate into a smaller share of dominance. They would ultimately turn on each other."

Larry nodded. "A lot of the folks sent here by secular authorities couldn't initially see beyond the fact that the annual flow of silver to Rome would now remain in their own lands. So the more narrow-minded ecclesiastics wept no small number of crocodile tears while counting the coin they and their rulers expected to realize from what is effectively a sustained papal interregnum.

"But the more farsighted folks realized that the short term gains of the Church's dissolution would have far greater long-term costs. Papal possessions and cities were actually more threatened by the Church's division than they ever had been by the Thirty Years' War. And now, with that conflict largely over, they could ultimately be absorbed into the most proximal and powerful secular states, since they no longer had any way to resist the forces of their much larger neighbors. As long as the power of the Church is effectively split between Borja and Urban, the Holy See is unable to provide military, financial, and diplomatic aid, because it's no longer collecting and distributing those assets to its far-flung conglomeration of possessions, client states, and free cities.

"So the trend in the discussions now is that an intact Roman Catholic Church is in the interests of all concerned, because without it, there would be an interval of dangerous instability and intrafaith strife— even as the specter of an Ottoman attack is looming in the Balkans. And ultimately, they all recognize that an intact Roman Church requires having Urban back on the *cathedra*."

Ruy sent a long sideways glance at Mazzare. "Your Eminence, I have heard you speak much on the differences between the Church in this world, and the one in yours. I am surprised to hear you supporting a future in which the Church retains its immense secular holdings and influence. I intend no impertinence, but have you not, on many occasions, cited the parable of the rich man and the camel's odds of passing through the eye of a needle when explaining why the papacy should be allowed, even encouraged, to return its attention to divine matters, rather than mundane possessions?"

Larry nodded. "And I still feel that way, Ruy, now more than ever. However, I also accept that, in these circumstances, the transition has to be gradual rather than abrupt. A sudden power vacuum in Europe would invite a rekindling of wars and atrocities as nations scrambled to gobble up the vulnerable papal possessions. And in that process, those warlike flames would almost certainly be fanned so hot and so high that they would reignite the hatreds that still exist between too many Protestants and Catholics."

Sharon sighed. "It's been five years since we got here, and I'm still waiting to see any easy answer for any of the problems we run into."

Ruy fell back a step, then paced forward to draw even with his wife's other side; now she was in the middle. "So," he asked with a mischievous twinkle in his eye, "there were many simply-answered problems in your wondrous up-time world?"

Sharon opened her mouth but nothing came out, as she evidently cast about for an effective reply.

"Sharon," murmured Larry, "don't lie."

Sharon closed her mouth and leaned against Ruy's arm.

All three completed their circuit of the cloister in silence.

Chapter 33

Klaus Müller was where he was supposed to be—right next to the door—when Norwin Eischoll slipped back into the overcrowded and squalid quarters that Ignaz von Meggen had secured for them. Although, in actuality, it had been the Swiss merchant with the squashed nose who had provided the tip that led them to their lodgings; he knew the town, and so knew where there were flophouses so mean and obscure that travelers never became aware of them.

"Well?" asked Müller.

"Hush," whispered Norwin, who slipped into a corner screened by a partial wall.

Müller followed. "Did you meet him?"

"Be quiet!" Eischoll ordered sharply. Then, in a low tone: "Yes." He uttered a sudden, incongruous chuckle. "Although, I have to admit: our handler is not the kind of person I was expecting."

"Who is he?" Müller persisted, but more quietly.

"That doesn't matter. What does matter is that he's given the word."

Müller forgot to keep his voice down. "Really? When? Where?"

Eischoll raised his hand, as if to cuff the much larger Müller. "That's your last warning, Klaus. Soft speech or none at all. We'll have the details well before dawn."

"How?"

"Our contact will come here once we're ready."

"We're ready now!"

"No, we're not. Not until we've completed two jobs. Before midnight."

Klaus had to keep thinking about how loud he might get; he forced himself to whisper. "What are these two jobs?"

Eischoll nodded approvingly. "First, we must contact that arrogant Occitan bastard Gasquet to bring his men here just before dawn."

"Before dawn?" Müller was already regretting the lost sleep. "Why?"

"Because that is when Gasquet and his men will need to change into their disguises—well, into the uniforms."

Klaus was now thoroughly confused, a feeling he experienced often enough to have learned a profound dislike for it. "What uniforms?"

Eischoll's index finger pointed through the wall, toward the back of their lodgings where the younger Swiss surrounded Ignaz, as they often did when he recounted one of his family's Swiss Guard stories. "Those uniforms."

"You mean, the ones they're wearing?"

Eischoll nodded.

"But...how do we get them?"

Eischoll smiled faintly. "That's the second job. Which you and the others will complete while I am off informing Gasquet when he has to be here." He produced two bottles of armagnac from his rucksack. "This should help you. Most of those farm boys haven't learned to hold their liquor." Eischoll rose, retraced his steps to the door, turned as he was about to exit. "And don't get any blood on the shirts."

As the darkness deepened, Pedro Dolor looked down into the walled grounds that ran back from the rear of the Palais Granvelle. It was lit unevenly by torchlight, but that was sufficient to facilitate the work necessitated by the banquet that would conclude tomorrow's final session of the colloquium. Consequently, the various foodstuffs and wine and other niceties had to be brought in quickly, during the hours when there was no particularly urgent concern with access, since none of the august personages who might also be targets were present.

So for now, the servants and hostlers had the run of those few parts of Palais Granvelle that were open to them. Freed of the endless round of security checks, their work proceeded swiftly. Wagons entered the garden gate to the south, and porters ran to and fro as the victuals and freshly cleaned linen were unloaded. Without any regular residents—a condition caused as much by the dissolution of the Granvelle's as by Bernhard's arrival—the palace's budget allowed only a small staff, and so, many of the services that might normally be expected on the premises had to be sought externally. The alternative, to quickly hire a full complement of additional staff, had not only been fiscally prohibitive, but functionally impossible. There were not so many unemployed persons with

the correct skills to be found in all of Besançon, and
none of the others could be enticed away from their
regular employment by a job that would not continue
beyond the colloquium and council.

Which, Dolor reflected, had been precisely the
opening he would have exploited, had he been tasked
with making the overt attack upon the pope. Apparently whoever had crafted the plan for Borja's men
had also perceived the opportunities inherent in an
after-hours surge of servants. One or two might be
new staff, hired to help with the increased demands
of a banquet, or it might be as simple as a porter who
lingered behind and could remain undetected, if aided
by someone already on the palace staff.

And getting them inside would be the work of a
moment. Surveying the activity down in the courtyard, he watched as the palace's overseers met each
group of porters, gave directions, then moved on to
the others. The meeting that would signify a contact
between an inside saboteur and outside infiltrators
would be slightly different, of course. It would probably resemble the one he watched even now, where a
small, bent hostler and his hulking porter were met
by one of the senior staff, an exchange like all the
rest, except for a brief moment when, left unobserved,
they glanced about furtively and stepped closer, their
ducked heads moving in time with a conversation that
became far more earnest and was quickly concluded.
After which the overseer and the provisioners separated,
evincing none of the words or gestures of departure
that would tell an observer that they had ever been
in conversation at all.

Dolor almost smiled. It was amusing to think that

he might have just witnessed the fateful exchange that would prime the perfidious mechanism of Urban's assassination. Wildly unlikely, of course. There was no shortage of roughly similar exchanges that took place as Dolor watched; trading rumors or tall tales or black market information would all have much the same appearance. Even though a handful of Burgundian soldiers were present, so long as nothing appeared out of the ordinary, they took no special note. If the men moving back and forth looked like hostlers and porters, then they were. If the boxes appeared to be full of foodstuffs and linens, then they were. They were probably keeping a rough count of each, but if they were off by one or two over the course of the evening, that would hardly strike them as a cause for alarm; that was just the kind of inaccuracy that they were accustomed to.

Dolor leaned away from the window, sealed the shutters, and began eating a small meal of sausage and cheese. He doubted Sanchez and O'Neill had liked the idea of the banquet, since they would have understood the dangers implicit in it. But clerics at official gatherings had their own expectations, one of which was to be fed at least one sumptuous meal by their host. And if the Wild Geese found nothing out of order when they ran the morning security check in the palace, all trepidation would be put aside. Particularly since two groups of assassins had already been foiled. It would sound alarmist to suggest that, despite all evidence to the contrary, a third attempt might be made.

Dolor idly pulled up one of the floorboards, the one that revealed a crawlspace that led under the rough wooden wall to his right, which did not, in fact, demark the far end of the attic room which he had rented almost three months ago. Beyond that false wall was a safe room: not large, but it would have held his men as they waited out whatever search followed Urban's assassination. A handy spot for hiding contraband, known only to a few smugglers, no sane person would think that it would be a suitable hiding place for a group of men: too small, too claustrophobic, lightless, and the stink of chamberpots would grow hourly.

But quicklime would eliminate the smell, and both fear and greed would have answered for all the rest: fear of trying to flee and greed for the princely sums that Olivares had provided for payment. Whether his men would have lived long enough to enjoy it was another matter, but Dolor had speculated that Olivares would have been likely to instruct him to retain their services if they had succeeded at killing Urban.

And it really had been such an elegant plan, particularly once Borja expressed his expectation that not just the pope, but cardinals and other clerics would become casualties in the attack. Of Urban's three possible locations—St. John's, its cloistered abbey, Palais Granvelle—only the last was a place where he would ever be collocated with those other targets. However, that was not why Dolor had presumed it to be the site the assassins would choose.

Since the security around Urban made a direct attack impossible, any successful plan had to solve the issue of gaining proximity to him without combat. St. John's and its satellite abbey were essentially hopeless. Urban and his many servitors would immediately detect and suspect any unfamiliar face, since both were served by religious communities that could not be infiltrated by outsiders. That left Palais Granvelle, where, because of the dozens of visitors and their staff, new servants, ostlers, and the like, unfamiliar faces were the rule, rather than an alarming exception.

So, with the Burgundian gear and up-time inspired weapons at the ready in the cellar he had retained, Dolor had hit upon a flexible plan that was largely based upon his opponents' assumptions, the most important of which was their reliance upon the tunnel connecting the palace to the Carmelite convent. In the event of an attack upon Urban in the palace, it was a surety that they planned to evacuate him there. Their multiple visits to the convent and then their attempts to locate those persons who had been most responsible for handling the subterranean and hidden constructions under it admitted no other explanation.

So, logically, once Borja's dogs attacked Urban in the palace, that would have the effect of chasing Urban into the convent—where Dolor and his team would never be suspected, at least not in time. Once sneaking inside, they would have enjoyed complete foreknowledge of both the overt and hidden elements of the groundplan. That would have made it relatively simple to both hide within the convent and observe much of the opposition's movement within it—at least until such time as the pope's security believed he had been deposited in a safe location.

At that point, it would have been simplicity itself to overpower his immediate guards, kill the pope, and then exit the same way they had entered—and with any luck, just as unseen. The up-time pattern shotguns would have given them a modest edge both killing Urban and fighting their way out if that became necessary. Given the close ranges, those weapons would have minimized the differences in training between his men and those of the opposition. And then, after returning to the cellar and shedding all their gear and weapons, they would have made their way separately to the room in which Dolor now sat. Of course, only he had possessed knowledge of its secret connection to a safe-room.

But that plan was ruined. All he could do now was remain where he was, quiet, until the Hibernians, aided by the Burgundian soldiery, finished sweeping the streets of Besançon after Borja's thugs made their attempt on Urban's life.

There had been a smaller manhunt earlier this day, no doubt precipitated by the discovery of Rombaldo's body. But, as predicted, the opposition could hardly spare any of their elite soldiers for such a task. Tensions and fears were high among the gathered clergy, and the collective reflex was to stiffen their defenses immediately. Consequently, the search for Rombaldo's missing killer was left to the Burgundians and the watch, which was the equivalent of sending a bull to find something in a china shop.

As Dolor finished the cheese, he found himself staring at the knife he was using. So different, and yet not so different, from the one he had used to kill Rombaldo. A knife was a knife, after all. But not all men are the same, nor are all their deaths. He had spent more time with Rombaldo than almost any other person since he had been fourteen. The Bolognese had not just been a relatively effective lieutenant, but loyal at moments when others might have shifted allegiance to a leader with more auspicious prospects.

But that might also have been a mark of Rombaldo's canniness, recognizing that there was often more to be gained by remaining in the camp of a promising newcomer. It was the kind of bloodless decision that Dolor himself might have made in that situation, in the ruthless ascension to ever greater power.

Admittedly, most of Rombaldo's ruthlessness was of a more base nature. He was possessed by pleasures that Dolor deemed perverse. For the Bolognese, violence had not simply been a means to an end, but a way of life, and frequently, an aphrodisiac. At least Rombaldo had not preyed upon children. But he did prey upon their parents without remorse, and had to be reminded, on occasion, to spare children who had seen what they should not have. The latter was a trait that Dolor silently abhorred: silently, because it was stupid to give warning to a colleague whose willingness to harm children might one day earn him a knife across his throat. So perhaps Rombaldo's death today was all for the best: a murder of necessity instead of what might have one day become an unavoidable killing on principle.

Yet, all things considered, his time with Rombaldo had actually been one of the most pleasant stretches of his otherwise rough and bloody life. Ever since Olivares had ordered him to mount and maintain a subtle investigation into who had helped Urban escape, and where to, and with what purpose, Dolor's daily duties involved managing information rather than assassinations. Madrid's preeminent puppet master also made sure to bring Pedro to court during one of those visits, ostensibly with the intent of acclimatizing him to the grandees and vice versa—a necessary precursor to using him as yet another means of spying on them.

It was an experience Dolor was not eager to repeat, having come within shouting distance of one of Philip's senior intelligencers and a person from whom he wished to maintain particular distance, at least until a time and place of his choosing: Zuñiga. Happily, the grandee never did see the much younger man, nor did he notice his efforts at careful avoidance.

Of course, Dolor reflected, further trips to the Escorial were now the least of his worries. His mission had failed. Olivares would very probably distance himself, and the attainability of Pedro's final goal would rewiden by just that same measure. All in all, it was quite frustrating, having been foiled by an esoteric detail of radio science.

He dusted off his hands over his blanket and scraped the crumbs together. Whatever else he did, he could not afford to leave anything that would attract rats and, thereby, attract human attention to what should be a completely unremarkable attic. Would that he could have achieved the same unnoticeability with the cellar, but it had not been possible. It had been necessary to stockpile rations and equipment there, preliminary to playing their secret role in the assassination of Urban. But given that the day's events had compelled Dolor to relocate swiftly, and that he needed to remove the radio and its batteries, he had been unable to carry any more than his own rations and a small bag of quicklime, lest he draw undue attention. Which meant that there were ten man-days of foods left there, no longer hidden under quite so much lime as before.

Pedro Dolor put all the crumbs he had found into his mouth, one by one; the window had to remain mostly shuttered now, lest someone become curious as to who was opening and closing it. A pity, really, as he was intensely curious to see how the last moves in this long game of covert pontificide would play out, and for which the window of his final refuge promised to offer an unparalleled view.

Part Six

Saturday
May 10, 1636

The firefly's quick, electric stroke

Chapter 34

Estève Gasquet glanced at Norwin Eischoll. The Swiss was already looking at him with an exasperated expression that probably mirrored the one on his own face. Chimo and one of Eischoll's men could no longer remember what they had been told—repeatedly—less than an hour ago.

Fortunately, there was a second opportunity to force-feed the two of them the basics of the attack plan. Since someone reliable had to be left on watch outside the one-room hovel, Brenguier had missed the presentation. And now that one of Eischoll's men had taken his place, he needed to be filled in on the details.

Brenguier pulled a stool over to the hovel's one table, sat, and stared at the rough map Eischoll's handler had furnished of the palace grounds and interior. "So what's the plan?"

Gasquet spoke before Eischoll could open his mouth. If the Swiss explained it a second time, everyone would look to him for leadership, regardless of what had been agreed upon. "There are three teams. One is outside the front of the building, another is at the rear, and the third goes in the main entrance."

"To receive Urban's blessing as the new Swiss Guard?"

Gasquet nodded. "That's the idea. Von Meggen"—he jerked his head toward the small heap of corpses against the back wall of the building—"was good enough to arrange that for us. It's to be Urban's first order of business after he concludes this colloquium of his. But what we don't know is where he will meet us."

Brenguier frowned. "Inside, of course."

Gasquet smiled. "Of course. His security hasn't allowed him to make a single open-air appearance since we've been here. So the question becomes where in the palace he'll meet us."

"I've got a question that needs answering before that one," Brenguier drawled, still frowning. "Why are they going to let us in the palace if von Meggen isn't with us, particularly since a lot of us don't exactly look like the fellows we're replacing?" He, too, nodded toward the corpses.

Gasquet thanked his stars that Brenguier had a good head on his shoulders. "That's been handled. Eischoll sent a messenger to the palace late yesterday, when von Meggen wasn't watching. The message was that Freiherr Ignaz von Meggen had apparently consumed some tainted food or water and was very disappointed to report that he might be indisposed on the day of the ceremony. However, he was sending his faithful lieutenant to stand in his place."

Brenguier glanced at Eischoll. "You?"

The Swiss nodded. "I've been careful to always appear with him whenever he speaks to the aristocrats, either in the palace or elsewhere. And he was good enough to point out the role I played in defeating the 'assassins' at St. John's."

Gasquet leaned in, gesturing at the faces around the table. "The rest of us don't have to really look like the Swiss. No one ever bothered to look closely at any faces besides von Meggen and Eischoll. And from our group, Chimo and Manel are about the same size as the farm boys they're replacing. Lastly, we have these." He held up a Spanish morion, rather worse for the wear.

Brenquier took it in his hands, scowling. "Where did you dig this up? From a mass grave?" Eischoll shrugged.

Gasquet leaned back. "Apparently, there's a lot of Spanish equipment here, left from when they used to garrison Besançon. That's why the helmets are falling apart and why the pope's people won't think them unusual. It's just the kind of thing that prat von Meggen might have done: some stupid gesture to try to make his pack of butt-scratching valley squatters look like soldiers. And of course, given the condition of these helmets, they'll have the opposite effect."

Brenquier nodded. "Meaning they'll take us even less seriously—and be unable to see our hair or much of our faces."

Gasquet almost sighed in relief at Brenquier's ready understanding. "Precisely. But they're more than a disguise. Look inside."

Brenguier turned the helmet over; fastened on either side of the interior were what looked like out-sized ear-muffs. He frowned, looked up. "We're going to be uncomfortably close to a bomb at some point, aren't we?"

From the corner of his eye, Gasquet noticed that

even Eischoll had to nod approvingly at that. Gasquet grinned at Brenguier. "Not too close, we hope. But we'll get to that later. The helmets are going to be worn by the third, or main, team: the one that goes in the front door."

Brenquier nodded. "And who's on that team?"

Gasquet struggled to remember the math behind their subterfuge. "Five of the real Swiss are gone. So that leaves seven. One more—Klaus Müller—is going to be with the outside team. So that leaves six Swiss for the main team. With von Meggen missing, the pope is going to be expecting only eleven recruits. So that means five of us have to take the place of the missing fools. That will be you, me, Donat, Chimo, and Manel. Huc will be on the outside team with Klaus. Peyre has the rear."

Brenguier rubbed his hands. "So I take it the main team is the one that gets to do the fighting. Where are the weapons?"

Gasquet shrugged. "Inside."

"Inside what?"

"Inside the palace. They'd never let us through the front door with anything more than daggers. If that."

Brenguier's face went through a quick evolution of expressions: surprise at Gasquet's answer, then anger, then a frown as he obviously realized the necessity of the arrangement, and lastly a look of dull acceptance. "Very well. And how do we get those weapons?"

Gasquet glanced at Eischoll before answering. "As I understand it, they will be served to us."

"Served? As in, on a silver platter?"

Gasquet shrugged. "That could literally be the case. At any rate, they will be there."

"And if they're not?"

"Then we'll hope the bomb does more damage than it's designed to do."

Brenguier leaned back. "Ah. The bomb that's going to come too close to us."

"That's why, when it comes through the window, you act surprised, then go low, one hand over your eyes. Use the other to jam the helmet down."

Brenguier scanned the map. "If I'm reading the symbols right, there are a lot of windows in the palace. Which one will the bomb come through?"

"The one we call for."

Brenguier looked up, his eyebrows halfway to his hairline. "And how do we do that?"

"By singing." When Brenguier just blinked, Gasquet explicated. "As you said, the only thing we know is that the pope will meet us inside. But there are three possible places. The entry hall or 'foyer' as they style it, the receiving hall, or the great hall. That last one is very unlikely, but no matter: once we see the pope, we start singing."

"And why would we do that?"

Gasquet indulged in a smirk. "For the same reason we'd wear these stupid helmets: because we're a bunch of Swiss yokels who are trying to show their appreciation and seriousness like a bunch of overgrown children. We start singing because that's a 'gift' we can give to the pope, and one that demonstrates our dedication to the Church."

"So: a different song for each window?"

Gasquet nodded. "*Te Deum* for the entry hall, *Dies Irae* for the receiving hall, *Deus Creator Omnium* for the great hall."

Brenguier nodded back. "And what sort of bomb is it?" He looked at Eischoll. "Or can't you tell us that, either?"

Norwin shrugged. "Not only can I tell you; I can show you." He reached down beneath the table and brought up a tube of black metal, open at one end. "It's what the up-timers call a pipe bomb."

Brenguier reached out carefully toward it. "Made of iron? Where'd you get that?" Metal pipe was a nearly unheard-of rarity. At least it had been before Grantville dropped out of the future.

Gasquet cut off Eischoll again. "From the up-timers." Seeing the incredulous look on Brenguier's face, he shook his head. "No, not from them directly. It just so happens that Bernhard brought a bunch of them here to start up some kind of metal shop in Bregille: the Silo Design and Construction Corporation, it's called. But they're doing more than that: they're making all kinds of fittings to carry water, grain, slurry." He jutted his chin at the bomb. "Eischoll was told that they were selling this, and about a dozen other pieces, for scrap, if you can believe it."

Brenguier looked from the Swiss back to Gasquet. "So no one here made the bomb? Then how do we know we can trust it?"

"Because the people paying us really want the pope dead, and a flawed bomb isn't going to help them achieve that. But they explained the design pretty thoroughly, so that if something happened to it before today, we could try to fix it and carry on."

Brenguier stared at grooves that had been cut into the pipe in a crisscross diamond pattern. "How long did it take to do that?"

Gasquet shrugged, remaining casual as he seethed with the necessity to refer the question to Eischoll. "Ask him."

Norwin's face was expressionless. "You know, I asked our handler the same question."

Brenquier frowned. "What did he answer?"

"'Don't ask.'"

"What sort of answer is that?"

"A bad one. But obviously, it took him a long time."

"Why did he do it—cutting those grooves?"

"He told me it makes the bomb more deadly."

Brenguier shook his head. Gasquet sympathized: crazy up-timer ideas always seemed to involve equally crazy activities and jobs. This was no different.

Gasquet settled the bomb back in the bag from which he'd removed it, twisting it so that it churned and sank down into the dense mix of nails and wire cuttings, ultimately filling it so that there was no slack in the fabric. "There are almost two pounds of reground, fine grain powder in there, the kind the up-timers use in their percussion cap revolvers. Compressed to the point where it's damn near solid."

Brenguier nodded at the bag. "Why not put the fragments inside the bomb?" Which was the customary practice.

Gasquet had to spend a moment recalling what Eischoll had told him. "More shrapnel this way, with more even spread and also less velocity."

"Less velocity means less killing power," Brenguier objected, folding his arms.

"True. And that's just what we want. Firstly, we could be pretty close to it. Secondly, we're not counting on this bomb to kill the pope or his allies. We just want it to make enough noise and inflict enough wounds to shock the defenders—long enough for us to get to our own weapons, and then theirs, and finish them off."

"You make that sound awfully easy."

Gasquet shook his head. "It won't be. If we didn't have the bomb going off first, I doubt we'd even make it to our weapons. In particular, don't underestimate those bog-hoppers, the Wild Geese. They may not know how to parade march and stand at attention for hours on end, but they know how to fight. Close and dirty, and with pepperbox revolvers, heavy rapiers or sabers, and wearing cuirasses. They're all veterans of the Lowland Wars and devoted Catholics; we can't expect them to run, and they'll be damned hard to kill."

"So I take it that, unless I have a shot at the pope, killing these Irish savages is the priority?"

"Actually, no. There will be some Burgundian troops in there as well. Probably restricted to the entry hall. They'll be the easiest to kill, the easiest to scare into running. Doing that should even the numbers. So we need to get them when they're stunned, disoriented."

Brenquier nodded. "Fine by me. How many Wild Geese can we expect to face?"

Gasquet picked his teeth with a blood-coated paring knife that had been used to kill one of von Meggen's true-hearted followers. "I wish we knew. There are about forty of them here in Besançon. But during the day, about eight are sleeping—the night guards for the cloister, along with the ambassadora's Marines. A few are on special duty. One's a surgeon. A few more are a reserve guard that we suspect are kept in a central location. The rest are scattered around the palace."

"Still, it sounds like we could face almost thirty."

Gasquet shook his head. "No, because a lot of them won't be anywhere near the pope. The Swiss tell us that, in Rome, most of the Pontifical Guards just stand watch over corridors and major entries. When the pope is moving, a much smaller number forms a barrier around him. We're guessing they'll do the same here."

"So, we'll still have to deal with a flock of these annoying Wild Geese."

"Yes," persisted Gasquet, "but a small one, and probably in the receiving hall. Although we might be enough of an embarrassment that they'll keep us out in the foyer . . . er, entry hall."

"Better than being tradesmen at the back door."

"Much better. It's best to take Urban as close to the front door as possible. The deeper into that damn palace we go, the harder to get out afterward. Besides, we don't want to draw attention to the back door."

"Why's that?"

"Never you mind." Gasquet smothered a small smile. "Anyhow, we wouldn't want to get in the way of the tradesmen working there."

"Why?"

"Because when we've killed Urban, we run out the back, through the kitchen."

Brenguier smiled. "So, out with the trash."

"If you like. At any rate, out toward the rear gate."

"There are usually four of the Irish there at any time."

Gasquet nodded. "Yes, and we have another bomb for them. Just like the first one."

Brenguier looked doubtful. "And the defenders inside

the palace are just going to let us stroll out through the rear gardens?"

Gasquet shook his head. "No, and that's why the second man on the outside team—Klaus—will be throwing a smoke bomb after the pipe bomb: to make it impossible to see where we are, and later, where we run."

"And is the smoke bomb similar to the pipe bomb?"

Gasquet produced one. "Very different, actually." It was longer, thinner, and made of wood. Its sides were lined with what looked like the finger holes of a fife, but plugged with wads of glue. "The mixture inside is six parts saltpeter and four parts finely ground sugar, mixed evenly into four parts of liquid wax and white dye and then poured into the interior tube."

"Interior tube?"

"Yes. What you're seeing is an outer tube, sleeved over the inner one. The holes along here—filled with plaster—are arranged so they are located directly over matching holes in the interior tube."

Brenguier shook his head. "And so what does that achieve?"

Gasquet had been careful to mentally rehearse this part ahead of time. "When the fuse ignites the mixture, it doesn't explode, but it burns fast, and that increases the pressure enough to pop the plaster plugs out."

Brenguier nodded. "So the smoke disperses evenly along the length and sides of the bomb. That's a nice trick. Could've used that three years ago in Lombardy." Which was where Gasquet had met him. It had been an assassination that had gone smoothly until the getaway—when the far more primitive smoke bomb they had been given to cover their escape had jetted all its contents out one end and off to the side, rather than directly between them and the pursuing household troops. Gasquet and Brenquier had been the only two who escaped. "So that's also what Peyre is going to throw to cover us before we run out through the grounds?"

"No. When Peyre hears the first pipe bomb go off inside the palace, he starts a two minute hourglass running. When it runs out, he tosses his own pipe bomb, charges the gate with a pair of double-barreled snaphaunce pistols, and puts down any of the bog-hoppers who are still able to fight. As soon as we come running out from the kitchen store rooms into the wagon bay, he lights the smoke bomb and drops it behind us as we scatter."

"Scatter where?"

Gasquet passed Brenquier a small, sealed wooden tube: a straw, really. "We've all been given one of these, which gives us directions to a place to hide. A one person hole, in most cases. Often enough, it's just a smuggler's false wall or what would pass for an oubliette. There are also directions to one of several hidden gathering points, once you get out of the city. Anyone who makes it there will find supplies, enough for a month if we're still being hunted."

"But what if one of us is caught getting away from the palace, or trying to leave the city?"

"Well, how could you tell them to find anyone else, since you don't know what information is in the other tubes?"

"No, but any of us can identify all the others and reveal that we're gathering outside Basel to get our pay."

"Well, you know how good that pay is, so you also

know that being identified is not a worry, because you won't need to be seen ever again if you don't want to. You will have free passage to a friendly nation and enough money to spend the next ten years living without a care, or for the rest of your life if you're careful with your coin. And as for our meeting place—well, when you get there, you'll see why having knowledge of it won't do them any good."

Brenguier frowned and leaned back from the table. "It's still a risky plan. A lot could go wrong. Some of us are sure to die."

Gasquet nodded. "Some surely will." *Thank St. Peter's left nut that you didn't say,* All of us might die, *because that's not entirely unlikely either.* "But those who survive will be rich men, maybe even pick up a meaningless title in Portugal or Mantua or the Basque country."

"Which might be another good way to get killed," observed Donat Faur with a sour smile.

Brenquier smiled back at him. "I don't need a title. I just want the money."

Gasquet saw the first glimmers of false dawn seeping around the ill-fit door. He rose. "We sleep until nine, get ourselves in our gear by ten, run over the plan again until eleven, stroll out as an unprofessional mob, and make it to the palace at noon."

Brenquier nodded. "And that's when we're to meet the pope?"

Gasquet shrugged and smiled. "Yes. And earn our pay."

Chapter 35

Larry Mazzare looked out over the uniformly male, and mostly aged, faces stacked in ascending rows, on either side of the long audience chamber. And although the hall was stately and tasteful, and although he had come to know the great majority of the attendees, he would be happy to bid them farewell and have a two week break from the room before returning to it for the Consistory Council. He would be happier still had he never had to see it again.

Not because the colloquium had been rancorous or frustrating. In truth, it hadn't. Most of the cardinals had come with a pretty fair understanding of what they were in for: hard questions about how things would be different, which were often thinly veiled admonitions for past deeds and decisions. Not all of the red hats had been able to endure that with good grace: Dietrichstein had stormed out twice, returning the second time only because Urban made a personal appeal, with Vitelleschi standing behind him like the Grim Reaper.

In their turn, the non-Catholic attendees managed to tolerate the occasional Roman reference to the "one

true Church," albeit with some very loud and distempered grumbling. Some of them were also active in
chastening their own members, particularly those who
seemed incapable of resisting the temptation to make
"general" remarks about pride going before a fall and
other poorly disguised suggestions that perhaps the
papacy deserved what had happened to it.

In truth, it was surprising that the now-concluded
Besançon Colloquium had gone so well. Of course,
that was partially because it really hadn't tried to
achieve very much other than establish a basis for
discussion between persons who, a year ago, would
never have tolerated being in the same room with each
other, except in the furtherance of homicide. So in
that regard, much had been accomplished. As Larry
Mazzare had seen in no small number of domestic
interventions (which shared no small number of simi-
larities with the colloquium), the real breakthrough
point was when people were just willing to stay in
the room and listen to each other.

But, just like an intervention, it had been emotionally
and psychologically exhausting. At any given moment,
the entire colloquium had always been ready to come
off the rails and fly into a hundred sectarian pieces.
And it had veered in that direction several times a
day, often without warning. So Larry, Wadding, Urban,
and increasingly von Spee, had had to be constantly
watchful for the seeds of that kind of contention in
order to defuse it before arguments got a chance to
spin up into full blown crises. Which meant that they
could never really relax, could never afford to take
their eyes off the process.

Von Spee concluded his review of the topics that

had been touched upon and the tentative resolutions that were to be addressed at the next colloquium and sat. Urban, who was sitting directly to Larry's right, rose. "I have been giving some thought to what history will say about what we accomplished here. Certainly the cynics will point out that we passed no resolutions, except to meet again, but that we did not even set a time or date. We will no doubt be criticized for being over-scrupulous in observing that old Roman axiom, 'make haste slowly.'" There were a sprinkling of smiles among the faces.

"However, in my contemplations, I also found myself going back to examine what other councils like this one accomplished. And in my readings I rediscovered a fact we all often overlook: that the last such council with vaguely similar ambitions—the Council of Basel—did an even worse job of coming to conclusions than we did. Because, since the Church of those years was almost as sharply divided as it is now, there is some debate as to whether it was ever formally closed." Murmurs, some of surprise, others of doubt, most of stirred recollections, troubled the silence of the hall.

Urban smiled. "It seems, therefore, that we may have actually set a new record for vigorously and swiftly achieving nothing to which we may put a name." Some actual chuckles, now. "However, in all seriousness, I would like to think that we are not only carrying on what they started, but their purpose for doing so: to achieve a greater ecumenical spirit, and where and if possible, reunification."

Johann Gerhard rose; his voice was cautious. "Fine sentiments and words, and I hope we may all be guided by them. But I must ask this: after almost two centuries of increasingly bloody discord have added to those impediments, why would our present be more hopeful than that past?"

Urban smiled. "Because that past did not also have a view to the future such as we have, such as came to us with Grantville." He gestured toward Larry, who wished he was invisible at that moment. "We have examples and visions of a world that evolved from our own, in which our faiths—all of those here—gathered and broke bread together, officiated at weddings together, were even martyred together as they stood, time and again, against savage and godless regimes."

He bowed his head. "And sadly, that future often recalled the Church of these years in no different terms. As a savage regime, and, if not godless, then seduced away from divine grace by power and mammon, following only the forms rather than the spirit of our sacraments and creeds."

Larry felt as much as heard a ripple of uncomfortable movement among the cardinals with whom he sat. The majority had not shared Urban's epiphanies, but they had come this far with him and, between their keen sense of political survival and whatever great or small conscience each possessed, they did not stir in rejection or revolt.

Třanovský rose, his face unreadable. "These are powerful words, but they are just that: words. Words that convey a personal sentiment, but nothing substantial, nothing that we may take back to our lands, our churches, and say, 'here is what is different now; here is a change upon which we may build our hope of some rapprochement and even, eventually, a possible partnership with Rome.'"

Urban nodded. "That is true and well said. So let me give you more powerful words, words from a future pope that you may take back to your lands and your churches and so quicken that spark of hope."

Třanovský, still standing, waved a contentious hand. "I am forced to point out that it is you, yourself, who decreed that the *ex cathedra* remarks of these future popes cannot be binding upon the pontiffs of this world, that they spoke in the context of their times—times that shall now never come to pass."

Urban kept nodding. "Again, true. But I am not referring to canonical teaching, to explicit directions of a pope who is invoking his infallibility in matters of faith and morals. I am invoking the words of a pope as a man, as a leader of Mother Church, speaking his mind. I am relating to the apologies made by Pope John Paul II, the same pontiff who ensured that the ecumenical resolutions that arose from Vatican Two became canon law. And if you have read those resolutions, then you know that these apologies are simply the logical, the inescapable, outgrowth of those ecumenical and ethical directives."

The room was very quiet as Urban lifted a paper from the lectern before him. "On behalf of the Roman Catholic Church, Pope John Paul II apologized for Catholics' involvement with the African slave trade, for the Church's role in burning persons at the stake and the religious wars that followed the Protestant Reformation"—a startled rumble arose from those seats not occupied by cardinals—"for the injustices committed against women and the violation of their rights as human beings, for the denouncement and execution of Jan Hus in 1415 since, in John Paul II's words, regardless of the theological convictions Hus defended, he 'cannot be denied integrity in his personal life and commitment to the nation's moral education.' He further apologized for Catholic violations of the rights of ethnic groups and peoples, and for showing contempt for their cultures and religious traditions, and for the Crusader attack on Constantinople in 1204, whose Patriarch of Constantinople he visited in the year 2000 to express these sentiments: 'It is tragic that the assailants, who had set out to secure free access for Christians to the Holy Land, turned against their own brothers in the faith. The fact that they were Latin Christians fills Catholics with deep regret. How can we fail to see here the mysterium iniquitatis at work in the human heart?'"

Urban put down the sheet. The room was so silent that Larry wondered if everyone was holding their breath. From the looks on their faces, they might well be doing just that. "Could it be chance, that this last apology was made mere weeks before Grantville spun back through time to land in our world?" He looked imploringly at the Greek and Russian Orthodox contingent. "Could it be any hand but God's own that sent such a message to us with such poignant timeliness, with such healing power, so that I might share it with you today?"

Cardinal Pázmány rose into the persistent silence, clearing his throat. "Let us suppose that this future pope was right to make these apologies, no matter how strange some of them may sound to us today. Is it only the Roman Catholic Church which must make apologies? Most of the offenses Your Holiness invoked through this future pope's words are not ours alone.

Should we be the only ones to own such failings?"
He looked meaningfully around the chamber.

Urban shook his head. "When Christ rebuked an
angry crowd by challenging 'let he amongst you who
is without sin cast the first stone,' he reminded us
that we all carry blame. But it is in the nature of free
will that confession and repentance, whatever shape
they may take in different churches, is ultimately a
personal matter. My friend Peter, if we see our faults
now, should we yet wait upon the actions of others to
declare them? That might be a sound strategy among
earthly states, but it subordinates actions of grace to
those of politics. It is by just such fateful steps that
the church, in its magnitude and worldliness, has forgotten that it must follow a different path, must aspire
to different deeds and wisdom. Christ said rightly,
'Render unto Caesar the things that are Caesar's, and
unto God the things that are God's.'

"That is good advice for righteous captains and kings.
But for us, His Own shepherds, it is not advice: it is a
sacred truth and duty. It is for us to seek the path to
grace, that others—including those captains and kings—
may follow the path to Our Lord's loving embrace. We
cannot do so if we remain too concerned by the things
which are properly Caesar's, for that which a man owns
can too easily come to own him, in turn."

Cardinal Wadding chuckled, did not stand. "Your
Holiness, have you been reading Francis again?"

Urban smiled at his friend. "With you ever at my
side quoting him, I have little need to do so." He
became more somber. "But the lessons of Saint Francis
of Assisi have been much on my mind of late. His
is only one of our Church's many voices which urged

it toward what was realized in Vatican Two...and I hope, what we may have taken some small steps toward here in Besançon."

Joasaphus rose slowly, the gold in his vestments catching a beam of sunlight from the chamber's high windows. "I have heard words of peace and reconciliation here, in this room, that I never expected to hear in my life. I nurture hope that they may effect change. But before I may let that hope fill me, and before I may raise a strong voice against those who will reject it, I must ask this: how do you see this change occurring? What steps must be taken?"

Larry looked at Urban, who, he discovered, was already looking at him. "I think our first step is to take no step at all. Rather, we must make our way through the door of this new hope, this new ecumenical moment, on our knees."

Joasaphus, whose face had never once betrayed an emotion, might have smiled slightly. "That is well said."

"I wish it was I who had said it," Urban admitted with a slightly theatrical sigh that summoned back a number of small smiles throughout the chamber. "But that also came to me from the future." He put a meaningful hand on Larry's shoulder as he continued. "I propose no specific resolutions because you, or certainly the rulers with whom you might share the proceedings of this colloquium, would rightly ask, 'how can a renegade pope have the temerity to propose anything, when he is not even sure where his next meal is coming from?'" There were chuckles again.

As Urban refolded his hands, Larry looked over at him: *he sure knows how to work a crowd. Leads them to the brink of an almost incomprehensible maelstrom*

*of papal admissions and apologies, and then hits them
with a few self-deprecating remarks and grins and the
room is smiling in relief and teetering on the verge
of actual bonhomie. The right pope in the right place
at the right time. Quite literally, "thank you, Jesus!"*

Urban spent a quiet second bringing his hands higher,
opened them slightly into an appeal. "What we can do,
what we must do, is to resolve ourselves to be ready
to embrace the change that is coming. But if we have
been too long burdened with the cares and woes of this
globe's flock to trust in the possibility of a new future
in which our faiths cleave closer, then here is a reason
rooted in the very dirt and mud of this material world."

He paused and stared around at the faces for at
least three seconds. "You may save lives. You may
call for tolerance where there has been none knowing
that, elsewhere, the rest of us are doing the same. You
may insist upon fair treatment of all God's children,
no matter their origins, knowing that similar exhortations are arising, not merely as a matter of individual
conscience, but as a collective resolve to make this
the bridge by which we shall ultimately reach each
other to join hands."

"And how shall we know that when we leave this
place, we are not alone in taking such contentious,
even dangerous stands?"

Urban smiled again. "Because we will still be sharing these words. On a daily basis if you wish. Because
the one thing you will all take with you, if you elect
to, is a radio. This is a gift from Grantville and
Gustavus Adolphus: a man of war who wishes to aid
us in forging bonds of peace between all our faiths."

Urban's voice became strained, rough. "How many

fields have been littered by the bodies of the Lord's own sons and daughters, blessed and cherished all, in His eyes? How many have been made homeless by those wars and now lie starving at the margins of fallow fields? And how many uncounted millions in the years and decades and centuries to come might feed the insatiable maw of this religious strife again and again and again—all of them chanting battle cries that it is their obligation to fight—and that the carnage is justified—because 'God is on our side'?

"What could be more practical, more effective, more essential than changing that, wherever and whenever we can? And here, today, the path through the door that leads from war and misery to peace and hope, stands open before us. Not merely as individuals, but as a collective, each of whom may communicate with and support the others on a daily basis, no matter how many miles separate us. You only need to choose to go through that door, but, as Cardinal Mazzare put it, you will need to do so on your knees, humble before both God and man." He stared around the utterly still chamber. "A small price to pay, I should think, to not only save untold thousands of lives, but to come closer to the holy message and mind of our Heavenly Father as we do so."

Johann Gerhard gestured his eagerness to speak. Urban nodded toward him and sat.

Gerhard's gaze shifted sideways: to Larry. "Cardinal Mazzare, I have acquainted myself with the official records of your up-time Church, at least those you brought back with you. However, at no point do they refer to these apologies of John Paul II. I wonder if you could explain that discrepancy."

Larry stood. "It's no discrepancy at all, Reverend Gerhard. Pope John Paul II made most of them in addresses, often during his travel to many countries in which each of the offenses occurred. They were reported in magazines and papers, both those affiliated with the Roman Catholic Church and other faiths, to say nothing of the public press."

Gerhard leaned his weight on the hands he had placed on the back of the bench in front of him. "I see. I gather then, that these, er, unofficial publications were not among those which you had copied and sent to Pope Urban?"

Larry nodded. "That is correct." *Where the hell are you going with this, Gerhard?*

"Then I must conjecture that it is you who suggested their inclusion in the pope's closing statement? It seems unlikely he could have come to awareness of them by any other means."

Ah. Now I see. "That is also correct, Reverend: I brought them to His Holiness' attention. He found them apt and so, incorporated them."

Gerhard leaned forward again. "More than apt, it seems. And more than merely 'incorporated' them: they became the very core of his ecumenical message to us today. Tell me"—and as Johann Gerhard said it, Larry discerned that the inquiry was propelled not by a desire to challenge the earnestness of Urban's appeal, but rather, a profound and puzzled curiosity— "what made you choose these words, these examples to show him? You certainly must have anticipated that it would make the senior clerics of your own faith . . . uncomfortable."

Larry smiled. "Actually, that's precisely why I brought

these words to His Holiness' attention. Because they would make Roman Catholics uncomfortable. And, if all the faiths of this time are disposed to look frankly in the mirrors of their own conscience, they will find their own sins reflected there, as well."

The non-Catholic rows in the council chamber were the source of unsettled rustling of frocks and other religious garments, but there were no mutters or whispers. *Yet,* Larry reminded himself.

Gerhard looked thoughtful. "Do you mean to suggest that our many churches are all as guilty of the same transgressions?" Larry did not hear an inquisitorial twist in the Lutheran's tone; rather, it sounded almost like just another step in an exercise in logic. *As if he's throwing me a slow pitch—*

Larry suppressed a smile. "As our Savior said, and as His Holiness quoted, we are none of us without sin. We need not make comparisons of which sins or how many each of us have committed for us to resolve to recognize, repudiate, and make amends for those of which we are individually guilty."

"And yet, if it was you who conveyed John Paul II's words to your present pope, surely you had in mind what has occurred today: a specific recitation of the sins of your own Church."

Larry lifted his chin. "That is an essential part of this process. Both that we may redeem ourselves in the eyes of God, and deserve credence in yours."

Gerhard seemed genuinely unsure. "I do not know if I understand your logic, Cardinal Mazzare."

Larry smiled. "Possibly that's because I'm just a basic country priest and have a correspondingly simple view of the relationship between sin and redemption.

Confession—whether to a priest, as part of a public ceremony, or in the privacy of our own room—is useless if it is not specific. We are not just vaguely guilty of wrongdoing. A sin is a specific act—or a slew of them—which must be recounted in all their ugly particulars. Anything else is not true repudiation; it's just a way to excuse ourselves. To truly repent, we must recall to mind the deed, the sin. Otherwise, how do we learn to regret the deed and sin no more? Anything less is an empty ritual, one in which we exchange a few minutes of shame and discomfort for absolution. And when it comes to entire institutions—my church or yours; it doesn't matter—John Paul II once shared a few crucial words on that subject, words that made me feel that the Roman Church had to own its transgressions openly, frankly, and fully, without any excuses."

Gerhard was smiling slightly. "And what were those words?"

Larry almost smiled back. "'An excuse is worse and more terrible than a lie, for an excuse is a lie guarded.'" Larry realized that his arms were straight, almost rigid at his sides. "We must be done with excuses, if we also wish to be done with lies. That is the nature of accountability, of truly repudiating sins. Repentance for them cannot be complete—or convincing—any other way."

The Lutheran nodded. "I thank you for clarifying this matter, Cardinal Mazzare—and for doing so with the same frankness that your words ask us all to adopt. 'The way through the door of this new hope, this new ecumenical moment, is on our knees.' That is well said."

Larry smiled. "I wish I had said it, but I owe it

to a priest named Yves Congar. In many ways, he was the architect of Vatican Two. It was he who gave that ecumenical gathering, and hopefully this one, its axiomatic image for action: 'The way through the door of unity is on our knees.' Prayer made in that spirit of humility is the kind that can change our innermost hearts, and if we are to save lives from further religious strife and walk in grace with God, then it is our innermost hearts that need to be changed."

Johann Gerhard cocked his head sideways and smiled as he sat. "For a 'basic country priest,' you are most peculiarly eloquent, Cardinal Mazzare."

Larry shook his head as he gathered his cassock to sit—and as his bottom hit his hard wooden chair, Urban was already back on his feet, making a gesture toward the closest entrance. Servants appeared, bringing in the first course of what Larry knew would be a rather elaborate lunch. "Now, let us break bread together, in the hope that, when next we meet, we may say that we are doing so as true brothers in faith." He sat.

Larry leaned over. "If you plan on giving those Swiss fellows your approval and a benediction, you won't get past the first course."

"I won't even get that far. Nor will you or the others who must attend me."

Larry stopped, his mouth half full of a salted roll. "Me? Others?"

Urban shrugged. "How could it be otherwise? Vitelleschi will insist on coming. That means von Spee, too. I'll need a secretary to record and duly post the Swiss fellows' entry into papal service, so that means my nephew Antonio. And any time I go someplace inside this palace, two of our three paladins—today, that would be Achille and Giancarlo—will surely follow, spoiling for a fight which no one will give them. By the love of Our Savior, they have already left this chamber."

"To go look for a fight?"

"No: to change back into their martial gear. They are about as priestlike as a pair of prowling tigers."

Larry waited. "And why do I have to tag along?"

Urban turned and smiled. "Because, my good friend, it is you who shall keep me sane in the midst of this improbable circus."

Larry finished his roll and speculated that, all other things being equal, Urban was probably right: that's just what he would focus on doing.

Now, as always.

Chapter 36

As Sharon passed the Palais Granvelle, she shot an annoyed glance at its double doors.

Finan must have seen it. "Wantin' to be in there today, Ambassador?"

"In there? Go—osh, no," Sharon said awkwardly, just barely managing to turn her originally intended "God, no" into something acceptable to Finan's devout Irish ears. As time went on, she had been informed how just about everything from the commonplace (and obvious) "jeez" to the archaic and obscure "zounds" ultimately traced their etymological roots back to a phrase that took the Lord's name in vain.

Finan's eyes crinkled and his mouth turned up at the right corner. "Not feeling a wee bit left out of the great proceedings?"

Sharon laughed. "Finan, I am so happy to be spared all that formal talk about the why's and wherefore's of ecumenical progress that I could dance right here in the street."

Finan's eyes never left her face. "So why aren't yeh, then?"

Sharon straightened her neck histrionically, sniffed slightly. "It's beneath my dignity."

Finan chortled. "'Scuse my laughing, ma'am." His smile dimmed a bit. "It's the radio, isn't it?"

Sharon felt her brow lower. "You're dam—darned right it is." *Another close call on the profanities front.* "Hastings had no business going behind my back and getting Ru—Colonel Sanchez to release it back to his unit."

Finan said nothing, perhaps because they were walking past a Hibernian checkpoint at that moment.

Sharon looked over at him. "You don't agree with me?"

Finan glanced away. "Hardly my place to say, ma'am."

"Unless I'm asking you. And I am, Finan. I trust you. And your judgment."

Finan stopped in the shadow of St. Peter's. "The fair truth of it is that there's something to be said for either side o' the coin. Having the portable radio made sure to put you where you were most needed, ma'am, and there's much to be said for that. On t'other hand, Hastings has a point when he says that the cutthroats we set sideways yesterday were ready to go, there bein' so little in their flat. So if there's more of 'em set to strike, they won't be long in coming out to play. Which means we want every radio in a bell tower, to send the word when they show themselves to our observers."

Sharon frowned, mostly because she had to agree with Finan: there was merit to both sides of the debate. And, truth be told, probably more merit to Hastings'. Whatever might or might not happen in the days to come, it was unlikely that there was anything to be gained by having Sharon Nichols roving around the streets of Besançon, hoping to be in the right place at the right time to see something suspicious. The accumulated leads and clues had either paid out or died out, like Lamy's killing. Everybody agreed that it remained suspicious, much in the same way that everyone agreed that there was still an enemy agent at large: the one who had killed de Requesens, the stonemason, and the guy who slipped out the window during the firefight. But even though the latter crimes were clearly connected with a plot to kill Urban, that did not mean there was anything to be done about them. In each case, what few uncertain leads they had ultimately led to nothing. So until and unless a new lead came to their attention, any further investigation was at a standstill.

All of which meant that Hastings was, regrettably, right: the radio that had been put at her disposal was no longer serving a crucial function. She was no longer notifying security and other staff of the arrivals of various dignitaries as they entered the city, nor was it needed to facilitate her timely contribution to various murder investigations. It was needed to put another observer—and sniper—in yet another overwatch position, thereby increasing the degree to which they could cover all the approaches to the Palais Granvelle.

Sharon resumed walking. "Are the radio logs we found in the flat decoded yet?"

Finan, short legs stretching to keep up with her longer ones, shook his head. "No. Your radio expert, Odo, is the only one who can do that work quickly, and he only got them after dinner last night. He says the codes have a nasty rub he hasn't tinkered with before. It's something he called a trapdoor cipher. It's not in the code books themselves, either. And this trapdoor seems to be opened by something small in each transmission. So, as best I conned what he was saying, he has to find the bit that is triggering the trapdoor before he can decode the messages." Finan frowned. "At least, I think that's what he was telling me." He swerved to follow Sharon as she began to cross the street. "Er... where would we be off to, ma'am?"

"We're going to pay a visit to Prioress Thérèse."

Finan looked wide-eyed at the door of the Carmelite convent, only ten yards away. "Shall I be waiting outside, then, Ambassador?"

"Outside? Nonsense: they have a room or two where they may receive lay men or women."

Finan looked relieved. "And if I may make so bold to ask, what's the purpose of your visit, ma'am?"

Sharon slowed as she approached the door. "To get a little more information." *And, if I'm being honest with myself, to see if Ruy and Owen might have missed anything that could become new leads into the murder of Baudet Lamy, and the disappearance of the mute stonemason who worked for Parsifal Funker.* It was a slim chance, but then again the conversations to date had always been between the prioress and two senior military officers. Or, more pertinently, between two frank and inquisitive men and one woman who, it seemed, had reasons to be less than forthcoming in order to protect the reputation of her house and its past or present nuns. Sharon had wondered if she might have disclosed more to another woman, speaking one to one. Particularly since that conversation would have been framed by an implicit understanding between them: of the difficulties and even dangers involved with being a female leader in a world not merely dominated by, but designed according to the will of, men.

Sharon drew up before the door and raised her hand to knock upon its heavy timbers. Even the best and most caring of men—such as her Ruy—forgot that every nun remained a woman, too, and that there might be things a woman would confide in another woman that she would never reveal to a man. *So, rather than make a direct inquiry, I'll just start chatting and, before long, we—*

The furious barking of dogs made Sharon start. The canine uproar was coming from behind the door of the two-story building that shared a common wall with the priory: a dilapidated flophouse. The baying of the dogs was punctuated by a few earnest snarls.

Finan put his hand to his holstered pistol. "What the divil—?"

The door to the flophouse flew open and, barking become whining yelps, two comically small dogs raced out, the proprietor of the place driving them with kicks and curses. "*Chiens idiots!* Shut up or I will kick your balls over your ears!" He came to a sudden halt when he noticed Sharon standing not ten feet away from him. "Pardon, madame! I apologize for my language, but these mongrels"—which even now were sidling back toward the door, eager to get inside—"are uncontrollable. And insane!"

Finan raised an eyebrow as the two dogs padded softly behind the proprietor and back into the house. "I've had a few pups in my time, monsieur, and I'm thinkin' they're soundin' more than narky. They're ready to set-to and draw blood. What set 'em off?"

"I cannot be sure," said the fellow, not meeting Finan's gaze.

Sharon stepped forward. "Oh? Maybe we should come in and have a look."

Finan glanced at her. "Now, madame, I'm not sure a pair of dogs are worth yer time—"

"Oui! Vraiment!" the landlord exclaimed too quickly, too emphatically. "I will settle them quickly enough with my boot!"

As if disputing the likelihood of such an outcome, the two dogs began baying again. There were more snarls than before.

Sharon frowned at the hint of an echo behind each howl. "Where are they? In your cellar?" Without waiting for an answer, she pushed past the landlord.

Who commenced wringing his hands. "Madame! This matter is beneath your dignity! It is but a few mangy beasts gone mad." His tone took on a theatrical tone of urgency as he followed her inside. "Mad... yes, mad! They could be dangerous, madame! You must not go down—"

Sharon was already ducking her head to follow the narrow staircase—if one could really call it that. The risers were more packed dirt than cobbles, now, and so worn and sloped that they were beginning to resemble a descending set of ridges. "Finan, we need your light down here. Hush, hush!" she shouted at the dogs. When that had no effect, she put a hand on one considerable hip and raised her voice—and she had quite a voice, in which she took no small amount of pride. "Shut your fool mouths this *instant!*"

The dogs cowered, whined, eyes rolling up toward her in the dim light, ears drooping in the classic position of canine contrition. One of them began pawing, then scratching at the crude door at the base of the stairs.

Sharon turned toward the landlord who had hastened down behind her, imploring hands reaching out toward, but not daring to touch, her. She fixed him with the same unblinking stare she had used on the dogs. "What's going on here?"

The fellow sat down heavily on the stairs, looked like he might cry. "Madame—Ambassador—please: I am not a wealthy man. This building is all I have in the world. If people learn, I will be ruined. They will—"

Sharon waved a hand to push his entreaties into silence. "If people learn *what*?"

"Rats," he groaned in response. "I can hear them behind the door. And if the tenants learn of this—"

"Stop." Sharon made her voice loud, dispassionate. The man stopped, looked up at her. "If you have rats in the cellar, why not just open the door and let the dogs in? Looks like that's what they're bred for."

"I would if I could, madame, but the door is jammed. I think the lock is broken."

Finan had edged past them and held the light higher to inspect the keyhole. "Not broken, exactly. Looks like the key snapped off in the lock. And hello; hold on"—he leaned closer, squinting—"not just broken." He straightened and met Sharon's gaze soberly. "There's another piece wedged in beside the tip of the key. Pushed over sideways, too. Jammed the mechanism."

Sharon turned to look at the door again, wondering if she should summon a few more Hibernians. *Damn it, woman: what are you thinking? Calling away some of the pope's protection just because you found a busted lock and decided you can't stop being Nancy Drew?*

But Finan's voice continued low and serious. "Something else, ma'am. Dogs don't go on so about rats, not unless they've gotten at a babby in a crib, or the like. They'll growl and scratch, but not this howling and such." He turned to the landlord. "When did they first start natterin'?"

"A day ago, maybe two. I can't really remember. They whined and fussed but not much more. Then, this morning! *Mon dieu*, they went mad."

Finan turned to Sharon. "To my way of thinking, ma'am, that's a savage sudden change."

Sharon nodded. She looked at the walls around her, aware that the basement of the convent was mere feet away. And as she did so, she recalled the last time she and Ruy had spoken about it, just two nights before. As if from a half-forgotten dream, she heard Ruy's voice recounting that part of his conversation with the prioress in which she revealed that the Carmelites had searched their own cellars for secret passages or the equivalent . . .

"Do you think the search was, well, sufficiently detailed?" Sharon had asked.

"Admirably thorough, from the sound of it," Ruy had answered. *"They searched all sides of the lower levels, excepting the one that they know abuts on an adjoining cellar in the only building that is built up against their own."*

An adjoining cellar . . .

Sharon stood back from the door, gestured to Finan. "Open it."

"Ambassador, I can't. The lock—"

"I mean bust it in. Get a hammer or—something. We need to get in there. Now."

Finan looked up the stairs, then handed his lantern

to Sharon. He unslung his rifle, glanced at the stock, then laid it gently against the broken lock. "Stand back."

Sharon did.

The little Irishman swung the rifle back gently and then rammed it viciously forward against the lock. A strained cracking sound accompanied the impact. Finan checked the stock of his gun, the lock, then stepped back. He raised his leg and kicked forward, the sole of his boot hitting about two inches to the side of the lock.

With a squeal, the door swung back and slammed into the wall. The dogs, atypically unbothered by all the loud human smashing and bashing, were inside as fast as had they been shot from twin cannons. No longer barking, they growled and chased about in the dark room beyond, exciting a sound of panicked skittering in response.

Sharon raised the lantern higher.

Rats ran in chaotic swarms, streaming away from a leaning heap in the far right-hand corner. They flowed toward apertures in the rough stone that framed the rest of the interior on all sides except for the rear wall. That, a haphazard aggregate of ancient-looking brick, apparently offered the rats no hope of escape.

Sharon, kicking at the slower rats, strode directly to the heap in the far corner as the dogs finished chasing the last of the rodents back into whatever invisible crevices they had disappeared. The two scruffy warriors, despite their short legs and lap-dog appearance, now resorted to trotting about the peripheries of the room, ruffs up and muzzles down, sniffing. They were still searching for a scent, even though the prey seemed to have disappeared. *Not entirely unlike me*, Sharon reflected as she kneeled down and gazed at the heap.

Which was, to be more precise, a much ravaged corpse. Judging from the long gray locks and frayed ends of the much-gnawed clothing, it was the body of an older male of very modest means.

She heard Finan's feet stop just behind her. "So this is what they were after."

Sharon glanced around, saw traces of lime leading away from the corpse, saw a light dusting of it on what was left of his clothes. "Yes. And I think I know who this is . . . or was."

Finan was silent, then breathed: "The mute stonemason."

Sharon nodded, looking at the square shapes under tarps positioned along the walls on either side. "Let's take a look at what else was left here. And be careful."

Finan snorted, a sound which eloquently expressed that he had already decided to be very careful indeed. Using the barrel of his Winchester, he started lifting the tarps off the angular objects beneath them: crates.

Sharon examined the body carefully, saw the hint of stains on either side of the neck and tracked them back to the almost surgically severed carotid and jugular. Meaning, from the precision and lack of either deep puncture or long slash, the wounds had been inflicted shortly after the stonemason was either dead or unconscious. The resulting exsanguination would have ensured that he'd never regain consciousness. She stood, feeling a chill run up her arms. The corpse smell was weak, but the sense of a professional execution was overwhelming. And that recalled other professional murders she had seen recently, conducted by an elusive left-handed killer.

Which meant, by all appearances, that this was his lair.

Chapter 37

Finan stepped closer to the rat-savaged tarp he had pushed back; he grunted restlessly. "Ambassador—"

Sharon moved to his side and stared down at what lay revealed in the first, large box. "Rations."

Finan nodded. "And the rats got at them just recently. The crumbs and the cheese are still moist."

Sharon studied the tarp more carefully. There was a faint gray-white dusting on it. "The tarp was either sprinkled with quicklime, or stored under bags of it."

Finan stared, then nodded. "So someone removed it and the rats came for a tuck-in. Well, *another* one: looks like they got to the stonemason sometime earlier."

Sharon nodded. "Seems so. What else did you find?"

"Quite a few shallow crates, Ambassador. I was just about to open them."

Sharon looked at them. "Could they be trapped?"

Finan shrugged. "Might be, but I doubt it. The lids are loose. But just to be safe—" He stood to the side, slipped his rifle's muzzle under the nearest lid, lifted. It flipped off without any effort or incident. They stared.

"Mother o' God!" Finan whispered finally.

Sharon could only nod as her assistant and body-guard started popping the tops of the other boxes. Revolvers that were copies of his own Hockenjoss & Klott. Double-barreled sawed-off shotguns that were down-time clones of up-timer weapons. Short, heavy swords. A box of what were obviously Grantville-influenced grenades. Buff coats and light helmets. Burgundian colors and gear, from the most commonly used boots to baldrics. And finally, a sizeable petard that could probably bring down the whole flophouse, and maybe a good part of the priory, besides.

Finan leaned in quickly, yanked the petard's fuse, staved in the side; powder spilled out.

Sharon watched the surety of his actions. "You've worked with explosives before."

Finan nodded as he defused the grenades, but was careful not to damage them. "I got my start soldiering for Colonel Preston in Spanish Flanders."

"So you were one of the Wild Geese, originally?"

"From the time I had whiskers, ma'am. Maybe before."

"Then why don't you know any of the ones assigned to Colonel O'Neill?"

Finan's smile was sardonic. "Because I'm half Anglo-Irish. That's why I grew up to serve with Preston, who's the same. Besides, he's the business when it comes to forts and sieges and the like. And you can guess the promise he saw in meself."

Sharon glanced at the modest distance from the bottom of Finan's boots to the top of his helmet. "Tunnels?"

Finan nodded. "Mining. Countermining. And the

nastiest fighting you've ever seen, in half lit tunnels always trying to fold in on your head. When the pistol fire got thick, it smelled just like hell in there. Pretty much looked like it, too."

"Is that why you left and joined the Hibernian Mercenary Battalion?"

"Aye, although it was just a company then. No more killin' and dyin' in tunnels. And better pay to boot. Besides, they needed a genuine Hibernian in their bliddy outfit."

Sharon nodded as she paced the room, observing other details. The most noticeable were the rodent-tattered remains of six sleeping rolls. So whoever had been here planned to use this room either as a refuge after an attack—unlikely, since a simple citywide search of all basements would have uncovered it—or as a staging area before an attack. Which meant—

Again, Finan interrupted her train of thought. "Ambassador, you'll want to catch an eyeful of this."

She swerved toward where he was standing next to the brick wall at the rear of the cellar, glanced where he was pointing: several piles of brick dust on the floor. Then his finger rose, drifted along what became the rough outline of a doorway upon the bricks. "They were drilling here, ma'am. You can see through to t'other side in a few places. One good push, and this part of the wall falls outward, into the priory's basement."

Sharon frowned. "But where are the tools?"

Finan shook his head. "You don't need big tools for a job like this one, Ambassador. My guess is, if we peered close among the guns in the crates, we'd find the tools right enough: small hand drills, files, and the like." He nodded a professional appraisal at the wall. "Whoever did this knew what he was doing. Probably cut a small hole first so he'd see if any light shone through. That way, he'd know when he had a potential audience on t'other side and couldn't work safely. But if the hole showed all dark and quiet over in the priory's cellar, then he could get to business, so long as he didn't make much noise. And the small tools used to undermine the brick here? If he went slowly, he'd have made less sound than the scurrying rats."

Sharon nodded, but was already walking back toward the splintered door, putting the pieces of the cellar's puzzle together. She stuck her head under the worm-eaten lintel and called up to the morose landlord. "Who had access to this cellar?"

The fellow looked up. "The man who rented it from me. How he knew I had it was a surprise to—"

"How long ago did he rent it from you?"

"A month ago. He paid it in full, up front. Which is strange; he did not look like a man of means."

"What did he look like?"

"He looked..." The man's voice tapered off; and he scratched his head. "I can only say that he looked average, Your Excellency. His hair was brown, he was of medium height and build. His dress was what one might see on a fairly well-to-do tradesman, or perhaps the lesser garments of a member of the gentry."

"So, neither rich nor poor."

"Precisely, madame."

Sharon nodded slowly: average indeed. In a world full of people who took pains to signal or exaggerate their social rank, this man did the opposite. Which sounded like it was not chance, but a carefully crafted intent. "Was there anything at all notable about him?"

The landlord frowned. "I do not think—yes! He had one odd requirement: that he be given all the keys. When I gave him the two I had, he asked for a third. Which I did not have. He was not satisfied I had given him all the keys until I went to the expense—which I had to prove to him—of having a third key made. Which, to tell the truth, never did work very well."

Sharon discovered her breath was coming more quickly. "Anything else?"

"Er...his eyes were light brown, what my aunt called hazel. And he moved—well, it is hard to describe. He did not move much, and never hastily, but when he did, there was a certain grace about him. As if he might be a dancer."

Sharon nodded and gestured for the man to go back up to the top of the stairs. "Don't go anywhere. I think we'll wish to talk further to you. If not me, then someone else."

"Oh, madame, please no! I promise you: the rats have never been here before this—"

"I don't care about the rats," Sharon snapped. "No one will even mention them. You're safe."

The landlord beamed: his teeth, although yellowed, shone in the dim light. "Ambassador, I am eternally in your debt. I cannot begin to—"

But Sharon turned away and reentered the cellar, pushing what was left of the door closed against the landlord's torrent of protestations of undying gratitude and service. As she walked slowly back to where Finan was inspecting the contents of the crates more closely, she finally had the silence to fit the puzzle pieces together.

So: before Besançon became overcrowded and overbooked, some man had approached the landlord to rent his basement. He had not even quibbled over the price, evidently. His only condition was that he had sole access to it, which he had confirmed by forcing the landlord to spend to have another key made. Not because the renter wanted a third key, but because he knew that landlords would rather part with their last key to a room than pay good money to have another one made. And so, given the tight-fisted nature of the owner's class, the renter was as sure as he could be that he did, indeed, have all the keys for the cellar.

And looking at what he stored in the cellar, and had done there, it was clear enough why he had taken that extraordinary step of insisting upon sole access. It was also clear why he had wanted to rent by the month: because it would be unclear when, precisely, his need of the room would become crucial. Which is to say, when the time would be opportune to attack the pope.

Sharon frowned. But something was still missing. Judging from what was stored in the cellar, this room and the necessary equipment had been here for days, maybe weeks. They had been in readiness, yet they still had not attacked. Why?

And then there was also the matter of numbers. Only six bedrolls were here, and the number of fire-arms suggested a similar number of attackers were to have hidden here. But, given the obvious security around Urban, how could anyone have thought that such numbers would be sufficient to—?

Sharon stopped, felt her breath catch in mid-exhale. This room, these attackers: they weren't the primary attack force. They *couldn't* be. Not only were their numbers insufficient, even with the Burgundian disguises: they were poised to enter the wrong building. The pope never entered the priory. Or at least, he *hadn't*. But the attackers clearly believed that at some point Urban *would* enter the priory. Nothing else made sense.

Sharon nodded to herself, seeing the inevitable begin to unfold before her. Clearly, they knew about the secret passage from the palace; that's why they could know that Urban had access to the priory at all. Which, in turn, meant that the leader of the assassins had known or suspected that Ruy and Owen meant to use that tunnel as an emergency escape route from the palace. That's why he had sought out the mute stonemason, who had no doubt confirmed the tunnel's existence before he died.

Sharon turned slowly, taking in the cellar and its contents once again. So, the leader of the assassins would not have devoted so much effort to securing this room and preparing it unless he was certain that another group would mount an attack upon the palace. And that explained why he had sought out the guild foreman Parsifal Funker; not only to find the mute stonemason, but to confirm, just as Ruy and Owen had, that there were no other subterranean ways in or out of the palace or the priory. In short, if Urban secretly fled the palace, they knew he could only flee to one place. And they prepared accordingly.

And, of course, Funker's interrogation had led the assassin leader to the mute stonemason, who had obviously known of the weakness of the brick wall separating this cellar from the priory's basement. And that was the beauty of it: it wasn't a secret passage or a buried chamber that might show up on some map somewhere. It was simply a wall that he had noted— or maybe himself had strategically weakened—which could be used to pass unobserved and unexpected into the priory.

She looked toward Finan. "They didn't mean to start the attack from here."

Finan cocked his head. "No? Well, they meant to end it here, sure enough." He pointed into one of the crates. "Naphtha or something like it. And since they don't need the petard for breaching, they must've meant it to collapse the place."

Sharon frowned. "But why?"

Finan shrugged. "Until the rubble was dug and sorted, who'd ever be sure they weren't killed by their own bombs, trying to escape? Harder to keep searching for a man when, with every passing day, most of your searchers secretly doubt that he's still alive."

Sharon repressed the shudder at the implicit willingness to destroy a flophouse full of innocent people— and perhaps no small number of Carmelite nuns—just to sow panic and uncertainty. And of course, that disaster would have diverted would-be searchers into emergency roles as rescuers and firefighters. Then again, given what she'd seen of war in this century, and the killing that her father had known both in Viet Nam and the south side of Chicago, Sharon Nichols told herself firmly that she simply had no reason to be surprised or shocked at all. Ruthlessness was a timeless human trait. Small wonder that an assassin would be its epitome.

Finan wasn't done, however. He held up one of the sawed-off shotguns. "I suspect you didn't notice this."

Sharon frowned. "Sure I did. Shotguns. Just like some of the ones that came back with us."

Finan shook his head. "No, ma'am. Sorry to correct you, but not 'just' like. This is *exactly* like that. It's one of ours—well, yours."

Sharon's skin suddenly felt very cold and tight. "What do you mean, one of ours? You mean they're up-time guns?"

"Just this one, Ambassador. All the others are copies. But this one went missing when the Wrecking Crew lost poor Felix."

Sharon felt her stomach plunge and fought against the kind of jitters she felt when she saw a particularly convincing horror film. "It can't be."

Finan simply held the weapon out to her. She saw the maker's mark—Remington—and the comparative fineness of the metal: thinner and yet so much stronger than the steel used in the copies. She saw crudely engraved initials, notches on the stock. "How can you be sure this is Felix's gun?"

Finan shrugged. "Because I watched him carrying it for weeks. You might recall, ma'am, that before I was attached to you, I was Colonel Thomas North's batman during the lively dance we were all doing in Italy, last summer. The first time I met Felix, he was cleaning this gun, right after the Wrecking Crew tidied up the Spanish who almost killed your Da and the others near Chiavenna. Feck, I can even tell you why he carved some of these notches into the stock."

Finan may have seen the persistent look of disbelief on Sharon's face. "I suppose it sounds strange, that we'd have such personal attachments to our weapons, ma'am. But just as a workman labels his tools, well, you might say a favorite weapon becomes part of a soldier's identity. The way lords and ladies are distinguished by their rings and jewelry or heirlooms of one kind or t'other."

Sharon opened her mouth, and for a moment, the words would not come. "But Felix was killed in Rome, during the trap they laid for you when you tried to rescue Frank and Giovanna Stone from the Insula Mattei."

Finan nodded solemnly. "So whatever hand was at work there may very well be at work here, ma'am."

Which would explain much, Sharon thought. If the same shadowy figure who had been behind destroying half of the Wrecking Crew, and behind the attack on the pope in Molino, had been running the assassination attempt here in Besançon, he would have had advance knowledge of the security forces: their equipment, their capabilities, their methods, and above all, their commanders. He would have studied his prey as carefully, as thoroughly, as relentlessly as he had obviously studied the Wrecking Crew and the rest of his adversaries in Italy.

As Sharon continued to study the gun and its copy, and thought back to the other copy she had seen on the bloodstained floorboards of the flat that Ruy and Hastings had cleared just yesterday, she realized: *Five killed, between the flat and the one stabbed—left-handed—in the street. So five dead and one other who remains missing.* She glanced back at the bedrolls. *Six bedrolls, or, to put it another way, five plus one.*

Sharon blinked. *My god; he's one of them! He killed his own man in the street! Killed de Requesens too, but the reason for that is less clear. But this much is certain: he's still at large.*

He was no longer a danger, of course. He had been waiting for an opportunity to strike and instead, was now presumably in hiding. But then, where were the forces which were to have attacked the palace, and moreover, how could anyone do that with less than a company of well-armed men? Between the palace's own defenses, and the snipers and reaction forces in all the churches, a frontal assault would be sheer suicide. Unless—

What if it isn't a frontal assault? But that would mean getting inside, somehow. And no one was going to be allowed into the palace except the colloquium's participants and members of the papal retinue, including Urban's own pontifical guards. Meaning the Wild Geese. And soon, the Swiss, too—

The Swiss—

Sharon felt her stomach churn sharply. *The Swiss. Only a few of them are well-known. Everyone has dismissed the majority of them like a pack of well-meaning, mangy puppies come to fawn around Urban's ankles. But what if they—?*

Sharon sprinted for the stairs. "Finan! The pope!"

"Eh—what?" the Irishman called after her, trailing as quickly as his legs allowed.

"Just follow me. And keep your gun ready!"

Chapter 38

Norwin and another of the Swiss were the first to go through the double doors of Palais Granvelle. Gasquet resented the entry order but could hardly argue with it; the Swiss were both known faces and voices, and as such, were essential to ensuring that the guards remained complacent. Feeling naked without any weapon other than a rusty old dagger from some long-dead Pontifical guardsman, the Occitan went over the threshold with a greater sense of unease, of being a pawn in the palm of Fate, than he could remember ever having experienced.

Gasquet almost paused as he entered; the entry hall was gargantuan. A short, wide staircase went up to the left and led toward the receiving hall. Beyond that was the still larger great hall in which the colloquium had been held and in which the attendees were apparently being served a luncheon banquet. Trays and salvers, both covered and open, were being carried up those stairs by a steady stream of servants.

Across the entry hall and to the right was a split stair-case with a wide landing. It was hung with papal banners and had three large chairs at its center. Probably the point from which Urban planned to accept their service. Gasquet suppressed a bitter smirk. Typical: all set up so that the riffraff didn't get any farther than the first room. Assuming they were allowed in the front door at all.

The defenders near the entry were Burgundians, as the report from Norwin's handler had indicated. Farther into the palace, however, they wouldn't see any of the local troops: only Wild Geese and the occasional Hibernian, the latter probably carrying messages or performing some other errand between the two groups.

Gasquet glanced quickly at the Burgundians as he walked into his prearranged place just behind the point of the wedge that would form up with Norwin at its head. They were marginally more alert than the soldiers he'd seen in the streets for months and were armed well enough for a military unit. But their swords were too long if they had to fight in narrow spaces, and those few who carried pistols were armed only with wheel-locks. One shot was all any of them would get. Their armor was an irregular collection of mismatched pieces and old leather gambesons. Like most rear echelon troops of the polyglot armies that had been chasing each other back and forth across Europe—but mostly Germany— for the past decade, their equipment was provided out of a fluctuating stockpile of outdated or captured materiel. And it showed.

Gasquet wondered if he'd been wrong instructing his men to go for the Burgundians first. They hardly looked worth the bother. But against his unarmored men, they were still dangerous, so since they were more vulnerable to the shrapnel from the pipe bomb, and would be more likely slain or broken outright by a first wave of fire, they remained the first targets. And if any of them ran, that might break the morale of the others while, conversely, boosting that of his own men.

Which might be exactly the boost they'd need, Gasquet reflected, turning his gaze surreptitiously upon the half dozen Wild Geese at the entrance to the receiving hall atop the left-hand staircase. Sturdy buff coats under cuirasses, lobster-tailed steel helmets, heavy swords, and pepperbox revolvers made them look even more dangerous than their professional, swaggerless demeanor. These were troops who had nothing to prove to anyone, least of all themselves. And they had the equipment and training to be steady in the face of a sneak attack and still return as good as they got. At least.

Behind him, the last of his faux-Swiss henchmen took their places in the wedge shape they had decided to adopt. One Burgundian yawned; two others snickered behind their hands. Two of the Wild Geese looked at the group, then noticed three servants taking covered trays toward the landing on the split stairs on the right, rather than toward the receiving hall on the left. Frowning, the tallest of the two headed toward them.

Danny O'Dee fell in step behind Turlough Eubank, who, as Sergeant de Campo, was the highest ranking officer of the Wild Geese after Owen Rowe O'Neill himself.

Eubank held up a hand to stop the first in a file of three servers. "Hold on, fellows. Don't those have to go to the great hall?"

The lead server shrugged as expressively as his burden would allow. "This is for the new—er, Swiss Guards, yes? For after the ceremony?" He looked toward the landing.

Eubank was frowning as Danny came to stand alongside him. "On whose orders? I've heard naught a word of this."

Another shrug. "I suppose the pope himself? I just do as I am told."

Eubank and Danny glanced back as the kitchen doors opened again. Almost a dozen servers filed out, angling toward the low staircase that led up to the receiving hall. "So many more dishes for the banquet, too? We had word it was almost over."

The little *besontsint* started sagging under the weight of his covered tray. "I do not doubt you, monsieur. But I am not informed of such things. I am just told to carry, serve, and fetch."

Eubank glanced from one group of servers to the next, nodded the fellow about his business, leaned toward Danny. "O'Dempsey, you go back and find Art McCarew. He'll be nursemaiding the pope with Jimmy MacDonald. Make sure His Holiness did in true order this new mess of victuals, and that the kitchen staff hasn't made a steaming melder of it."

"Right y'are, Sergeant." And Danny O'Dee was off at a trot.

Sharon Nichols was not a gifted sprinter but, she reflected as she arrived breathless at the steps of St. Peter's, today was probably her personal best.

The sergeant in charge of the watchpoint—Kuhlman, if she remembered correctly—reached out toward her as if she might collapse. "Ambassador! What is—?"

"Watch...that house," Sharon gasped, pointing back at the flophouse. "Don't let...anyone...in there."

"Ambassador, why—?"

"Just do it. The assassins—the basement."

"Assassins in the basement?"

Sharon shook her head. "No assassins . . . there now. But . . . they could be . . . in the palace."

Kuhlman blinked, looked around as if he expected black-cloaked cutthroats streaming out of every window along the length of the street. "But Your Excellency, we've been watching. We've seen no danger to the palace."

Sharon gritted her teeth, panted through them. "Swiss," she tried to gasp out, but it sounded as if she was trying to imitate a snake while wheezing.

Klaus Müller glanced at Huc, who was strolling about ten yards ahead of him. Like Klaus, he was dressed as a tradesman, a sack carried over one shoulder. And every so often, he stared up at the tops of the taller buildings, let his eyes linger for a fraction of a second longer on the high windows that ran the length of the northwest wall of the Palais Granvelle.

Klaus envied Huc his easy, relaxed stroll. This kind of playacting was not to his own liking; he preferred a straight up fight. And yet, here he was, assigned to the one task—the *one* task—which probably would not involve any fighting at all. All because he had a strong and accurate throwing arm. Which made him feel a little better in light of his self-comparison to Huc: Klaus was a bit taller and broader, and definitely the stronger of the two. On the other hand, he reflected irritably, Huc was the more athletic; whatever he might lack in raw strength, he was likely to make up for in efficient form and motion.

Again, Huc glanced up at the sequence of palace windows, and Klaus suddenly realized, with a panicked chill, that he had once again forgotten which windows communicated with the entry hall, the reception hall, and the great hall respectively. Did the entry hall have just one window, or was it two? Or was the second window the one that was supposed to overlook the landing on the split staircase? Or was that where the receiving hall started?

Klaus realized that he had started walking faster, and that Huc had noticed and was changing his own course to be more divergent from the Swiss's own.

Damn it, he's scared I'm going to give him—us!— away. Norwin should never have put me out here. I'm a fighter not a—a bomb-thrower! And he knows, knows, that I have a hard time remembering . . . well, things.

Things like which window goes to what room.

Danny O'Dee wondered when he'd see his Ma and Da next, so he could tell them that he, *he*, was the point guard for Pope Urban!

Oh, sure an' it was only a seventy-foot walk from the main entry of the council chamber, through the receiving hall, to the foyer. But the pope himself had smiled at Danny when the young Irishman approached and asked about both the new luncheon courses and the food for the Swiss. "Well, let's go and find out," were the words the earthly saint had spoken and then gestured that Daniel O'Dempsey should take the lead in the bodyguard triangle that would protect him during those seventy feet.

No matter that there was nothing to protect him from. The pope had chosen Daniel Q. O'Dempsey to lead and now—poor bog-hopper's son that he was—he could almost feel the holy breath on the back of his neck. So what if it came with a faint hint of garlic and nerves? It was the breath of a *pope*!

Turlough met them halfway across the receiving hall. "Your Holiness, I'm sorry to be troublin' yeh, but did you order food for the Swiss? And another course for the guests of the colloquium?"

Urban waved a blithe hand. "I did not, but I am grateful to whoever had the presence of mind to do both."

"Er . . . of course, Your Holiness, but we just want to be sure that everything is, well, as safe as can be."

Urban smiled. "I suspect a few more treats shall not be the death of us, Sergeant. And those Swiss fellows always strike me as being a few meals short of health."

Eubank's expression took on that square-jawed tightness that Danny O'Dee had seen often enough, and it meant one of two things: either he was digging his heels in against stupid orders from an officer, or about to put one of those same heels in the arse of a slacker recruit. "Your Holiness," Eubank restarted, his voice a register lower, "I am very sorry to continue to trouble you on this point, but I must insist—"

"Holy Father!" The shout came from the man at the head of the Swiss, who had remained in their wedge shaped formation, awaiting Urban. "We thank you, and, poor as we are, would honor you in the only way we may—with our voices!"

Ah, fer Chrissakes, thought Danny O'Dee, *the buggers are going to* sing? *Please Lord; anything but that.*

Sharon straightened up, drawing in great wracking breaths—*okay, having lost weight is not enough; I* have *to exercise more!*—and lifted an arm to point at the palace. But as she did, her attention was drawn to one of the tradesmen walking near it. He seemed, well, twitchy somehow, like he wasn't at home in his own skin. And now that she watched more closely, he seemed to be veering to stay close to another trades-man. The second fellow's own gait and demeanor were not noteworthy in any way, but he did share one unusual behavior with the other: they were both stealing quick glances up at the second floor of the Palais Granvelle, or at its high windows.

Sharon started walking in the direction of the palace. "Finan."

"Ma'am?"

"What do you make of that?" she said, pointing.

"Er...the tradesman, Your Excellency? Or the two, I guess? Both from out of town, maybe, staring at the big buildings. It happens, you know."

"Hastings is at this station, isn't he?"

"Yes'm."

"Get him now. Right now."

And she started walking out into the street, her breathlessness forgotten. She heard Finan's feet thump-ing away. "Watch officer?" she shouted behind her.

"Ma'am?"

"I need you and your men to follow me."

"But Ambassador, those two fellows are just—well, now that you mention it—"

"They could be assassins," she said. And then, in the hope of startling the Hibernians into action, she repeated herself so loudly that it was almost a shout: "Assassins."

❖   ❖   ❖

Above the irregular noise of the midday bustle on Besançon's main street, Klaus heard a woman's voice asserting, rather than shouting, "Assassins." He looked around quickly but realized a moment later that that had probably been the worst thing he could have done: people stared at his reaction.

Huc uttered a low oath and sprang forward, his backpack coming off in a single smooth sweep. But, but—what could Huc do? No one was singing yet! How could he possibly know which window—?

And then, again too late by a second, Klaus understood: Huc was going to throw the bomb through the middle window. Gasquet had mentioned something about this when they'd been going over the plan just before starting out for the palace. If, by some chance, the street team was spotted, the best odds were to put the bomb through the windows into the receiving hall. It was uncertain that the pope would come all the way out into the foyer, and even if he did, a lot of his guards and support staff would probably be lingering back near the great hall, near the rest of the dignitaries.

After touching the pipe bomb's fuse to a long-burning match Huc had kept curled in a pierced tin container, he pulled the bagged explosive out of his satchel, and swung it around his head. Two leaping steps forward as the bomb spun and then he let it fly—a beautiful arc, Klaus had to admit as the smoke-trailing bag flew up toward the fourth window.

The window I'll put mine through as well, thought Klaus as he pulled the smoke bomb out of his own satchel.

❖   ❖   ❖

Even as Norwin lifted his chin to start the *Dies Irae*—which annoyed Gasquet, because the three chairs on the landing all but assured them that Urban would actually come out to the foyer for the induction—there was a change in the faint street noise that leaked in through the closed door and the small, street level windows: an indecipherable shout, which seemed to spawn others. Something was going on out there, and Gasquet had a bad feeling about what it might be. So, yes, the receiving hall and the *Dies Irae* were the right choice, after all.

There were some surprisingly good voices amongst his own men—odd: cutthroats who could have been choir boys—and the low, somber melody of the hymn was just right for the collection of baritones and basses that had come to kill the pope.

"Dies irae—" Gasquet smiled: it was an appropriate song for massacring the wealthy, sanctimonious bastards who had spit on him, his family, and kept taking and taking what they had until there was nothing left to take. Yes, the day of wrath indeed.

"—dies illa."

The first bomb crashed through the middle window of the receiving hall with a triumphant shattering of glass. And Gasquet thought:

Time to meet your nonexistent maker, you hypocrites.

Klaus looked up from fumbling the match against the fuse, saw:

—Huc's bomb splinter through the fourth window;

—three Hibernians running at him, led by that damned Moorish ambassador of the USE;

—faces and then more faces, turning toward him,

mouths opening, shouts emerging, accusing fingers rising.

He loped toward the same window as Huc sprinted away, began swinging his smoke bomb by the wooden handle with which it had been fitted, and thought: *I won't miss. I won't. I can do this. And then—*

—then I'll run like hell.

"Down, Ambassador!"

Before Sharon could react, a Hibernian—one she'd never met and whose name she didn't know—had tackled her from behind. Despite a mouthful of dust, she prepared to give the man a short but vigorous tongue-lashing—

And couldn't think of words—any words—as two .40-72 Winchesters started roaring only a few feet overhead.

Somehow, the big assassin who was swinging the second bomb managed not to go down right away, although he was being hit by slugs made famous for their ability to stop lions, and even water buffalo.

But on the fourth or fifth clothes-shredding, blood-misty impact, he stumbled with a childlike whimper and the bomb spun out of his limp fingers just before he stretched his length upon the dry street.

By which time, the screaming panic of the noonday traffic made it almost impossible to hear the warning that Sharon was now chorusing with the Hibernian who had tackled her:

"Bomb! Bomb!"

Ruy Sanchez de Casador y Ortiz had just emerged from his unsuccessful attempt to convince Achille d'Estampes de Valençay and Giancarlo de Medici that, since they were now both nobles and cardinals, they owed it to their respective nations and Church to not go marching around in military gear and risking their necks as Urban's unofficial bodyguards. Maybe he could at least persuade Léonore to do differently when he relieved him back at the cloister this evening.

As they left the small sitting room, Ruy again prevailed upon their apparently nonexistent sense of balance in the universe. "My lords, but the pope has guards. Many of them."

"A pope can never have enough guards," Achille retorted flatly as he led the way out of the room—and stopped as the middle window on the opposite side of the receiving hall exploded inward, a smoking bag at the midst of that glittery storm of knifelike shards.

"Bomb!" he cried, even as gunfire erupted out in the street.

Ruy, eyes always scanning, already knew where the pope was: about twenty feet beyond the midpoint of the receiving hall, where he had stopped, hands folded, to listen to the irregular musical offering of the new Swiss Guard. Ruy's eyes fixed their positions, picked out subtle differences in posture and size, noticed the new helmets that possibly concealed more obvious differences. But that realization and its implications, all registered in a fraction of a second, had to wait. He charged around Achille, whose reflexes kept him only a few feet behind Ruy, and screamed, "Shield the pope!"

The bomb hit the ground with a thump—perhaps eighteen feet behind the rearmost of the pope's guards. Who performed as Owen and he had trained them.

The one at the front of the triangle—Daniel O'Dempsey—spun around, grabbed Urban by the front of the cassock, and twisted into a fall so that the pontiff went under him. The two in the rear spread themselves wide as they dropped to their knees, becoming overlapping human shields. Sergeant Eubank threw himself on top of Daniel, shouting orders to the other Wild Geese—

Which were never heard.

The bomb went off with a broad, earsplitting boom. The two kneeling Irishmen went down, shrapnel tearing a bloody ripple across the closest one's neck and back, despite his cuirass and buff coat. The sound in Ruy's ears was suddenly displaced by muffled silence and daggerlike pain. The hangings on the walls, the furniture, the servants, two of the other Wild Geese and one of the Burgundians went down under a hail of small projectiles—which, Ruy realized, had sliced into his own arms and legs, spalled off his cuirass, clipped the end of his nose, all in the same instant that the shockwave staggered him back a step.

Achille stood impassive in the storm, bleeding from half a dozen wounds of indeterminate severity.

Giancarlo's fury came out as a hiss. "My face! They cut my face!"

Ruy started forward again, saw Achille shouting, even as he did the same, but was unable to hear his own cry any better than the Frenchman's, but knew he was howling the same thing:

"The pope—does he live?"

Chapter 39

Gasquet once again envied Norwin the speed of his tactical reflexes: the Swiss was up and moving even before the last of the weak fragments had finished spattering harmlessly into the entry hall. Shouting warnings against assassins coming in from the street, Eischoll waved the servants back into the kitchen—even while he set about opening all the covered trays that had been tagged with a short band of red ribbon. He'd have the weapons in hand in a second, but until then—

Gasquet made for the main door, where the two terrified Burgundians kept turning from the acrid smell of the bomb inside the palace, toward the sustained gunfire outside. He stood straight, put all the military hauteur he could muster into his voice: "Bar the door, you fools! They mean to get in among us!"

One of the Burgundians hopped to the task immediately, and had run the beam halfway across the doors before he paused, then turned back toward Gasquet, perplexity rapidly converting into doubt. In a moment more, it would become suspicion.

Gasquet closed the distance in a single step, had his dagger out and in the man's throat before a cry escaped him.

The other soldier, still paralyzed by surprise and fear, snapped out of his trance with a start. He drew his sword into a wide backhanded cut at Gasquet—who bent and snatched the wheel-lock off the belt of his first victim. He had it up, cocked, and leveled as the second Burgundian's blade arced in toward him. But rather than rush—undue haste defeated more men in combat than the skill of their foes—Gasquet took the time to dodge the cut. As he'd thought, the Burgundians were like most rear echelon troops: no better than their equipage.

Before the man could recover from his wide round-house slice, Gasquet leveled the gun at the center of soldier's chest and pulled the trigger. He had a vague impression of a bloody splatter as the large ball tore through ribs and lung, but didn't stop to look. Sightseers on a battlefield rarely lived to fight again.

Gasquet scanned the room: more than half of the men had clustered near Norwin, scrabbling for whatever weapons had been concealed in the covered trays. A few more were bearing down on the remaining Burgundians, who seemed to have realized that even though they had swords and their attackers only had daggers, that they were severely outclassed.

Finally, Gasquet's eyes grazed across the trays that had been abandoned on the landing—two of which had red ribbons tied about their handles. He sprinted toward them.

Larry Mazzare charged out the door of the great hall two seconds after the last of the shrapnel had

finished peppering and chipping the scenes painted
on the receiving hall's walls. To his surprise, vinegary
old Vitelleschi, who had started at his heels, had over-
taken him by the end, arriving at Urban's side one
stride sooner than the up-timer. As von Spee brought
up the rear, Ruy joined them, and—speaking slowly
and loudly—admonished them: "Eminences, you are
running in the wrong direction."

"I shall not leave my pope," Vitelleschi almost spat.

Turlough Eubank ignored the exchange; he was
busy checking the dogpile of three Wild Geese atop
one pope. He rolled a bloody-backed Irishman off
the heap. "MacDonald is dead." A quick check on the
next. "McCarew is breathing, but he's got more holes
in him than a sieve."

Danny O'Dee shrugged out from under his unconscious friend, shouted. "I'm okay!"

Nodding, Eubank reached down and helped Urban
to his knees. "His Holiness is alive."

Urban, wincing at every sound, looked at the faces
around him, and, seeing Larry, grabbed his arm. "Lawrence, you must ensure the safety of the attendees.
Go. Now." And, seeing the frown that Larry could
feel growing on his face, added: "No argument."

Turlough Eubank had grabbed Danny by the collar
and waved over two of the Wild Geese who had been
on the outer periphery of the bomb. He pointed at
the short staircase leading down to the foyer, where
there was a chaos of movement, some of it apparently
violent. The sound of a single gunshot rebounded from
the palace's stone walls; they all looked up.

Ruy rattled out orders. "Sergeant, take your men
and hold the staircase." Achille and Giancarlo made

to follow Eubank. Ruy barked at them as if they had been raw recruits. "No. The three of us guard the pope until O'Neill arrives."

Achille sneered. "Arrives? What do you mean?"

Ruy drew his .357 magnum revolver and rapier in a single, fluid, cross-body motion. "It is a contingency plan. The colonel has a group nearby, to ensure the evacuation of the pope."

Urban, shaking his head and fighting to get his legs under him, stopped to stare at Larry. "Obey me, Cardinal Mazzare: protect our guests."

Larry, bitterly hating the task that would take him from the pope's side, also discovered a quick pang of gratitude bound within the regret: it seemed, at least for the moment, that he would not have to kill as he had at Molino. He turned and sprinted back to the council chamber, shouting for two newly arrived Wild Geese to help him secure the doors.

Gasquet turned at the sound of gunfire: Norwin had snatched up a pistol and fired it at two of the Burgundians who had been retreating toward the kitchen. Hit in the torso at point-blank range by the large caliber balls, one fell spurting blood and shrieking. The other slumped over with a curse, trying to maintain a hold on his sword. One of the Swiss was there, leaped past the faltering blade and was atop the soldier, dagger raised high. It fell. The struggle ceased.

Gasquet, leaping up the stairs to the landing, half expected what he found when he flung away the lid of the first ribboned tray: three pepperbox revolvers, identical to those used by the Wild Geese. A clever choice, given it was the only rapid-firing gun with which any of them were already familiar: both he and Norwin had drilled their men on the dangers of the gun, and also how to operate it. He got one in either hand, reached behind; Donat and Manel were there. Each grabbed one.

Meanwhile, Gasquet, checking on the rest of the fight in the foyer, saw it was already resolving. Brenguier had been trailing Norwin, saw the two Burgundians go down, saw the last three shy back toward the staircase leading to the receiving hall. The big Occitan grabbed Chimo by the collar and charged them. Although the two assassins were only armed with daggers, the soldiers did not wait to try their chances; they fled up the stairs, one throwing down his sword.

Which was the reminder Gasquet needed. "Grab a sword!" he shouted at his men. "You've got five shots and then you're out."

"He's right!" shouted a new voice. Two porters emerged from the kitchen, each armed with a bloodied meat-cleaver. "The back door is clear," continued the older one, who was bent and had an alarmingly disfigured face. He swung around toward Gasquet. "Don't forget the grenades."

Gasquet blinked, turned toward the second tray, opened it, and discovered several pots of hardened jam. Except that each one had a wick protruding through their tightly fitted covers. But lighting them? Maybe a candle from the trestle table would do—which was when he noticed that embedded in the wax along the back of the candles was another cord: a slow match.

Gasquet grabbed them all and jumped down toward where the rest of the men were arming themselves with pepperbox revolvers from the serving tray and swords from the dead Burgundians' hands. The sight made him smile.

So far, so good.

Sharon Nichols ducked her head as the second bomb went off, its fuse having burnt down over three seconds that felt like an eternity.

But instead of detonating with the same brutal roar that had resounded within the palace mere moments before, this one went of with an anemic pop—at which, smoke began gushing out of it. By the time she was back on her feet, Sharon could barely see the palace.

She started toward the growing smoke, but a strong hand grabbed her arm. She turned, annoyed.

It was Finan. "Pardons, ma'am, but now yer jes' being foolish. This is our job." Hastings, looming behind the little Irishman, nodded sharply.

Sharon shook her head. "I'm perfectly fine, and we need to get those—"

"Ma'am, it's us, without *you*, who need to get the assassins. Your job is to make sense of all this mess when the shooting's over and use your gift of diplomatic gab to settle all the ruffled feathers. An' it's true enough you won't be able to do either job if you're dead. Which would slay me sure enough, too."

Hastings nodded again. "He's right. Your husband would kill us if we allowed you to get any closer. Now, stay here. Please, Ambassador." And together, he and Finan led six other Hibernians toward the smoke.

Sharon, fists clenched, was still searching for a rebuttal when they vanished into the thick white haze.

❖   ❖   ❖

Norwin sped around to the men, making sure each had one of the pepperbox revolvers, or, in two cases, double-barreled snaphaunce pistols. Gasquet split the grenades between himself, Brenquier, Donat, and one of the Swiss who he knew had a good arm.

The disfigured porter trotted over, limping and listing, the other—a round-shouldered ox of a man— trailing in his wake. "Aren't you ready, damn it?"

Gasquet lifted his chin. "And who are you to ask?"

"The handler who got you the guns, damn it. Now, let's kill this bastard pope."

The hulking fellow behind him nodded, touched a much larger grenade to a slow match hanging at his belt, and threw it with surprising grace up the stairs into the receiving hall.

Danny O'Dee was right behind Turlough Eubank as they neared the stairs, drawing his pistol a moment after the sergeant did—and just before a fuming gre- nade crested the top step. It took a surprisingly high bounce, headed straight toward them—

The sergeant dove for the smoking bomb. Danny blinked: *is he tryin' ta kill himself?*

But Eubank's long dive allowed him to get to the bomb before it could hit the ground again: he swat- ted it with one hand, sent it wobbling toward the left-hand wall—

The grenade exploded before it got there: a ragged bark that sent out smoke and fragments along with a shock that felt like a kick to Danny's chest.

He hit the ground, heard bits of metal keening overhead like distant bees, got half a breath back into his constricted lungs, reeled to his feet.

A man—one of the Swiss fer feck's sake!—was charging up the stairs, a double-barreled pistol in one hand, a sword in the other. Closer to him, one of the Wild Geese was on his back and not moving, and the other rising slowly, shaking his head. Eubank was pushing himself off the floor as if he was fighting up through a pool of half-frozen molasses; his arms were quaking as if he was trying to lift a millstone.

The world still tilting and muffled as if by a foot of cotton, Danny cocked the hammer of his pepperbox. He swung it toward the man who had just reached the top of the stairs, put the front sight in the hammer's triangular aperture, drifted it up to his target's abdomen, and squeezed the trigger.

The pepperbox hardly jumped—its heavy cylinder/barrel combination had been cast as a single piece of metal—and the man staggered, the ball splashing a red hole into his left shoulder. Danny worked the cocking handle on the pepperbox, brought it up—but not before the wounded assassin discharged his own pistol straight at Danny's head.

Danny O'Dee, like most young soldiers, had imagined his death. It had taken hundreds of forms—but never involved being shot between the eyes at close range. He felt a ringing impact above his brow, saw a brief, bright flash, and then felt himself falling backward. And as he did, a greedy, swallowing darkness came at him.

And gulped.

Gasquet saw Manel totter at the top of the steps, blood streaming out of the wide, ragged hole in his left shoulder, a piece of his scapula showing like the stub of a broken tooth.

The other four who were already armed reached the top of the stairs, pistols at the ready.

Ruy kneeled and waved the others lower as several shots were traded at the head of the stairs. The only one of the Wild Geese who'd been on his feet—Danny O'Dee—staggered and then fell his length on his back.

Achille was incredulous. "We are crouching like cowards. Why? To surrender?"

"No, to become smaller targets."

Eubank had reeled to his knees and was scrabbling uncertainly after his pepperbox. The other Irish trooper knocked down by the grenade had risen, gun in hand. He began firing just as four more of the assassins crested the stairs, pepperbox revolvers in all their hands.

Mierda! Ruy drew aim with his .357, regretted not being a better marksman with the admirable weapon, felt movement at his back.

The soldier in him wanted to fire; the security chief for the pope forced him to glance around.

Von Spee was still trying to get the somewhat disoriented Urban down to his knees. And Vitelleschi had stood again—stood straight upright and directly between Urban and the assassins, his chin raised, his eyes closed.

Mother of God, no—!

Ruy threw himself backward against Urban's shins. The pope dropped with a startled cry at the same instant that the enemy's pepperboxes roared in a savage sustained chorus.

The Irishman at the head of the stairs, already specked with blood from the fragments of the bomb and then the grenade, was hit at least three times, red mist marking where each of the point-blank bullets went through his buffcoat and body, more rounds spanging into his cuirass. Eubank leveled his weapon at the enemy line, firing steadily, bullets chipping dusty white chips of marble from the lip of the stairs, others going over the heads that ducked in response. Dazed, he kept cycling his weapon even after the hammer fell and nothing happened.

Ruy, still crouching, crept forward, revolver at the ready.

Giancarlo's voice was hoarse. "Don Ruy, that is not valor; that is suicide."

"You wished combat, my lords? Now you shall have it. We shall advance together. Why do you stare? You each have a piece. And you each have longswords and heavy armor. We shall charge them before they may organize to fire again."

The only reply was from a new voice: a sob. Ruy gritted his teeth; he hadn't the time to turn again, but he had to.

Von Spee was kneeling over Vitelleschi. The wizened Black Pope had fallen backward, arms out. There were at least five large gunshot wounds in his torso and limbs, and more blood on the marble floor than Ruy believed the vinegary old Jesuit could possibly have still had in his perpetually pale body.

Achille's voice was thick. "Is he—?"

"He lives," wept von Spee. "But I think not for long." Urban looked on, tears streaming down his cheeks.

Ruy gritted his teeth. "Father von Spee, you must leave Father Vitelleschi and escort the pope to the escape tunnel. Go now."

"But if the assassins are behind us as well—?"

Which Ruy admitted was a possibility: *why else had O'Neill failed to show up?* But there were no other options left. "If you encounter assassins, then you must fight as well as you can and save the pope. But he may not stay here. Now go—"

Feet pounded on marble behind them. Ruy turned: it was either more assassins or—

Owen Roe O'Neill, Tone Grogan, and five Wild Geese had emerged from one of the two halls that led away from the front of the council chambers in a tee—but from the wrong hallway. "They have bombs and revolvers," Ruy shouted at them. "Stay low."

But O'Neill had already motioned for his men to approach at a fast crouch. "I know the feckin' drill," the Irishman grumbled when he drew close.

"Do you?" Ruy snapped. "Then where have you been? Napping?"

"No, running like scalded cats."

"What?"

"Damned 'dignitaries' came flooding into the hall as we were trying to reach you. So we had to go upstairs, cross over, come down the other side."

Ruy smiled. Despite the endless planning, they had never considered how the colloquists might become an obstruction, not merely a stationary body to protect. "Then I am doubly glad to see you at all. They have the foyer."

"Numbers?"

"We have not seen—"

Eubank, who evidently had not only recovered from two deafening explosions, but possessed extraordinarily robust hearing, whispered loudly. "I saw seven or eight at least. Main doors are shut. Probably no more than twice that number all told, mebbe less."

O'Neill's voice was calm but tense. "Stay down, Turlough. You fit to fight?"

"O' course . . . now that I'm reloaded." He cast away an empty cylinder.

"Then you're with me."

Ruy nodded his appreciation at the calm courage of the sergeant. "Since the most direct route to the music room is blocked—"

O'Neill nodded. "We've got to use the fifth evacuation contingency. Can't say I like our odds of charging down into the foyer, then up past the landing on the right-hand staircase."

Ruy shrugged. "At least they will not expect it—any more than they will expect us to charge them." He glanced at Achille and Giancarlo. "You are ready?"

He did not wait for an answer: he charged.

Chapter 40

Gasquet turned to the others. Everyone had been armed, the hasty attack plan worked out. Nothing complicated: a few more grenades over the top, then a volley from the revolvers and a charge. Swords and pistols at arm's length was how the day was always meant to be decided.

Gasquet turned to look at them. "Now," he screamed, "at them and finish the job!"

Howling their approval and blood lust, all twelve of them—the two porters and the ten remaining assassins—rushed up the stairs, two throwing grenades as they went.

As the smoke started to clear, Hastings got the last of his command gathered on the stairs leading up to the Palais Granvelle's main entrance.

The last two who had emerged from the mists looked quizzically at the door. "Sir?" they said. Hastings could almost hear what they really wanted to say: *Are we waiting for someone to answer the door?*

Hastings shouldered his rifle. "They have barred

the door against us—at least partially. It may take all of us to break it down."

"Where's a battering ram when you need one?" Finan quipped.

Hastings almost grinned. "Sling arms. Line up here. Finan, you stay back. No, not because you're small, but because I need someone with a gun already out who's got the sense and the aim to pick off any assassins who might be trying to hold the door against us when we come through."

Finan snapped off the safety on his Winchester. "I'm yer man fer that, Lieutenant."

"I knew you were. Now, men, altogether—"

Ruy heard the charge coming up the stairs, sprang forward, heard Achille and Giancarlo keeping pace with him on either side.

"Why not wait for them?" Giancarlo panted; not as heavily built as Achille, he found the armor more tiring.

"They'll throw grenades, and throw blind. Which means long."

Sure enough, by the time they had closed half the distance to the stairs, two grenades came arcing high over the top riser, landed behind them, continued rolling.

He could hear O'Neill's men following close behind, speeding up as the grenades went past. They had to get clear before—

The grenades detonated, distinctly smaller blasts than the first one, but enough to make them duck. Ruy felt a single fragment smack the back of his cuirass weakly.

That was the same moment that the first wave

of attackers came over the stairs, pepperboxes firing wildly as they came.

Ruy stopped, slipped into a sideways profile and raised the .357. He hated wasting ammunition, but right now it was more important to buy time than take lives. He began squeezing the trigger.

The thunderous discharges of the heavy up-time handgun had an immediate effect: the charge slowed. One man went down on the second round, another was wounded by the third. Ruy let instinct guide him: *one more round should do it.* He fired, missed—but the attackers crouched down, returning fire almost blindly as they did.

Ruy looked back. Achille was taking a hand away from his breastplate; it was stained red. Seeing Ruy's look, he shrugged. "Flesh wound."

Ruy hoped he was right, had no time to do anything but glance at Owen Roe O'Neill's group, who were rushing over the edge of the stairs. "Now," said Ruy calmly to the armored cardinals on either side of him, "it is our turn."

As Turlough Eubank fell in behind Owen Roe O'Neill, his feeling of regret at leaving Ruy and the two cardinals alone to clear them a path vanished instantly.

The flying wedge the Wild Geese had formed around the pope came over the crest of the stairs straight into the front rank of the assassins. Fortunately, the flank closest to the left—the pathway to their escape up the main stairs—was now the weakest: the man Danny O'Dee had wounded had been killed by the trooper who had died during the first fusillade, and evidently, Ruy had wounded another on that side. But now, rising to plug that gap were the assassins in the second rank.

Pepperboxes discharged on both sides. Bodies fell. Some were Turlough's mates, some were the bastard assassins. Then they were through, just as it sounded like a giant was knocking at the double doors to the outside. Owen himself was bleeding from a wound to the leg and the Jesuit—von Spee—was half carrying Urban despite a ball going through his own arm.

But getting through the second rank of attackers did not mean they were free and clear. The assassins veered after them as they raced around the corner to the main stairs and made their way up. But, slowed by the pope, the Wild Geese had to turn, and a second furious exchange of sustained volleys dropped one of the attackers, wounded several more on each side.

The escape had slowed, which meant, if Ruy and his two paladins were not able to hold the other flank in place, they might still be overwhelmed.

Turlough glanced back in their direction—

Ruy let his empty .357 drop on its lanyard, pulled at his main gauche. Firearms also empty, the four remaining assassins of the first rank surged up the stairs, pushing away from Giancarlo. Two pressed Ruy back just as his second blade cleared its sheath, but neither of them came within range of an easy riposte. The better and older of the two—von Meggen's evidently traitorous lieutenant Eischoll—was competent enough not to fall for any of Ruy's attempts to appear unprepared.

However, that was enough to keep Ruy from intervening on behalf of the weakened Achille, whom the other two rushed, hacking fiercely.

Normally, they would have been quick work for the Frenchman, but his armor slowed him and his wounds weighed upon him even more. He fell back before them, managed to slash one's leg before a heavy blow to his helmet laid him out. Jumping into the opening in the line, the assassins turned Ruy's flank.

Giancarlo, panting under the weight of his armor— *more a would-be warrior than an actual one, are you?*—swung around Ruy to defend his other flank more directly, pushing back Eischoll and his companion. Now, rather than the three defenders holding the top of the stairs against four attackers who were several steps lower, the line of engagement ran down the middle of the stairs, top to bottom.

One of Ruy's new opponents—the one who had felled Achille—leaped in, swinging savagely. At last, an easy kill: Ruy parried the cut, rolled his wrist, his rapier ready to skewer the fellow, saw that it was the disfigured porter. But it was also a familiar face. From the day the Swiss had arrived. It was the supposed ironmonger and trader. The bent fellow whose nose had resembled a squashed turnip. The one who had intervened on behalf of von Meggen. "You!"

The man used Ruy's moment of distraction to pull back. His mouth a rictus of animal hatred, he spat, recovered his footing, and brought his blade around for yet another cut.

Ruy had less than a second. He did not need to glance around the foyer to know what the rhythm of this combat signified: war to the knife. Men who would do anything to kill the pope facing men who would do anything to protect him. There was no pause, no quarter, and each side had already started to steal a moment here or there to deliver a coup de grace to a fallen foe.

But this enemy was, in all probability, too important to kill.

Ruy reaccelerated the swing of his rapier, turned his thrust into a wholly unnecessary feint. The man with the squashed nose was an enthusiastic but wholly untrained killer and changed his cut into an attempted parry.

Ruy almost smiled as he dropped out of the feint and ran his blade through the man's right outer thigh, then twisted outward. The bent man shrieked as the steel bit through skin and muscle to rip free, dropped his sword to clutch the welling wound; bloody, but not arterial.

But the extra fraction of a second that it cost for Ruy to check his first blow and shift to inflicting an incapacitating wound instead, was all the opening the other attacker needed. A competent swordsman, he waited for the Catalan's rapier to sink deep into Turnip-Nose's leg, feinted with his sword, and as Ruy caught it with his main gauche, he brought up the dagger he held low and ready.

Ruy twisted away from the upward thrust aimed at the open left armpit of his cuirass, managed to get his body out the way, but not his arm. The dagger left a deep seam from his tricep to his elbow even as his rapier was clearing the turnip-nosed man's thigh. He slashed then, rolling his wrist into a backthrust at the arm holding the dagger: clipped it enough to inflict a wound that was almost the match of the one he'd just suffered.

For a moment, the men on the stairs stared at each other, panting: Giancarlo and Ruy, guards up against the three remaining assassins, who were less wounded and exhausted.

This, Ruy reflected was about to get very interesting. Possibly in the very worst sense of the word.

Turlough Eubank's stomach sank, seeing the three assassins on the stairs, and the big oaf with the meat-cleaver mounting the stairs, apparently meaning to get overhead, maybe behind them. "M'lord," he grumbled at O'Neill.

The colonel turned, eyes measuring the scene as he did. As he drew his sword—even he, with two pepperboxes, was dry—O'Neill shrugged a slung rifle off his other shoulder. "Use this. First to help them, then us." And he turned away to parry an assassin's blade as the weapon slid into Turlough's rough hands.

It was the SKS that the Hibernian commander, Thomas North, had gifted to Owen in respect for what he had achieved during the seizure of the Castel de Bellver in the Balearics, less than a year ago. And almost identical to the one with which Eubank himself had gunned down more than a dozen of the Spanish defenders.

Turlough brought the weapon up quickly, breathed deeply: not the right weapon for these tight quarters, really. But with a momentary knot of his mates keeping the enemy off him...

Eubank squared the sights. He had to fire over the heads, or even the shoulders, of Ruy and Giancarlo in order to get at the enemy. Whispering a silent and shockingly profane prayer, he sighted on the attacker who had just cut a bloody groove in Colonel Sanchez's arm. He cheated the sight a little higher, saw Ruy step backward, giving ground—

He fired three fast shots into the top of the sniper's triangle in the moment before the assassin could once again close with Ruy.

Turlough Eubank didn't know how many shots hit, but at least one had; the man slumped over as the weapon's distinctive up-time report—sharp and reverberant—seemed to paralyze both sides for the space of one eyeblink.

Then the giant who'd been knocking on the front door smashed it in.

Hastings pushed through the gap between the doors, the rest of the shattered cross-bar splintering where it had been incompletely slid into the retaining hooks on the right-hand side. For a second, the crash seemed impossibly loud, then Hastings realized it was rifle fire. Up-time. SKS, from the sound of it.

The room, filled with gunsmoke, was a tableau of carnage and weary men. More than a dozen bodies were already on the floor, and there was no telling how many were friend or foe. But it was clear enough that the Wild Geese on the stairs, with Owen Roe at the point of a reduced wedge, were almost all wounded, holding back their attackers while one priest—von Spee—helped a man up the stairs...

A man *in a cassock*...

The pope!

"Rifles!" Hastings screamed. "Flank right!"

In less than a second, three had leaped to the right, drew a bead. But didn't fire. "Blue on blue!" shouted Kuhlman.

Damn it; still no clear field of fire. "Further. Fire when clear!"

One second, two more leaping steps, and the first of the Winchesters began to fire.

Half of the assassins pressing O'Neill's knot of defenders went down like sacks of grain. Another tried running for the kitchen. Finan, weapon raised to cover that flank, fired five times, working the level so that it sounded like a triple-time metronome. Three red holes appeared on the assassin's back, the last ugly crater erupting even as he fell.

The remaining assassins—a mere handful—broke in all directions.

Except for Sergeant Eubank, O'Neill and his men ducked low; Ruy and Giancarlo did so a moment later. Now with a clear field of fire, the Hibernians' Winchesters and Eubank's SKS spoke again in combined, remorseless thunder. Invisible bolts of death cut through enemies only a few yards distant. Then, there was only smoke and silence—

—until the moaning of the wounded began.

When Otto had seen his friend Heinz fall, his leg butchered like an Easter lamb, his only thought had been to kill: to kill the small, fast man with the mustaches and quick sword, the man who had cut Heinz so badly. Heinz was Otto's only friend. Heinz fed him, clothed him, scolded those who teased him for being slow-witted. So, kill. Otto happily forgot the other plans. They were no longer important.

But before he could get to the top of the stairs, and maybe sneak around behind the swordsman who moved as smoothly as a traveling acrobat, a loud gun began shooting from near the foot of the other stairs. It was a bad sound, and it killed one of the not-Swiss men, went through his body and blasted out a big chunk of the stone wall behind him.

And then the big doors crashed open and more men came in: the dangerous ones with the long guns. Otto wanted to weep; now if he stayed to kill the fast little swordsman, he would probably die. Besides, although the swordsman's arm was bleeding, he did not act like he was hurt at all. He was still looking around, very alert, like a fox making sure that there was no trap nearby.

So Otto ran. Because what else could he do? He couldn't run back out through the kitchen, because the bad-sounding gun could shoot him if he went back down the stairs. He had only one choice: to run toward where the pope-lovers had come from.

He ran past a dead-looking man who had been a priest, but probably not one of the really bad ones, because his black robes were plain, as was the cross that was covered with blood from the many bullet holes in him.

When Otto got to the end of that long hall, he found big double doors sealed before him. He looked right and then left. A hall either way. Then, sound: voices, speaking with the same accent used by the pope-loving men that Heinz said came from Ireland— wherever that was. The voice came from the right, so he ran to the left—and heard more voices coming from that direction.

Trapped! Otto felt sweat under his arms, saw what looked like a small cave in the wall to his left, jumped for it, stumbling over a trestle table filled with table cloths and dirty napkins, like after a big meal at a fancy inn. He fell forward, crawled quickly into the little cave, the linens falling on and around him, and then curled up. There were too many to fight. And since he had come to kill the worse of the two popes—Heinz said so!—they would surely kill Otto if they found him.

The voices from the left met the voices from the right just a few feet away from where he was hiding. They talked about searching the palace, and then faded toward the room that Heinz called a foyer: the room where all the shooting had been, but had now stopped.

Again, Otto thought he might cry. He couldn't hide well: he was too big. Falling into and under the linens in the little wall-cave had just been lucky. He had to either find a way to run away from the palace, or at least a better place to hide.

Otto rose up out of the tablecloths and napkins, wondered which way he should go, chose the right because he was right-handed and proud of it. He might not think well, but he wasn't a child of Satan, at least.

Otto crept as quietly as he could into the hallway to the right, staying on tiptoes as he did.

Just like Heinz had taught him.

O'Neill kneeled down next to Ruy, who was holding the bloody seam on his arm closed with a strip of cloth from one of the assassin's sleeves. "Dr. Connal's too busy?"

"He just arrived with the last of your men, from back near the great hall."

"And?"

"And he is quite occupied keeping Father Vitelleschi alive. And after that, several of your other men."

O'Neill nodded, hung his head. "A lot of good blood spilled today."

Ruy grumbled. "Perhaps not enough good blood was spilled."

O'Neill looked up, frowning. "Eh? Whose blood would you be referring to?"

"My own, Colonel. Because at a crucial moment, you apparently forgot your primary duty: to save the pope!"

O'Neill turned red, leaned forward, then leaned back. His color began returning to normal. "Exactly how," he asked calmly, "did I fail in that duty?"

"By giving Sergeant Eubank the up-time rifle to save me! You should have used it on the assassins impeding you on the stair."

"And in time, that is exactly what he would have done. By killing the bastards who'd tangled you up on the other stairs, Eubank would have been able to swing round to the side of the ones going sword-to-sword with us."

"Unnecessary! He could have fired directly at them!"

"Ruy, you are a wonder with a sword and have one of the quickest battlefield minds I've ever met, but you've not spent much time acquainting yourself with the particulars of the larger up-time weapons, have y'now?"

Ruy squirmed a bit, told himself it was due to the pain in his left arm. "I am familiar enough."

"No, y'stubborn Spaniard—"

"Catalan!"

"So then: no, y'stubborn *Catalan*, you just don't understand some of the limits of up-time rifles. Yes, they're very deadly. Yes, they shoot very rapidly. Yes, they're very accurate. But what they're not so good at—no better'n our own rifles—is working in close. I needed to get Turlough off the stairs, where we weren't in his way. And with you and Giancarlo freed up, you could have stood guard on him while he blasted into the flank of the bastards who had us pinned on the stairs. To say nothing of keeping them off him when he had to reload: that rifle only takes ten rounds at a time. Besides, by the time I gave him the SKS, he was just the backup plan."

"It seems to me he was the *only* plan."

"Sorry to contradict yer esteemed self, but yer just flat wrong, Ruy. The knocking on the main doors started before we had made it to the main staircase. We all had three guesses who was comin' in, and the first two didn't count. Right enough, it was Hastings and the artillery. And that was the end of that. Sergeant Eubank was just icing on the cake."

Ruy elected not to share the possibility that Eubank's choice might very well have been right: fighting one-handed against three reasonably skilled assassins while Giancarlo was barely holding his own could have had a most disappointing resolution. Instead, Ruy said, "And you are apparently failing in your sworn duty yet again: the pope has not yet been moved, I observe."

"Yer powers of observation are greater than yer memory today, my friend. Have yeh forgotten what the protocol is if we had assassins inside the perimeter, particularly if their access might have been other than just the front door?"

Ruy wished he had a free hand so he could smack his forehead; it wasn't like him to lose track of something so basic. Then again, it wasn't like him to lose so much blood—"A lead team has to check the evacuation route, ensure that there are no enemies lying in wait."

"Precisely, and rather than send the pope all the way up the stairs, I've sent two of my less wounded lads to see if the main hallway is still clear of the colloquium's many honored and obstructive guests. If so, we'll go to the priory that way. Easier on the pope. And my walking wounded."

As far as Ruy could tell, that included almost all of the Wild Geese, including O'Neill himself. "A prudent choice. And I see they're reloading while they wait."

O'Neill nodded. "And not just our arms, either. We've got almost two pepperboxes for every man, now, thanks to the murderous bastards who are no longer in need of theirs. If there's more of 'em, we won't have another situation like this one, where we shot ourselves dry because there was never enough time to swap cylinders."

Ruy nodded. "That was clearly part of their plan. To trade casualties one for one if they could with the revolvers, and then close to range so it was blade against blade. That was their greatest strength." He looked around the foyer. "But not great enough, evidently."

O'Neill smiled, looked up as one of his men trotted down the short flight of stairs that descended into the receiving hall, dodging pools of blood as he came. "Escape route is clear, sahr."

O'Neill stood. "That's my cue." A commotion at the door made him turn. "And apparently it's your lady-wife's cue as well." He waved toward the entrance.

"Doctor, we've got a wounded Spaniard over here— pardons, a wounded *Catalan*." O'Neill's smile was warm, if wicked. "I believe his ego has been cut through and through."

With a laugh, O'Neill left—and Sharon filled the spot he left, eyes on nothing but Ruy.

Who leaned back and sighed: *and now, everything is right with the world.*

Chapter 41

Kneeling next to Ruy, Sharon tried to keep the tears from escaping her eyes but failed. "Damn you," she wept softly.

"Damn me?" Ruy replied, his eyes wide. "But why, my love? We have saved the pope!"

"Yes, and almost died doing so. I'm not going to be a widow, Ruy Sanchez. Not again, and especially not *your* widow."

Ruy's strong teeth unveiled yet another of his maddeningly irrepressible smiles. "Ah, I see: it would be unfair to any suitor who might follow me once your mourning period is over. Yes, I suppose it would be inconsiderate to die, since who could follow in my footsteps, or my—?"

Even now, with his arm looking like a gutted fish, he can slip in a double-entendre. What an insufferable, maddening, resilient, wonderful man. She hugged him hard, once, then stood back up. "And now I have to go."

Ruy nodded. "Vitelleschi. He will require all your arts, I suspect."

"More than mine," she said in a low tone. "I'm going to need to keep Sean Connal with me as well. And I don't even know if we can risk moving him. But if he has a major bleeder—well, nothing I do is going to matter." She kissed Ruy's hand. "Gotta go."

Turning to Finan, she ordered, "Find Leo Allatius, immediately."

"He's the Greek Roman Catholic, yeh, ma'am?"

"Cretan, but yes. He was trained as a physician. I need his hands out here." Sharon stared at the bodies around her. "I won't be able to perform enough surgeries fast enough to save all these men, not if he can't stabilize them. And find Larry—er, Cardinal Mazzare as well."

"He's a physician, Ambassador?"

"No, but, at some point, he took a course in first aid."

"First what?"

"Never mind." Sharon began moving up the stairs toward Vitelleschi, her core quivering with trepidation over what she might find. "Just get them here, and anyone else who knows how to bind a wound or stop bleeding. Otherwise there will be more dead men before this day is out." She looked behind her. "A lot more."

Turlough Eubank shook his head, trying to clear it. *Damn it but those bombs were loud enough to wake the dead. Or even me old Da.* And in this bloody tunnel, just the noise of their boots slapping down and their gear clanking was enough to make a man ready to stick a badger in each ear, if that would keep the sound out.

O'Neill turned back toward him, keeping his voice low. "Sergeant, you fit and able?"

"Right as rain, m'lord."

"Then keep up. The priory is just ahead. And pass the order: seal the tunnel behind us."

"Aye, sir. Seamus?"

"Sahr?" came a stone-dulled but echoing reply from the back of the line.

"Time to close it up. Make it lively."

"Yes, sahr!"

After a few moments, Eubank heard the distant door shut with a bang and a sharp snap: a sound of great finality, more so than usual.

Satisfied, Turlough shuffled forward.

Otto, having found refuge in a closet of the music room, had held his breath while men clanked past. The Irish, probably: only the floppy metal plates that stretched down their necks from the back of their helmets made that sound.

Otto crept out—still on the tips of his toes—and saw a door standing open to the basement, where the clanking sound had gone, and was getting fainter with each passing second.

Then he heard more voices approaching from the hallway: many different accents this time. And coming toward him.

Otto stared around, thought he might start crying. He didn't want to follow the Irishmen down into the basement, but that was the only way to escape the others who were coming. And maybe he'd find another place to hide down there. Otto, still on his toes, ran to the open cellar door and went down.

The cellar was not particularly large—it was the smallest room he'd seen in the palace. But somehow, the Irishmen had disappeared. And there weren't enough places for them all to hide. So where had they gone? Had they vanished into the air like the spirits in the stories that he loved but which also frightened him? Were the Irishmen magic?

A sharp clack, with a faint squeal right at the end, came out of one of the tall dusty wardrobes at the far end of the cellar. Wishing he hadn't forgotten his cleaver back in the little cave where he had been hidden by the tablecloths, he crept forward, both curious and fearful.

The wardrobe was slightly ajar; he stuck a finger in, opened it a little wider.

And there was the answer to the mystery: the Irishmen hadn't disappeared. They had gone through a narrow door hidden in the back of the wardrobe, which went directly into the wall. Otto looked closer, noticed a thin line of light leaking around one side of the door. It grew fainter as he watched. Feeling at the edge of the secret door with his finger he found that this one, too, was ajar.

He swung it open carefully, silently, saw a distant light dwindling in the blackness of a narrow, low tunnel, one which he would barely be able to fit through. But it was better than staying in the palace. There were too many of the pope-lovers there.

Otto slipped inside, snatched his finger away from something that cut him as he grasped the door to close it behind him. Annoyed, he pressed on, never noticing the slivers of rust that had lodged in his flesh like tiny shark's teeth, shed from the ancient—but freshly broken—lock.

✧　　　✧　　　✧

Pedro Dolor had not been able to resist watching the rear of the palace when the attack started. He had told himself that it was worth the risk of emerging from his hidden hole in the wall, that what he witnessed might provide important clues as to how successful the attack had been.

But in truth, Dolor also had to admit that watching the attack was a matter of professional curiosity, of how well Borja's thugs had planned it. What he saw was about what he had expected.

After the large blast announced the start of the attack—and called Dolor out of his rathole—there had been a short delay. Then a tradesman appeared running down the road that led almost to the foot of the house in which he was hiding, faint sounds of gunfire trailing after him. However, despite the assassin's attempt to stay close against the buildings on the southwest side of the street, the Hibernian sniper in nearby St. Vincent's Church obviously spotted him and knew him for an enemy.

When the man was about forty yards away, the Winchester in the bell-tower began a relentless series of slow, aimed shots. The first kicked up dirt, the second tore a horizontal gout of mortar out of a building's wall, and the third seemed to have no effect whatsoever—until, two seconds later, the man fell face down in the street and did not move.

Approximately a minute after that, another figure appeared from the other direction, and on the street that passed directly beneath Dolor's vantage point. He was a completely nondescript and unremarkable figure except for two details that were significant to an experienced assassin's eye. Firstly, this fellow was also dressed as a tradesman, and had a satchel over his back. Not too uncommon; similar figures could no doubt be found on almost every street of Besançon. Secondly, however, he was strolling casually—despite the muted sounds of gunfire now emerging steadily from the palace behind which he was walking.

Shortly after walking past the rear gate to Granvelle's gardens and grounds, the man doubled back, casually producing a small sack from the larger one he'd carried over his shoulder, and then lighting a fast-burning fuse which protruded from its top. A few more steps and he slung it over the low wall; it landed with admirable accuracy right between the two guards at the gate.

The blast knocked both of them over. One did not move. The other did so, albeit feebly, and was going for his pepperbox revolver when the man came through the battered gate and put a bullet through his brain.

—and then stopped, looking around suspiciously.

That was the instant at which it became apparent that the Wild Geese had plans and contingencies of their own. What Dolor had noted, and the strolling fellow could not have seen, was that, moments after the first, muffled explosion had occurred, and right as Dolor was emerging from his hiding spot, two of the four guards who had been near the gate had fallen back. They had taken concealed positions in a small grove, one hidden between a suitably stout tree trunk, the other behind a strategically placed—and reinforced—cart.

As the fellow who'd thrown the bomb began crouching, realizing that half of the anticipated guards were missing, those same guards opened fire. It was long

range for their pepperbox revolvers, but their target
had only two barrels on his pistol and after discharg-
ing the second, he cursed audibly and bolted back out
the gate—which was when a ball hit him in the back.
He went down in the dust, heaved himself up, made
it around one of the two tall stanchions on which
the garden doors hung—and promptly came under
fire from the belltower at St. Vincent's. He tried to
run, slumped against the outside of the garden wall,
pushed off again.

He had gone two steps when the fourth rifle round
hit him in the back. The fine red mist was quickly
lost in the small eruption of dust made by his body
hitting the ground.

Moments later, the intermittent gunfire in the palace
was drowned under a sustained surge of larger weapons fire: big, quick firing rifles like the Hibernians'
Winchesters, and another, sharper tattoo from what
was, unmistakably, an up-time shoulder weapon.

And then all was silence.

A predictable outcome, Dolor reflected, as he slipped
down into the crawl space and made sure the floor
board above him was securely wedged in place so
that it would neither rattle nor give way easily. He
crawled back toward his hole in the wall. They might
have killed the pope, but he doubted it. Which was
unfortunate, but all would not be lost so long as at
least one of the attackers lived and was capable of
implicating Borja.

But even that would only be corroboration. Because
if the enemy's radio experts had not done so already,
they would soon crack the trapdoor code which protected the radio records he had allowed them to

discover. Which contained every bit of evidence one could wish to establish Borja as the architect of the assassination plots, save his name.

All in all, that would be enough for Olivares' purposes.

And more than sufficient for his own.

Chapter 42

Ruy Sanchez de Casador y Ortiz looked up as the door to the small salon opened; O'Neill sauntered in, a small wrap on his left hand, a larger one binding his right thigh. Ruy smiled. "Feigning injury to better play the part of the hero, are you, Colonel?"

O'Neill smiled back. "Monstrous piece o' shrapnel did this," he said, patting his leg. "The size of the biggest gnat you ever saw."

"And the hand?"

"One of those bastards cut me deep with a dagger. Must have gone in—oh my, let's see now—a quarter of an inch."

Ruy reached out for his glass of wine. "Legendary wounds, good sir. My own pales beside them."

O'Neill looked meaningfully at the glass. "Any left?"

Ruy nodded toward the bottle at his feet. "There is."

"Feelin' generous?"

"I am."

"Is it rioja?"

"Sherry."

O'Neill made a warding gesture. "And why would you be drinkin' shite like that?"

Ruy sighed. "Because, my good Colonel, all my many virtues aside, I have succumbed to, and ultimately acquired, the tastes of my homeland's oppressors."

O'Neill grunted. "Well, I guess we Irish know a thing or two about that, too." He sat beside Ruy. "Just heard back from Grantville."

Ruy sighed. "And are we well chastised?"

"No, we seem to be feckin' heroes."

"Heroes? We almost allowed the pope to be killed. That's a second time, for me, I might add."

"Well, I guess they're feeling shockin' generous. Some of them, anyhow."

Ruy raised an eyebrow. "And whose opinion of us is not so high as the others'?"

"Well," Owen murmured. "Not so much a lower opinion, but a clear desire to get personally involved."

"Ah." Ruy smoothed his moustaches. "That would be our intelligence chief, Estuban Miro."

Owen glanced over. "He was right, y'know."

"Please do not remind me. I wish to enjoy my wine."

"Well, enjoy all you like, but he was the one who said the one thing we couldn't control was infiltration, not unless we were in Grantville itself."

Ruy shook his head. "Perhaps, but even then—"

O'Neill nodded. "Aye, even then. There's always enough money, or enough dirty secrets to expose, to get some damned idjit to break his word, to let the wolf in the door. Particularly if it's a wolf that bleats like a sheep."

Ruy turned. "You have learned something?"

O'Neill shook his head. "No, but I think I'm on the scent." He stood. "You ready to take a walk?"

"For what?"

"For asking a few pointed questions of that ugly bastard whose leg you filleted."

Ruy was on his feet before O'Neill had finished his sentence. "Let us go at once."

The prisoner was being kept isolated in a narrow room in which the night-servants usually napped as they shared shifts.

The moment the man with the squashed nose saw Ruy enter the room behind O'Neill, he sneered. "Here to finish the job, Spaniard?"

Ruy simply smiled. "My associate is unlikely to allow me that singular pleasure."

O'Neill sat on the bed. He patted the bloody wrappings on the fellow's leg; the man winced, went pale. "Still stings a bit, eh? A shame, that is. But as to your fears of imminent demise. I'm happy to say that my good friend is correct: there'll be no killing you today. And not tomorrow. Not for some time, I expect. If ever."

The man did not look relieved. "And whose clemency is this? Your soft-headed pope? I almost think I liked him better when he was a favor-peddling fop without the nerve to do his own murdering."

"Ah, an' sure that he has a high opinion of yourself, as well. But enough pleasant chatter; down to business, then. You'll not die because it's clear you know who sent you here, and why. At least, that's what the others tell us," O'Neill lied.

"Which others?" the fellow asked.

"Now, see, that's where you lack understanding of this process. We ask the questions; you answer them."

"Or what? You'll disembowel me? You think I didn't consider that beforehand? You think I care?"

O'Neill glanced at Ruy, then back at the man. "Y'know, I'm not the one in this room that you have to worry about. I said you'd not be killed, and I meant it. But whether you find living a pleasant alternative . . . well, I can't answer for that. Not in my hands alone, y'see."

Ruy just smiled.

The man actually threw his head back and laughed. "Oh, you *are* fools. Greater than I thought! You think I'd lie to protect the bastard who promised me silver, more than I could carry, to manage the murder of your precious Roman Pimp—I mean, Pope?"

O'Neill frowned. "Can't say as I know one way or t'other about that. Seemed to me you were straight serious enough when you said you'd given thought to what might happen to you."

The man shrugged, looked away. "I was prepared for death, I was prepared to live with more silver than I could spend. I was ready for anything in between."

O'Neill exchanged quick glances with Ruy. "But you weren't prepared to die to protect the identity of who sent you."

He looked back. "That's right. Because if Urban isn't dead, then it's all the more important that you know who was behind this."

Ruy took another step into the room, hand on the hilt of his main gauche. "And who would that be, you murderous dog?"

"Who do you think, you Spanish pig-fucker? The next hypocrite-who-would-be-pope: Borja."

Ruy stopped. This was too easy. "And why would you betray your employer?"

"My employer?" The turnip-nosed man threw back his head and laughed. "More like my tool."

"Your tool? To achieve what?"

"Idiot! To ensure the destruction of popery: to put an end to the greed, the hypocrisy, the mammon that oozes out of Rome like pus from a buboe."

O'Neill studied the man closely. "You know I'm an Irishman. So you know it's coming on half a millennium that our country hasn't been our own." His face lost its ironic animation. "I have no small amount of familiarity with the sound of righteous indignation. Particularly the kind that's just high talk to conceal the personal grudge beneath. To hide a wound that won't heal, a wound in the heart. As when one loses one's kin to an invader, a usurper, a thief with a crown."

"Or a miter." The words came out like an animal snarl. The misshapen face looked upward, contorted in an arresting mix of vicious hatred and emotional agony. His verbal rage came out through a mist of distempered spittle. "Can you guess how I knew who that prat von Meggen was? Or how I fooled those farm boys into thinking they could become the new Swiss Guard? Because my own grandfather was one and died at the battle von Meggen went on about. I didn't tell them, of course. I just needed to stay close enough to introduce them to Norwin's thugs, who were smart enough to work for coin, rather than for their taskmasters in Rome. And then I faded away, neither group the wiser."

"That's what Borja hired you to do?"

"More than that. They needed someone to make

556 Eric Flint & Charles E. Gannon

the bombs, to sneak in the weapons. Pity you didn't open all my barrels when I came through the tollhouse, Spaniard. You might have recognized the pieces of the pepperbox revolvers. But then again, I doubt you'd have dirtied your hands with it, and only you and a few others would even recognize the parts, mixed in with all my ironmongery."

It was a contention that Ruy could not contradict, no matter how much he wished to. "Go on."

"I don't need your prompting, Spaniard. Any more than I needed prompting when Borja's agents approached me. They suspected I'd work for them. What they didn't guess was that I would have done this all for free, even if I knew that, at the end of it, I'd be drawn and quartered for my trouble."

"I've heard men say such things before," murmured O'Neill. "Back in Ireland. After their towns are burnt, or their families put to the sword."

The man's nose became very red. "Don't think to get cozy with me, you shit-brained bog-hopper. We'll not be weeping together at the end of this conversation or any other. I know what you think of me. And I don't care. But it's true enough that there's plenty of misery in the lands beyond your muck-loving Ireland. You see, I too was born Catholic. That's the height of the joke, don't you see? At least in your land, it's the other side—the Protestants—who make your life a living hell. But in my canton? It was my own church.

"They taxed me like a serf. I didn't protest. They— meaning the Spanish who marched through the Valtelline to the German wars—took my two oldest boys and fed them to the Protestant cannons. And I mourned, but still prayed.

"But then my youngest, he married a Lutheran. And could you blame him, seeing what his own kind had done to him and his family?" He settled back, his eyes narrow, his voice becoming cool, detached. "News got around, of course. It always does. So the next time the Catholic armies came marching through, my youngest and his wife fled to my house. And mind you: I never missed Sunday mass, was generous at the poor box, and never spoke an ill word against the local priests or Rome.

"But none of that mattered. The Spanish came to my farm. Dragged the two of them out and killed them in front of each other, made sure each one was alive long enough to know that the other was dying. I tried to stop them; the captain galloped straight through and over me. I can still remember him laughing as his horse's hoof came down on my face.

"My wife wouldn't stay in the root cellar when she heard the screaming; she came out and grabbed a broom to start beating them off. Before she landed a single blow, they cut her to ribbons—literally, to thin bloody strips—with their halberds. When I tried to get up, to stop them, the officer rode over me again, but instead of killing me outright, he just left me with this bad hip as a parting gift. I screamed every Spanish curse I knew at him, told him to kill me like a man, to finish what he'd started."

The man smiled. "Do you know what he said? Death would mean the end of my suffering. It was a better punishment for me, and a better example for the good of the Church, that I should live with the disfigurement that would also be my badge of shame until the day God himself took me. And in whose name did he do it? Surely you can guess."

O'Neill murmured, "Pope Urban VIII."

"Well, I guess not all the Irish are as stupid as they say. But either way, you weren't smart enough to stop me."

Ruy came a step closer. "No, we weren't. So why don't you show us just how smart you are?"

The man spat at the Catalan and missed. Which, Ruy allowed, was fortunate, because he wasn't sure he could have stayed his hand in time. "You don't need to trick me into telling you how I worked this. I want you to know. I want you to be able to check every fact, trace every lead back to Rome."

O'Neill nodded. "Because then there can be no peace among the Catholic nations of Europe, or even the Hapsburgs."

"My, you *are* smart for an Irishman; I'll bet you don't even have a tail. Of course that's the point, you dullard. And it will happen no matter who sides with whom, in the end. Spain can either protect or disown Borja; either way, someone will have to march into Rome and unseat him. With any luck, they'll destroy what little he's left of the Holy City. And if Spain supports him? Why, I saw none other than Bedmar, the cardinal-protector of Spanish Flanders, in the line in front of me when I entered Besançon this time. So, what will his leash-holder, Fernando, the presumptuous 'King in the Lowlands' do? Support Philip his brother and king of Spain, or take a stand against him? And given that his wife is the sister of the emperor of Austria—and so, another Hapsburg—all is set fair to split that dynasty right down the middle, with all of Europe taking one side or the other." He leaned back; his smile would have been a suitable decoration on a tombstone. "I just hope I live to see it: to see it all burn, become the pyre that finally consumes the Roman Church and all its depravity."

"So, you understand politics. And are well-informed. Atypical for a farmer."

"I haven't been a farmer since I lost the ability to steer a plow, to work a hard day in an alpine field, you idiot. So I made my trade ironmongery. I had always been good with languages—you get a lot of experience at that, in the cantons—and with turning a profit, no matter how poor a year we had. Before long, I was traveling past Zurich, up to Basel, to Constance, even to Besançon."

"Which is how you were known here, had the contacts and information you needed."

"Ah, so the Spaniard has a brain, too. And uses it for something other than cheating and buggery. Impressive. Of course, when Borja's agents contacted me last year, I knew that contacts and information wouldn't be enough. I would need leverage."

Ruy frowned. "Ridiculous: Borja could not have known that there was a colloquium being planned last year, much less that it would have been in Besançon."

The man sneered. "So maybe I was hasty presuming you had a brain. Of course he didn't know that, yet. But he knew Urban would turn up somewhere, and Rome has deep pockets. From what I can tell, Borja contacted someone like me in every region: someone who hated Urban, who would be willing to take coin to assist in an attack on him. I just volunteered to do more than he expected, and was in the right place— and had the right leverage—to do it."

O'Neill nodded. "What leverage?"

The man smiled. "When you're on the road a lot, as I am, you notice changes in traffic. The new balloon traffic to Basel increased, then began going even further west. Turned out they were mostly landing in Besançon. Now, most people wouldn't hear much about that. But it turns out that wherever up-timers go, they are always bringing or buying metal. It's their lifeblood, it seems. And there was a lot of metal moving in the direction of Besançon, just like the airships. So off I went to see what I could see.

"At first I thought it was all due to this new up-time company that Bernhard the Pretender had brought in: the Silo Design and Construction Corporation. But a little more time in town made me think otherwise. I started seeing your Wild Geese and the Hibernians. Then I heard word that your Moorish wife had been here for months. Not seen often, but still often enough to establish that she wasn't merely traveling to and from Besançon frequently: she was living here. And that told me all I needed to know."

Ruy nodded. "That Urban was here, or would be soon. And that therefore, you needed to procure leverage to infiltrate one of the places where he would appear."

The man gestured all around him. "And where else would he appear, where else could he hold a colloquium, but in this palace? No other place in Besançon is large enough, and conveniently, the Granvelle's are a dying line, at least insofar as the ones who should live here are concerned. All of them live elsewhere. So I knew where I needed to find the leverage: amongst the staff of this place, with whom I had already traded and so, knew their names and faces.

"That was where I had to do a little extra work. Greed would not be enough of an incentive. Any person with enough authority to be useful would be making a reasonable living as a retainer in this palace. They might wish more money, but I had no way of being sure that, when push came to shove, their greed would be greater than their fear. No, I had to find someone who had something to hide, something that, if revealed, would endanger them, force them to flee as far as they could. *If* they could. That is the sort of threat I needed to hold over them: that not cooperating with me carried a greater surety of disaster than agreeing to help."

Ruy hoped his smile looked like a predator baring its teeth. "It seems you yourself have excellent skills in depravity and cruelty."

The man smiled back just as mirthlessly. "I had excellent tutors. At any rate, it took a little while frequenting the less reputable establishments of both the Buckle and the Battant, but I eventually I came across what I was looking for: one of Palais Granvelle's heads of staff lurked around the most despised spot along the waterfront. Its depravity is so great, it doesn't even have a sign. It is only known among the thieves, swindlers and perverts of this town—of which there are a fair number.

"From there on, it was a simple matter of following him—Delgado, the head of the kitchen staff who was also, as luck would have it, the assistant major domo—and confirming what was said of him, and which my observation suggested: that he was inordinately fond of youths at that point of life where their peach fuzz is about to become a man's bristles.

"Mind you, he was careful about his buggery. Never with locals: usually young apprentices, sent here by their families to finish their tutelage under another master. Or new hands on the river boats. That sort of thing. Never for long, and never seen together in public. They prearranged rooms in which to rendezvous: usually in flop houses, sometimes in a tavern, but that was riskier.

"Delgado maintained the appearance of preferring women, went so far as to hire prostitutes to disappear into rooms with him: discreetly, but still publicly. He was careful with his money, lived alone, had no close friends, was not a *besontsint*. In short, he was perfect: on his own, hiding his depravity, and guilty of a crime that would certainly destroy him figuratively, and maybe literally, if it were to become common knowledge. And no, I doubt you'll find him: the pervert fled the moment he saw what w—what I had put on the covered trays."

O'Neill leaned forward. "Was that what 'we' or what 'I' put on the trays?"

"Mostly just me. But the grenades that were disguised as jam pots, I had a young fool help me with those. He was so green and from such a shithole that he'd never seen a jam pot before. Probably never had jam."

Ruy wasn't sure if there was more to the man's stumble over the singular versus plural pronoun, but there wasn't time to examine every question detail in this first interrogation. "So Delgado was not aware that he was aiding and abetting assassins?"

"Of course not, imbecile! Telling him would have been as foolish a risk as announcing it on the street, no matter how terrible his perversion. I just made it clear that a certain victualer wished to gain the favor of the house, and that the major domo was receiving bribes from the current provider. So Delgado only had two jobs: first, to ensure that the major domo was removed, which involved the minor matter of planting false evidence. Which you two apparently swallowed whole, thank you very much. The second job was to allow me to bring in and oversee a shipment of special delicacies from the new victualer, to be received the night before today's banquet, and then served to all the dignitaries today. Who were expected to rave about it and so bring about the desired change in victualers."

O'Neill frowned. "And he believed that?"

The man chuckled. "When a fool can't be found, one can usually be made. Just give a desperate man a reasonable sounding explanation for why a single, modestly dishonest act will produce an outcome he very much wants. Or needs. A man in that position can convince himself that the most improbable scenarios are true." He shrugged. "A few leading conversations, a few drinks, and I got the rest of what we needed from him: the daily schedule of patrols in the palace."

Ruy turned to leave. "And the attack on St. Jean? A way to convince us that the Swiss could be trusted?"

"Of course. Easy enough, since they killed the attackers."

"You are a brute."

"Why? Because we hired men I meant to send to certain death? Tell me, Spaniard: in your time, have you not seen your precious Empire—or even yourself—do the same?"

Electing not to answer the main question, Ruy retorted, "It is not my Empire. It never was."

"No. Of course not. You'll take anyone's coin, I suppose."

Ruy smiled. "Enjoy your stay with us. And expect to repeat your tale many times in the coming days."

Ruy stepped out of the room quickly, but not before the man could shout at his back: "I'm looking forward to it!"

Ruy did not slow down until he had left the servant's wing, had emerged back into one of the main hallways. He folded his hands behind his back, let O'Neill catch up before asking, "Are there any other survivors?"

O'Neill shook his head. "Not many." He sighed. "That's the problem of having troops who are good at what they do: the Hibernians and my Wild Geese are a tad too gifted at killing. And the bastards who didn't get an extra bullet or blade in 'em, well, your lady-wife has had her hands full of our own men's guts. So most of the assassins she could have saved have gone to their deserved judgment in the meantime."

Ruy frowned. "That is a pity." He let his lips straighten. "But not a very great one. Now, where did I leave my wine?"

Chapter 43

Turning the corner and entering the salon from which they'd begun, Ruy found that he and O'Neill were not alone. Corporal Finan stood to attention, as did the soldier behind him—

Ruy blinked, then grinned more broadly than was probably appropriate for so senior an officer as himself: "Daniel O'Dempsey! I am delighted to see you! But surprised."

Danny O'Dee saluted, letting a lopsided smile creep onto his face. "With respect, Colonel, I think yer asking why the divil I'm not dead?"

Ruy chuckled. "Well, yes, I suppose I am."

Danny tapped the rim of his helmet: there was a deep dent in it. "Hit the metal, knocked me cold, but here I am."

O'Neill slipped around Ruy, clapped his man on the soldier, took a seat. "I always said that hard head of yours would come in handy one day, Danny."

O'Dee turned a baleful look on his commanding officer. "Sahr."

"Yes?"

"Surely a man of yer wit and breedin' can do better'n that."

O'Neill sighed. "I'm afraid that's the best I've got at the moment. Judging from the look of you two, and that you were lying in wait here, I suspect you have reports?"

"That we do, sahr." Danny O'Dee paused. "Seems a tad ironic, me carrying the final casualty tally, Colonel."

"On the contrary." As Ruy sat, he felt the smile ebb away from his face. "Who better than a man back from the dead?"

"Aye, sir, as you will. We count fifteen attackers including the inside man and the ones out front and back. All dead except for two."

"We just had words with their handler. Who is the other?"

"Don't know, sir. He's still unconscious."

"Very well. Our losses?"

"Counting the dustup at the rear gate, five of our own lads dead, six too wounded for duty, sir. I doubt two will serve again."

O'Neill nodded glumly.

Ruy raised his chin. "The Burgundians?"

"Six dead, one wounded, sir. Might not see the dawn, though."

"The Hibernians?"

"Except for a few bruised shoulders from a frontal assault on the door, all fit and ready for duty, sir."

"Minor wounds among our men?"

Danny looked abashed. "Sorry, Colonel Sanchez. Haven't got the count on it yet. But I think it's safe to say, 'almost all.'" He absently rubbed his own wrappings.

"Thank you. Corporal Finan, what news from you?"

"Medical update, sirs. Your wife, m'lady Nichols, is still operating on Father Vitelleschi. Dr. Connal is assisting her. Father Alatius has er, em—'stabilized' the rest, along with Cardinal Mazzare."

"Any casualties among the staff?"

"One minor wound to one of the servers who was in the foyer when the shooting started. And the major domo—well, the assistant major domo—is missing."

Hardly a surprise. "Very well. Anything else?"

"Yes, sir. Technical intelligence report, sir."

Ruy eyed the little corporal narrowly. "Did my wife teach you to use that term?"

"Aye, sir. She did, sir."

"I see. Well, what have you to report?"

In answer, Finan held up a pepperbox revolver.

Ruy stared at it. "I do not understand."

"Sir, this is ours."

"Yes, they were clearly procured from the same source—"

"No, sir. I do not mean 'like' ours. I mean it *is* ours. Well, more accurately, it's yours, Colonel O'Neill." He paused. "From Rome. From the ambush at the Insula Mattei."

O'Neill—who, like Finan, had been there personally—was out of his seat in one rapid motion. "Impossible," he said, but his voice was one of denial, not conviction.

"I wish I could say it was, sir, but . . . well, here: look for yourself."

O'Neill took the weapon in his hands, looked it over, stopped when his eyes fell upon the grip. "It can't be."

Ruy rose also. "What is it, Owen?" When his friend did not respond, the Catalan looked to Finan. "What is it?"

"The initials, Colonel—they're his cousin's: the late Earl John O'Neill's."

Owen's hands had tightened and whitened around the weapon. "Is this a message from Borja? Is this a jab back at us?"

"Or," Finan added in a low tone, "it may simply be a matter of using the most advanced weapons they could bring to hand. All the other guns lost there were recovered from the assassins, sir."

Owen, still grasping the gun, turned on his heel, made for the door. "Well, I think I know just who to ask—"

Ruy intercepted him. "Owen. My friend. Not now. Let us think on this, first."

Finan shifted his feet. "Sirs, there's something else you'll want to be knowin'."

Ruy turned back to him. "And what is that?"

"Yer wife and I: we found more of our equipment in the cellar next to the priory. That's how she knew the attack was comin'. That's why she ran up in the street, had already rallied some of the Hibernians when the bomb-throwers stepped forward."

"What do you mean, 'found more of our equipment?'" Finan told him.

Ruy and O'Neill exchanged long stares. Ruy frowned. "Six bedrolls, you say?"

"Aye, sir: six."

O'Neill rubbed his chin. "And all unused? Could there be another group of assassins at large here?"

Finan cleared his throat. "Begging the colonels' pardons, the ambassador thinks there's just *one* more assassin at large."

Ruy snapped his fingers. "Of course. Six bedrolls,

and the guns were a match for the ones used by the dogs we eliminated at the flophouse overlooking the cemetery. But, including the one we found dead in the street, there were only five of them."

O'Neill nodded. "So one is still on the loose: the one who knifed the bastard who got out the window."

Finan's tone was deferential. "Seems so, sir. And it seems the missing one went back to the cellar at least once. Looks like he grabbed some of the quicklime that had been left there to ward off the rats."

"So," Ruy mused, taking up his wine again, "we apparently have at least one assassin left in Besançon."

O'Neill, his anger cooled by grappling with the new and broader mystery before them, sat. "Aye, and if he's the ruthless bastard who almost killed the lot of us in Rome, then he's the most dangerous of all. We need to double the guard on Urban. Now."

Finan looked down slightly. "Of course, sirs. Although, if we do, then there won't be enough left to oversee the house-to-house search for this slippery fish, or any other thugs who might still be hoping for a shot at the pope."

O'Neill shook his head. "Much as it pains me to say it, Finan, we're here to provide security troops, not investigators. We let the Burgundians do the searching."

"Pardon my saying so, Colonel, but that means no real searching at all."

Ruy and Owen smiled crookedly at each other, after which O'Neill regarded the corporal carefully. "You've been doing a wonderful job, Finan. There's always room for you back in the Wild Geese, if you get tired of the Hibernians."

Finan folded his hands behind his back. "Now, that's a very kind offer of you, sir. But as you might recall, I served under Colonel Preston." He cleared his throat. "A matter of my family background, as it were."

O'Neill shook his head, his smile growing more crooked. "A lot has changed in a few years, Corporal. Not the least of which is that my cousin John"—he hefted the revolver meaningfully—"is no longer in charge of my tercio. So his—well, shall we say religious preferences?—no longer determine recruitment." O'Neill put down the pepperbox and folded his hands. "I suppose we're all getting a bit more ecumenical, these days."

"As you say, sir," answered Finan carefully. "And I'll think on your offer with much gratitude, m'lord. But for now, I'm happy where I am. And after all, without me, they can't properly call themselves the Hibernians, can they? I'm practically the only bog-hopper in the lot."

O'Neill chuckled, saluted. "Carry on, Corporal. You too, Danny. But be sure not to say a prayer tonight."

Danny stopped, dumbfounded. "But . . . but, sahr: it's the day I should be prayin' hardest, yeh? Thanking the Lord for a wondrous strange deliverance, I'd be."

"Yes, and letting His angels know right where you are. Who knows? Cheating death that way, they might come back after yeh."

Danny O'Dee gulped, saluted and hastened out on Finan's heels.

When they were both out of earshot, Ruy frowned at O'Neill. "Owen, that was cruel."

"Nah; that was just keepin' 'im on 'is toes. Now, where's that wine of yours?"

"It is sherry, and you do not care for it."

"It's wine and it's been a long day. Now, give it here."

❖   ❖   ❖

Standing next to the door at the other end of the long, tight tunnel, Otto heard women's voices on the other side. But this time they were there for only a minute and then faded away. They spoke very quickly, and in French, a language Otto had a very hard time remembering.

But at least they weren't men's voices, the dangerous ones who spoke with the accent of Irishmen. It had been a long time since he had heard those voices. Maybe they had left?

On the other hand, each time the women's voices had come and gone, he had also detected the faint smells of food, particularly hot bread, from the other side of the door. That made Otto very happy, both because he liked bread a great deal and because he was very proud of his sense of smell. Heinz had often called it the very best of his six senses. Which confused Otto, since there were only five senses. He had asked Heinz, one time, what the sixth sense was. "Common sense," Heinz had said seriously, then laughed and slapped him across his broad round back and said it was just a joke. Otto had smiled, because he liked Heinz, his friend. But he didn't really get the joke. At all.

As Otto continued to smell the bread, he discovered it was now making him sad, because it made him realize how hungry he was. Maybe, just maybe, this tunnel came up in a bread shop, and the Irishmen had come to search it several times, but had now given up? It seemed as good an explanation as any other, and besides, if it was a bread shop, Otto could eat and figure out where to go next.

That thought frightened him all over again. And made him even more hungry.

As Otto did when he was distracted by too many confusing thoughts and feelings, he stopped paying attention to any of them and simply acted: he pushed open the door.

Or tried to: it seemed to be held on the other side. But he could feel that the resistance had been weak; the door had wobbled outward away from him almost half an inch before it refused to budge further. So Otto stepped back and leaned into it with this shoulder. Hard.

The door sprang open and Otto almost fell into the dimly lit room. Not a bread shop, but a kitchen, lit by a single, dim oil lamp: an old open one with a wick floating free at its center.

There was no bread around—it must have been taken away—but he could smell food. And best of all, there were no Irishmen or anyone else.

But as he crept around the kitchen, still on his toes, searching for where the food smell was strongest, he heard movement. Overhead. On the next floor. And now, he heard feet on a staircase. Maybe they were coming down; maybe they were going up. He couldn't tell.

And he didn't wait to find out. Creeping through the kitchen, he came upon two linen closets: too small to hide in. Then a hallway that led out into a big, dark room: that could be dangerous.

Finally, just as he arrived at the very back of the kitchen, he saw a door between two large casks. It was a light door, the kind he could easily break if he was not careful. So, very slowly, and using just the tips of his fingers, he tugged on it, and after the gentlest of pressure, it popped open.

It was a pantry, filled with food. Particularly hard cheeses and hard sausages, which, he realized, had been the source of the food smell he had been following.

Leaning the door almost entirely shut behind him, he wandered to the back of the storage room, where a number of barrels and casks stood. His nose told him there were winter vegetables in them—beets, radishes, maybe even rutabagas—but his eyes told him what he really needed to know: this was a good place to hide. He started to wriggle carefully in amongst the casks, then paused. He was still hungry.

Otto reversed his path, reached out, clutched a length of hard sausage and a mountaineer's cheese to his round chest, was about to hide himself again, realized he wasn't done. He stepped back out, peered around the dim room, found what he was looking for: a cheese knife. He grabbed that, tiptoed to the door, closed it, and felt his way back to and between the barrels and casks.

He would wait a while, until he could be sure it was night. Then, he would try to sneak out. But until that time, at least there was food. He sighed, cut into the cheese, lifted a sliver to his mouth and smiled for the first time in hours.

Chapter 44

Larry Mazzare looked around the room, satisfied with the furnishings, with the two Wild Geese at the equivalent of parade rest with weapons drawn, and with the utter lack of any way into or out of the room other than the door toward which he was drifting.

Urban looked up from the large, cushioned chair in which he had sat while Father Leo Allatius had extracted two unnoticed bits of shrapnel. One had cut into the pontifical left buttock, one into the right thigh. "I should be by Muzio's side."

Larry shook his head. "No, you should be here under close guard, with troops along all the corridors."

Urban almost smiled. "I can only imagine the prioress's discomfiture."

Larry almost smiled back. "She's bearing up quite well. I suspect she may want one of those pieces of shrapnel as a relic."

Urban actually laughed at that. "A relic? That would have to come from a truly holy being, not me." He put on a theatrically somber face. "She may have the fragment from the leg. The other lacks, well, sufficient papal gravity. Although it certainly has more comic value."

Larry nodded. "I'm sure she'll make do with either. Now, I must be going. Is there anything else you—?"

Two knocks on the door.

Larry paused. The Wild Geese waved Urban out of his chair, set up behind two tables in cross-fire positions.

As they did, another knock sounded, then a long scraping noise down the jamb, then two more fast knocks.

The leader of the two Wild Geese, Turlough Eubank, said, "Enter," at the same moment he cocked the hammer on his pepperbox revolver.

The door opened slowly, revealing Tone Grogan. "Some visitors for His Holiness, Sergeant."

Eubank frowned. "His Holiness is not to have visitors."

"I know, but the colonels passed these on. Matter of state, as it were."

"Well, then, don't leave the door open: come in."

Tone stood aside: Cyril Lucaris, Johann Gerhard, and John Dury entered, hands folded in front of them, their heads bent in what looked like a synthesis of contemplation and respect.

Urban waved away objections. "You are very welcome here, gentlemen. I have little variety of refreshment to offer, but I am sure a bottle of wine could be loca—"

Gerhard shook his head, waving away the offer. "We do not wish to intrude for that long. We are here to bear the good tidings of the colloquium and...and to share a few words."

"Then please be seated."

Larry resumed his move toward the door, nodding to the newcomers. "Excuse me, but I wish to ensure you have the privacy you requi—"

Lucaris held up a hand. "Your presence is not merely anticipated, but much desired, Cardinal Mazzare. Please: we shall not begin until you, too, are seated."

Larry smiled tightly and took the seat he had hoped to avoid taking.

Urban folded his hands. "Now, what are these words you wished to share?"

Gerhard smiled. "Well, naturally, we wished to express our relief and gladness at the news that you had not been harmed, a sentiment shared by all of—"

Lucaris interrupted with almost savage abruptness. "My Roman brother, my thoughts of you have not always been . . . charitable. Indeed, even since arriving here as your guest, pride and suspicion have kept me from asking our Lord and Savior to forgive my unkind spirit and hostility. But now"—Lucaris squared his shoulders—"I wish to say that I consider it a great blessing upon all of us that you were saved from the work of assassins this day."

Urban bowed his head. "It is not a simple thing, to throw off long-held distrusts and animosities. I am honored and humbled that you are willing to entertain the possibility that, despite my many flaws, I am honestly and earnestly attempting to fashion my deeds and words according to my best, if imperfect, understanding of Christ's will and vision for us all."

Gerhard smiled. "I will promise not to convey that confession of imperfection to the others."

Urban waved his hand. "As a man, I am far more imperfect than most. And as for speaking *ex cathedra*— well, I think I shall do so as sparingly as I might, henceforth. It is hard to believe I could truly be a vessel for His Voice and Wisdom. But subtle pride can hide within the guise of humility. It is upon me to remain the pontifex, so I must accept that I am unworthy of my position even as I carry out its responsibilities."

Gerhard leaned back as if to get a better look at the pope seated before him. "It is strange, is it not, how our Lord ensures that even the agents of Satan ultimately become the means whereby His Will is realized?"

Urban frowned. "I am not sure I take your meaning, Reverend Gerhard."

"I simply mean that, if there was any uncertainty among the colloquists when we ended our proceedings just before lunch, today's events have eliminated that."

Urban shook his head. "I still do not understand."

Dury threw out an impatient hand. "You were almost martyred. But perhaps more importantly, we all know who paid those assassins their thirty pieces of silver: Borja. And if we must deal with the Roman Church, and we must, then the choice between the two of you became not merely conceptually, but viscerally, clear today.

"Do not look so surprised. You know the weakness of all men: that we are quick to forget, both what we have seen before, and the resolutions made because of what we saw. Specifically, who could be surprised that Borja would attempt to assassinate you again? But today, it was not some distant event. It happened right before our eyes. And we can hardly doubt that Borja would have been happiest if no small number of us might have been within the reach of the bombs and grenades."

Urban's reply was quiet, almost a whisper. "If the fine soldiers who gave their lives protecting me thereby ensured that we—all of you and I—might truly put an end to sectarian strife, then they should indeed be memorialized as martyrs, as men who fought and died so that untold millions would not have to do so in the future."

Lucaris and Gerhard made a chorus with Larry, murmuring, "Amen."

After a moment of silence, a small grin grew on Gerhard's face. "I hoped, as the colloquium went on, that you might indulge me by answering a question before we departed." His smile became wider. "It is not theologically significant."

Urban shrugged. "Ask."

—a response which, Larry noted, invited the inquiry but offered no promises about making an answer to it.

Gerhard nodded, no doubt having decoded the same subtext. "You know, of course, the kinds of questions we will face upon returning to our homes, to the rulers who will look to our report of the events here as a guide and barometer for how to deal with the Roman Church in the coming months, even years."

Urban smiled. "They are as predictable as a miser's grab after a falling coin."

"Just so. But there is a question I am sure we will be asked for which we have no answer. Specifically, you have spoken much about your change of heart, and determination to chart a course back toward grace. But what prompted it, finally? What passage from scripture, or writing by John Paul II, was the fulcrum point for you?" Gerhard reacted to Urban's quizzical expression by explaining in greater detail.

"What you describe is, for all intents and purposes, an epiphany. But you have spoken of it in generalities. The more exact and concrete its description, the more likely that the secular leaders of our nations and cities will believe it."

Urban nodded. "It is a prudent question. I wish I had a more illuminating and intellectual answer for you. But, if we are fortunate enough to get a fleeting glimpse of the face of God, it usually comes suddenly, unbidden, from places and events where we were least likely to look for it. So it was with me.

"Over the winter, as we remained in hiding here in Besançon, Ambassadora Nichols became concerned for everyone's mental and emotional well-being. She was fearful that we would all—staff, soldiers, clerics— contract a malady she called 'cabin-fever.' This, I later learned, was a euphemism for the increasing boredom and impatience that comes along with snow, cold, and shorter days which commend us to our hearths. So, determined to raise our spirits, Donna Sharon sent to Grantville for what they call a film projector and several films, both from the high school library and private collections."

Urban grinned at Larry. "Cardinal Mazzare owned one such film. It was the first one we 'screened,' just two nights before Christmas, after completing our devotions. It is called *It's a Wonderful Life*. I do not wish to detain you with a synopsis of it. Suffice it to say that it is a morality play, set in their miraculous and confusing future world. Neither the discourse nor the circumstances are lofty or particularly inventive. Indeed, I suppose some would consider the main character's dilemmas to be trite and contrived.

But somehow, that only adds to its charm and to its Everyman applicability to all persons, regardless of their social station."

Urban either did not notice or was not concerned with the increasingly surprised expressions on the faces of his three visitors. "Ultimately, the protagonist—a rather Job-like character—contemplates suicide, but before he can plunge into an icy river, he sees and rescues a man in the current beneath him. This fellow turns out, most improbably, to be an angel in disguise, who becomes his guide through the world as changed by the protagonist's despair: the world as it would have been had he never lived.

"Predictably, in the course of his travels, he rediscovers his love of his actual life, which kindles renewed hope and a repudiation of the suicide he was considering. And then, again reprising Job, he is rewarded by having his ills removed by the same Divine Providence which originally inflicted them. A predictable, even childish, tale, I know.

"And yet, in its simplicity, it spoke to me more eloquently than any learned treatise about how we choose the future we come to inhabit, and what occurs when we become too bitter—or jaded—to be guided to it by hope and grace." Urban looked down, rubbing his hands together slowly, meditatively. "I had abandoned that long ago. Maybe before I had to shave. It was all I was taught; it was all I knew. This simple film brought me face to face with the fact that although I preached poverty and grace, I had never repudiated my materialism, my hoarding of the appurtenances of secular power.

"So yes, Urban VIII, or better, Maffeo Barberini

speaks of greed. And who better? For the up-time books showed me what my intimates would not, and which I refused to see in my own mirror: they depict my vanity and selfishness. And they do so in such matter-of-fact terms—so dispassionately, and at such a great remove from the years of my papacy—that it is clear that this is not the voice of partisanship. This is the long-settled judgment of history upon the kind of pope, and man, I was.

"So it was ultimately not the theological treatises of the up-time world that saved me: it was Grantville's films and history books. And now I must act in accordance with what they revealed to me."

He stood. "Your concern and solicitude leaves me in your debt, gentlemen. Now, I do not mean to appear rude, but the events of the past hours have been somewhat fatiguing and I have my sermon to deliver tomorrow in St. John's."

Dury actually wrung his long, pale, hands. "Might it not be more advisable to...well, continue to minimize your exposure, Your Eminence?"

Larry wanted to nod vigorously; no one had been able to talk Urban out of officiating at the cathedral's Pentecost Sunday service.

Urban's smile was almost sly. "Firstly, I think that we have now exhausted Besançon's surprising supply of assassins, and I refuse to be cowed by the fear of them anymore. But secondly, did I hear you correctly?" His left eyebrow rose: "'Your Eminence?'" he repeated quizzically.

Dury stiffened slightly. "We all use terrestrial titles without suggesting that their holders have precedence over us in the eyes of our one true Lord. It is no different in this case. I simply used the title for the archbishop of Rome."

Urban's smile broadened as Gerhard rolled his eyes at Dury's lack of humor. "I understand, Reverend Dury. I had thought a moment of levity might be yet another step forward."

Dury blushed. "I am . . . not accustomed to levity in matters of faith and God. But as you say . . . well, it is another change to which I must become accustomed." His smile looked more like a brief spasm of indigestion. "Better smiles than swords, I suppose."

"Yes," Lucaris murmured with a nod, "I think we can all agree with that. And upon the lateness of the hour." The three stood along with him. "Thank you for receiving us."

"Truly, it was my pleasure. And yes, Cardinal Mazzare, you may go with them. And do send word on Father General Vitelleschi's condition."

Larry Mazzare found Sharon sitting with a cup of black tea in the bedroom adjoining the prioress's, which had become both the operating theater and recovery room for Muzio Vitelleschi. "How are you doing?" he asked, entering with as soft a tread as he could muster.

Sharon looked up. Her eyes were so bloodshot, it looked like an overdone special effect rather than reality. "Nothing that a few hours of sleep couldn't fix."

Larry nodded and glanced toward the door that communicated between her bedroom and Vitelleschi's.

Sharon saw the look. "Connal is in with him. That guy is becoming a damned good surgeon. Did a tricky removal; could've easily nicked an artery but didn't.

He's on watch for another forty minutes. Then I go back in. It's nip and tuck."

"So, if you're on duty again in forty minutes, why aren't you asleep?"

Sharon looked up at him. "Ever been so exhausted by a nonstop crisis that it takes you hours just to relax enough to go to sleep?"

"Once or twice."

"Well, this is one of those times."

"Should I have them send you more tea?"

"Nah. The next guard rota has promised to bring me a pot of honest-to-God coffee." Seeing Larry's eyes drifting back toward the leader of the Jesuit order, she sighed, "Don't ask, because I don't know. If he makes the night, I give him fifty-fifty odds for tomorrow. If he makes that, and no sepsis sets in, I think he'll make it. But he lost a lot of blood."

"Thanks. I'll send word back to Urban."

"Well," sighed Sharon as she leaned back in her chair, "the pope probably has more power over the outcome now than I do."

"How so?"

"Because if the stories and claims are right, he's got a hotline to the Big Guy upstairs. And from here on in, Vitelleschi's life is truly in God's hands."

Part Seven

Sunday
May 11, 1636

The basic slate, the universal hue

Chapter 45

Owen Roe O'Neill glanced behind to check the carriage that had moved the consistory's scribes and lesser assistants from their gathering point at the steps of the Palais Granvelle to St. John's, and now back. And somewhere, mixed in among them, was a scribe as old as any other there, and a Franciscan monk, judging by his simple, hooded habit.

Except that the scribe was in fact Urban VIII who had not, contrary to appearances, returned from St. John's to the abbey and cloister by one of the three predictably shrouded sedan chairs. Instead, he had once again blended in with the lowest members of the consistory's support staff. A handful of out-of-uniform Wild Geese accompanied the carriage. It was all they could muster, with their numbers temporarily reduced. The Hibernians had taken over all the security at the cloister, and, unbeknownst to anyone else, a good deal of the hallway watchpoints in the Carmelite priory, where the majority of the combat-ready Wild Geese remained, making sure that the pope was safe.

Despite the prudent shifting of their forces—half of

the snipers and overwatch teams in belltowers had been redeployed—it hadn't made Owen or Ruy much happier with the day's military state of affairs. They knew, as few others did, just how understaffed they now were, and would not rest easy until the next detachment of Hibernians arrived by balloon, sometime later this day, or the next if the weather failed to hold.

Ruy Sanchez had been uncustomarily grim-lipped as they had watched two columns of the dour Hibernians walking on either flank of the sedan chairs, rifles at the ready. If that hadn't been enough to deter any possible assassins, half of Joasaphus' Russian guards were riding at the front and the back of the formation, faces wearing fierce, suspicious scowls for anyone who had the temerity to meet their eyes. The same parade had made its way back to the convent, without Urban in any of the chairs, and without Ruy there to watch the charade: the long wound on his arm been swelling and was now warm enough to the touch that Sharon hustled him out of the cathedral as soon as the service was concluded.

So now it was Owen and two of his men, Tone Grogan and Dermot Carty, who walked back to the priory alone, catching up with the carriage just as it drew up in front of the Neptune fountain. O'Neill scanned for Urban, caught sight of his habit still in one of the seats, then spotted the man he'd hoped to find: "Turlough Eubank!"

The tall sergeant turned, possibly with a hitch in his step as he did. "Colonel?"

O'Neill drew up to him; Grogan and Carty hung back. "Turlough, has Connal released anyone from the infirmary yet?"

"Sorry, sir, but it's gone the other way, I'm afraid: Dunnigan near fell over with fever just forty minutes ago. He'll not be able to stand the next watch in the pope's chambers."

O'Neill shook his head. "I was afraid of that. So I've sent the only man I've got free to replace him: Danny O'Dee. He's with the pope now."

Turlough balked. "Sir? Danny?"

Owen frowned. "There's a problem with Danny?"

"Well...nothing other than he's not likely to stand up to a priest, let alone a pope. You know 'im, sir: good lad, but just that: still a lad. Like as not to genuflect every time he comes within spittin' distance of a church."

O'Neill nodded, but had no alternatives. "As you say, Danny's a good lad. Which means he'll follow orders. Better than having him sitting by McCarew's sickbed, wringing his hands. I've got to have two men on that detail. So you can do the bossing and Danny can do the shooting, if it comes to it." He glanced more closely at his senior sergeant. "You seem awfully pale, Turlough."

Eubank grunted through a lopsided grin. "You've got no rosy bloom in your own cheek, Owen O'Neill."

Owen shrugged. "Well, I can't argue that. When did you last sleep? Twenty-four hours ago?"

"Erm, don't know exactly, sir. Been a while, though."

Owen clapped a hand down on his sergeant's shoulder. "Damn, but it's been a hard day for all of us. Now best you catch up."

"Catch up?"

"Aye. Just saw the pope get down from the carriage and head into the priory. Danny's already in his chambers. So get stepping, Sergeant."

Turlough may have winced as he nodded and turned away. Owen frowned. Eubank was usually among the more stoic of his men. But long days and aches and pains could overcome all of them, like as not. Besides, there was more duty shuffling to do, if he was to make sure that there would be adequate security for all the attendees, as well as Urban.

Turlough Eubank kept himself from stumbling as he reached the stairs leading up to the pope's rooms. It was urgent that he get there—not so much for the pope's safety, but Danny's sanity. The lad would likely wet himself if the pope so much as frowned at him.

As Eubank thought about Danny wetting himself, he realized he'd better pay attention to the same need. At least. And he couldn't very well ask to borrow the pope's own chamberpot. Seemed vaguely like he'd be defiling something. Nonsense, of course. But he admitted there was probably a little bit of Danny O'Dee in every man who'd ever been brought up in an Irish parish, no matter how old and grizzled he became.

Turlough swung away from the stairs, bracing himself before walking through two rooms of what his men had dubbed "nun-country:" the part of the priory that the mother superior had set aside for her convent's exclusive use during the pope's stay. He sped through the two chambers: a sitting room and the kitchen itself, where two of the Carmelites were working and did their best not to notice the large, rough, armed man who stalked around them and out toward the privy.

Eubank almost missed the first step down from the kitchen, barely caught himself. Yes, it had been a long time since he had gotten any sleep. And while he hadn't technically lied to O'Neill—he couldn't say exactly how long it had been—he knew that it was before breakfast yesterday. So, coming up on thirty hours without a wink. Almost half that time since he'd even sat down: with so many wounded, he'd had to oversee the guard shifts in the priory all night long.

He reached the jakes, closed the door behind him, turned, undid his buff-coat, his belt, sat, stared down at his hands—

—and felt his hair stand up. He was covered in blood down to his knees. Most of it was dried, but Jayzus—

He put his hand under his shirt, felt for the source, found two small punctures just above his belt—or, just under it, when standing. So he'd been bleeding, steady and slow for half a day or more. The belt must have held back the flow, but then, as it just shifted, the wounds had opened.

He probed each one with a tentative finger: they were sore and hot. Why hadn't he felt that before now? Maybe he had, he realized in the next second, but had just dismissed it along with the other aches and pains and agonies of being on duty, hand perpetually on hilt, for the last day and a half.

Either way, he had to get to the pope. But he had to find a guard along the way, to carry word that Owen had to assign a replacement—any replacement—who wasn't wounded or likely to keel over from continuing blood loss. Cutting his visit to the jakes far shorter than he'd intended, he rose, cold hands going to refasten his shirt and other clothes—

But the cold suddenly became numbness. He slumped against the side of the privy, grabbing for anything that might hold him up. The world swam. Blackness rose.

He pushed open the door to the jakes, all pride gone in the urgent need to contact someone, to make sure that Owen, that anyone, knew that he might not make it to his post.

He was halfway out when the vertigo hit him like a ringing tornado, swirling up from his gut into his head. His eyesight tunneled down; he flailed with his hands, but there was nothing to catch hold of.

Eubank fell his length, his forehead whacking sharply against one of the paving stones that led from the back of the kitchen out into the convent's winter garden.

Otto flinched awake as the door to the pantry shut, eyes opening to darkness. Out in the kitchen, women's voices were discussing foods they were preparing and other topics he didn't really understand. But none of that mattered. He had no way to escape as long as they were out there. And they might come in again, might need to search for a cheese or a sausage where he was hiding. And then what?

Otto rose from the floor, bits of cheese and sausage falling off his shirt in the dark. He couldn't remember how much he had eaten of each, but it was a lot. And now, it was churning in his belly, making him even more nervous.

The door opened again; a shaft of light cut into the darkness like a knife.

A woman—a nun, from the outline?—entered the pantry at a brisk pace, glancing about.

Otto pushed back as far as he could—and felt the wall give slightly behind him.

The woman or nun found what she needed, glanced back in his direction, but her glittering eyes were aimed at the floor, not at him. "Marie! We have rats again, and they've been at the cheese!" She stalked out. The door shut. Darkness returned.

Otto turned as quietly and carefully as he could, felt for the part of the wall that had moved, just behind him. It shifted again when he pressed against it, but did not go back any further. It was if there was a door in the wall that would not open.

Otto almost gasped in surprise, and felt excited delight even through his fear: another secret door! Maybe a secret passage to freedom! Just like in the stories that Heinz told him on cold nights around the campfire when he found it hard to sleep. He almost shed a tear; he missed Heinz. He'd never been separated from him for this long in—well, maybe in forever. And how would he find him once he was free?

Otto put his big, fleshy lips together until they felt hard. If he was going to find Heinz, he had to get out first. And that meant getting through the secret door. But if he hit it hard, then the nuns might hear. So, bracing his feet against the floor, he leaned against the secret door and pushed, both with his legs and his shoulders. The wall began to bend inward a little more—

It gave way with a rasping squeal. Otto, unable to catch himself in time, fell into an even darker passage of some kind. Almost immediately, he felt the urge to cough: dust had risen up around him, like that one time he had helped Heinz open a big stone casket in a building filled with them, to get something from a corpse. An uncle of his. Except Otto wondered how Heinz would have an uncle with a Spanish name.

Otto stood up, tried to close the door, but it wouldn't stay shut. In the dim light that came under the pantry door, he saw why: the outline of a twisted and snapped lock told him that, yet again, he'd broken something that wasn't his. Well, Heinz wasn't here to yell at him, and there wasn't anyone to tell, so he didn't need to worry about that. But if he did get hungry again... he reached back into the pantry, grabbed the small cheese he'd been eating when he got so full he had fallen asleep. The knife fell out; he leaned in, picked it up, closed the door softly.

Otto felt along the wall to his right, back in the direction of the kitchen. It ended after three feet. No way out there. He turned, felt along the other wall for five, ten, fifteen feet—and almost cried out when his shin hit something. He reached down and felt around.

Stairs. And small bones. About the size of a rat's or even a cat's. And so much dust that—

Otto sneezed, scolded himself. He had to stay quiet if he was going to escape!

He extended his foot to detect the next riser. And so, step by step, Otto began ascending the stairs, which were barely any broader than he was.

Maffeo Barberini, known better as Urban VIII, unleashed his secret weapon.

He pouted.

It was an excellent pout; no quiver, but just soft enough to be expressive and yet remain manly.

Well, as manly as any pout could be.

Urban even felt a slight tinge of guilt as he used it. It was a powerful weapon against devout Catholics, and had moved the hardened hearts of many a bishop and priest. But this might be overkill, he admitted to himself, akin to using a cannon to kill a mouse.

Urban looked up to see what effect it had had.

Daniel O'Dempsey, who everyone else seemed to call Danny O'Dee, had flushed a bright crimson, a trait that seemed particularly pronounced among the fairer-complected Irish and Scottish. "Your Holiness, as God is my witness, please believe me: if I could, I'd get you those pills. But I can't leave you; I am under orders." He tapped a nervous foot. "And I'm not supposed to be alone here. A sergeant, probably Eubank, was to be here by now."

Urban assessed the amount of desperation in the young man's tone, estimated that the time was right to add in another level of complexity and stress. "You and the sergeant have been posted here to prevent me from being killed, correct?"

"Aye—yes, Your Holiness. That's the truth of it."

"Then you must make a decision, Daniel."

"Your Holiness?"

"How do you prefer I die?"

"What—what are you talkin' about, Your Holiness?!"

Urban shrugged. "Well, I am feeling faint, which may be a sign of increased pressure upon my heart. In which case, I need the tablets that Ambassadora Nichols said I should ingest in such a circumstance. Otherwise, my heart might stop. I did not wish to burden you with this information, but either you shall go and get the tablets from Ambassadora Nichols, or you shall stay here to protect me against imaginary assassins and watch me as I very possibly die."

Urban regretted creating this terrible dilemma for the poor young Irishman—he seemed a decent fellow and as devout as one could wish—but the alternative was intolerable. Urban had sacrificed every last shred of pride but this most basic of human needs for privacy. And once it became obvious that the young Irishman would not, under any circumstances, leave him unobserved for even a scant second, well, a little white lie surely wouldn't harm anyone. Given the layers of guards between Urban and any assassins—pairs of them at every entrance in the convent, at every major intersection of halls, and at the bottom of the staircase—it was a certainty that he was quite safe without having a young fellow within the room, and within arm's length, at that. A pope had the right to more dignity than that, surely! "You must choose, Daniel. But I implore you: please get the tablets. I feel weak."

Daniel O'Dempsey seemed ready to bite himself in a fit of hopeless frustration and uncertainty, and then finally bolted from the room, crying over his shoulder, "Hide under the bed. Er . . . an' it please you. Your Holiness." By which time his feet were thumping down the stairs.

Urban sighed, smiled, rose, walked to his bed to fetch his chamberpot.

After all, even popes had the right to relieve themselves in private.

Otto rounded the corner on the landing and immediately smelled the change in the air: not so dank or dusty. The change was subtle, but unmistakable. At least to *his* nose.

He felt his way quickly up the staircase, felt a landing spread out under one searching hand as he clutched his food and utensil to his chest with the other. And there was a draft from the left. He felt along that wall and his fingers hit the side of another secret door, set flush with the wall. At last! The way out!

Feeling around eagerly, he located the lock, a simple turnbolt. He rotated it one-half counterclockwise turn and tugged inward.

Clothes. Shirts, trousers, cassocks were arrayed in front of him as if he was on the edge of a jungle grown by tailors. He put a hand between two of the cassocks, parted them, saw another door. But this one was very light and wooden. And suddenly Otto understood: this secret door opened into the back of some kind of wardrobe. How clever! Just like in some of Heinz's stories, and like the one in the palace!

He reached for the door, turned the small oval knob, pushed it outward and almost gasped for joy when light and fresh air came in. Otto stepped through the wardrobe, imagining how, for once, it would be Heinz who would sit openmouthed and eager when he told the story of his escape through a secret door hidden in the back of a wardrobe!

Urban straightened, mildly delighted to find that one of the many servants had apparently changed the chamber pot when he wasn't looking. Being constantly in peril gave one a renewed, almost childlike appreciation for various small conveniences and comforts.

The door creaked open, and Urban prepared to make his apologies to young Daniel O'Dempsey— but then realized it wasn't the door to the hallway that had opened. It was, improbably, the door to the wardrobe. As Urban straightened in surprise, a large, round-shouldered man emerged from it, scratching his ass and carrying a much-diminished round of cheese, a knife embedded in it.

Both as a young noble and a rising cleric, Maffeo Barberini had always prided himself on never being at a loss for words. But this time, he could not manage more than a surprised splutter before realizing that he should make no noise whatsoever. However bizarre this near-giant's appearance was, his first reaction should not have been one of wonder at the surreality of his emergence from the wardrobe, but of realizing the unmitigated danger it represented.

The large, soft-lipped man—almost an ogre in build and hirsutism—had heard the pope. His small round head turned around; his eyes fixed on Urban, first surprised, then wondering.

Urban remained motionless, but his eyes moved swiftly across the other's clothing: the partial livery of the palace staff, the type worn by hostlers and victualers. But the staff of the palace had no business here in the convent, which meant—

Urban's eyes flicked toward the knife, and before he could stop the reflex, his eyes widened and he took a step backward. Which quickened a memory he had not recalled in many decades—

When he was but thirteen, the Barberinis had been invited to visit the estate of a prospective business partner in the Little Dolomites. Naturally, Maffeo and his brothers had wanted to go exploring, hoping to encounter good game that they might bring to table. But the oldest of the guides had been full of sour warnings, one of which had been about the more dangerous animals they might encounter in the upslope forests.

"Should you come upon a black bear, young signor," the gray-locked borderer had warned with slow gravity, "make no hasty movements. When it is calm, you may calmly leave. Do not run until it can no longer see you. And above all, show no fear."

But, Urban realized, he had shown fear.

The bear awakened in the large man's eyes. Surprise became almost mindless ferocity, and with a single growled word that sounded like, "Evilpope," the ogre leaped forward with surprising speed.

The knife came out of its cheese scabbard. Urban tried keeping his face to his attacker while retreating, felt his heel catch upon the rear hem of his gilt cassock, went down backwards, hit the base of his skull against the hardwood floor.

A single dazed moment. Then his vision straightened and he tried to rise—just as the ogre leaped upon him and drove the knife down into his chest.

Again and again and again.

Sharon heard the repetitive thumping halfway down the stairs from the pope's room. "C'mon!" she cried and began racing upward, Larry Mazzare at her heels.

But Danny O'Dee sped past them like they were standing still. Sprinting up two risers at a time, he didn't stop when he reached the door: he burst straight through. As they got to the head of the stairs, he let out an animal howl.

Sharon raced to the door, shoulder to shoulder with Larry and just three steps ahead of the guards from the bottom of the stairs, but was stunned into immobility on the threshold.

There was a large man in the middle of the room,

rising from the bloodied form of Urban VIII, turning toward Danny O'Dee, menacing him with what looked like an absurdly small paring knife.

Danny raised his pepperbox—

—"NO!" yelled Sharon in chorus with Larry—

—as Danny fired twice before the gun jammed. The big man staggered back a step, almost tripping over Urban, from whose lips blood was dribbling.

Larry rushed in to grab Danny, but was a moment too late. The young Irishman let out a tortured scream-sob as he drew his sabre into a rising backhand cut that sliced a groove into the ogre's chest, opened his cheek, bisected an eye and raised up a patch of his scalp. The huge man bellowed—more like a bull than a human—and struck out with the knife that was almost unnoticeable in his immense fist.

Danny O'Dee jumped aside, feinted a cut to the body, but dropped his wrist at the last moment: the faint whistle of his sword ended with a dull thud as it hit the assassin's femur.

Sharon angled around toward Urban, who seemed—impossibly—alive. Larry couldn't get close to Danny without endangering him—and was then pushed aside and to his knees as the other two Wild Geese made room to draw their swords and help their comrade.

But they were not swift enough: Danny had used what was left of the sweeping momentum of his sabre to slide it out of the wound as the big man shrieked with pain and staggered back, clutching at his spouting leg with one hand and waving his knife with the other. Danny, tears streaming down his face, leaped forward, removed two of the ogre's fingers—and the knife—with his blade, then swiftly rolled his wrist and thrust the full length of the steel into and through the great fleshy chest before him.

The big man did not scream but whimpered and then fell off the blade, blood gouting up as he crashed to the floor.

By then, Sharon was on her knees at Urban's side and had to hold back her own tears: the pope was bleeding too quickly from nearly a dozen wounds in his chest. Both lungs were flooding and with three sucking chest wounds, there was nothing she could do in time. "Larry," she murmured. "Come here. Quickly."

Larry was there, asking as he came, "Why aren't you—?" And then he saw what Sharon had and fell quiet. "Your Holiness."

No response. Sharon, startling out of her daze, grasped for and found a pulse: steady but fading.

Larry leaned in toward the pope. "Maffeo. Maffeo Barberini!"

Urban's eyes flickered open, as if he'd been on the verge of a very deep sleep. "Lawrence. How good that you are here."

"Don't talk. We have to try—"

"Lawrence, I am called by God. I go without regret. But I go with shame."

"Shame? Why?"

"Be-because I tricked that poor young boy into leaving me alone." Urban laughed, coughed up a jet of alarmingly bright blood. "Pride and a lie. Always my downfall. You'd think I'd have learned by now." He coughed again. Sharon was surprised to see Larry turn his head away, and then realized, with a painful catch in her throat, that he wanted to ensure that Urban would not see, or feel the dripping of, his tears. "Your Holiness... my friend... I must ask: should the circular—?"

Urban burbled blood as he shook his head, his eyes closing momentarily. "The circular stands as written. Unless you feel it needs more... more... more revision." He coughed out the words.

Larry turned back to face the pope. "No: it is a great document, a great legacy."

Urban may have smiled. His eyes were open but as blank as a blind man's. "Then let its words be my last."

Larry nodded, squinting against the tears. "Your Holiness, may I offer you the rite of extreme unction?"

Urban's only response was a sigh. And then silence, his chest still.

Sharon felt the thin pulse falter and stop. "He's gone."

Pedro Dolor looked down upon the center of the Buckle from his attic perch. He had not anticipated how quickly the search for other suspected assassins would be mounted. Before dawn, the attic adjoining his safe room had been visited by imperiously thumping troops, whose words and gaits were marked more by self-importance than competence. Clearly, Burgundians. Just as he had expected.

So Dolor had emerged earlier than he originally planned, deeming it wise to get a feel for the mood in the city and listen to the radio. Perhaps he would be able to leave sooner than he had thought. But he wouldn't be able to determine that immediately. The throngs who had turned out to see, or at least get close to, Urban's celebration of the Pentecost service would have to diminish. So he settled in for a light lunch and some slow careful stretching of his muscles.

Just when he thought the streets had settled down enough that he might be able to read the social undercurrents that ran through them, there was some kind of commotion near the entrance to the priory. He could not make out exactly what it was: the front of the convent faced away from him. However, he had seen guards and servants sprinting there in response to an apparently urgent summons. And then all was quiet, but the guards were both alert and subtly agitated.

Radio on, Dolor began turning slowly through the frequencies. He soon detected an unprecedented flurry of secure radio traffic, both outbound and then inbound, in one of the Grantville codes he had not yet been able to crack. And then nothing. It became a Sunday like any other.

Except now, none of the Wild Geese were anywhere to be seen, either on guard or at liberty. And the street watchposts of the Hibernians had been withdrawn to the interiors of all the buildings at which they were stationed, beyond where townspeople might reach them.

Dolor leaned back, considered. So perhaps Gasquet's attack had not been a complete failure, after all. Perhaps Urban had been wounded, evacuated to the priory—that much seemed obvious—and then had taken an unexpected turn for the worse and expired. Or perhaps some remainder of the attack—the notional equivalent of a booby trap—had lingered behind long enough to eliminate the pope.

Dolor paused, putting a check upon the unwarranted optimism of that last conjecture. It was difficult to imagine that any of Borja's clownish men had shown such inventiveness and presence of mind to leave behind a hidden dagger, as it were. But *something* unexpected had occurred just after noon, something which necessitated high level radio exchanges with Grantville and compelled all the security forces to be withdrawn from public contact. And the latter meant that this event was also something which his opponents desperately wanted to keep silent.

Perhaps, then, not all was lost. Although it was not logical, a successful assassination attempt always became more of an outrage than a failed one. And if Borja's henchmen had, somehow, managed to kill Urban, then Olivares would have what he wanted: a pretext whereby he might convince Philip to openly renounce ties with his renegade cardinal and thereby at least preserve the situation in Naples.

And if Olivares got what he wanted, that translated into greater power and access for Dolor to pursue his own objectives. First, the destruction of Marques de Villa Flores et Avila, Don Pedro de Zuñiga. And then, eventually, the stage would be set for Pedro Dolor—or more properly, Wilbur Craigson—to wreak his final vengeance upon the true culprit behind Zuñiga, Borja, and Olivares; upon the beast that had spawned all the well-heeled murderers and pimps who predominated in Philip's court:

Imperial Spain itself.

Chapter 46

There was a knock on the door of the salon that the last lord of Granvelle had been wont to use for meetings of his privy council.

Larry looked over at Sharon, whose wide eyes met his. "You ready for this?"

"As ready as I'm ever going to be." Sharon shrugged her considerable shoulders. "Okay, then: here we go." Raising her surprisingly dainty chin and her surprisingly powerful voice, she called, "Come in!"

The door opened, admitting white-haired Luke Wadding, and then, after dismissing two guards with a wave, Cardinal Alfonso de la Cueva-Benavides y Mendoza-Carrillo Bedmar. They both nodded at the two up-timers and sat.

Larry didn't waste any time. "Maffeo—Pope Urban asked that I speak to you in the event of his death. The two of you, specifically."

They nodded again.

"He also asked that Father Vitelleschi be here, but that is not possible."

Wadding leaned forward anxiously. "Does he continue to improve, or—?"

Sharon smiled, waving a calming hand. "He is already doing much better. Very weak, not awake much. But when he is, he's as sharp as ever. And even more short-tempered."

Wadding's eyes got shiny at the same moment his smile widened. "Thank God on high for that gift!"

Sharon's smile widened as well. "I don't mean to sound a heretical note, Your Eminence, but I'm not sure the weapon has been made yet that can kill Father General Vitelleschi. He's about as tough and stringy as they come."

That made Bedmar smile. "When a physician can make jokes about his—erm, *her*—patient, it means they are out of danger. Or the physician is a brute. Which is so very clearly not the case. At least that's what Achille insists, and he is almost as hardheaded as Vitelleschi."

Larry nodded. "Well, although you're not a physician, Your Eminence, I suspect your comment about Achille tells us something similar: that his wound is not too severe."

"It is not; no major surgery was ultimately required. He insists on calling it a scratch, and is scheduled to depart on the morrow, under the watchful eye of his brother. Who, of course, blames himself for not being at the battle."

Larry sat up straighter. "Can they delay their departure for a week?"

Bedmar shook his head. "They cannot. There are matters in France, matters pertaining to the crown, which require Achille's immediate attention. Indeed, they have contracted one of your balloons to take them on the first leg of their journey." He frowned.

"Lawrence, I take it you wish him to remain to maximize the numbers of the consistory—that now you mean to call a Papal Conclave."

"I do."

"Well, I doubt any one vote will become too important. And after all, this process could take months—"

"No," Larry interrupted. "It can't. It has to take place immediately, and it has to run concurrent with the Council to establish Urban's ecumenical vision as canon law."

Bedmar and Wadding exchanged long looks. "Lawrence," began Wadding, "this is most—irregular."

Larry nodded. "It is, my friend, but we are living in irregular times. Desperate ones, in some regards."

Bedmar frowned. "Those are dire words. Please explain them."

Larry let out a long sigh and clasped his hands before him. He didn't mean to affect the appearance of praying, but maybe it was appropriate, anyhow. If this scheme didn't work out—well, he didn't dare think about that. "So, you're aware that you two are the only clergy who've been informed of Urban's death?"

They both nodded.

"That's not just because you were close to him. We've sharply limited the news of his demise so that we can manage the fallout—er, the aftermath—and minimize the damage."

Wadding, whose instinct for politics was often as limited as his talent for theology was vast, screwed up his face. "'Minimize the damage?' What does that even mean, Lawrence? The pope has been slain by an assassin. What more damage can there be?"

"Plenty, Your Eminence," Sharon put in. "This could

impact a number of sensitive political and international situations. And not in a good way. Not unless we exert some control over the news of the pope's death. Immediately."

Bedmar folded his arms, stared at Larry. "You said that the pope wished you to speak with us in the event of his death. But you have not told us what about."

Larry drew in a deep breath. *No time like the present to drop the bombs.* "He left me with two sets of instructions. One regarding the circular he authored that sets out the new canonical laws for ecumenicism—"

"A circular? Not an encyclical?" Wadding swallowed. "But Lawrence, he cannot posthumously impose a complete—!"

"—and the other instruction," Larry continued, riding over the top of the Franciscan's stunned outburst, "has to do with the process and outcome of the Conclave."

Wadding's eyes widened; Bedmar's narrowed. "How," asked the latter, "can the late pope have offered any comments on the outcome of the process whereby his successor will be chosen?"

"By making it clear to me, in no uncertain terms, that, in the event he was killed, that you, Alfonso de la Cueva-Benavides, must be the next pope." Larry held up a hand. "I know how it sounds. Hell, I know what it means. But Urban was emphatic about this: that only you, Bedmar, could survive being Borja's opponent. And the next pope we decide upon will be his mortal enemy, no matter what we might wish. You are a Spanish cardinal. Borja will not dare to go after you."

Bedmar smiled mirthlessly. "Unless I fall from Philip's favor. Which I suspect is only a matter of time."

Sharon nodded. "Because eventually you will have to choose between Philip and Fernando."

Bedmar shrugged. "I was made the cardinal-protector of the Spanish Lowlands: my course is set. And while I confess no great attachment to the ecumenicism that has so energized the rest of you, I know disaster when I see it—and Borja and his rapine and persecution are that disaster. We need to come to a *modus vivendi*, to some kind of peace, all us Christians. After all, we do not exist in this world alone." He glanced meaningfully to the east.

Larry nodded. "Which was another one of the reasons that Urban insisted upon commenting upon the outcome of this conclave: that it cannot be unmindful of the threat from the Ottomans."

"Well, with that I can certainly agree!" Wadding exclaimed with a thump on the arm of his chair.

"Good, then hopefully you'll see why Urban had, on the sidelines of the colloquium, already approached some of the more influential voices among the consistory, singing Bedmar's praises. And most of them agreed—in part, because he can do something that no other man wearing a biretta can currently do."

Bedmar nodded, understanding. "I can wait out that bloodthirsty dog. He sits upon the *cathedra*, but surrounded by eyes filled with hate and bellies hungry for vengeance. I sit in Brussels at the pleasure of the Hapsburgs, accepted by the populace, and deemed tolerable—at least!—by most of the nations of Europe." Bedmar ran his finger beneath his small, pencil-thin moustache. "Urban's moral epiphanies did not blind him to political practicalities, I see."

Larry leaned forward. "So, if the conclave were to choose you, you would have no reservations?"

Bedmar laughed. "I would have more reservations than we have fingers and toes in the entirety of this city! But I have more reservations, and fears, about what Borja would do to any of the others in this consistory. And therefore, what he would do to the need for Christian unity in the face of a Turkish threat. A threat that Philip seems less than wroth about, I may point out."

Wadding gulped back a horrified gasp. "Is this true?"

Bedmar nodded. "Oh, quite true. And not at all surprising. Think on it: Spain's Hapsburgs have been all but spurned by the Austrian Hapsburgs. Who, of course, will bear the brunt of a Turk attack. And who will come to their rescue, and thus be bled dry of men and treasure? The USE certainly," he answered, nodding at Sharon, "Venice possibly. The Knights of Malta assuredly. In short, all of Madrid's greatest foes or irritants. And if I know Olivares, and I do, he will find a way to turn a profit on it, bargaining for trade garnishments from the Turks in exchange for standing aside and letting the rest of Europe bear the brunt of Murad IV's attack."

Sharon smiled. "Have you been talking to Mike Stearns?"

"No," he said, returning her smile, "have you?"

"Enough to know that this will have repercussions for your immediate liege, Fernando, as well."

Bedmar frowned. "Yes. To be frank, I fear for him most of all. This will push the conflict between him and Philip to the edge of, or possibly past, the breaking point. It goes well beyond the provocative title Fernando has selected, King in the Lowlands, and his refusal to answer, simply and unequivocally, whether

Philip is still his suzerain. There are whispers—whispers which I understand originate from your own radios, Ambassadora—that Madrid has reason to expect a most disappointing report regarding this year's infusion of silver from the New World, to say nothing of the state of the Flota that was sent to carry it."

Wadding frowned. "I claim no great knowledge of such things, but would not the Flota have just arrived in the New World? How could its fate already be known? At this time, it would be carrying a mere fraction of its silver."

"That is true," Bedmar agreed. "And yet, there are the whispers. Aren't there, Ambassadora?"

Sharon's smile was somehow both friendly and feral. "No comment, Your Eminence."

Bedmar chuckled. "I see that we shall get along famously. At any rate, if, for some mysterious reason, Spain does not get the New World silver she expects this year, that shall send her down into a financial maelstrom. She will be more desperate for Ottoman trade and coin, and will have to give greater concessions to get it, since Istanbul will have heard of her fiscal vulnerability. And so, the *reales* that Spain sends to prop up the occupation forces in the Spanish Lowlands will become twice as dear. Philip's patience with an upstart brother who refuses to bend his knee may very well fray to the point of breaking. And if that occurs . . . well, it is difficult to see how my King Fernando will fare."

Sharon nodded. "This has been considered. Contingencies, many related to ongoing enterprises and developments in the New World, are in place. Also, however dire circumstances become for the Spanish Lowlands, they're going to be a lot worse for Borja's

Italy. Every cardinal he killed there was also a major member of a noble family. And in those places that were never too fond of the Spanish presence in Milan and Naples, it's worse. Much worse. He's angered every noble family in Florence, Tuscany, and Venice. And the commoners in a lot of the other regions hate him just as much. So, as we see it in the USE, Borja is poised to become Macbeth in the final scene of the play of that name, all alone on the ramparts of Dunsinane. The Spanish won't want to touch him because of his murderous papal ambitions, and, with a few exceptions, the cardinals of his 'consistory-held-at-gunpoint,' are just waiting for an opportunity to cut and run."

Sharon leaned back. "Our assessment is that before two years are up, the Spanish are going to be having a hard time just holding on to Naples, and the cost of doing so is that Oruna will have to leave Borja out to dry."

Bedmar grinned. "When you put it that way, the notion of becoming pope almost sounds, well, appealing."

Larry nodded. "Good. But there's a catch."

Bedmar frowned. "And what is this 'catch'?"

Sharon shrugged. "We need to keep Urban's death quiet. As in, *completely* secret."

"What? How?" Wadding exclaimed.

"I believe," Bedmar said slowly, looking from one up-timer face to the other, "the most pertinent question is 'why,' Cardinal Wadding."

The Franciscan nodded vigorously.

Larry shrugged. "Because we need to elect a new pope—you—before anyone knows Urban is dead. And then, we have to give his work here time to take hold."

"But—"

Larry held up a hand. "Luke, I've come to think of you as my older, kinder brother, but please: hear me out."

Wadding blinked, nodded, and sat back in his seat.

"So, most of our guests are going to return to their homes at a whole lot more leisurely a pace than they came. And there's no way around that. We tied up most of the USE's hot air balloons for months and we just can't do it again, particularly given what's happening down along the Hungarian border."

"So you feel certain that the Turk's attack upon Christendom is so imminent? Even if the kings of Europe can quickly put aside their childish bickering?"

Larry nodded. "I don't for a second think that Murad IV is undertaking this out of religious fervor, though. Sure, that's his rhetoric, and I'm sure he believes it at some level, but he's an autocrat who can detect weakness and seize a moment, and he has both the money and manpower to do it.

"He knows that our nations are already in disarray. But if he then sees half of them swinging first in the direction of Urban's ecumenicism, only to learn that Urban has since been assassinated by Spain and that all his transformative work might die with him, that's a further encouragement to Murad. And the last thing we want the sultan to think is that this is the time to accelerate his campaign, to take advantage of our internal debates. If Urban's ecumenical initiative is going to take root and unify us, it needs some time to do so, time before the news goes out that its creator is dead."

Bedmar hid a thin smile behind steepled fingers. "That does not sound like you talking, Cardinal Mazzare. Again, that sounds much more like Michael Stearns."

"It should—which, by the way, just goes to show how useful radios really are."

"So, practically speaking, what does this mean?"

"It means that the cardinals will be tied down here for several months. Luckily the consistory sometimes closets itself during Councils, particularly when the matters being discussed are particularly sensitive. Since the matter of ecumenicism may be the most provocative topic that could be raised right now, closed sessions and removal from the public eye shouldn't raise many eyebrows. Otherwise, this would be impossible."

Sharon sighed. "Of course, that in turn means we're going to have to increase security. We can't have any of the cardinals being snatched and debriefed, or any of their staff, or scribes gabbing around town. At the same time, we're going to have to share the information with some parties that we'd rather not, and that's going to require us committing to the normalization of diplomatic relations before we really wanted to. For instance, Bernhard has to be told. This is his capital and he'll figure out pretty quickly that something fishy is going on, what with all these cardinals here under tight security. So tight that they are always under guard. That means there's going to have to be more quid pro quo with Bernhard, and trust me, you don't want to be in that man's debt."

"And what might come of that?"

Sharon shrugged. "He'll probably get more bold about grabbing land on the western banks of the Rhine. Not USE territory, but there are lots of little principalities or independent cities that he might like to gobble up. We've been trying to make that financially, politically, or in some cases, even militarily unattractive to him.

But if he's got to keep our secret—well, then he's going to have leverage. And he'll use it."

Bedmar nodded. "I see. Lawrence, you said something about a second directive from Urban—a papal circular?"

Larry bowed his head. "Yes. Urban has been working on it for months, with some help from Cardinal Wadding and myself."

Wadding shook his head. "Lawrence overreports my labors and underreports his own. Profoundly."

Larry smiled. "Don't listen to the crown prince of blarney over there. We both put a lot of work into this."

"And what, exactly, is it?"

Larry was trying to find the words when Wadding raised his chin and let flow his particularly Irish eloquence. "It is the essence of the grace and charity that God granted the fathers of the up-time church, tried and then titrated through the contemporary alembic that was Pope Urban VIII's fine mind, and reformed into a tonic suitable for this day and age. It is neither too ambitious in its directives, nor so general that it can be avoided, forgotten, or reinterpreted into meaninglessness. It is an ecumenical elixir, one which we may all sip, and which we shall all survive." He glanced, maybe glared, at Larry. "However, it was to be an encyclical, a matter for discussion, not a *fait accompli*."

Larry shrugged. "In the last few days, Urban decided otherwise. After the ambush at St. John's, well, I think he realized he might not be around for the discussion. So he made it a straight up legacy: a circular."

Sharon nodded. "I've seen it." She returned Bedmar's surprised stare. "If the consistory confirms it as canon, I think the majority of the other churches will go for it. And equipped with those radios, I think they'll want to start discussing it, and comparing their experiences trying to put it into practice."

"Which could be quite difficult. Even bloody," Bedmar observed.

Larry nodded. "Yes, it probably will be. But they won't be experiencing that alone; they'll be trying it together, suffering together, persevering together. They'll share strategies for introducing it at every social level, from a prince's court to a peasant's hovel. And wherever the USE's Committees of Correspondence have a toehold, there's ready-made support for the basic proposition that is its foundation: freedom of religion."

Bedmar folded his arms and looked down; it was clearly a posture he had learned as an officer, not a cleric. "This is all well thought out. However, although I do not anticipate a challenge from Madrid regarding my election, I am quite certain that when I publicly aver that Urban is a martyr of the Church and that his ecumenical directives should become dogma, Philip and his cardinals will charge me with the same deviation from faith that led them to supporting Borja's rape of Rome."

Wadding nodded. "Just as occurred when Urban exonerated Galileo. The door was opened to considering the matter of the up-timers as something other than the agents or creations of Satan, a proposition that many cannot renounce."

"Precisely," agreed Bedmar. "And I will be tarred with the same brush." He turned to Mazzare. "I have read the arguments you advanced in Molino against the proposition that Grantville is the work of the devil. They are compelling, but there is one problem with them."

Larry raised an eyebrow. "And what is that?"

Bedmar sighed. "None of them are mine. If I simply repeat your arguments, it will be easy—indeed, natural—for the clergy of my country to accuse me of following the Satanic up-timer path as blithely as did Urban. I need additional arguments, arguments I may represent as my own, which shall preempt that accusation." He smiled. "In short, I am asking you to be the theologian that I most certainly am not. But that I shall take the credit for being."

Well, at least he's honest about it. "Very well, Your Eminence. There is a line of reasoning which I did not use at Molino, in part because I did not have the time, and in part because it was so provocative. You might say it follows the reasoning that the best defense is a strong offense."

"Excellent. I welcome such an approach."

I expected no less. "So, let us project the inevitable. They will make their argument not against the particulars of any one doctrine, or even the religious documents which came from the future; they will attempt to attack the problem at its root. In short, they will assert the Satanic nature of Grantville itself."

"Without doubt," Bedmar agreed. "Despite the level of superstition required to maintain such a belief in the face of all evidence to the contrary, you might be surprised—or more likely, alarmed—how many otherwise learned men in the Escorial and in the churches of Spain are able to remain steadfastly behind such a conclusion."

Alarmed yes, surprised no. "My arguments in Molino were made before more reasonable men. So I refrained from the most aggressive riposte I could make, which points to how such a belief actually contradicts long-standing Church positions. It forces them to either overturn those time-honored beliefs or accept that Grantville's identity and appearance are both natural, rather than supernatural, in origin."

Bedmar nodded vigorously and lowered his head, as if prepared to butt his way through a dense web of theological sophistries.

Larry managed not to smile. "If it is argued that the creation of Grantville, its inhabitants, and the profound and even prophetic accuracy of the information it brought into the world are all within the scope of Satan's power, which he has only now fully shown, we must then ask: why is it that Satan was so tardy exploiting these powers, unless God was restraining them? But then why would He restrain them no longer? Perhaps He has grown so weak or inattentive that Satan was able to overpower His protection?"

The stiffened spines among the clerics in the room demonstrated just how the mere suggestion of God's infirmity or forgetfulness prompted a fiercely oppositional reaction.

"Of course," continued Mazzare, "Spain's theologians will insist, loudly, that such a proposition is absurd. And once they do so, Cardinal Bedmar, they have handed you your victory. For then *they* must answer why Satan has not attempted this ploy until now, and also why God would permit it—and that therefore, the revered exegetes of the past several centuries have evidently been uniformly wrong in their explanations of why the age of great miracles is past. Because clearly, it isn't."

Bedmar was nodding fiercely, smiling at the end. "The most ardent among them will, of course, attempt to concoct rebuttals. But they will be at considerable pains to do so convincingly, and shall no doubt become entangled in their own theological bickering as they attempt to finalize their counterposition. Which shall buy us the time we need. As you no doubt foresaw."

Larry smiled. "In the up-time game of football, this is known as running out the clock. We don't have to score again; we just have to keep them from doing anything useful until it's too late."

Bedmar smiled back and put out his hand. "I will hope to have your counsel, Cardinal Mazzare, should the conclave decide as you suspect."

"As I suspect and as Mother Church must hope." Larry bowed slightly. "And as for my counsel, you have it now as my brother in Christ, and later, as the Prelate of Rome."

Bedmar nodded, then frowned. "I must confess I do have a worry about this strategy, though." He looked down.

Larry had never seen Bedmar do such a thing. "You have a reservation regarding the efficacy of this argument?"

Bedmar shook his head. "Not the argument, but where its success might lead us."

"And where is that?"

Bedmar looked up. "To a godless world. After all, is that not where yours was headed?"

Before Mazzare could answer, Wadding swept in: strange to think that the man who had made precisely this argument was now ready to inveigh against it. "Your fear today was mine last year in Molino, my brother. After all, we find in Grantville's collected volumes explanations for the majority of natural phenomena which we attributed to God's touch upon the firmament of His creation. Thus, the mysteries of the universe shrink so profoundly that, to the layman, it will seem as though they have disappeared, even though philosophers of science ensure me that the remaining miracles, while more subtle, are also more profound."

Mazzare smiled faintly. "I seem to recall that you spent some time grappling with the concepts of relativity, special relativity, and quantum mechanics."

"And I can still feel the vestiges of the headache they inflicted upon me, Lawrence. But as I spent more time contemplating these wonders, I came to see that perhaps they are an incomparable gift. Consider: we have them *and* a world based on faith at the same time. Perhaps here, in this reality which Grantville forever changed, if we are bold enough, we may seize upon these without the controversies of your world, Cardinal Mazzare. Perhaps, we will not see these revelations as evidence that God need not exist, but rather, that His Creation is woven from such fine and elegant forces that they themselves are the enduring proof that what surrounds us cannot be without an architect, cannot be happenstance. We and the entirety of the material universe were made with purpose, and it is His Words which shall guide us to the point where worldly mysteries meet and fuse with divine miracles that, together, make up the very face of God Himself."

The passion in Wadding's voice and eyes made

Mazzare wonder if, had the old Irishman been around up-time, he would have become the lead spokesperson for the concept of intelligent design.

Bedmar glanced up. "Cardinal Wadding, your optimism can almost sway a cynical old warhorse like me, but really: do you think it shall work the way you hope? These mean profound changes to the Church and the faith of its flock. Consider how these shall sound: that most natural phenomena are scientific in nature, but do not diminish the centrality of godhead; that it is consistent with God's will that we beat our Counter-Reformational swords into the ploughshares whereby we shall raise up a new crop of truly ecumenical attitudes."

Larry leaned back. "I grant you, it won't be quick and it won't be easy. But on the other hand, Urban VIII died for his beliefs and for the hope and promise of ecumenicism, of peace. That makes him a martyr of the first order. We can't underestimate the power of that. In my world, an American president by the name of Kennedy set our nation the challenge of boldly exploring outer space, shortly before he was assassinated." Larry folded his hands. "And so, we went to the moon in record time, carrying Kennedy's memory with us all the way. So, will the pope's martyrdom create an analogous, extra measure of passion for and curiosity about the ideas for which he died? For finally putting aside the grudges that have divided Christendom?"

Although the question had been rhetorical, Sharon took it at face value. "My guess? You'll find all the people with common sense, or reason, or just plain open-mindedness on one side."

Bedmar frowned. "And on the other?"

She looked him straight in the eye. "All the reactionaries, fanatics, and hatemongers. In a word: all the assholes."

Bedmar blinked and then beamed. "Ambassadora Nichols, if I am selected in the conclave, I wonder; would you agree to remain as the ambassador to the legitimate papacy?"

"And work with my husband's former boss and fellow troublemaker?" She smiled back. "I'll have to think about that."

"That's all I ask."

Larry very much doubted that that was all that Bedmar would ask for.

But it was as good a start as any.

Epilogue

Monday
May 12, 1636

There is a substance in us that prevails

Standing on the front steps of the Palais Granvelle with Bedmar, Larry Mazzare waved his solemn farewells to the slow but persistent trickle of colloquists who passed, making their way to the Pont Battant and, ultimately, to their respective homes.

Bedmar leaned slightly toward Larry. "Lawrence, do you think they know? They appear...concerned."

Larry shook his head. "No. But we told them that the pope required rest and also wished to remain at Father Vitelleschi's bedside, whose condition is very grave."

Bedmar sighed. "I wish no ill upon the father general, but I must say, I wish the roles you have assigned them were reversed."

Larry resisted the urge to glance at Bedmar's mournful tone. "I wasn't aware you were so fond of the pope." He couldn't yet bring himself to say "the late pope."

Bedmar shrugged. "He changed greatly in the

last two years. In some ways, I thought it was for the worse . . . until I came here and realized that he had not grown irresolute or weak, but had acquired the strength of the convictions that define our faith. And in so doing, he has left us an example we must emulate. For if Maffeo Barberini can reject the allure of earthly power and riches, then surely it is within the scope of us all."

Several of the colloquists parted from the main stream and made toward the stairs: Komensky, Lucaris, and Manasseh ben Israel. The latter was the first to speak. "I wish to extend my particular thanks and gratitude for the invitation to participate in the colloquium." A smile quirked the left side of his mouth. "In the past, those of my faith have typically received a different kind of summons from Church authorities. Far more insistent . . . and pointed." He glanced at a Burgundian guard's halberd.

Larry allowed himself the luxury of a small, rueful smile. "Yes, well, changing the nature of, and reason for, those invitations is a large part of what we're trying to achieve. I hope you'll consider returning."

Manasseh bowed very deeply, placing his hand upon his heart. "If I am invited, I shall be honored to attend." He straightened. "Might I—we—leave a message of special gratitude for the pope, as well as our wishes for his continued good health?"

"We would be happy to convey both those sentiments," Bedmar replied with a nod of his head.

Komensky gestured backward toward his small entourage. "I wished to add a special thanks for the radio. A most generous, and useful, gift. I wonder, though: if we should have problems with it, or, for some other reason, we fall silent, is it possible that you shall know in an, er, timely fashion?"

Larry smiled at his carefully indirect words: the radio was an important, but frail and vulnerable, lifeline for any of the colloquists who had reason to fear the disapproval of their home authorities. "The first thing that shall be established with each of you is what is called a 'radio check schedule.' We will agree upon a reasonable interval in which we expect to hear from you. If you should go silent, we will know to mount inquiries, either to discover the nature of repairs your radio might require, or any other impediments that you might be experiencing."

Komensky smiled and bowed himself away as Lucaris stepped forward. His tone was as brusque as his words: "In the first blush of enthusiasm for this new ecumenicism, no one has yet bluntly spoken these crucial words: we may fail. Some of us may die."

Larry nodded, thought, *If only you knew how powerfully we experienced that truth just yesterday.*

However, before Larry could reply, Bedmar folded his hands and said, "Theophilestatos Lucaris, as you certainly know, I am what is called a 'political cardinal.' My command of theology, or even a modest degree of religious eloquence, is woefully wanting.

"However, I commanded men on battlefields, so I understand wars: not just wars involving swords and cannon, but those involving ideas and beliefs. And that is the experience I draw upon when I tell you: yes, we will have casualties. Yes, we will lose some battles. But we are no longer merely individuals, hoping for change. We are the leaders of a new army. An army not just of hope, but survival. Certainly, the carrot of peace and brotherhood is a strong incentive, but the stick—the threat of being defeated in detail by the resurgent Turk—that will serve to marry the idealism of this colloquium with the practicalities of survival. Yes, similar things have been said before, both by prior idealists and prior pragmatists. But never before have these things been spoken so frankly, never before has the need to accept them been so great, and never before have they had a handmaiden as powerful as the radio. This is a war we shall win." He smiled. "That is the opinion of a general, not a cardinal, but I hope it counts for something."

Lucaris' dark eyes were unblinking, their focus upon Bedmar almost alarmingly intense. "It counts for a great deal, Cardinal Bedmar. A great deal indeed. I hope we shall meet soon again."

Larry smiled, put out his hand. "That's the plan. Safe travels."

Lucaris took it in a firm shake, his gaze softening. "And safety to you as well. Cardinal Borja will no doubt try once again to remove this growing thorn from his paw. I pray that your lion-slayers shall do no less than they did this time."

Larry smiled, waved farewell, and felt like his heart had turned to stone.

"That," Bedmar said in a thick voice, "was difficult to hear."

Larry stared after Lucaris. "Tell me about it."

Estuban Miro shooed the radio operator out of his office, sending him on an errand that would take him to the other side of Grantville. "I'm alone now, Mike."

Michael Stearns sounded distracted. "Yeah, okay. I don't have a lot of time here. Got some uncooperative southern neighbors to set straight. So what's up?"

"Me. Literally. I'm taking a balloon to Besançon within the hour."

One of the unnerving features of voice-grade communications—and the radios capable of it were few and far between—was that one had to endure what the up-timers dubbed "pregnant pauses." During telegraph style signaling, a long silence could mean so many different things: a distracted operator on the other end, the other sender's need to phrase his reply so that it was as succinct and complete as possible, or even a brief equipment failure. But with voice transmissions, the circuit remained open, the constant crackle a reminder that the other party was there, had heard, and could reply whenever they chose. Except they hadn't yet chosen to do so. Which often signified a potential dispute in the offing.

When Mike Stearns' voice finally emerged from the speaker, his tone had become more measured, even determined, in its patience: not a good sign. "Estuban, I thought we went over this. The first rule of running any organization is that you have to be able to delegate, to trust the people who are carrying out your orders. It ruins their morale, and costs you time you can't afford, if you go flying off to fix a problem whenever one of your plans goes wrong."

Miro cleared his throat. "I'm not going because of what went wrong in Besançon."

Another pause, but not quite pregnant. When Stearns' voice came back it was somewhat mollified. "Oh. You're not? Then why are you going?"

"To make sure that the new mission is a success. Because if we can't both protect the consistory and keep it from revealing Urban's death to the rest of the world, we'll have an even bigger disaster. So, I figured that this time, I should go and oversee it myself. Because we can't afford another failure, can we?"

There was a silence on the line, then: "Well, if you're going, you might as well take a few notes for when you speak to Bernhard."

"Me? I should speak to Duke Bernhard? But why? Dr. Nichols is the ambassador."

"Yes, but she's the ambassador to the papacy. Which is job enough, particularly if Bedmar gets the miter. He's a tough customer and is not as big a fan of up-timer knowledge and influence as Urban was. So Sharon is going to have her hands full. You, on the other hand, are going to have to dance around Bernhard and keep him quiet. Which will mean keeping him happy, but without giving him the farm in the process. That kind of diplomatic wrangling isn't exactly in your job description, of course."

"No," agreed Miro, "but it would be excellent cover, to go as a special envoy to Burgundy."

"Well, yeah, how about that?" Stearns sounded quite pleased with himself. "You going to go alone?"

Miro nodded his head, for which he immediately chided himself: Stearns was hundreds of miles away. "Yes."

"That might be a pretty hefty project to handle on your own, Estuban."

Miro smiled. "I only said I am traveling alone. Fortunately, I already have agents on the ground."

Kuhlman, one of the Hibernians' apprentice wireless operators, looked up when Finan came into the command center in the basement of the abbey. "Boss-man wants a radio check from you."

"Which Boss-Man? North or Donovan?"

"Donovan. Odd frequency he gave for the radio

check, though." Kuhlman got up, handed the slip of paper to Finan.

The little corporal read it, shrugged. "Always keepin' us on our toes, I guess." Finan took the seat Kuhlman had vacated, began retuning the radio. "Yeh might as well take a break, Marcus. I could be at this a while."

"You wouldn't mind watching the post for me?" Kuhlman looked like he was ready to run out the door.

"Nah. Where else am I going to go, anyhow?" Finan began tapping his transmission code. "Now, be off with yeh."

Kuhlman nodded his thanks and bolted.

Finan finished entering his code and leaned back. As he expected, he didn't have long to wait. The clacker started chattering out the secure-coded message:

```
MESSAGE BEGINS.

TO FINAN, C., CORPORAL, HIBERNIAN
MERCENARY BATTALION. STOP. YOUR
EYES ONLY. STOP. REMAIN ADJUTANT
TO AMBASSADOR NICHOLS. STOP. NEW
MISSION REQUIRES SECURE SEQUESTRA-
TION AND OVERSIGHT OF CONSISTORY.
STOP. ACTIVATE AGENTS DELTA AND
OMEGA TO PROVIDE ASSISTANCE. STOP.
CONTACT DONOVAN IN EVENT HASTINGS
ATTEMPTS TO REASSIGN YOU. STOP. AM
ARRIVING BY AIR WITHIN 24 HOURS.
STOP. IF I AM DELAYED, NEXT CON-
TACT CODE IS FT9XV. STOP. SIGN IS
GRAY. STOP. COUNTERSIGN IS ASH. STOP.
ESTUBAN MIRO.

END.
```

✧   ✧   ✧

The man who still called himself Pedro Dolor raised one eyebrow when, upon turning the final corner separating him from the Pont Battant, he discovered a line of persons waiting to cross the river and depart Besançon. Just before the old Roman bridge, a cluster of soldiers, mostly Wild Geese and Hibernians, formed a gauntlet through which everyone had to pass.

A dragnet. Dolor shifted his rucksack, dusted another trace of quicklime from its bottom, and suppressed a pleased smile. There was no single definitive reason to validate the conjecture that rose up when he saw this attempt to detect departing assassins, but, after long years in his bloodstained and blackhearted trade, he had learned that there is a rhythm that builds in the wake of incidents like successful assassinations. In the aftermath of such events, there evolves a pattern in the demeanor, reactions, and even posture of those who have been apprised of the disaster, a mood that communicates itself from whatever inner circle first handles the confidential information and gives appropriate orders, on down to the lowly spear-carriers who carry out those orders without any real understanding of why they were given. And if Pedro Dolor's instincts were correct, this dragnet signified that Urban VIII had in fact perished, albeit not during the attack itself.

That provisional realization sent a pang of surprising regret through him. It was a shame that it had to be done, really, particularly since Urban had repudiated his past nepotism and materialism, and had seemed to genuinely desire reconciliation among many faiths. But there had to be a trail of blood that led to Madrid. And, sadly, Urban's rehabilitation and embrace of true brotherly love was more likely to be emulated because of his martyred example rather than his late exhortations—which sharply contrasted with his deeds as the pope most associated with the Catholic atrocities of the last ten years.

Even so, Dolor did not revel in Urban's probable death. In fact, he discovered that, for whatever small difference it made, he was glad that it had not been his own hand that struck the presumed mortal blow. Still, it was also cheering to speculate that his mission had not been a complete failure. Only time would tell: time that Pedro Dolor would spend on a circuitous road back to the Mediterranean as he waited for news of Urban's final fate to overtake him.

And so, guide his next action and thus, his next destination.

Owen Roe O'Neill turned to Ruy Sanchez and said flatly: "Ruy, go home."

Ruy acted as though he had no idea what his friend might be referring to.

Owen rolled his eyes: it was not one of the faux-hidalgo's best performances. It was, rather, very possibly his worst. "That arm is still inflamed. Yer white as a banshee. And for a man of yer complexion, that's truly saying something. So go home."

Ruy shook his head. "I will wait until the end of this watch. It is not long. And the colloquists have almost all departed."

Owen elected not to point out what Ruy would certainly have remembered had he been right for duty: that they were screening for murderous thugs, not sending clerics on their way home. "Then stay the watch, if yeh must. But there's no reason for both of us t'be on our feet. You sit, now. When your turn comes, I'll get you to your lazy feet again. The men are doing all the work, anyway. We're just wielding the whip, and one whip is plenty."

Ruy muttered something about sitting higher so he could still observe the departure line, found a chair, sat down heavily.

O'Neill turned back toward the line, ensuring that his men were reasonably thorough in their checks. They were, and they certainly had an eye for overtly shady-looking characters. But what most of them lacked was a sense of how a subtler criminal would adopt an appearance as unremarkable and nondescript as possible.

Like the fellow who'd just come abreast of Tone Grogan, waiting while the Irishman sorted through his knapsack. He'd be exactly the kind of person you wouldn't look at twice: medium height, medium build, light brown or hazel eyes, and hard to see how fit he was in his loose tradesman's clothes. The only noteworthy thing was that he was well-groomed, particularly for his station.

One by one, Grogan was taking equally uninteresting items out of the man's ruck: a plate, a spoon, a pair of old sandals, a comb, a bar of coarse brown soap—

Owen felt his thoughts quicken, jolted out of the rut they had fallen into beneath the unrelenting sun and the unending parade of completely innocuous clerics and common folk. For so well-groomed a commoner, the man had a surprisingly modest collection of hygiene-related items.

"Hold there," he called to Grogan, watching, as he did, for any change in the posture or demeanor of the average-looking man. There was none.

As Grogan finished emptying the rest of the ruck's

wholly unremarkable contents, Owen looked in the man's eyes. Yes, they were hazel, and that was all he could really say about them. Which was a bit odd: O'Neill prided himself on being able to tell a great deal about a man by looking in his eyes, particularly regarding intelligence or the lack of it. In this case, the eyes were unreadable—so much so, that he felt a small tingle of doubt that it could be natural. "You keep yourself very presentable, I see."

The man nodded. "I try."

"So I'm wonderin' how yeh manage to remain so clean and well-groomed with no more'n that?" Owen hooked a thumb at the soap and comb laying on the table before Grogan.

The man shrugged. "It's difficult with those. But in the city, a man may spend a sou or so, and do much better."

Well, that made sense. And he wouldn't be the first commoner who'd suffered enough at the hands of soldiers or aristocrats to learn how to become unreadable. "I see. Fair journey, then."

Grogan finished reloading the ruck, handed it across to the man—which was when Owen noticed a dusty smear along one of the shoulder straps. "Let's have it here," he said, intercepting the sack. He ran a finger along the dust, raised it to his nose, touched the powder-fine deposit with his tongue. "This is quicklime, isn't it?" O'Neill remembered what had been found in the basement next to the priory and was suddenly and coolly very conscious of the precise location and angle of his sword hilt relative to his right hand.

The man nodded. "Yes." He might have been a little perplexed. "I'm an assistant to stonemasons, sometimes."

"And other times?"

The man seemed to repress a grimace. "I carry things. I dig. I can use a hammer well enough." He ended with a small, expressive shrug.

O'Neill looked for any hint of prevarication in the man's face as he felt down around the lining of the bag. Nothing unusual in either place. He palmed the spoon before he closed the bag. He handed it back to the man by its strap. "Be on your way, then."

The man took his rucksack carefully, slowly, as if moving swiftly might extend the unwanted attention from the armed men. He offered a shallow nod of respect, turned, walked away.

O'Neill let him get five paces before yelling, "Hey, you!" As the fellow turned, Owen threw the spoon at him. The man blinked, and just barely caught it, bobbling it before firmly grabbing it with his right hand.

His *right* hand. Not his left, O'Neill noted. Well, so much for finding the missing assassin. "Sorry for the trouble," he muttered. He turned back to the line a moment after the man turned back to his own path out of the city.

And who, facing away from Owen Roe O'Neill, indulged himself with a small, very brief smile.

Gaspar de Borja y Velasco stared angrily at the radio. It remained silent. As it had for more than two days now. He felt rage building in him anew. "It is possible, Maculani, that at this, the penultimate hour, our men go silent? Could they have been caught?"

Maculani rubbed his heavy nose. "Only time will tell, Your Eminence."

"I do not expect time to tell!" Borja snapped. "I

expect that foppish whelp de Requesens to tell. Or the other one, the Swiss that you recommended. But silence? We had regular communications with the handlers of both groups! Both! Is it possible that they could both have been discovered? Or defeated?"

Maculani paused, seemed to be choosing his words carefully. "Without having any knowledge, all things are possible, Your Eminence. But that does not mean that all things are likely. As you point out, they were in regular communication right up until they advised us that the moment for them to strike might be at hand. If they did so, and escaped, they are unlikely to be able to stop long enough to set up their apparatus to send a signal. But until they signal, we cannot know that either. So we must wait."

"Yes, yes, Maculani. I know it is so. You may go; I have no further need of you today."

"As you wish, Your Eminence. Until tomorrow, then." Maculani bowed himself out of the large, wood-paneled office.

Borja turned his chair the other direction, looked out the window at the increasingly sluggish Tevere, then glanced at the wheeled serving cart at his side. A decanter of rioja sat upon it, waiting to finish breathing. It would be best in half an hour, and that was, after all, a more appropriate time to indulge in more than a small glass. But with his trials and tribulations unresolved, Borja saw in the wine both strength and consolation, a reinforcement of both the determination and the calm required to resolve to try again in the event that Urban had still not been eliminated.

Borja needed that calm, that determination, immediately, not in half an hour. He grasped the decanter hastily, but poured the wine out slowly, anticipating and watching it fill his crystal goblet with a rich, dark red. It reminded him of blood.

A pope's blood.

Sharon Nichols was surprised, but also reassured, by the speed with which Ruy rose from the dinner table in the refectory of the chapter house.

He offered his right arm. "Shall we take in the evening air, my love?"

Sharon rose, lightly, gracefully. "I thought you'd never ask."

As they exited, she stole a quick glance at where his other arm hung across his chest in a sling. Better: much better. Three hours ago, Ruy had returned from manning the outbound traffic checkpoint at the Pont Battant. He was escorted by two Burgundians whom Owen had sent along for the express purpose of making sure he went straight to his physician wife. And it was a good thing he did: Ruy had arrived drawn, pale, and, for him, alarmingly weak. But once in the cool of the basement, and with a little surgical prompting, the wound in his left arm finally drained, his fever dropped, and his appetite returned. Given his almost inhuman constitution, he had been back to his old self by dinner, of which he had two helpings.

They emerged into the cloister just as the sun was setting. Burnished gold glinted off the ivy that twined about and climbed the columns all along the southern colonnade. Evening flowers released their scents as birds dipped and swooped after invisible insects.

"It's so peaceful," Sharon murmured.

"Blessedly so, yes."

After they had walked the length of the first colonnade, Ruy led her gently out into the diagonal that bisected the garden: not their usual path, but welcome.

"I wonder what comes next?" Sharon whispered, just before they reached the small central fountain.

"Who can tell?" Ruy smiled. "For the present, I am satisfied to be walking in a garden. With you."

Sharon kept herself from starting and staring. It was not Ruy's typical tone. It was not filled with his usual buoyance, or the alternative low-voiced prelude to wooing. It was reflective and—what?—relieved? Content? Not tones Sharon had come to associate with her husband.

Then he turned, his smile dimming but his eyes unusually still and expressive, giving them the appearance of being larger than usual. And Sharon understood that this night, the mix of lewd innuendo and playfulness that often marked their time together would remain absent. In its place, there was a quiet thoroughness of glance and even, arm to arm, touch. It seemed as if the seriousness of what had recently transpired—and of what now had to be concealed— had pervaded this night like the scents of the flowers.

Or, perhaps, more like the premonitions of ghosts from a future where the lives of thousands of innocents could yet be forfeit due to Urban's murder, as well as the perfidious deeds which had preceded, and would surely follow, it.

Together, in silence, Sharon and Ruy walked.

Cast of Characters

Achille d'Estampes de Valençay, cardinal *in pectore*, captain of France, knight of the Sovereign Order of Malta

Alfonso de la Cueva-Benavides y Mendoza-Carrillo (formerly Marqués de Bedmar), cardinal-protector of, and Spain's special envoy to, the Spanish Lowlands

Cormac Finan, corporal in the Hibernian Mercenary Battalion, bodyguard and communications specialist for Sharon Nichols

Daniel O' Dempsey, soldier in the O'Neill tercio of the Wild Geese

Estève Gasquet, Borja's chief assassin from Provence

Friedrich Spee von Langenfeld, Jesuit, assistant to the father general

Gaspar de Borja y Velasco, cardinal, would-be pope

Gaspar de Guzman, count-duke of Olivares

Giancarlo de Medici, cardinal *in pectore* and nephew of Claudia de Medici of Tyrol

Ignaz von Meggen, freiherr of the Swiss Cantons, descendant of a Papal Guard commander

Javier de Requesens y Ercilla, Spanish intelligencer and handler of Borja's assassination team

Lawrence Mazzare, up-time priest, now cardinal-protector of the USE

Luke Wadding, cardinal, Franciscan theologian, and former Guardian of the College at St. Isidore's

Maffeo Barberini, Pope Urban VIII

Marwin Hastings, senior lieutenant in the Hibernian Mercenary Battalion

Muzio Vitelleschi, father general of the Society of Jesus (Jesuits)

Norwin Eischoll, Borja's chief assassin from the Swiss Cantons

Owen Roe O'Neill, colonel of the Wild Geese and chief of the Papal Guard

Pedro Dolor, intelligence operative for Count-Duke Olivares

Rombaldo de Gonzaga, chief of Pedro Dolor's assassins

Ruy Sanchez de Ortiz y Casador, colonel and chief of Papal Security, former Spanish officer and husband of Sharon Nichols

Sharon Nichols, up-time EMT/physician and ambassador to Rome, wife of Ruy Sanchez de Ortiz y Casador

Turlough Eubank, sergeant de campo temporarily assigned to the O'Neill tercio of the Wild Geese

Vincenzo Maculani, bishop, secretary and executive to Borja, former chief inquisitor

Author's note

On poetry in the Ring of Fire series

Readers who have followed the Ring of Fire series are by now probably familiar with my habit of using verses from various poems or other literary sources to accompany the different parts of each novel. I started that practice in the very first novel of the series, *1632*, more or less on a whim. And then—also more or less on a whim—I continued doing so in succeeding novels. The whimsical nature of this enterprise is perhaps best demonstrated by the fact that three of the novels have no verses accompanying them. Why? Because I forgot to do it.

As whimsical as they may be, I do try to use poetry or other verses that in my opinion capture something of the novel's spirit. Perhaps the most obvious and clearest illustration of this guiding principle (using the terms "guiding" and "principle" oh so very loosely) are the verses cited in the novel *1636: Mission to the Mughals,* which are from the great Hindu epic *The Ramayana.*

I realize that some readers may not feel any particular

set of verses is really appropriate to the novel to which it is attached. Such readers are, of course, entitled to their opinions—just as I am entitled, of course, to ignore them.

For those interested, here are the verses cited:

1632: William Blake, "The Tyger"

1633: W. B. Yeats, "Sailing to Byzantium"

1634: The Galileo Affair: Robert Browning, "My Last Duchess"

1634: The Ram Rebellion: verses from the *Book of Ezekiel*, the Bible (King James)

1634: The Baltic War: W. B. Yeats, "Meditations in Time of Civil War"

1635: A Parcel of Rogues: Robert Burns, "Such a Parcel of Rogues in a Nation"

1634: The Bavarian Crisis: William Wordsworth, "Intimations of Immortality from Recollections of Early Childhood"

1635: The Cannon Law: nothing

1635: The Dreeson Incident: John Milton, "Paradise Lost"

1635: The Eastern Front: William Wordsworth, "Lines Composed a Few Miles above Tintern Abbey, on Revisiting the Banks of the Wye During a Tour, July 13, 1798"

1636: The Saxon Uprising: Alfred, Lord Tennyson, "Ulysses"

1635: The Papal Stakes: Edna St. Vincent Millay, "Renascence"

1636: The Atlantic Encounter: Wallace Stevens, "The Idea of Order at Key West"

1636: Commander Cantrell: William Shakespeare, *Troilus and Cressida*

1636: The Kremlin Games: nothing

1636: The Cardinal Virtues: Not poetry but depictions of the four virtues

1636: The Ottoman Onslaught: Robert Browning, "Andrea Del Sarto"

1636: Mission to the Mughals: verses from the *Ramayana*

1636: The Vatican Sanction: Wallace Stevens, "Le Monocle de Mon Oncle"

1637: The Volga Rules: nothing

1637: The Polish Maelstrom: "Völuspá: The Prophecy of the Seeress" from *The Poetic Edda*

1636: The China Venture (forthcoming): Rudyard Kipling, "Mandalay"